The Krays & Freddie Foreman: Read All About It!

By
Freddie Foreman, Steve Wraith, Neil Jackson
and Wayne Lear

Published by Media Arts
For more copies of this book, please email: info@media-arts.com Tel: 0844 3577120

Designed and Set by Media Arts www.media-arts.co.uk
Cover design by Andrew Brewster.
Printed by Tandem Press in Great Britain

A Note From The Authors

People seem to be as fascinated with the Krays today as they were when they were pictured brushing shoulders with film stars and royalty in the sixties.

Even when incarcerated the Krays made headlines.

Whether it was the infamous 'I Don't Pay Tax I'm Mad' story about Ronnie or the interviews Reg gave on his deathbed or Charlie's drugs charge in 2000 the Krays have been providing copy for our tabloid and broadsheet newspapers for over five decades.

And wherever the Krays were, Freddie Foreman was not far away.

It was Fred who was tasked with making the body of the unfortunate Jack The Hat disappear.

It was Fred the twins turned to when their disasterous plan to break Frank Mitchell out of HMP Dartmoor went wrong and he had to be silenced.

Fred stood shoulder to shoulder with the Krays and their associates in the dock in 1969 and remained a firm friend and ally for the lifetimes of the three brothers.

In this book we've included clippings from newspapers spanning from the 50's through to the present day. As well as the well known headlines we've tried to include some lesser known stories and articles that feature the Krays and Freddie Foreman.

Because of their age some of the old publications are hard to reproduce in perfect detail and may be difficult to read in full. We have tried hard to keep this to a minimum.

Our thanks go to Micky Nesbitt and Paulet Wilkes for supplying some of the articles.

There are also over 30 unseen photographs included in this book from the personal collections of the authors as well as some fantastic colour images of Reg and Frances from her own

personal photo album. We are grateful to Louise Potts for allowing us to use these in the book.Also included are the passport photos of Ron, Reg, Charlie and their parents Violet and Charlie Senior along with many others.

A special thank you has to be noted to Freddie Foreman's godson Christian Simpson for his helpfulness and willingness to make so much happen for this project. Heartfelt thank you from the three of us for all you have done in helping with meetings in London and other behind the scenes arrangements.

Finally we would again like to say a huge thank you to you, the reader for purchasing this book. We hope you enjoy reading the articles we've selected and looking at the photos.

Your support and encouragement is very much appreciated and we hope to see you soon on our website www.thekrays.net or our Facebook groups.

Steve, Neil & Wayne
October 2015.

Special Thanks

We are grateful to the following people who purchased one of the first 100 copies of this book:

Mark Bowman
Paulet Wilkes
Neil Buckley
Stephen Cross
Wanda Wells
David Last
Julie Russell
Andrew Bryan
Louise Potts
Kat Devai
Gill Bamford
Craig Alderson
Tracey Wilcox
Shaun Preston (x2)
Chris Lovell
Julie Douglas
Lisa Durham
Brian Moffat
Colin Rowan
Mick Smalley
Alan Warren
Lindsey Jones
Deano O'Hara
Richard Sykes
Danny Gordon
Adam Ayling
Craig Thorneycroft
Simon Liddell
Leon Rix
Susan Wiles
Charlie Sparks
Shaun McGrath
DJ Rust

Roger Slocombe
Lee Martin
Peter Crocetti
Chris Walton
Matt Ball
Ryan Ball
Melissa McGuire
Sparrow Harrison MBE
Neil Smith
Robert Hopcroft
Alasdair Geddie
Craig Cox
Rod Harrison (x2)
Jill Higgins
Dave Potter
Max Thompson
Andrew Jones
Lisa Smeaton
Jayne Surman
Frances Salter
Judith Jones
Sian Kelly
Micky Nesbitt
Mark Rodgers
Keighley Vogel
Stephen Ashley
Robbie English
Maureen Curme
Michael Metcalf
Janet Taylor
Mark Fisher
Yvette Raybone
Roy Hickman

Sumeet Virdee
Paul Cox
Martin Jackson
Mark Fisher
Sharon Parker
Steven Ware
Loretta Richardson
Lindsey Pollard
John Robb
Mick Connor
Gary Behagg
Connor Robb
Christopher Norris
Wayne Radnedge
Kathy Pamenter
Leonard Veal
Melvyn Swinscoe
Linda Leigh
William McBeth
Michael Oates
Michael Sullivan
Darren Craven
Garry Elton
Andy Evans
Martin Abrahamson
Jamie Cunningham
Kevin Bright
David Gibson
Stephen Rowbotham
Wayne Brindley
Simon Povey
Albert Oliver

Contents

Foreword

Here is the book that I know, due to the many hours of research and tireless work on this project by the three outstanding authors - Steve Wraith, Neil Jackson and Wayne Lear and also my Godson Christian Simpson, who was a huge help from the very beginning, has been a very long process in bringing to life.

I'm very happy with the final completion of this book.
Rather more so than my recently published book called 'The Last Real Gangster', which should have been titled 'Last Man Standing.'

I'm always very happy to do any projects with my dear trusted friend John Blake, who is a world leading book publisher.
I felt 'The Last Real Gangster' was ruined from the title and the front cover to the misrepresentation of actual events placed in the book by the ghost writer, who only spend one hour of his time with me and never returned to work alongside me further on the book.
This I felt was was shockingly unprofessional and showed a huge lack of respect.
I'm not happy with some of the misquoted comments in that book about certain people and friends, many of whom I have had to personally reach out to and let them know that I had no intention of offending them as many of the quotes used in that book were not mine but rather those of the ghost writer.

Here is a book that I'm very pleased about and to be honest, reading through the first draft copy of the book and viewing the many newspaper headlines over the years it has brought back a lifetime of memories and thoughts of years gone by.

Freddie Foreman
October 2015.

1950's

"We were fearless in those days, fighting was our game"
Reg Kray

"I loved my life in the late fifties. I made a lot of money and was a good club owner"
Ron Kray

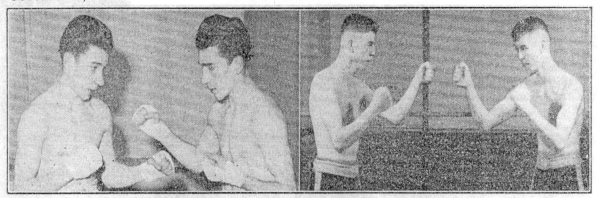

No you're not seeing double, just identical twins. On your left: The Krays, Ron and Reg. On your right: The Smiths, Jackie and "Southpaw" Albert.

TWINS

Why not match the Krays and Smiths? asks 'Ringwise'

IF any ambitious matchmaker is at a loss for a couple of attractive supporting contests may I suggest the Smiths v. the Krays. Never heard of them you may say. Quite rightly, neither match will make a lot of difference to British or even Area championships, but it offers probably a unique opportunity of matching a pair of identical twins.

We have had a glut of boxing brothers lately: the Turpins and the Buxtons and now within the last few months on to the professional scene has stepped the Krays, Ron and Reg from Bethnal Green, and Albert and Jackie Smith from Elland in Yorkshire.

CAN'T TELL 'EM APART

Should the match ever materialise opticians and doctors in the district will certainly have a stream of customers for the facial resemblance of both is amazing. Tommy Miller, manager of the Smiths, admits he still cannot tell them apart and smiles as he recalls the night of Albert's professional debut.

He shared the verdict and Miller, offering advice after the show, said he should have got the decision. Imagine his surprise at the reply, "I'm Jackie and won!"

The Smiths caused some confusion in cadet boxing before joining the Army and since their demob have each had three professional contests. Only difference appears to be their weights for the shorter Jackie, who is the eldest by twenty-five minutes, scales half a stone lighter than his "southpaw" brother. Both are boxing lightweights however.

HALF A POUND ONLY

Such a distinguishing aid for ringsiders is not offered when Bethnal Green's dark-haired unbeaten lightweights are on view, for although Ron is a little more aggressive than his brother, both have similar styles and always weigh within half a pound of each other.

Reg and Ron do everything together. At 10 they made their first appearance in the ring and earned five bob for a fairground exhibition. Two years later they stepped along to the local boxing club and began chalking up an impressive list of victories.

Apart from their fairground exhibition the seventeen year old Krays have met on four occasions but except for sparring in the gymnasium those days are over, for their mother has barred any meeting in the professional ring.

For the record only one member of a twin boxing family has won a world's title. That was Irish-American Mike Sullivan who captured the welter crown over forty years ago. America, too, have their twins with Mexicans Rudy and Jesse DeHoyos and coloured Henry and Bobby Holt from Danbury, all campaigning at the moment.

MILE END—July 31

If the seventeen-year-old Bethnal Green twins. Reg and Ron Cray go far up the fistic ladder, it's going to be mighty confusing for referees and reporters. for these two lightweights look alike, dress alike and even fight alike!

Both made their professional debut on this programme and Reg (9.11) outpointed Bob Manito, Walworth (9-11) in a tough six round bout while Ron, who of course also weighed 9st. 11lb., had a slightly easier task and beat Bernie Long, Romford (9-7) who retired in the interval following the second round.

MILE END—August 21

Reg Kray, Bethnal Green (9-11½), beat Johnny Starr, Canterbury (9-12), who retired at the end of the third with a damaged thumb.

WEMBLEY—September 11

The lightweight twins from Bethnal Green, Reg and Ronnie Kray, scored another "double." Reg beat George Goodsell, Cambridge (9-12), when the referee stopped the bout in the third round and Ron beat Bernie Long, Romford (9-6¾), when the referee stopped the bout at the end of the third round.

SHEPHERDS BUSH—October 29

Ron Kray, Bethnal Green (10-1¼), ko'd George Goodsell, Cambridge (9-11), in the fourth to confirm a previous win a week ago. He had Goodsell down twice in round three and twice in the fourth.

His twin Reg (9-11½), had a much rougher time against last minute substitute, Billy Sliney, Kings Cross (9-12), whom he outpointed over six rounds.

Various boxing reviews featuring the twins in 1951.

ALBERT HALL—December 11

Lew Lazar, Aldgate (10-7-10), displayed a varied selection of punches before knocking out Charlie Kray, Bethnal Green (10-9¼), in the third round.

The Kray twins from Bethnal Green had mixed fortunes over six rounds. Reg (9-13) turned in the most workmanlike performance of the pair to outpoint Bobby Manito, Clapham (10-1½), but Ron (10-0) never found an answer to the speedier leading of Bill Sliney, King's Cross (9-12½), and was well outpointed.

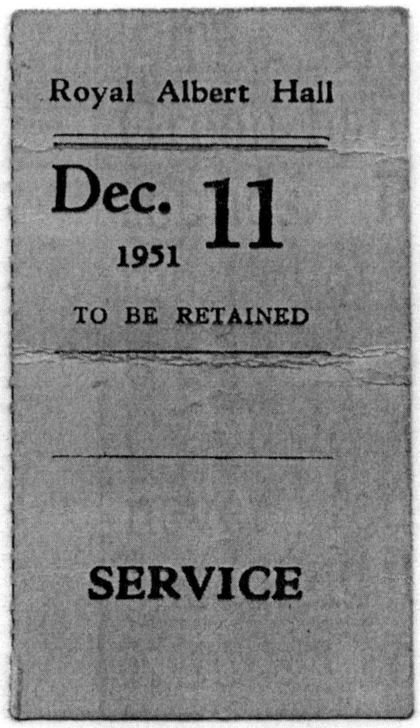

Royal Albert Hall

Dec. 11
1951

TO BE RETAINED

SERVICE

Above: A review of the now famous evening where the three Kray brothers appeared on the same bill at the Albert Hall.

Left: A ticket stub from that night.

BOURNEMOUTH—May 5

Over six rounds, Charlie Kray, London (10st. 3lb.), outpointed Ray Howard, Bournemouth (10st. 7lb.).

WALWORTH—April 11

Over four rounds, Charlie Kray, Bethnal Green (10st. 7½lb.), outpointed Doug Eland, Sheffield (10st. 13¼lb.); Bert Sinclair, Jamaica (9st. 1¼lb.), and Mick Long, Welling (9st. 2lb.), fought a draw.

Freddie Smith, Morden (9st. 12½lb.), had Joe Barton, Mile End (9st. 12lb.), on the deck several times during the course of their six-rounder, but could not keep him there, and had to be content with a points verdict.

Over four rounds, Vic Phayer, Woolwich (11st. 9lb.), outpointed Frank McGowan, Ireland (11st. 5lb.); Jim Blackburn, Walthamstow (10st. 1¼lb.), and Charlie Kray, Bethnal Green (10st. 3½lb.), boxed a draw, and Bernie Long, Romford (9st. 9½lb.), outpointed Tommy Trinder, Mile End (9st. 7lb.).

Some of Charlie's boxing results.

Results of the welterweight competition were as follows: *First Series*: Leslie Wood, Brighton (10st. 5lb.), beat Cyril Carrey, Edgware (10st.), on points; Ossie Wilson, Northampton (10st. 5lb.), k.o.d Rene Delaney, Watford (10st. 7lb.), in the second; George Smith, High Wycombe (10st. 7lb.), beat Arthur Field, Luton (9st. 11½lb.), on points; and Charlie Kray, Bethnal Green (10st. 6lb.), beat Johnny Fraser, Hackney (10st. 9lb.), on points.
Semi-finals: Wood beat Wilson on points, and Kray beat Smith on points.
Final: Kray beat Wood on points. All contests were over three rounds.

While much is rightly made of the boxing careers of the three Kray brothers Freddie Foreman was also an accomplished boxer. Here in his own words he explains:

When I was sixteen I joined Battersea Boxing Club at the Latchmere Baths and I would also go along to Jack Solomons' Sunday Morning Nursery Club in Soho.
The actor Stewart Granger presented me with shorts and training boots and I had fights with other clubs as well as the army, navy and police teams.
I got to the final of the London Federation of Boys Clubs, only to be beaten by a guy named Simon. The very next day I came down with the flu and was out of action for two weeks.
I knew that night I wasn't at my best as my legs felt like lead and that was where my amateur career finished.

In 1954 I turned pro and trained at the Thomas a Becket gym under Tommy Daly, who was the brother of famous boxer George Daly, who had taken part in 192 professional contests at flyweight, bantamweight, featherweight, lightweight and welterweight.

I had one pro fight against Del Breen at Walworth Baths at the end of 1954.
After my performance in that fight Jim Wick, who would go on to manage heavyweight champion Henry Cooper said I would never have an easy fight again.
Big mistake, I was put in star rankings too early.

I continue to enjoy the sport and in 1987 it was my great pleasure to organise for the Eltham Boxing Club to come over to Marbella to fight a team of Spanish fighters. The show took place at the football stadium in Puerto Banus and the British and Spanish teams won 4 bouts each.
I still regularly attend boxing shows whenever I can.

"One guy who deserved to be paid 100 notes was Freddie Foreman, who had his one and only pro fight, against Del Breen. Best supporting scrap I ever saw! They hit each other with everything but the corner buckets. Nobbins were still coming in five minutes after the fight ended. After such a fistic baptism Freddie never again drew on a glove. Look where he is now, though. He owns half the Costa Brava!"
"I knew that name should ring a bell," I said. "The boys in blue at Scotland Yard have asked the Spanish authorities to extradite him. It was on the TV News last week."
"I've said before that I speak as I find," insisted Stan. "Freddie was a lovely guy. He fought his heart out and packed the place out to the rafters with his supporters."

Excerpt from the book 'Down Memory Lane' by Stan Baker where he describes Freddie's professional boxing debut.

1960's

"In all clubs you get the occasional drunk, you know and sometimes they have to get slung out"
Reg Kray

 "I think most clubs are respectable you know, and I don't think there's any trouble at all in any of them...
except occasionally."
Ron Kray

CRIME OF PASSION says writer

POLICE officers investigating the shooting of "Ginger" Marks this week were handed a letter linking the shooting with that of another man.

The letter, which was sent to the Editor of the Advertiser group of newspapers, threw light on both shootings, and said that it was a crime of passion.

The letter alleged the shootings were a crime of passion involving an unfaithful wife and an illegitimate child.

Information in the letter ties in with information already known by the police and reporters, but it does also throw additional light on the matter.

Police officers are still checking out the fires at the Beulah Hill 'House of Peacocks' and the "Advertiser" office and the letter that was published two weeks ago.

They have taken several dozen specimens of handwriting and these are being checked against both letters.

Working from the East End's Commercial Street Police Station detectives are checking and re-checking statements made by the scores of people interviewed since the investigation started.

At Scotland Yard, Detective Superintendent Ronald Townsend and senior officers are also reviewing the facts that have already come to light.

Yesterday, Wednesday, police were digging in Whitechapel for the body of 'Ginger' Marks, following a tip-off.

BET SHOP CLERK IS SHOT BY GANG

GEORGE FOREMAN, the bets shop clerk who was shot when he opened the door to five men at his Bland House, Vauxhall-st., Lambeth, home on Thursday is still in hospital, although his condition is not so serious as when he was rushed there for an operation.

Police are still searching for the men who shot 44-year-old Mr. Foreman in the groin with a shotgun, and investigations into an "protection racket" have proved negative.

Someone might have shot Mr. Foreman to settle a personal grudge it is thought.

Both Mrs. Foreman and Mr. Foreman's employer know of no reason for the attack. Mrs. Foreman was not at home when the shooting took place.

Well known

Mr. Foreman is well known in Vauxhall and New Cross betting circles.

There have been a number of "fire bombs" thrown through bets shop windows, but it is unlikely that such an attack would be made on an employee.

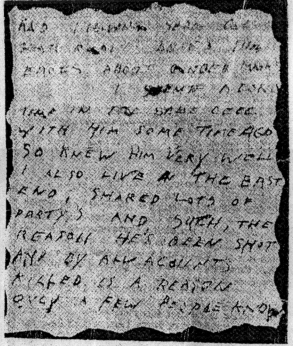

EVANS IS REMANDED

COURT ROOM DRAMA OVER BAIL

GEORGE JAMES EVANS, 34-year-old owner of the "House of Peacocks" at Upper Norwood, was remanded in custody at Lambeth Court yesterday (Wednesday) after a "very strong" police objection to bail.

Evans, a fruit machine proprietor, of Beulah Hill, Upper Norwood, was charged with shooting at bookmaker's clerk, George Foreman, at Bland House, Vauxhall Street, Kennington, on December 17 with intent to do him grievous bodily harm.

'Marks was wrongman'

A BARRISTER suggested at the Old Bailey on Tuesday, that George Evans, owner of the House of Peacocks on Beulah Hill was the target for the gunman who shot Ginger Marks.

"Ginger Marks was shot by mistake," said Mr. John Lawrence.

William Stevens, a 29-year-old street trader, of Cavendish Road, Wimbledon, denies breaking into a jeweller's shop in Bethnal Green Road.

Mr. Lawrence, defending Stevens, told the jury: "Outside the jeweller's someone took a pot shot at Evans, but Ginger Marks was the man who was shot."

The case continues.

THREAT TO RADIO LONDON

Police were this week investigating a series of threatening "lay off" telephone calls to Radio London — made by the thugs that threatened and petrol-bombed the "Advertiser".

The telephone calls — there were two of them — were made by a man with a gruff, Cockney voice who told a member of the Radio London staff at their head offices in Mayfair to "stop advertising the South London Advertiser — or you'll get the same as they did."

It was only three months ago that the offices of the "Advertiser" were petrol-bombed following an exclusive story linking the "House of Peacocks" with the disappearance of East End car dealer "Ginger" Marks—still missing, despite an extensive search by police.

In the last week threatening telephone calls have also been received by members of the "Advertiser" probe team.

Peacocks' man in court again

'EVANS WITH GINGER MARKS'

GEORGE James Evans of Beulah Hill, Upper Norwood and Thomas 'Ginger' Marks were two of three men seen in a Bethnal Green public house one Saturday night in January, Thames Court was told yesterday (Wednesday).

Evans and 29-years-old street trader Henry Walter Long of Cavendish Road, Wimbledon, appeared at the court charged with being concerned with others in breaking and entering a jeweller's shop in Bethnal Green on January 2.

THERE is still no sign of Ginger Marks, the car dealer who disappeared after a shooting incident in a London street. And the News of the World's offer of £5,000 reward for his discovery dead or alive still stands.

THE PICTURE WE MUST NOT PRINT

Brothers talk of picture in flat

NO OBJECTION TO SEEING IT PUBLISHED, SAYS PEER

BOOTHBY WITH KRAY

Lord Boothby and Ronald Kray—picture taken in the peer's flat on their second meeting

Lord Boothby talks of picture with ex-boxer

BY DAVID THURLOW

LORD BOOTHBY left Cambridge last night after spending the weekend with friends and taking a rest on doctor's orders. Today he will return to London for a consultation with his lawyers.

They would decide on any action which might be taken about recent rumours concerning him, he said.

Ronald Kray alleges libel

Solicitors for Mr. Ronald Kray, former boxer, of East London, said yesterday that they had received instructions and would issue a writ for alleged libel against the International Publishing Corporation in respect of articles in the Sunday Mirror and The People.

PICTURE BY EXPRESS CAMERAMAN ROBERT MAGWELL

Lord Boothby yesterday: A visit to friends

15

Has 'House of Peacocks' a link with Thames nude murders?

NORWOOD RIDDLE

Advertiser Exclusive

ON Tuesday an "Advertiser" reporter passed on to a senior Scotland Yard detective information linking an Anerley man with the Beulah Hill "House of Peacocks" raid, the disappearance of "Ginger" Marks, and the Thames nude murders.

The "tipster" explained that the man in question is believed to have controlled the activities of three of the murdered prostitutes — Hannah Telford, Margaret McGowan and Gwynneth Rees.

He was detained at Kensington police station by detectives inquiring into the murders, but later released.

The name cropped up again after last week's Flying Squad raid on the "House of Peacocks" during the massive London hunt for the missing East End car dealer "Ginger" Marks.

The "grass" — the underworld's name for a "tipster" — said that the name of the man owning the "House of Peacocks" was known to criminals as an alias of the man questioned about the nude murders.

The "grass" also said that the man had done some "crooked" car deals with "Ginger" Marks.

One of the two cars still standing in the driveway of the "House of Peacocks" — the blood-red Ford Classic — belongs to the man. The other, an American convertible, is known to criminals as belonging to an associate of the man.

Dumped in the Thames

In a third conversation the "grass" cast further light on what might have happened to two of the prostitutes the night they died.

Gwynneth Rees died of an abortion — not as the result of a sexual assault, as such;

One of the other prostitutes he said, died in a bath in a house in Marylebone Road before being dumped in the Thames.

The "grass" then alleged that the man bossed a chain of brothels and call girls, and held the lease of a house in Curzon Street, Mayfair, formally owned by the notorious Messina brothers.

He gave the reporter names of two South London prostitutes, the addresses of houses in Notting Hill Gate and Bloomsbury used by prostitutes, and the name of a South London public house used by an unnamed prostitute — she arranged to meet the man at the "House of Peacocks" — all the women were controlled by the same man.

The "grass" said the man, knowing he was known to police, had provided himself with an escape route to Dublin.

The "grass" then said that the underworld generally believe that the man was in hiding, abroad.

"But" said the "grass", "I know that he is living at Number .... Road, Anerley."

He added, "My underworld friends tell me that 'Ginger' Marks is not dead, but seriously wounded."

BULLION RAID

Today's robbery is the largest gold bullion theft in London for many years. Gold robberies as such are rare because of the extra precautions usually taken when gold is under lock and key or in transit.

February 1962: Thieves stole £30,000 in gold coins and medals from the offices of a coin dealers in Great Portland Street.

December 1961: Attempt to rob bullion van with £120,000 in Bow Common Lane, Leytonstone, foiled by security guards.

November 1961: £15,000 in gold stolen from aircraft at London Airport.

May 1957: £20,000 in gold stolen from BEA van on Great West Road at Brentford.

September 1954: £46,000 bullion robbery from KLM van in Theobalds Road, Holborn.

£5,000 REWARD FOR GINGER STILL STANDS

Ginger Marks and his wife

'Menaces' charge: No bail for Kray brothers

REGINALD KRAY . . . a £4,000 bail plea was refused.

TWIN brothers Ronald and Reginald Kray, described as company directors, were accused yesterday of demanding money, with menaces.

The 31-year-old brothers, who had been arrested the night before, at a London hotel, were refused bail.

They were remanded in custody for eight days by the magistrate at Old-street, London.

The magistrate, Mr. Neil McElligott, heard that £4,000 sureties were available for each brother. But he told them:

"I am satisfied, so far as I can be at this stage, that there are other persons at large, who are in a position to interfere with witnesses and impede the investigations—and would perhaps be in a better position to, were you at large."

The name of the person alleged to have been menaced by the Kray brothers was written down by Detective Chief Superintendent Frederick Gerrard.

'Brief'

Chief Superintendent Gerrard — one of Scotland Yard's "Big Five"—told the magistrate that he arrested the twins in a basement bar at the Glenrae Hotel, Seven Sisters-road, Finsbury Park.

Reginald Kray was said to have shouted to a group of people at the bar: "Get us a brief, Charlie!"

Chief Superintendent Gerrard agreed with the magistrate that this meant: "Engage legal representation."

At City-road police station, Ronald Kray was alleged to have said: "It's taken you long enough.

"This is all down to the Mirror. It was the same with Spotty."

When Ronald Kray was charged, he was alleged to have said: "Ridiculous. I want to see a solicitor."

Reginald Kray was alleged to have said: "It's one of those things. You've got your job to do."

Chief Superintendent Gerrard said that other inquiries were being made. And, he said, two other men, who disappeared after the twins' arrest, were being sought.

RONALD KRAY . . . he is alleged to have said: "Ridiculous."

TWIN KRAY BROTHERS ARE SENT FOR TRIAL ON MENACES CHARGES

By FRANK HOWITT

A LAWYER speaking about the meaning of the word "protection" was told by a magistrate yesterday: "I am at the moment trying to protect you from yourself."

Defending 31-year-old twins Ronald and Reginald Kray, who were sent for trial charged with demanding money with menaces or force, Mr. Ivan Lawrence told Mr. Neil McElligott, magistrate at Old Street court:—

"The word protection has a number of connotations which may be sinister."

Sitting in the dock with the Kray twins was 32-year-old television scriptwriter Edward Richard Smith, also committed on the same charge. They plead not guilty. All three were committed in custody.

Mr. Lawrence, who submitted the prosecution had not established a case, said: "It is well known that protection rackets, as such, existed and perhaps still exist in this part of London."

Then he said: "If all the defendants were trying was 'If we put two doormen on your door and give you a receptionist who is well known to villains who might come in to demand protection money or smash up your club.'

"And if for that treatment a percentage of the takings was returned—would that be no more than a legitimate business enterprise?"

Knife

He was continuing his argument when Mr. McElligott said: "It is well to consider the limits to which this submission should go."

A "man called Jack Spot" was mentioned by Detective Inspector Leonard Read, who gave evidence of arrest.

He said that when Ronald Kray was charged at City Road police station he replied: "It's taken you long enough. You have been after us long enough. This is down to the Mirror. Spotty was the same."

In a police car, alleged Inspector Read, Ronald Kray said: "Somebody must have put the finger on us. We have not been out 'blacking' people, you know."

The inspector said "blacking" meant: "blackmailing people or demanding money."

Later, when a sheath knife was found on Ronald Kray—who was also charged with possessing an offensive weapon—he was alleged to have said: "That will be a bit more aggravation, I suppose."

When Smith was arrested, the inspector claimed he said: "I have not been with the Krays. I am a writer. I manage a few singers for them, but have not been having anything to do with them."

Lord Boothby at his London home last night

BOOTHBY:
Why I am asking about the Kray brothers

Express Staff Reporter

LORD BOOTHBY plans to ask a question in the House of Lords tomorrow about the Kray twins who are in prison awaiting trial.

He explained at his London flat last night: "I have not been in touch with the two brothers since last July and hold no brief for them.

"They did not ask me to put the question. It is simply that I am opposed to a legal situation which permits the Kray twins to be held in custody for nearly five weeks without trial."

WRONG!

Lord Boothby, who was a Scottish M.P. for 34 years before becoming a life peer, will ask the Government "whether it is their intention to imprison the Kray twins indefinitely without trial."

He said last night: "For years I have fought this system and will continue to do so. It is quite wrong that they and other people can be held in prison like this.

"I would like to see the same procedure adopted as used in Scotland. That would mean a person could only be held in custody for a specific length of time without trial.

"At the moment all they know is that their trial has been postponed indefinitely and they remain in jail."

NO BAIL

The Kray brothers, 31-year-old Ronald and Reginald, have been in custody since January 7. On February 1, with a third man, Edward Richard Smith, they were committed for trial, charged with being concerned with others in demanding money by menaces or by force from a West End club owner.

At the Old Bailey on Monday an application for bail was refused. The brothers have pleaded not guilty and reserved their defence.

Krays' bail refused

Three High Court judges yesterday refused to grant £18,000 bail to the Kray twins, Ronald and Reginald, who are in custody accused of demanding money with menaces.

Bail was also refused for Edward Richard Smith, a 32-year-old writer, who is jointly accused with the Krays.

HUBBUB IN THE LORDS
Yes—it was rough, says Boothby

A HUBBUB from peers engulfed the words of Lord Boothby in the Lords yesterday as he spoke about the twin Kray brothers.

Krays used the 'weapon of cowards'

By ARNOLD LATCHAM

HEW McCOWAN
"Certain overtures"

THE price of the "protection" service offered by the Kray twins to the owner of a new Soho club was an eventual 50 per cent of the takings, it was alleged at the Old Bailey yesterday.

But later, after "certain overtures" had been made to him, the club owner, Mr. Hew McCowan, had the courage to go to the police, said prosecuting counsel, Mr. John Mathew.

The Kray twins, 31-year-old Ronald and Reginald, of Seven Sisters Road, Finsbury Park, London, and 32-year-old writer Edward Richard Smith, of no fixed address, pleaded not guilty to conspiring together and with John Francis to demand with menaces or by force property capable of being stolen from Mr. McCowan, with intent to steal.

NEW NAME

Mr. Mathew said: "This is a case about Soho club life. The allegation here is that the Kray twins, assisted by Francis, who is not in the dock because he has not been arrested, and Smith plotted to get protection money from the owner of a Gerrard Street night club."

The club was originally known as the Bonsoir, but when Mr. McCowan decided to buy it last autumn, he renamed it the Hideaway Club and spent a substantial sum of money on it.

Ronald Kray told an associate of Mr. McCowan that he would put two doormen in the club "and guarantee no trouble from villains," Mr. Matthew went on.

That would be provided free for the first month of the club's existence. Then they would want 20 per cent of the takings, then 30 per cent and finally 50 per cent every month.

'CORRUPTING'

Mr. Mathew told the all-male jury: "Fear is an ugly word. It is a wicked and corrupting weapon. But it is also the weapon of cowards."

When Francis made suggestions to Mr. McCowan, the new club had not even then been opened.

Mr. Mathew added that Francis said the Krays were prepared to provide doormen to keep out undesirable people who might otherwise try to get into the club.

Mr. Mathew continues his opening address today.

REGINALD KRAY
Accused ...

RONALD KRAY
... with brother

EVANS SUES FOR LIBEL

George J. Evans, of 283 Beulah Hill, S.E.19, has brought a claim for alleged libel against the 'Advertiser' arising out of stories published in this newspaper just prior to the 'Advertiser' being bombed, and in the two issues following the bombing.

QC tells of parish priest and a 'forced' witness

KRAY TWINS: NO BAIL, SAY 3 JUDGES

REGINALD KRAY

RONALD KRAY

ACCUSED twin brothers Ronald and Reginald Kray, 31, were again refused bail yesterday—by Lord Parker, the Lord Chief Justice, and two other judges in the High Court.

A similar application was refused by Judge Griffith-Jones at the Old Bailey on Monday.

The brothers, described as company directors, are awaiting trial at the Old Bailey with Edward Smith, 32, a writer, on a charge of demanding money with menaces or by force from a West End club owner. The brothers have been in custody since January 6.

Passports

Mr. Petre Crowder, Q.C. for the Krays, told the judges that they now offered £18,000 bail—£6,000 more than the sureties offered at the Old Bailey on Monday.

The brothers would surrender their passports, report to the police twice a day and undertake not to interfere with witnesses.

If bail were granted, added Mr. Crowder, the brothers would be in a position to trace witnesses—people in Soho clubland whom they knew only by their first names and who could only be found in the early hours of the morning.

Mr. Crowder alleged that a prosecution witness had said he was

Evidence not true — defence

being forced by his employer—the complainant in the case—to give untrue evidence.

This admission was made, said Mr. Crowder, when the witness went to the home of Mr. Charles Kray, brother of the twins.

The local parish priest called on a courtesy visit during the interview—and it was proposed to take a statement from him.

Refused

After a two-minute consultation between the judges, Lord Parker said bail was refused for the Krays—and also for Smith.

● A question due to be put by Lord Boothby in the House of Lords today will ask the Government "whether it is their intention to keep the Kray brothers in prison for an indefinite period without trial."

CURATE TELLS COURT OF "TALK ABOUT PERJURED EVIDENCE"

DEFENCE WITNESS IN KRAY TRIAL

The Rev. Albert Edward John Foster, of The Vicarage, Bethnal Green Road, E., priest in charge of St. Matthew's Church, Bethnal Green, was called as a defence witness at the Central Criminal Court yesterday in the trial of the Kray twins and a third man who are alleged to have been concerned in a plot to demand protection money from a West End club owner.

Mr. Foster said in his presence Mr. Sidney Vaughan, a Crown witness, had stated that if he did not give perjured evidence against the Krays his allowance of £40 a week would be cut off.

Ronald and Reginald Kray, aged 31, of Seven Sisters Road, Finsbury Park, N., and Edward Richard Smith, aged 32, self-employed writer, of no fixed address, have pleaded Not Guilty to conspiracy to demand with menaces or by force property capable of being stolen from Hew Cargill McCowan with intent to steal, and conspiracy dishonestly and with menaces to extort from Mr. McCowan such money as he might be persuaded to part with.

The prosecution have alleged that the accused, assisted by a man named John Francis who has not been arrested, plotted to demand protection money from Mr. McCowan, who opened the Hideaway Club in Gerrard Street, Soho, W., on December 16 last year.

None of the three defendants went into the witness-box.

"AID OF £40 A WEEK"

Mr. Foster, who was called on behalf of Reginald Kray, told the Court he had known the Kray family for four years. On January 20 he went to Brixton prison to see Ronald Kray, who had been refused bail. Later that day he returned to Vallance Road, Bow, where the Krays' parents lived. "I was shown into a back room", he said. "Already there were a Mr. Noble, Charles Kray and someone who was introduced as Sid. (Sidney Vaughan.)

"Mr. Noble said 'This young man (pointing to Sidney Vaughan) says he has given some evidence to the police about the Kray brothers which was not true.' There was a long conversation and Sidney was asked whether he had actually heard the Kray brothers demanding money and he replied that he had not."

Mr. Paul Wrightson, Q.C., for the defence of Reginald Kray.—What happened then?

Mr. Foster.—Mr. Noble asked Sidney whether he was willing to give evidence in court and so perjure himself. Sidney said he was getting £40 a week financial aid and if he did not give this evidence that financial aid was going to be cut off. He said the money was coming from someone whose name sounded like McGowan. Sidney added that he had two flats to keep and a wife and child to support. Mr. Noble also asked him if he was frightened that the Krays might take reprisals if he did give perjured evidence and Sidney said he was not frightened of the Krays at all.

Mr. John Mathew, for the Crown.—You appreciated that someone who was going to be a witness for the prosecution was saying he had told untruths about this matter to the police. I suppose you advised him to go to the police and tell them at once?—I did not join in the conversation at all.

NO REPORT TO POLICE

Mr. Mathew.—Having heard that, did you advise him to go to the police and make a clean breast of it?—No, sir.

Did you report this matter to the police yourself?—No.

Mr. William Noble, of Shipwright's Drive, Benfleet, Essex, for 20 years a Metropolitan Police officer and now an inquiry agent, said on the afternoon of January 20 he was at the home of the Kray family when Sidney Vaughan arrived. Vaughan said to Charles Kray: "I am very sorry but I cannot help myself. McCowan told me if I did not make a statement he would withdraw his financial support. McCowan gives me about £40 a week financial support. I have two flats to keep. My wife and children (or child) live in one of them". Vaughan went on to ask: "What can I do if I do not get the money from McCowan." Vaughan also said the police told him that if he did not make a statement they had enough to subpoena him. He then made a statement which the police wrote down.

Mr. Noble said he then asked Vaughan: "Do you seriously say that in order to save your £40 a week you are prepared to give perjured evidence regardless of the fact that it might mean men will be sent to prison? He replied: 'I have to think of myself . . .'"

Mr. Wrightson.—Did he say anything about McCowan working with the police?

Mr. Noble.—Yes, he said McCowan had been telling everyone he had been working with Superintendent Gerrard on this case for five months and he had been promised a citation from the Queen and an O.B.E. or something. Vaughan went on to say "I have come here so that you can know my position and help prepare the defence, if you know what I mean."

'WOULD BE IN RIGHT MESS'

Mr. Noble said that Vaughan concluded: "I would be in a right mess if McCowan stopped his financial support, so I must go along with him or say I forgot when I get into the witness-box. What would you do if you were me?" Charles Kray told him: "Just tell the truth, Sidney, that is all." Vaughan retorted: "That is not so easy when you are dealing with McCowan" and he described McCowan as a pathological liar.

Mr. Mathew, cross-examining.—This was a matter of the greatest importance obviously?

Mr. Noble.—I gathered so.

Mr. Mathew.—Did you communicate any of this information to the police?—No, I passed it on to the solicitors acting for the Kray brothers.

The trial was adjourned until today.

CLOSING SPEECHES MADE IN KRAY CASE

Mr. Petre Crowder, Q.C., in his final address to the jury on behalf of Ronald Kray, at the Central Criminal Court yesterday, appealed to them to put out of their minds any prejudice following what he called the tremendous publicity there had been in relation to the Kray twins.

Reginald and Ronald Kray, aged 31, and Edward Smith, aged 32, self-employed writer, have all pleaded Not Guilty to conspiring with John Francis to demanding money with menaces from Hew Cargill McCowan, and extorting money with menaces from him.

Mr. Crowder said that the only witness the jury need have heard was Mr. McCowan. The jury were entitled to look at the evidence of Mr. Vaughan in so far as it assisted the defence.

About Mr. McCowan, he said: "Here you have got this man obviously leading a most unusual, unhealthy, unattractive existence. Here you have a man who has paid the penalty on former occasions for homosexuality."

Mr. McCowan was a rich young man in a predicament who thought that in being friendly with the police " in cropping up time and again to give evidence in blackmailing actions and in trying to assist in this matter " he would help himself.

Mr. Paul Wrightson, Q.C., for the defence of Reginald Kray, said to the jury in his closing speech: "This case is a matter of atmosphere. Let me remind you how carefully that atmosphere has been built up

"Have you not got the impression in this case that everybody, with some exceptions, is against everybody else? One might almost use the phrase that one witness used of 'having the needle'. That is the way this case has developed."

Mr. McCowan, he said, was hopping mad with Mr. Vaughan and against the Krays. The police were hopping mad with the Krays and Detective-superintendent Gerrard had a thing against the Krays.

Mr. Kenneth Richardson, for the defence of Smith, said in his closing address to the jury that the case was opened on the basis that there were threats and fears.

"But there is an uglier word than fear in these courts, and it is injustice. It would be an injustice if Smith were to be convicted on the evidence you have heard ", he added. If the case against the Krays was flimsy and unsatisfactory, then the case against Smith was non-existent. "It should never have been brought."

The trial was adjourned until today.

WITNESS SAYS, "NO THREAT BY TWINS"

Mr. Sidney Vaughan, a Crown witness, told a jury at the Central Criminal Court yesterday that as far as he was concerned the Kray twins never threatened Hew Cargill McCowan, son of a wealthy baronet, and part owner of the Hideaway Club in Gerrard Street, Soho, W.

After trouble with the customs over watches there was an occasion, he said, when McCowan wanted a man "cut up" and the name and address of the man was handed to Ronald Kray.

Ronald and Reginald Kray, aged 31, twins, of Seven Sisters Road, Finsbury Park, N., and Edward Richard Smith, aged 32, self-employed writer, of no fixed address, have pleaded Not Guilty to conspiracy to demand with menaces or by force property capable of being stolen from Hew McCowan with intent to steal, and conspiracy to dishonestly and with menaces extort from Mr. McCowan such money as he might be persuaded to part with.

BASEMENT PROPOSAL

Answering further questions Mr. Vaughan said Mr. McCowan was in favour of the basement at the Hideaway Club being turned into a casino. He wanted it decorated as a castle. "The Krays were to take over the basement and we were to take the profit on the drinks, and they would pay us a rent ", the witness added. Because the lease of the premises was not in Mr. McCowan's name Ronald Kray lost interest in the proposition. The Krays never made any threats to McCowan.

Mr. Paul Wrightson, Q.C., for the defence of Reginald Kray, said to Mr. Vaughan: "Mr. McCowan says he was threatened by one or other of the Krays through you. In other words, you were the person who was conveying the threats?"

Mr. Vaughan.—That is untrue.

The trial was adjourned until Monday.

CLUB OWNER WAS WITNESS FOUR TIMES IN BLACKMAIL CASES

DEFENCE QUESTIONS IN SOHO CLUB CASE

Mr. Hew Cargill McCowan, part-owner of the Hideaway Club in Gerrard Street, Soho, W., one of the principal witnesses for the prosecution in a case involving an alleged plot to demand protection money, stated at the Central Criminal Court yesterday that on four occasions since 1955 he had given evidence for the prosecution in blackmail cases. Three of those accused were convicted but the fourth was acquitted.

Mr. McCowan, of Great Cumberland Place, Marble Arch, W., was giving evidence in the trial of Ronald and Reginald Kray, aged 31 twins, of Seven Sisters Road, Finsbury Park, N., and Edward Richard Smith, aged 32, self-employed writer, of no fixed address.

All have pleaded Not Guilty to conspiracy to demand with menaces or by force property capable of being stolen from Mr. McCowan, with intent to steal and conspiracy to dishonestly and with menaces to extort from Mr. McCowan such money as he might be persuaded to part with.

The prosecution has alleged that the accused, assisted by a man named John Francis who has not been arrested, plotted to demand protection money from Mr. McCowan who opened the Hideaway Club on December 16 last year. After certain overtures had been made Mr. McCowan went to the police.

Cross-examined by Mr. Petre Crowder, Q.C., for the defence of Ronald Kray, Mr. McCowan denied that he asked Ronald Kray on October 29 last year if he would be able to get Judy Garland to sing or entertain at the Hideaway Club. "If I had wanted Judy Garland I could have booked her myself", Mr. McCowan added.

MOTIVE DENIED

Mr. Paul Wrightson, Q.C., for the defence of Reginald Kray: Am I right in thinking that you have a motive for what you have been saying to the Court today ?

Mr. McCowan.—No.

Mr. Wrightson.—Do you think in your mind that you are unmasking people who you think have not behaved correctly ?—I am not trying to unmask anyone.

You have considerable experience of that sort of thing, haven't you, and this is not the first time you have been a witness in a case of blackmail ?—That is correct.

I am wondering how it is that you have been in this unfortunate position three times. Did you think you would get public acclaim for giving this evidence ?—I am not interested in public acclaim.

Did you tell your friends that you have been working with Detective-superintendent Gerrard for five months on this case ?—No, the first time I met Gerrard was the day after the Krays were arrested.

Answering further questions, Mr. McCowan agreed that he knew Detective-sergeant Donald at Marylebone, who had been involved in two other cases in which he (the witness) was concerned.

Mr. Wrightson.—Did you let your friends know that because of your great assistance in this matter you were going to get the O.B.E. ?—That is quite untrue.

It may sound silly, but I am wondering if that is the way your mind works ?—It is not the way my mind works.

Is it true or untrue that you applied improper pressure upon Mr. Vaughan (Mr. McCowan's agent) to go to the police station to substantiate your story ?—Totally untrue.

"DIABOLICAL FRAME-UP"

If Mr. Vaughan were to say that here, that would be wrong ?—It would be a lie.

If he said it in front of a vicar it would be even more wrong ?—It would still be a lie.

The fact is you have a fairly rich father ?—Yes.

And you have been allowed certain sums of money for your own businesses ?—Yes.

Is the situation that you have not been all that successful in business in the past ?—That is true.

And as a result your father, or the people responsible, have told you that this club venture was your last chance ? No. It was my own money in my own trust.

Mr. Wrightson.—Were you annoyed that Mr. Vaughan had not given the same evidence that you had given at the lower court ?—Yes, I was.

Mr. McCowan was then questioned about a Mr. Peter Francis Byrne. He said he knew him as someone who worked on a postcard stand in Piccadilly Circus.

Mr. Wrightson.—Is it correct to say that you have been to his flat ?—No. That is totally and utterly untrue. This is a diabolical frame-up.

The suggestion is that you knew Vaughan had been to see Byrne about you and you wanted to know what Vaughan had said to him ?—That is not correct.

I suggest that you asked Byrne to forget what Vaughan had said to him ?—Why should I care what he said. No, I did not.

It is further suggested that you threatened Byrne if he did not tell you ?—That is a lie.

CASE IN SCOTLAND

You know that Byrne was beaten up in March and had to go to hospital ?—I heard he had been slashed.

Have you threatened Vaughan similarly ?—Never.

Mr. Wrightson.—Is it right that in March, 1955, at Glasgow Sheriff Court you gave evidence in the case of a man whose name I won't mention ?—Yes, you are quite correct.

That was a blackmail case and the defendant was acquitted ?—Yes, that is true.

That makes four occasions on which you have given evidence ?—The other three were not acquitted.

Asked why he had not mentioned the case in Scotland when asked earlier, Mr. McCowan said: "That was 10 years ago and I had completely forgotten."

Mr. John Mathew, in re-examination.—Mr. McCowan, do not let us shy away from this matter. Did the blackmail relate to alleged homosexual activities of yourself ?—Yes.

Mr. Mathew.—Were you being blackmailed on these previous occasions in relation to substantial sums ?—Not that much, £500.

The trial was adjourned until today.

THE KRAYS TO BE RETRIED

JURY DISAGREE AFTER 4 HOURS

After considering their verdict for four hours the jury at the Central Criminal Court yesterday were unable to agree in the trial of three men who are alleged to have conspired to demand protection money from a West End club owner, Judge Aarvold, the Recorder of London, discharged them from returning a verdict.

A retrial was then ordered "to take place as soon as possible", but not before Tuesday next.

The accused were Ronald and Reginald Kray, aged 31, twins, of Seven Sisters Road, Finsbury Park, N., and Edward Richard Smith, aged 32, self-employed writer, of no fixed address, who had pleaded Not Guilty to conspiring to demand with menaces or by force property capable of being stolen from Hew Cargill McCowan, with intent to steal, and conspiracy to dishonestly and with menaces to extort from Mr. McCowan such money as he might be persuaded to part with.

The prosecution had alleged that the accused, assisted by a man named John Francis, who has not been arrested, plotted to demand protection money from Mr. McCowan who opened the Hideaway Club in Gerrard Street, Soho, W., on December 16 last year.

The Recorder, summing up, referred to the fact that none of the accused had gone into the witness box. "It has been very properly pointed out that that in no way proves anything against the defendants", he said.

RIGHT OF ALL

"They had no need to go into the witness box if they did not want to. There was no compulsion upon them at all. They are only exercising the right of every one of us when they say : ' You prove it if you can but I am not going to say anything. The result in this case is, however, that you have not had the advantage of hearing their explanations about the meetings which took place after October."

Dealing with a Crown witness, Mr. Sidney Vaughan (described as Mr. McCowan's agent or manager), the Judge said : " On his own admission he is prepared, or at any rate at one stage was prepared, to give false evidence on oath, to perjure himself regardless of the effect of such evidence on innocent people if by so doing he could secure for himself a continued payment of £40 a week. And he is a man, you may think, who was prepared to admit to other people that he was going to commit perjury in order to safeguard his own financial future.

" Do you think that Vaughan cared a fig for the truth ? Do you think he is prepared to say anything when his own personal interests are involved ? The prosecution do not ask you to rely upon a single word he has said. If you think that Vaughan's evidence makes it impossible for you to rely on the evidence of McCowan then that is the end of this case.

" Do not make the mistake of thinking Vaughan has been got at by the defence. That would be quite improper. There is not the slightest evidence of that."

Krays: We may sue

An Old Bailey jury yesterday found the Kray twins, 31-year-old Ronald and Reginald, and writer Edward Smith not guilty of a night club "protection plot" charge.

Later a solicitor acting for the three men said : "The opinion of counsel is being taken on the question of High Court writs being issued for false arrest and malicious prosecution."

Not guilty: The Kray Brothers' welcome home

There was Auntie May and redhead Frankie and jubilant 'Cannonball' Lee

AFTER 90 days in jail, Ronald and Reginald Kray—the ex-boxing twins from Bethnal Green who made a name for themselves in London's West End—went home in triumph to the East End yesterday, freed by an Old Bailey jury.

Home for keeps too. For both of them—found not guilty of a "protection" plot—have decided to give up their West End life.

Standing smiling on the doorstep of their parents' tiny terraced house, the twins said: "It's the quiet life for us now.

A desire for peace

"Peace and quiet—right away from the West End. That's all we want, now, today, and every day.

But in Shelley Vallance Road, the Bethnal Green of the Krays, there was little peace and quiet. The acquittal of Ronald and Reginald, with 33-year-old Edward Richard Smith, brought all the Krays out in full.

They've been kept like wild animals in a cage all this time all for nothing, he said.

Grandpop added: "As Jimmy Lee I was known as the Southern bantam-weight champ and I've watched my grandsons grow up as boxers. They're good lads.

As the new judge brought them back home from the Old Bailey outside a standstill crowd in a pink-curtained Kray headquarters came to the door for a bear hug from her men.

She was kept in her slippers and cuddled Mitzi, the family Pekingese.

They will wed soon

Reginald slipped an arm tightly round her waist. They smiled into each other's eyes. And he said simply to her: "We're to marry very soon, maybe next week."

NEXT came Mum, Mrs Violet Kray. She drew both

sons into her arms and could only say: "Wonderful. Wonderful.

THE MAY from next door ran out to give them a kiss.

THEN out bounced Grandpop Jimmy Lee, a spry 68-year-old man and once a boxer, giving his grandsons a shadow-boxing welcome.

The Kray twins and Smith, who was alleged by the prosecution to have coaxed stamps of the "protection" plot, all were found not guilty of all the charges against them.

GRANDPOP WAS THERE

stage to tell me you do not wish to hear any more."

The jury of 11 men—a 12th juror having been dismissed—then retired for 12 minutes to consider the judge's suggestion.

When they returned the foreman said: "We didn't with the case to go on."

building, rich young Mr McGowan walked away looking very upset.

"It was a double brandy in the public house opposite the court, he said: "I told the truth as I saw it. All I want to do now is to go away somewhere for a holiday to forget this whole case.

Now I want to forget

Through their counsel they both asked for costs and were refused. "A dead liberty it was they look with you."

After they had left, the

The club will go on

"It is still my intention to continue with my night club as possible. There is a dispute on at the present over the lease and a court case pending."

Mr McGowan, who said during both trials that he was a fundamental mound: My one regret is that my family may

... in braces and a bonnet when his 'good lads' Ronald (left) and Reginald Green got home to the neighbours and the family in Bethnal Green

REGGIE'S GIRL, 19-year-old Frances Shea, was there. 'We hope,' he said, 'to marry very soon—perhaps next week'

keep the Kray brothers in prison for an indefinite period without a trial?

"I can only say that I hold no brief for the Kray brothers, one of whom I have never met and the other only twice in my life.

'Matter of principle'

But that approach and even an application to the Lord Chancellor two days later failed to get the Kray bail while they were awaiting trial.

When he heard yesterday's verdict Lord Boothby said: "I'm delighted. It shall go on fighting to see that no one is kept in prison without a quiet trial. It is a matter of principle."

Waiting for the bride

Above: Former British feather-weight champion Terry Spinks (with wife, son Jarvis)

Right: Former world flyweight champion Terry Allen (that was in 1950)

'After this, no more limelight'

Outside St. James the Great—a large group of large men ...   ... waiting for Reggie Kray's bride

KRAY TWIN WEDS REDHEAD FRANCES

New job for Krays

BROTHERS ARE TAKEN ON AS PARTNERS IN SOHO CLUB WHICH FIGURED IN THEIR TRIAL

THE Kray twins have been taken on as partners at the Soho club where, an Old Bailey jury was told, they had plotted a protection racket. The jury found them not guilty.

RONALD KRAY
"A good clientele".

REGINALD KRAY
Back from honeymoon

Last night, 25 days after their acquittal following a re-trial, the lights went on again outside the Hide-a-Way, in Gerrard Street.

It was the first time since twins Ronald and Reginald, and writer Edward Smith, were cleared of demanding money with menaces from Hew McCowan, when he was running the Hide-a-Way club.

NAME

The club has been re-named the El Morocco. Running it are Mr. Gilbert France, who owns the premises, the Kray twins and elder brother Charles; Edward Smith, and Mr. Fred Foreman.

Reg Kray flew back from his honeymoon in Greece to be at the opening.

Said Ronnie Kray: "McCowan wanted us to go into partnership with him when he was running the club but we refused.

"Now we have been cleared and it's all behind us. Mr. France has decided to run it himself and has asked us to join him.

FACES

"There will be no membership as such. People's faces will be their membership card. We want to build up a good clientele and run a high-class, respectable club.

"Charlie is managing a young pop group from Yorkshire, called The Shots, and they will be playing here to start with. We shall be having some top-line acts."

GUN MURDER AT THE 'BLIND BEGGAR' PUB

A MAN was shot in the head last night as he stood drinking at the London pub called The Blind Beggar. Two hours later he died.

By then, detectives were already at work, trying to find out if the shooting was connected with Tuesday's early-morning shotgun-gang battle at a gambling club, in which another man died.

Police believe that last night's killing is part of an underworld war which has been going on for months.

It was about 8.40 p.m. when death came to the saloon bar of The Blind Beggar—the East End pub in Whitechapel-road, Stepney, where car dealer Thomas ("Ginger") Marks often used to drink before he vanished, two years ago.

As 38-year-old George Cornell stood drinking in the bar, a man walked in. Three shots were heard. One hit Cornell in the face.

Nursed

Cornell fell to the floor. The gunman fled. Five of the pub's regular customers ran outside. But they were too late to see the car in which the killer drove off.

A barmaid and barman nursed the dying Cornell as they waited for an ambulance and the police.

Cornell was taken to the Mile End Hospital, then to the Maida Vale Hospital. Surgeons began an emergency operation.

But at 10.40 p.m. he died.

At 11.5, Mrs. Cornell—mother of a young boy—arrived at the hospital with friends.

Pistol

She told the police that at 9.30 p.m. at home in Masterman House, Elmington Estate, Peckham, she had an anonymous phone call from someone who said: "Your husband has been shot."

During the emergency operation, a bullet had been taken from Cornell's head. It was thought to be from a nine-millimeter pistol.

Detectives investigating the killing talked to The Blind Beggar's licensee, Mr. Patrick Quill, and his staff.

Two men who had been talking with Cornell could not be traced.

A regular customer, 70-year-old Thomas

The scene .. *Police outside The Blind Beggar pub after last night's shooting in which a man died.*

Continued on Back Page

Man shot down at the Blind Beggar bar

GANG WAR NEW KILLING

Blind Beggar victim 'set up for death'

THE killing of small-time criminal George Cornell has set London's underworld on edge

It now seems certain that he was shot in the Blind Beggar pub, Stepney, as a direct result of the gun fight two days earlier at a casino in Catford.

That battle—in which 36-year-old "Dickie" Hart died, and at least four other men were wounded—was between two mobs struggling to control fruit-machine gambling.

Cornell — who had twice been jailed for violence, and was also known as Myers—was a friend of at least one of the wounded men.

REVENGE?

Detectives suspect that he was "set up" on Wednesday night for a revenge killing in the bar of the Blind Beggar —a favourite pub of vanished car-dealer Ginger Marks.

It is thought a phone call lured Cornell from his council flat in Elm-Ington Street, Peckham.

FACT: He was sitting at the bar chatting to two men on either side of him when the killer came in.

Cornell, father of two children, showed no panic as the man walked 20 paces to reach him.

THEORY: Either the gunman was someone he trusted, or a stranger hired for the job.

SILENCE

There was no fight. Just the wicked crack of an automatic— believed to be a 9mm. Luger.

The killer ran out to a waiting car. Cornell's two companions vanished. The underworld's wall of silence has swallowed up all three.

Now the fear is that a new round of revenge shootings may begin.

● Detectives want to see two men about the Catford shooting. One is 24, and possibly wounded in the head. The other is 37, and heavily tattooed.

MAIL ROBBERY CASE CHIEF TO PROBE GUN KILLINGS

SCOTLAND YARD, faced with the threat of more murder reprisals by gun-law gangsters, took an unprecedented step last night.

Chief Superintendent Thomas Butler, head of the Flying Squad, was appointed co-ordinating supervisor of the investigations into this week's two London killings.

Primary reason for this unusual step is the now almost 100 per cent proof that the murders are connected and that both are linked with the protection and gambling rackets.

An additional reason for the departure from police routine is a suggestion from a reliable underworld source that there will be at least one more murder bid this weekend.

Dedicated

Mr. Butler — who directed the investigation into the £2,500,000 train robbery—is a tough, dedicated 52-year-old bachelor with many underworld contacts.

He probably is the one man who can break the wall of silence which has gone up around the gangland murders.

His operational headquarters will be Leman Street police station, Stepney, and he will have hour-to-hour contacts with Detective Superintendent John Cummings and Detective Superintendent James Axon.

Superintendent Cummings is the officer who has been investigating the murder of Richard Hart in a Catford gaming club last Tuesday.

Superintendent Axon has been heading the inquiries into the shooting of George Cornell at the Blind Beggar public house, Stepney, on Wednesday.

Fear

Both men, who were known to police, were killed by heavy calibre bullets.

Fear of violent reprisals has made these the cases of frightened witnesses.

A £20 FINE was imposed at Greenwich yesterday on Leonard James Parsons, aged 22, who was found with an unloaded .22 revolver in Mr. Smith's club, Catford, scene of Tuesday's shooting.

Detective Sergeant Russell Harris told the court that he found Parsons on Thursday night with the revolver tucked into his belt. He explained: "I heard about the bothers and I just wanted to be flash."

GANG WARFARE

This battle is mostly over control of 'one-armed bandits'

ANOTHER KILLING BY GANG GUNMEN

TWO shots at midnight signalled yesterday the twenty-first shooting in London this year and the fourth killing by the gun-gangs.

The victim was 42-year-old Ernest Arthur Isaacs, known as "Jovial Ernie," a street trader who had some criminals among his friends.

He was found shot in the basement living-room of his terrace home in Penn-street in the tough district of Hoxton—a district regarded by the police as the centre of London's underworld.

The police believe that Isaacs invited two men—who were to be his executioners—to his home soon after 11 p.m. on Monday.

Two floors above the basement, 35-year-old Mrs. Vivienne Isaacs and two children — Patricia, 4, and Caroline, 2—were asleep.

Silencer

They heard nothing of the murder—the killers are thought to have used a gun with a silencer.

It was not until 5.45 a.m. yesterday that Mrs. Isaacs went down into the basement and found her husband dead.

The detectives know that Isaacs left his home at about 8 p.m. on Monday.

He went to a number of pubs and ended up at his local—the Merry Monarch in Murray-grove, Hoxton.

The police have learned that he left at 11 p.m. with a fair-haired man who was slim, aged 25 to 40, and smartly dressed.

That, so far as the detectives know, was the last time anyone but his killers saw "Jovial Ernie" alive.

Last night the detectives appealed to the fair-haired mystery man to come forward.

Friends

Isaacs was known to have a number of underworld friends among the notorious "South London Mob." He was also on Christian-name terms with George Cornell —shot dead in the Blind Beggar pub—and with another man involved in a shooting at Mr. Smith's Club in South London.

Apart from their inquiries in the underworld, the police interviewed business associates of Isaacs.

A few hours after the murder was discovered yesterday, a friend of Isaacs, Mr. Cyril Brown, 38, called

4th VICTIM THIS YEAR

at the house in Penn-street.

Mr. Brown said: "I have known Isaacs for twenty years. He was a good friend of mine and worked for me in companies I had.

"He was inclined to be rather a loudmouth. I shall tell the police all I know."

Mr. Brown added: "I fear I may be the next person on the list to be murdered.

"I am very scared and feel quite sick. I am frightened to say more about it."

Mr. Brown, who arrived at the house in Penn-street carrying a camera, said he had come to take some photographs of Isaacs and his family. Then he heard of the shooting.

DRIVE HOME TO MOTHER—

Express Staff Reporter

THE Kray twins Ronnie and Reggie left separate East End police stations yesterday after 36 hours of helping police with inquiries into the murder of George Cornell.

Cornell was shot five months ago at the Blind Beggar public house, Stepney.

Ronnie left Commercial Street police station at noon. Four hours later Reggie walked out of Leyton police station.

PARADE

The 32-year-old twins were driven in separate cars to their flat above a barber's shop in Lea Bridge Road, Walthamstow.

The twins, former East End boxers and well known in the West End's clubland, talked about what had happened to them since police raided a party at their flat in the early hours of Thursday morning.

Ronnie said: "Myself and a friend were taken to Scotland Yard where we were told an identity parade was being arranged at Commercial Street in connection with the murder of Cornell.

"At the police station we were put in a cell and not allowed to see solicitors until this morning.

"At midday we were lined up with about 13 other men and I was told that if I was picked out

I would be charged with the murder of Cornell.

"There were two witnesses—a young man and an old man—and both of them walked straight past. The police let us both go."

Reggie said: "The police told me I could have been the man seen in the car in which the killer got away. They said they were looking for a witness who would identify me.

"The first night at the police station I slept on an office floor, then I sat 18 hours in a chair. It was only last night that I got a cell and a blanket.

"Finally today they said they were letting me go and during that time I was not allowed to see a solicitor. They said they could not find the witness.

"Of course Ronnie and I knew Cornell—who didn't in the East End? But the first we knew of his death was when we read of it in the newspapers."

BIRTHDAY

Reggie was driven to the flat in a Jaguar by Mr. Tom Cowley who was arrested with him on Thursday morning. He was released at the same time.

Added Reggie: "Thank goodness they have let us out today. We are going to have a drink with our mum. It's her birthday.

"We had nothing to do with the murder of Cornell. It's not the first time we have been picked up as suspects. We are getting fed up with it."

YARD SWOOP ON PARTY IN BIG GUNMEN HUNT

KRAY TWINS SPEAK

By MIRROR REPORTERS

THE twin Kray brothers, Ronald and Reginald, went home yesterday after long sessions in which they had both tried to help police inquiries into the Blind Beggar pub murder.

Ronald Kray, 32, said he and a friend had taken part in an identity parade during his thirty-six hours at Commercial-street police station in Stepney.

Witness

"I stood there in line," he said later, at the twins' flat in Lea Bridge-road, Leyton. "Two men walked past, and didn't pick me out. I was released."

He added: "They've had months to find witnesses. It shows they were on to the wrong people."

Brother Reginald, who spent forty hours at Leyton police station, said: "They said a witness was missing.

"I didn't go on parade. But I was told I would have to, if they found the witness."

The victim in the Blind Beggar murder, last March, was 38-year-old George Cornell. He was shot dead while drinking at the pub, in Stepney.

Ronald Kray said last night: "Reg and I both knew George. He was well known in the East End.

Party

"But the first we knew of his death was through reading about it in the newspapers."

The Kray twins were called on to see if they could help Scotland Yard's inquiries, while they were having a party at their flat, early on Thursday.

"My brother," Ronald Kray said last night, "was taken to Leyton station. I was taken to Commercial-street.

"I thing they separated

'It was all about the pub killing'

us because they didn't want to mix us up."

Ronald Kray were on: "The police didn't ask many questions. They said it was about the George Cornell affair.

"They just said I was going on parade. And they kept me thirty-six hours waiting for it.

"They didn't tell me of any charge they wanted to make against me—or anyone else."

He added: "They looked after me all right. I had sausages and mash and—another time—pie, beans and chips. And there was tea when I wanted it."

Before he left the Commercial-street station. Ronald Kray saw the Yard's Flying Squad boss, Chief Detective Superintendent Tommy Butler.

"Mr. Butler told me," Ronald Kray said, "that if they wanted to see me again, he'd get in touch."

Worried

Brother Reginald said that the police told him they were investigating the Blind Beggar shooting.

"It's getting a bit strong, the coppers involving us in all this," he complained.

He added: "Our Mum has been very worried about all this.

"It's her birthday today —she's fifty-six.

"So we'll be having a little drink, and cheer her up."

DETECTIVES from Scotland Yard's Flying Squad made a series of swoops early yesterday in East London.

The raids were organised by Chief Detective Superintendent Tom Butler, who has been investigating gangland shootings — including the murder of 38-year-old George Cornell last March at the Blind Beggar public house in Stepney.

Seven men went with detectives to police stations. Last night three were still helping inquiries.

Before the raids, Flying Squad men and East London detectives met for a secret briefing by Chief Superintendent Butler.

Troops, helicopters hunt jail terrorist

Searchers: Commandos, jail officers and police

ESCAPE: WHY IT HAPPENED

MITCHELL

By ALFRED DRAPER
on Dartmoor
MAURICE TROWBRIDGE
in the Commons

AS Commandos and helicopters joined the Dartmoor hunt for violent giant Frank Mitchell yesterday Home Secretary Mr. Roy Jenkins came under fire from M.P.s and prison officers.

A "calculated risk" was taken, Mr. Jenkins told the Commons, in allowing Mitchell to go on outside working parties.

But Mr. Fred Castell, secretary of the Prison Officers' Association, said: "The calculations are made by those in authority and the risks are taken by the prison officers. Mitchell should never have been allowed out."

Dartmoor staff said they repeatedly objected but were overruled.

It was reported that Mitchell terrorised fellow prisoners into being his " servants " and that he used to visit a pub while out on working parties.

THE TEST

Mr. Jenkins disclosed that in fact the question had been raised of releasing Mitchell— who was serving life for robbery with violence.

Sanction for him to work outside was given in May 1965 after he had been in prison six and a half years.

"The object of outside working parties," said the Home Secretary, " is to test the trustworthiness and develop the responsibility of a prisoner in conditions of less than maximum supervision when his eventual return to the community is contemplated.

"The former governor of Dartmoor had recommended on several occasions that a date should be given for Mitchell's release.

"The general view of the authorities at the prison was that Mitchell had matured considerably and his conduct on the working party since 1965 had given reason to expect that he would not abuse the degree of trust employment in an outside working party entails."

Mr. Jenkins added: " I very much regret that this trust proved unfounded."

WARNINGS

Tory Mr. Michael Heseltine, whose Tavistock constituency is near the jail, mentioned two warnings given about Mitchell. And Shadow Home Secretary Mr. Quintin Hogg asked what account was taken of them.

Mr. Jenkins said: "There was nothing in his conduct over the past 18 months that gave

MINISTER
Calculated risk

WARDERS
Warnings overruled

TORIES
Big protest

POCKET CARTOON
by OSBERT LANCASTER

"How about all of us going out on an honour party to Primrose Hill!"

down a Commons motion for an inquiry into the Mitchell affair, backed by 40 Tories.

It seems that on working parties Mitchell sometimes had something stronger than tea.

Mr. Edgar Roberts, landlord of the Peter Tavy Inn, said that over the last two weeks a man he thought was Mitchell " came in at lunchtime and drank cider."

Mr. Roberts added: "He boasted about his strength and showed me his muscles. He

Mitchell hide-out tip starts search

By PERCY HOSKINS and ALFRED DRAPER

DETECTIVES concentrated in the East End last night after a tip that Dartmoor runaway Frank Mitchell was "holed up in a disused building."

A reliable informant told Scotland Yard that he was being harboured by two hoodlums.

The place: " Within a square mile of Hackney town hall in Mare Street."

Detectives used commercial vehicles as observation posts on suspect addresses.

AXEMAN: YARD SEEK 2 GANGSTERS

MPs DEMAND MAD AXEMAN 'AT ONCE'

FRANK MITCHELL, the "Mad Axeman" of Dartmoor, was still on the run last night—after a day of drama on the Moor and uproar in the House of Commons.

Helicopters and 100 Royal Marine Commandos were called in to help 200 police in a massive hunt over rain-lashed Dartmoor.

By MIRROR REPORTERS

But there was no sign of 37-year-old Mitchell, who vanished from an outside prison working party on Monday.

He was serving a life-sentence in Dartmoor for robbery with violence.

As the search went on, a furious row broke in the House of Commons over the escape.

Home Secretary Mr. Roy Jenkins faced cries of: "Resign!" from angry Tory MPs.

The MPs, led by Mr. Michael Heseltine (Tavistock), tabled a motion demanding an immediate inquiry into why Mitchell, a man with a record of violence, was allowed to join an outside working party.

Warned

Their motion asked: Was it true that prison staff and others had warned against putting him on an outside party—and if so, who overruled them?

Mr. Jenkins told MPs that Mitchell had been a model prisoner for the past eighteen months.

He added that the former Governor of Dartmoor had several times recommended that a firm date should be set for Mitchell's release.

He said that the decision to put any prisoner on an outside working party was a "calculated risk."

Regret

But placing a criminal on trust like this was necessary—"rather than to let them out among the public on licence without any trial as to how they might behave."

Mr. Jenkins went on: "I very much regret that this trust proved unfounded."

Mitchell has already escaped from Rampton and Broadmoor mental institutions, and from Hull jail.

He was called the "Mad Axeman" after he used an axe in a robbery when he was on the run from Broadmoor in 1958.

At 6ft. 1in. tall and 16st.

Continued on Back Page

The hunters . . . A commando and a police inspector check a map of the search area.

Jail governor to check 'Mitchell in pub' stories

By KENELM JENOUR

THE Governor of Dartmoor jail is to investigate reports that escaper Frank Mitchell has been visiting a pub while working outside the prison.

A Home Office spokesman said in London last night: "We have no knowledge of Mitchell going into a public house. It seems a most unlikely story, but it will be investigated fully."

Earlier, Mr. Bob Roberts, landlord of the 15th century Peter Tavy Inn, about six miles from the prison, spoke of the huge man in green denims who has been popping into the pub for a drink and a meal over the past two months.

Fifty-six-year-old Mr. Roberts said: "As soon as my wife Mary saw Mitchell's picture in the papers, she said that it was the man who has been coming into our pub at lunch times and early evenings.

"He was always with a small man who wore horn-rimmed spectacles. This man also wore denims."

Upset

Former prisoner Christopher Williams, freed from Dartmoor three weeks ago, claimed yesterday that Mitchell used to visit a pub on the moor.

Williams said in Plymouth: "For the past three months Frank has been slipping away from his working party to a pub at lunchtime for a drink and a bite.

"Nobody ever grassed on him. I remember one screw upset him, so he gave him a bear hug and the screw just crumpled to the ground with broken ribs."

Helicopter in big Moor hunt: Page Two.

Did the underworld threaten him?

POLICE NET TIGHTENS

EDWARDS DRAMA

From this phone box (pictured below) off Southwark Bridge Road, Ronald "Buster" Edwards made the dramatic call to New Scotland Yard last week which led to the meeting, "over a cup of tea" between Edwards and Chief Superintendent Tom Butler, head of the Flying Squad.

After the talk, at which Edwards was alleged to have said, "I have been thinking of giving myself up for some time," he was driven to Aylesbury for further questioning in connection with the Great Train Robbery of three years ago.

It was in one of the flats in the block in background of our picture that the dramatic confrontation took place in the very early hours of the morning.

Edwards was also alleged to have said: "There are a dozen and one reasons why I want to give myself up. On their own they don't mean much but, put together, they do."

According to Chief Superintendent Butler, Edwards has been co-operative and has answered all questions put to him.

HID IN SOUTH LONDON?

Police believe that he has been hiding out in South London for some time.

Now the intensive hunt continues for Ronald Biggs, who escaped from Wandsworth Prison, and Charles Wilson, who got away from Winson Green Prison in Birmingham.

And the hunt for these men, as well as a third man, Bruce Reynolds, who is still wanted for questioning in connection with the robbery, is concentrated in South London.

Police are keeping a special watch on the block of flats where Edwards gave himself up.

Watches are being kept on all main roads out of London. A police spokesman said that Edwards' action may precipitate moves by Biggs, Wilson and Reynolds.

"We are ready for them," he said.

● It is believed that one of the major factors in Edwards' surrender was the Underworld itself. Criminal circles in South London into whose hands some of the proceeds of the Great Train Robbery undoubtedly found their way, were desperate to ease the intense police pressure that has produced many recent arrests and may have forced Edwards to come forward

Ex-'House of Peacocks' owner on conspiracy charge

GEORGE JAMES EVANS, former owner of the "House of Peacocks," at Beulah Hill, Upper Norwood, was allowed bail when he appeared at North London Court last Friday.

JENKINS TO ORDER BIG JAIL SECURITY SHAKE-UP

Dartmoor warders in plea to Mitchell

By DOUGLAS SLIGHT

AN appeal to runaway prisoner Frank Mitchell goes out today—from a group of Dartmoor prison officers.

The warders think that 37-year-old Mitchell, who escaped from a Dartmoor outside working party last Monday, may want to give himself up by now. Yesterday, they asked the Daily Mirror to publish this plea to Mitchell:

If you let us know where to meet you, we will be quite willing to pick you up.

One prison officer told me: " It is quite on the cards that Mitchell is keen to get back, but frightened to give himself up to the police.

" We think he would be far more inclined to give himself up to people who know him and he knows he can trust.

Meeting

" We appeal to him to get in touch with your paper, so that we can bring the matter to a close without anyone getting hurt."

This unofficial offer is likely to be supported by the local Prison Officers' Association branch at a meeting tonight.

A statement which the unofficial group of warders issued last night said: " Despite contrary statements made by people outside the prison, there is a feeling among prison officers that Mitchell will not be offering any violence.

" During his absence there has been no report of any crime, nor indeed any sighting of him since he was reported missing.

" Prison officers believe he might easily surrender to someone he trusts. There is a growing feeling among the prison staff that Mitchell, wrongly, of course, may be trying to prove something.

Trusted

" He may surrender to a member of the prison service, and thus prove himself to be the person those in charge of Dartmoor believe he had grown to be."

The statement added: " If he does this, he will not only gain reasonable consideration for himself, but will also vindicate those who trusted him and were proved wrong—and prove wrong, indeed, those who have condemned him."

Mitchell—he is 6ft. 1in. tall and weighs 16st.—was serving a life sentence in Dartmoor for an axe attack on an elderly couple while he was on the run in 1958 from Broadmoor mental institution. He had also escaped from Rampton institution.

Late last night, police at Shoreham, Sussex, searched yachts and motor-cruisers in the harbour, after a report that Mitchell had been seen calling at the Schooner Hotel, in nearby South-wick.

DARTMOOR PROBE STARTS

And the pantomime season opens one week early

WITH THE AMAZING PRISON LIFE OF FRANK MITCHELL

MURDER

Does the word mean anything to YOU any more?

HERE are 10 names: Ivor Pearce, William Barnett, Alice Bunn, Ramon Bravo, Tadeusz Szpotanzici, Agnes Standing, Ernest Isaacs, Frederick Bradshaw, George Cornell, and Richard Burnett.

They are the victims of London's forgotten murders—although they were all crimes committed within the last six months. Forgotten by practically everybody ... except relatives, close friends, and a handful of detectives.

Police chief in Axeman probe

Daily Mirror

4d. Wednesday, December 21, 1966 ✦ ✦ ✦ No. 19,594

I escaped so everyone would know of my plight

A LETTER TO THE MIRROR–SIGNED FRANK MITCHELL

The final break with Rhodesia

By VICTOR KNIGHT

A FIRM pledge that rebel Rhodesia will not now get independence except under African majority rule was given yesterday by Premier Harold Wilson.

It means that all offers of a settlement made to Ian Smith's rebel regime have been withdrawn.

This announcement by Mr. Wilson in the Commons fulfils the undertaking given to the Commonwealth Premiers' conference last September.

Mr. Wilson told M.P.s he still believed that Mr. Smith wanted a settlement along the lines worked out aboard the cruiser Tiger earlier this month.

But the Premier declared: "It is now clear that he is a prisoner of some very racialist and fascist-minded people."

Uproar

And he said that there was no future in any further talks with "that crowd of people."

Any future legal government in Rhodesia would be free to take up negotiations, Mr. Wilson said.

There was uproar when Opposition spokesman Sir Alec Douglas-Home said that Mr. Wilson's statement would be "bitterly regretted" and appealed for a reopening of talks.

For the first time last night, the British Government revealed a detailed record of the Tiger talks.

The account shows that during the first day Mr. Smith appeared willing to reach agreement.

But the following day his attitude hardened after he received a telegram from Salisbury.

In the final minutes, Mr. Wilson told Mr. Smith that Britain had not reversed her earlier undertaking not to use force to end the rebellion.

But, he warned, the regime should not assume that the British Government "would necessarily be able to maintain this position."

The Letter

Mitchell—"unhappy."

This is the letter which arrived at the Daily Mirror office in London yesterday .. signed Frank Mitchell and bearing an ink finger-print in the top right-hand corner.

By TOM TULLETT and EDWARD VALE

A LETTER signed "Frank Mitchell" arrived at the Daily Mirror office in London yesterday.

And last night, it seemed almost certain that the letter had been sent by Dartmoor jail runaway Frank Mitchell, 37.

The letter, addressed to the Editor of the Mirror, said:

"Sir, The reason for my absence from Dartmoor was to bring to the notice of my unhappy plight. To be truthful I am asking for a possible date of release.

"From the age of nine I have not been completely free, always under some act or other.

"Sir, I ask you where is the fairness of this. I am not a murderer or sex maniac, nor do I think I am a danger to the public.

Punished

"I think that I have been more than punished for the wrongs I have done."

The letter added: "I am ready to give myself up if I can have something to look forward to.

"I do not intend to use any violence at any time should I be found, that is why I left a knife behind with my prison things.

"Yours sincerely, Frank Mitchell."

In a postscript, the writer repudiated a Sunday newspaper article which said that according to an "old friend and former prison companion," named Denny Darling, Frank Mitchell would surrender after Christmas.

Mitchell escaped ten days ago from a working party outside Dartmoor jail, where he was serving a life sentence for robbery with violence.

The letter which reached the Mirror yesterday had Monday's date.

The envelope was postmarked "Ilford and Barking," on the same day.

The letter was written on cheap lined paper. In the top right-hand corner was a blue-ink fingerprint.

Last night, Scotland Yard fingerprint experts were checking it.

The handwriting in the letter looked similar, in many ways, to the writing in letters which Frank Mitchell had sent from jail to his family.

Mitchell's father, fishmonger Sam Mitchell, 64, of Old Ford-road, Bow, East London, said: "There seems little doubt that my boy has written this letter."

Clue of a fingerprint

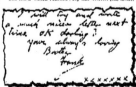

Part of a letter which was written by Frank Mitchell when he was in jail.

Another note from Mitchell

By MIRROR REPORTER

ANOTHER letter from Dartmoor jail runaway Frank Mitchell was handed to Scotland Yard last night.

The letter had been sent to The Times newspaper in London—the day after other letters from Mitchell reached the Daily Mirror and The Times.

In the latest letter, Mitchell, 37, repeats his demand for a possible date of release from his life jail sentence.

"If I must be buried alive," the letter says, "give me some reason to hope."

"It is obvious I have moved since posting my last letters," the latest message says. "I am sorry that my absence has caused certain people to think badly of men like Mr. Roy Jenkins, who I am sure is trying to use modern methods of dealing with prisons.

"What Mr. Jenkins had said is true . . . treat people like animals and they will react like animals. But treat them like human beings and they will act like human beings."

Posted

The letter was posted in Birmingham on Tuesday. The two earlier letters were postmarked Ilford and Barking, Essex.

Mitchell thanks the Dartmoor prison officers who—through the Daily Mirror—have offered to meet him and take him back to jail.

His letter ends: "Trusting in the goodness of others. Yours sincerely.—Frank Mitchell."

Mitchell escaped eleven days ago from an outside working party near Dartmoor jail. He had been serving a life sentence for robbery with violence, imposed in 1958—and a concurrent ten-year term for robbery.

Escaped

He had previously escaped from mental institutions at Broadmoor and Rampton.

A few hours before the arrival of his latest letter was revealed, the Home Office announced this unprecedented offer to Mitchell:

"As Mitchell has completed his ten years' sentence, less remission, it is open to the Home Secretary to release him on licence whenever he is satisfied that there would be no risk to the public in doing so.

"If, after his return to prison, there is good evidence that he no longer constitutes a danger to the public, fresh

Continued on Back Page

The Mirror replies to FRANK MITCHELL

ANOTHER letter from escaped prisoner Frank Mitchell, pictured above, who figures prominently in the Mountbatten report, has been received by the Daily Mirror.

Mitchell has now written four letters to the Press while he has been on the run.

The first two were received by The Times and the Mirror on Tuesday. They were post-marked Ilford and Barking, Essex.

The second letter to the Mirror, which had been delayed, was received yesterday. It was posted in Birmingham and was similar to a letter received by The Times on Wednesday.

Today the Editor of the Mirror replies to Frank Mitchell. This reply and Mitchell's latest letter are on the BACK PAGE.

By ARNOLD LATCHAM

WARRANT OUT FOR MISSING RONALD KRAY

A WARRANT was issued at the Old Bailey yesterday for the arrest of 32-year-old club owner and ex-boxer Ronald Kray, one of East London's well - known Kray Twins.

He has been missing for more than a month.

Mr. Justice Widgery was told that Kray, of Vallance Road, Bethnal Green, refuses to give evidence against a detective he has accused of corruption.

The warrant was applied for by Mr. John Mathew, counsel for the Director of Public Prosecutions.

He said Kray alleges that 33-year-old Detective Sergeant Leonard Alfred Townsend, of Dereham Road, Barking, Essex, and of Hackney C.I.D., demanded a £50 a week bribe from him.

After an investigation of Kray's complaint Sergeant Townsend was arrested and charged with that, on October 3 last year. Kray wrote to the Director of Public Prosecutions indicating he did not wish or intend to give evidence in the case.

He failed to appear in court on December 13 to give evidence.

Counsel for Detective Sergeant Townsend, who is on bail, said the arrest application was not opposed.

Mitchell hunt

Armed detectives hunting Dartmoor escaper Frank Mitchell searched a large Victorian house in Cazenove Road, Stoke Newington, North London, yesterday. They found nothing.

Home Office denies 'deal' with Mitchell

By JOHN BALL

THE Home Office denied last night that it was entering into a bargain with Dartmoor fugitive Frank Mitchell to persuade him to surrender.

'THE NOTORIOUS KRAY TWINS' BY A COUNSEL

By GEORGE GLENTON

TWIN brothers 'Ronald and Reginald Kray were described as "notorious characters" at the Old Bailey yesterday.

"They are persons of the worst possible character," said Crown counsel Mr. John Mathew. "They have convictions between them for violence, blackmail and bribery."

The activities of the brothers, added Mr. Mathew, were always of interest to the police.

Ronald Kray was to have been a prosecution witness at the trial of a detective sergeant before the court—Leonard Townsend, 36, stationed at Hackney, London.

Townsend, of Dereham-road, Barking, is accused of attempting to obtain £50 from Ronald Kray as an inducement to show favour, and of corruptly accepting £50 through a publican for showing favour to Ronald Kray.

He has pleaded not guilty to both charges.

Mr. Mathew told the jury that, after making a complaint against the detective sergeant, Ronald Kray later refused to give evidence for the prosecution and disappeared.

He had not been found, though an arrest warrant was issued by an Old Bailey judge so that he could be brought to court as a witness.

But, Mr. Mathew went on, evidence by Kray could still be put before the jury.

Recording

This was because a tape recording of the actual attempt to obtain money from Ronald Kray was taken at a public house, the Bakers' Arms, Northiam-street, Hackney, last August.

Ronald Kray had contacted a private detective—a Mr. Devlin—and a tape recorder was hidden in a potato crisps tin.

Kray was also fitted with a personal tape recorder, with a microphone hidden under his shirt.

In the recording it was alleged, Townsend said he appreciated that Kray needed a little place to work quietly and said Kray could use the public house —it was on his "manor."

Mr. Mathew said that Townsend asked for "a little bit of rent ... a pony a week each"—£25 each for himself and another officer.

Ronald Kray was said to have replied: "I will have to discuss it with my brother, because everything I do, I do with my brother."

Eventually, added Mr. Mathew, it was arranged that Townsend should collect £50 at a rendezvous with the pub licensee. This meeting was arranged in co-operation with the police—who closed in on Townsend.

The trial goes on today.

The Kray brothers . . . Ronald (left) and Reginald.

Kray put bribery demand on tape fitted to chest, jury is told

By ARNOLD LATCHAM

RONALD KRAY had a tape recorder fitted to his chest when he met a detective sergeant who was trying to obtain a bribe from him, it was alleged yesterday at the Old Bailey.

Mr. John Mathew, prosecuting at the trial of Detective Sergeant Leonard Alfred Townsend, of Hackney C.I.D. described Kray as "one of the two notorious brothers who between them have convictions for violence, blackmail, and bribery."

Sergeant Townsend, of Dereham Road, Barking, Essex, pleads not guilty to two charges of corruptly attempting to obtain £50 from Kray on August 11 last and accepting £50 on August 15.

Mr. Mathew said that at the meeting, in the Baker's Arms public house, Northiam Street, Hackney, another tape recorder was hidden in a potato crisp tin.

He said that although Kray originally reported the alleged bribery attempt, he later refused to give evidence and had disappeared. A warrant was out for his arrest.

A MEETING

Last July, Kray and some of his associates began using the Baker's Arms. On August 9 Sergeant Townsend and another policeman entered the public house.

Mr. Eric Marshall, the licensee, said he did not like the police visiting his premises and causing customers to leave. Sergeant Townsend, it was alleged, replied: "There is no reason why the Kray Twins should not use your public house, provided they accept my terms."

A meeting was arranged between Ronald Kray and Sergeant Townsend.

Before the meeting Kray contacted a private detective and a tape recorder was hidden in a potato crisp tin. Kray also had a tape recorder fitted to his chest.

In the small room, said counsel, Sergeant Townsend said: "You can use the pub on my manor for a little bit of rent. There are two of us in it—a pony (£25) a week each."

It was agreed the money should be paid each Friday.

The tape recording of the meeting was handed to Scotland Yard.

The trial continues today.

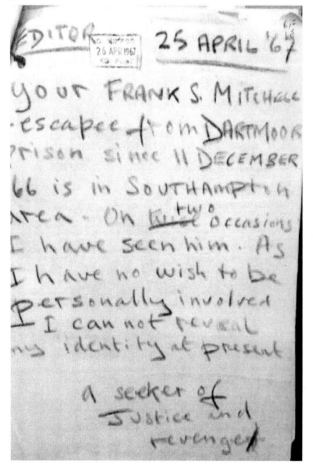

EDITOR 26 APR 1967 25 APRIL '67

your FRANK S. MITCHELL escapee from DARTMOOR prison since 11 DECEMBER 66 is in SOUTHAMPTON area. On two occasions I have seen him. As I have no wish to be personally involved I can not reveal my identity at present

a seeker of Justice and revenge

35

Wedding day . . . Mrs. Frances Kray and her
husband Reginald.

Wife of a Kray twin found dead

MRS. Frankie Kray, wife of one of the Kray twins, was found dead at home yesterday.

She is believed to have died from a drugs overdose.

A police spokesman said last night: "Crime is not suspected."

Frankie, 23, married Reginald Kray in April, 1965. It was the wedding of the year in East London, attended by 200 guests. The couple lived in Wimbourne-court, Hackney.

KRAY TWIN'S WIFE KILLED HERSELF BY DRUGS

By EDWARD VALE

THE wife of Reginald Kray, one of the East London twins well-known in sporting circles, killed herself with an "enormous" overdose of drugs, a coroner said yesterday.

The coroner, Mr. Ian Milne, also said of the wife, Mrs. Frances Kray, 23: "She had a two-year history of personality disorder.

"Her marriage was on the rocks, though there seems to have been recent hopes of a reconciliation."

The inquest, at St. Pancras, London, heard that Mrs. Kray was married in 1965. She reverted to her maiden name when she started to live with her married brother at Wimbourne-court, Shoreditch, last January.

Her brother, haulage contractor Frank Shea, said his sister had been given tablets regularly by her doctor.

Holiday

Dr. Julian Silverstone, a consultant psychiatrist, said Mrs. Kray had been in hospital for "a personality disorder" and was later twice admitted for drug overdoses—once after being found in a gas-filled room.

The doctor added that, when he saw Mrs. Kray two days before she died, she talked about a holiday and seemed much better.

The Kray brothers who were detained yesterday. . . . Reginald (left) clasps hands with Charles and Ronald in a picture which was taken in April, 1965.

KRAYS HELD IN DAWN RAID

By TOM TULLETT and EDWARD VALE

TWIN brothers Ronald and Reginald Kray, well known in London sporting and club circles, were among twenty men detained by Scotland Yard detectives yesterday.

One hundred detectives and twenty policewomen took part in a series of raids—one of the biggest and most secret operations in the Yard's history.

The first call by the police was on the 34-year-old Kray twins and their brother Charles, 41, at dawn.

All three were detained at the home of their mother in a council flat on the ninth floor of Braithwaite House, City-road, Finsbury.

After the three brothers were taken to West End Central police station—where other detained men were also taken later—the flat was put under guard.

Boxers

The Kray twins, both with notable records as amateur boxers, are known for the support they have given to charity affairs. Their names have been associated with several clubs.

Reginald Kray, who with his twin brother was described as a director of a hotel in Finsbury Park, was married in April, 1965. The wedding guests included boxers Terry Spinks and former world flyweight champion Terry Allen.

The swoop yesterday followed two years of intensive undercover activity by Yard detectives, directed by Commander John du Rose.

The special team of detectives he appointed—led by Detective Superintendents Leonard Read and Donald Adams — moved away from their offices in Scotland Yard and worked

Kray brothers held

from another police building in the West End.

Then at 1 a.m. yesterday, Commander du Rose called a "raid conference."

At 2.45 a.m. the teams—between four and ten strong—left in cars and vans. Throughout the morning, a stream of men with detective escorts arrived at West End Central.

Several more raids were made at midday, and two more men later went to West End Central. By 10 p.m. two of the twenty detained men had been allowed to leave.

Kray brothers: new moves today

The Krays: Three-way handclasp for, from left, Reginald, Charles, Ronald.

By PERCY HOSKINS
JOHN BALL, FRANK HOWITT

CHARGES are expected to be made today following London's biggest-ever series of police raids in which 21 men were roused from bed and arrested.

Last night three of the men were released from West End Central police station in Savile Row.

Those arrested included the club-owning Kray twins and their elder brother, and an American who was staying at the May Fair Hotel.

Preparations that began six months ago in a small office in Tintagel House on the Embankment were climaxed just before dawn yesterday.

Behind the planning was Det. Supt. Leonard Read, 42, whose nickname is "Nipper" —and that was the code name given to the massive operation involving more than 100 detectives, in some cases outside London

Just after 3 a.m. yesterday Superintendent Read led 10 men to a ninth-floor flat in a block of flats named Braithwaite House, in Finsbury, on the edge of the City.

In bed

Glass splintered over a red-carpet and a door collapsed off its hinges.

The 34-year-old Kray twins, Reginald and Ronald, were in bed. An hour later they were at West End Central.

On the other side of the City, in Tower Hamlets, another squad went to the flat of the elder brother, Charles Kray. He too got dressed and went to the police station.

All found London Superintendent Read's men carried out their raids. Some men on their list were out of town, and pick-up orders were switched to places like Bournemouth and Southend.

One of the last to be taken in was an American named Joseph Kauffman, who the previous day had taken a room at the May Fair.

After the men came the documents — piles taken from offices, gambling houses and hotels — for examination by officers who included Fraud Squad experts.

Guards

At the modern seven-storey police station in Savile Row, special guards were on duty. An interview room was set aside for solicitors.

Mr. Ralph Haeems and Mr. J. Charman of City solicitors Sampson and Co., called there last night. Afterwards Mr. Haeems said: "We were not allowed to speak to the Kray twins whom we represent. They passed out a message asking for cigarettes. We shall be returning to see a number of the detained men later."

Meanwhile, police conferred with the Director of Public Prosecutions.

Commander John du Rose was in overall command of the operation. Apart from Superintendent Read, Superintendent Don Adams of the Great Train Robbery team took over one aspect of the inquiry and Chief Inspector Cator of the Fraud Squad another.

Court move in Kray case

A DRAMATIC new move will be made in the High Court tomorrow by defence lawyers in the Kray case.

Mr. Ivan Lawrence will ask detectives to name the victim in a case of alleged conspiracy to murder.

The Kray twins, Ronald and Reginald, with Richard Morgan, 35, of Midlothian-road Stepney, are on one of the alleged conspiracy to murder charges.

THE Kray twins Reginald and Ronald have been charged with two offences of conspiracy to murder.

Accused with them on these charges is 32-year-old Thomas Peter Cowley, of Malford Court, The Drive, South Woodford, Essex.

All three will appear in court at Bow Street today—along with 15 others.

Senior officers at West End Central police station spent nearly eight hours reading a total of 14 charges to various of the 18 men, finishing after 2 a.m. today.

The charges range from the two of conspiracy to murder to demanding money with menaces, causing grievous bodily harm, fraud, and presenting false bonds.

The 34-year-old Kray twins and their 41-year-old brother Charles are accused on two charges of demanding money with menaces—one mentioning £5,000, the other £500.

No names

The conspiracy to murder charges mention no names of the alleged intended victims. Both accuse the Kray twins and Cowley of conspiring "with other persons."

One charge covers various unspecified dates between January 1 and May 6 this year, the other various unspecified dates last year.

Ages of the 18 men range from 32 to 63. They had been in custody for 36 hours.

Just before Det. Supt. Leonard "Nipper" Read, and Det. Supt. Don Adams began the charging procedure last night nearly 40 C.I.D. men were put on guard in and around the charge room at West End Central station.

A relay of shorthand typists worked to prepare the 11 pages of charges.

38

NAME 'MURDER PLOT' VICTIM SAYS KRAY TWINS' QC

A LAWYER defending the Kray twins, who are accused of plotting to murder "a male person" made a vain attempt yesterday to find out the name of the alleged victim.

The lawyer, Mr. Paul Wrightson, Q.C. asked Detective Superintendent Leonard Read, in court at Bow-street, London:

"There is one charge of conspiring in 1966 to murder a male person—what is the name of that male person?"

Before the Superintendent could answer, Mr. David Hopkin, Q.C. prosecuting, told the magistrate Mr Gerald Rees:

"I do not see how my learned friend is entitled at this stage to ask this question of this officer."

Justice

Mr. Hopkin added: "He can apply to the Director of Public Prosecutions. At the moment, I am not in possession of that information."

Mr. Wrightson told the magistrate:

"The reason for asking is the latest of all nature—that a man is entitled to know what is levelled against him.

"To say you conspired to murder gives him no information."

Later, Mr. Wrightson asked the magistrate to direct Mr. Hopkin to give the information before the case is sent for trial.

The magistrate refused.

Earlier, Mr. Wrightson—appearing for the Kray twins, their elder brother Charles and another man—had applied for reporting restrictions to be lifted in the case.

This normally would mean that the magistrates' hearing would be reported in full.

The 34-year-old Kray twins, Ronald and Reginald, of Braithwaite House Bunhill-road, Clerkenwell face two charges of conspiracy to murder.

Faces

Thomas Cowley, 32, of Milford Court, The Drive, Woodford, Essex, faces the same charges.

Charles Kray, 41, of Townfield House, Rosehill-gardens, Birchfield Estate, Poplar, is accused —with the twins—of demanding money with menaces and other crimes.

Five other men were also in court, in custody on various charges. Another nine are on bail.

All nine men in court were remanded in custody for a week.

HELICOPTER CRASH

Three crew members were rescued unhurt when a Navy helicopter plunged into the sea 150 yards off Weymouth, Dorset, yesterday.

KRAYS ACCUSED OVER 'AXEMAN' JAIL ESCAPE

THE three Kray brothers were accused yesterday of helping to arrange the escape of axeman Frank Mitchell from Dartmoor jail.

The 34-year-old twins Ronald and Reginald Kray, with their brother, Charles, 41, were also alleged to have harboured Mitchell after the escape, seventeen months ago.

Four other men were in court at Bow-street on the same charge.

All seven men were remanded in custody for a week.

The Kray twins—with Thomas Cowley, 32, of Milford Court, The Drive, Woodford — were also remanded in custody for a week, on two charges of conspiring to murder "a male person."

For a second time, the defence tried in vain to find out the name of the alleged murder-plot victim.

Mr. David Hopkin, prosecuting, said: "I am still not in a position to furnish that information."

Two accused with Krays

Two men were accused at West End Central police station last night of an alleged fraud with which the Kray brothers and seven other men have already been charged.

The two men are David Levy, aged 41, of Turners Road, Bow, East London, and John Albert Chappell, 45-year-old driver, of Brabrook, Basildon, Essex.

'Axe-man' murder charge

ONE of the Kray twins, Reginald, was charged yesterday with murdering "axe-man" Frank Mitchell. He was already accused of helping Mitchell escape from Dartmoor. Another Londoner faced the same murder charge—Albert Joseph Donaghue, aged 32, of Devons Road, Bow.—Full story: Page 5.

The Krays' escort

HEAVY
POLICE
GUARD
AS
TWINS
AND
THEIR
BROTHER
STAND
IN
DOCK

PICTURE BY EXPRESS CAMERAMAN RONALD GERELLI

In Bow Street yesterday, the motor-cycle escort waits for the police van to leave the court yard with the Kray brothers

NINE men, among them the three Kray brothers, peered through the half-frosted windows of a police van as it sped yesterday from Bow Street Court to Brixton Jail.

In a major security operation, the van was led through the London streets by motor-cycle policemen, three special patrol vans each packed with eight constables, and two police cars.

For the 26-minute court appearance of the Krays—Charles, Ronald and Reginald—and 15 other men accused of a variety of offences, 12 constables ringed the iron-railed dock. And 20 Scotland Yard and

By ARNOLD LATCHAM

regional crime squad detectives, with their chief, Commander John du Rose, lined one wall of the court.

Reginald and Ronald Kray, 34-year-old twins, of Braithwaite House, Bunhill Row, Clerkenwell, are accused of two conspiracies to commit murder, demanding money with menaces, fraud, and two other conspiracies involving Canadian shares and securities.

Elder brother Charles, 41, of Rosehead Gardens, Poplar, faces the same charges except for the alleged murder conspiracies.

Charles Kray, dressed in a grey pin-stripe suit, crumpled after 30 hours at West End Central police station, was the first to step into the dock.

He was followed by

Reginald and Ronald, both in blue suits, and Thomas Cowley, 32, of Melford Court. The Drive, Woodford, Essex, who is also accused of conspiracy to murder.

They were remanded in custody with five other men, including 38-year-old Joseph Kaufman, American arrested at London's May Fair Hotel—until next Friday.

Bail

The nine freed on bail were remanded until May 31.

BAILED were: David Forland, 64, of Fontley Way, Roehampton, S.W.; Samuel Lederman, 63, of Wicker Street, Stepney; Harold Charles Clarke, 42, Eagle public house, Lizzard Street, Islington; Alfred Charles Willey, 46, Mostyn Grove, Bow.

William Henry Exley, 45, Woodsear Street, Stepney; Frederick Bird, 39, Bow Common Lane, Bow; Marshall Goldblatt, 33, of Abercorn Place, St. John's Wood; Mark Kennedy, 44, of Fairacres, Putney; Arnold Davis, 34, of Bedford Court Mansions, Bloomsbury.

IN CUSTODY, additional to the Krays, Cowley and Kaufman: Charles Mitchell, 39, of Ellersley Street, Fulham; Robert Gould, 38, of Bude Green, Fyfield, Ongar, Essex; Gordon Anderson, 37, of New Dover Road, Canterbury, Kent; and Thomas Welch, 51, of Rheola Close, Tottenham.

Magistrate Mr. Kenneth Barraclough told counsel for the men held in custody that they could apply to a judge in chambers for bail.

Krays face 'Axe Man' hearing today

By ARNOLD LATCHAM

THE full hearing in the case of the three Kray brothers, charged with murdering Frank "Axe Man" Mitchell, opens at Bow Street Court today.

Reginald and Ronald Kray, aged 34, and their brother Charles, aged 41, are charged with murdering Mitchell, who escaped from a Dartmoor Jail working party in December 1966.

Also accused of the murder are Albert Donaghue, aged 42, of Devons Road, Bow, London, and Cornelius Whitehead, aged 30, of Bigland Street, Stepney.

Between them—though not all face the same charges —the Krays and 15 other men are also accused of a variety of charges, ranging from conspiracy to murder, causing grievous bodily harm, and fraud.

These will be presented to the court in stages during the four months which the committal proceedings are expected to last.

At previous remand hearings defence counsel asked for the ban on newspaper reporting of proceedings to be lifted. This is expected to apply again today.

KRAYS WILL ASK JUDGES: TELL US THESE SECRET NAMES

Express Staff Reporter

THE names of two "male persons" whom the Kray twins and another man are accused of conspiring to murder are being kept secret for fear of interference with witnesses, said a Q.C. yesterday.

Mr. Kenneth Jones, Q.C., for the Crown, said in the High Court: "As soon as the Crown is satisfied that the risk of interference with witnesses will be minimal the information will be given."

Mr. Ivan Lawrence, for Reginald and Ronald Kray, Thomas Cowley, and Richard Morgan, had asked Lord Parker and two other judges for leave to seek an order requiring that they be given the names.

Leave was given. A hearing was fixed for tomorrow week.

The four are among a number of men who have been remanded several times at Bow Street. Mr. Lawrence said that the Kray brothers and Cowley are charged with conspiracy to murder in two cases and Morgan is charged in only one case.

SIX TIMES

Six times, said Mr. Lawrence, the defence had asked in vain for the names of the "male persons" to be disclosed.

The most they had been told was that the names would be disclosed during committal proceedings due to begin next Tuesday. But many charges were to be dealt with, and there was no assurance at what stage the names would be given.

Meanwhile the possibility of bail applications and preparation for the defence were being prejudiced.

Said Mr. Lawrence: "A remand hearing every eight days is not to be a mere hollow sham to prove that the accused is alive and to show him to people in the public gallery and to provide an exercise for lawyers.

"If it is to be an opportunity for a legitimate inquiry, then counsel is entitled to ask and the magistrate is under a duty to require he be told the nature and substance of the charge against the accused.

"That appears to be so fundamental a principle of natural justice that one is astounded to see it so blatantly contradicted in this case."

Mr. Jones: "I am mindful that this information should be given to the defence at the first opportunity."

NIGHT-LONG GUARD ON 2 GIRLS IN THE KRAY CASE

Guard put on axeman's 'love girl'

THE KRAYS IN COURT

A GIRL whose name is being kept secret faces the prospect of sacrificing a year of her life—because she is a key witness in the "Mad Axeman" case.

It is estimated that the committal proceedings, which opened yesterday, will last at least five months.

Then, after a month's gap, there will be an Old Bailey trial that may well last a further six or seven months.

In the meantime Miss B—one of four witnesses whose identities are being concealed—will go back each night to a secret, heavily guarded country hide-out.

And until the trial finally ends her private life—and that of Miss A another key witness —will be practically nil.

Miss B is the girl who it is alleged was ... provided ... for Frank Mitchell in a London hide-away flat where he was kept after being "sprung" from Dartmoor.

'Prisoner'

Prosecution counsel Mr. Kenneth Jones, Q.C., told of her when the hearing opened at Bow Street, London, yesterday of a murder charge against the three Kray brothers and other men.

It is claimed that he was rescued from Dartmoor and then shot outside a flat where he spent four days with Miss B.

All this time, said Mr. Jones, Mitchell was virtually a prisoner—and so was Miss B.

Then when pressure was put on Mitchell to return to jail he refused—one reason was a deep attachment he formed for Miss B during their four days and nights together.

Finally he left the flat thinking the girl was joining him later, said Mr. Jones.

A little afterwards she heard four or five bangs outside.

And, alleged Mr. Jones, one of the two men who had taken Mitchell out returned to the flat and made a phone call.

The news

He just said: "The dog is dead," and put the phone down. The four words, claimed Mr. Jones, were to give the information that Mitchell had been killed.

Afterwards Miss B was paid more than £100.

And Mr. Jones said Reginald Kray threatened that if she told anyone of the happenings at the flat they would get her, no matter where she went.

● Shortly before the case started yesterday, Ronald Kray, aged 34, was separately charged with the murder of George Cornell who was shot dead at the Blind Beggar public house, Stepney, in 1966.

Evidence concerning this charge will be given at a future hearing.

● Shortly before the case started yesterday, Ronald Kray, aged 34, was separately charged with the murder of George Cornell who was shot dead at the Blind Beggar public house, Stepney, in 1966.

Evidence concerning this charge will be given at a future hearing.

By TOM TULLETT, EDWARD VALE and BRIAN McCONNELL

POLICE directed by Commander John du Rose, the C I D chief at Scotland Yard, were last night mounting a round-the-clock guard on three court witnesses at secret addresses.

The three—two young women and a man—are giving evidence in the hearing at Bow-street involving the three Kray brothers.

One young woman told the court yesterday that she was taken on visits to Frank Mitchell—known as the "Mad Axeman" —while he was serving a life sentence at Dartmoor.

Mitchell escaped in December, 1966. For eleven days afterwards it was alleged in court yesterday, he was kept virtually a prisoner in a council flat in London's East End and then taken outside and shot dead.

The escape and the murder, said Mr. Kenneth Jones, Q.C., prosecuting were engineered by the three Kray brothers—twins Ronald and Reginald, 34, and their elder brother Charles, 41.

After the shooting, Mr. Jones also alleged, one of the Krays' "henchmen" made a phone call with just four words: "The dog is dead."

Accused

The three Kray brothers are accused with two other men of murdering Mitchell on or about December 23, 1966.

The two other men on this charge are Albert Donaghue, 32, and Cornelius Whitehead, 30.

The five men are also accused with four others—Thomas Cowley, 32, Wallace Garelick, 26, John Dickson, 38, and Patrick

Court story of Mitchell killing..'The dog is dead'

Connelly, 39—with conspiring to aid Mitchell's escape and later harbouring him.

The Krays and the other accused men arrived at Bow-street yesterday ninety minutes before the hearing began. They were escorted by police motor-cycle outriders and radio cars.

The motorcade drove against one - way street signs and policemen regulated the traffic as it passed.

Around the court—and inside — were policemen with walkie-talkie sets.

As the procession drove into the court yard, relatives and friends of the accused men gave the thumbs-up sign.

As the court adjourned last night, Commander du Rose was standing among members of the public and watching security arrangements being put into operation.

Court Story—Centre Pages.

KRAY TWINS TOLD NAME SECRET

'WE HAVE DONE ONE MITCHELL ALREADY.. IT COST 1s 9d'

A WITNESS in the "Mad Axeman" murder case said yesterday that Reginald Kray put a gun under his chin and told him: "I am going to blow your ―― head off."

The witness, Charles Edward Mitchell, said the threat was made while he sat with the three Kray brothers in a Jaguar car near London's Hyde Park.

Mitchell also alleged that Reginald Kray added: "We have done one Mitchell already. It's easy. It only cost 1s. 9d."

Mitchell went on: "I said, 'Think of my wife and children.'"

The Krays—twins Reginald and Ronald, 34, and their brother Charles, 41—are accused with two other men of the murder of "Axeman" Frank Mitchell after he escaped from Dartmoor in December, 1966.

In his evidence at the Bow-street court yesterday, 39-year-old Charles Mitchell said the Jaguar car incident happened about the middle of last summer.

Involved

He added that he knew a man named Leslie James Payne, with whom he and the three Kray brothers had been involved in transactions.

On the day of the gun incident, Mitchell added, Charles Kray phoned and said he wanted to meet him outside a Kensington hotel.

After meeting, they drove in Mitchell's car to a parking lot by the restaurant in Hyde Park. There he entered a Jaguar car and Charles Kray got in behind him.

Mitchell continued: "Reggie Kray pulled out a gun and put it under my chin. It was a big gun, an automatic.

"He said, 'You have been seeing Payne, you bastard. I am going to blow your ―― head off.'

"I was frightened out of my life."

Mitchell then spoke of the remark: "We've done one Mitchell already . . . "

In cross-examination by Mr. Petre Crowder, Q.C. for Ronald Kray, Mitchell was asked what

A meeting in a Jaguar—'I was frightened'

the reason was for a pistol to be pointed at his head.

Mitchell replied: "Because they thought I was seeing Payne. They had the needle to him."

In further cross-examination, Mitchell spoke of his discharge at the Bow-street court last week after the prosecution offered no evidence against him on charges alleging conspiracy concerning American and Canadian bonds.

He said the prosecution's move was a "complete surprise" to him and it was untrue that he had made a bargain with the police to give evidence in the present case.

Mitchell—who admitted he had "a very bad record"—alleged that he was "intimidated" while in Wandsworth Prison on remand.

He was cross-examined about his time in Wandsworth by defence counsel Sir Lionel Thompson, for Thomas Cowley, one of nine men charged with aiding Frank Mitchell's escape from Dartmoor.

Message

Charles Mitchell alleged that while in the exercise yard at Wandsworth, Cowley gave him a message.

The message, he added, was: "The Kray brothers want you to put up five grand to give somebody to take care of two witnesses."

Sir Lionel asked: "The witnesses supposed to be squared for £10,000. . . . do you know their names?"

Mitchell wrote down names. "They are big police informers," he added.

On the "Axeman" murder charge, the three Kray brothers are accused with Albert Donaghue, 32, and Cornelius Whitehead, 30.

The five are also accused with four others—Thomas Cowley, 32, Wallace Garelick, 26, John Dickson, 38, and Patrick Connelly, 39—of conspiring to aid Frank Mitchell's escape and of afterwards harbouring him.

The hearing goes on today.

KRAY SAID GIRL MAY HAVE TO GO —WITNESS

By BRIAN McCONNELL

REGINALD KRAY, one of the twins accused in the "Mad Axeman" case, was alleged yesterday to have said of a night-club hostess: "It looks as if she might have to go too."

QC TELLS OF FOUR-WORD MESSAGE THAT SPELT THE MAD AXEMAN'S END . .

'The dog is dead'

THE KRAYS IN COURT

A girl was provided in hide-out flat for man 'sprung' from The Moor, court hears

LIFER Frank (The Mad Axeman) Mitchell, "sprung" from Dartmoor jail by "The Firm" —a gang bossed by the Kray brothers—found himself just transferred from one prison to another, a Q.C. alleged yesterday.

For during Mitchell's 11 days in an East London hideaway flat—provided with a girl to keep him company—he was guarded by "minders," the Bow Street, London, magistrate was told.

By ARNOLD LATCHAM

The girl at the flat, it was said, went there in fear of the gang and was forced to stay, almost a prisoner herself.

And she, sleeping four nights with The Axemen, felt pity for him — while he became deeply attached to her.

Gifts

He gave her the grubby 3in-square calendar, clipped from a newspaper he kept in his cell for marking off the days and months of his sentence.

And a comb in a plastic case which he used for keeping himself spruce while in the Moor.

Then, flanked by two of the gang's henchmen, he walked out to his death. It is alleged—shot four times in the head in a car parked outside the flat—in Barking Road, East Ham.

One of the "minders" returned to the flat to make a telephone call. He said: "The dog is dead." And replaced the receiver.

This dramatic story of how freedom then death, is said to have come to The Axeman—whose body has never been found—on his escape from the Moor on December 12, 1966, was given by Mr. Kenneth Jones, Q.C.

Reginald Kray, one of the 34-year-old twins, of Bunhill Road, Clerkenwell, is alleged to have said that Mitchell was causing them as much trouble as George Cornell—shot dead in the Blind Beggar public house, Whitechapel, on March 9, 1966.

In the court cells yesterday, 40 minutes before proceedings began, bespectacled Ronald Kray was accused of Cornell's murder.

The girl who was moved to feelings for The Axeman—6ft. 1in., 16-stone and serving life for robbery with violence—will not be identified when she tells her story from the close-guarded witness box.

Nor will the owner of the flat —a man said to own an East End street-market bookstall—where she and The Axeman are alleged to have found tender moments together.

Initials

Mr. Jones said they would only be given initials—just as a dark-haired girl witness of 21, in green suit and lime jumper, was referred to as Miss B. She told of visits, with two of the alleged gang, to Mitchell in jail.

Five men are accused of the murder of Mitchell; and conspiring to effect his escape, and harbouring, comforting, and assisting him with intent to prevent him being taken into lawful custody.

They are: Reginald and Ronald Kray; elder brother Charles (41) of Rosefield Gardens, Tower Hamlets; Cornelius Whitehead (30), and Albert Donaghue (32).

Also accused of the escape plot are: Thomas Cowley (32), Wallace Garelick (26), John Dickson (38), and Patrick Connelly (33).

Mr. Jones opened the prosecution case by telling of :—

THE ESCAPE Mitchell, sentenced in 1958 to life jail for robbery and violence, vanished from Dartmoor on December 12, 1966, and was taken to a flat in the East End of London.

Involved in the escape itself, or the final plans for the escape, were Garelick, Connell, and a third man who would be referred to by the name of "Smith," said Mr. Jones.

He went on: "Having been kept in close custody in that flat for 11 days, on December 23 Mitchell was taken out of that flat by Donaghue and Whitehead and was shot in the street—in all probability in a car outside the flat where he had, in effect, been imprisoned.

"The case for the Crown is that the whole of the operation, which started with the plan of his escape and ended in his death, was organised and supervised by the three Kray brothers."

The other men in the dock, he said, were the Krays' henchmen.

The Krays themselves had been careful to keep in the background and they appeared rarely in the evidence.

But when they did appear, said Mr. Jones, it was in a decisive role of supervising, organising, and ordering what should happen.

Dealing with events leading up to Mitchell's escape, Mr. Jones said Mitchell apparently received few visitors.

But in the spring of 1966 Connelly, Garelick, and a girl went to see him. Mitchell said he wanted to be home for Christmas and the answer he got was: "You won't be here for Christmas."

Later both Connelly and Garelick told the young woman that "they" were going to get Mitchell out.

Vanished

Mr. Jones went on: "In June Garelick paid a further visit to Mitchell and told him arrangements were being made for his escape."

Then on December 11, Garelick and Connelly, he said, arrived at an hotel near the prison.

The next day Mitchell, outside the jail with an "honour party," vanished after a warder had allowed him to take some bread to some horses.

The magistrate heard of the alleged escape car —a Humber hired by a man named Exley—and Mr. Jones then told of :—

THE FLAT in Barking Road, East Ham, where he said Mitchell was taken on escape day.

Mr. Jones said the flat was owned by a man who some time in the past had offered Reginald and Ronald Kray the use of this flat.

On December 12 Charles Kray asked if he could have the keys and later that day Mitchell arrived.

Said Mr. Jones: "He remained there for 11 days until Friday, December 23.

"There was always at least one man in the flat to guard him. What apparently had happened was that he had exchanged one prison for another.

"The two men who were particularly charged with keeping him in the flat were Exley and the defendant Dickson. Exley was given this job by the three Kray brothers and in fact was physically taken there by Charles Kray.

Letters

"There were visitors to the flat — Connelly, Donoghue, Whitehead, and the three Kray brothers from time to time.

"During his period of incarceration, Mitchell communicated with the Press, and we know that some four letters were written by him to the Press. They were exactly similar in each instance.

"They were written by Mitchell, although they were the product of a combined effort by a man named Smith, Exley, and the owner of the flat.

"Orders had come from above that these letters should be written. Mitchell had been sentenced to life imprisonment and his great concern was the indeterminate nature of his sentence.

"He wanted a date of release."

Mitchell, said Mr. Jones, was anxious for female company, and the magistrate then heard of :—

THE GIRL who was provided for him. Said Mr. Jones: She was at the flat from December 19 and remained there for four nights and was there on December 23 when Mitchell finally left.

"She was forced to remain in the flat. If she left, then one of the minders went with her.

"During the time she was there, she talked with Mitchell and there is no question about it she slept with him. It appears, and this may be of some importance in the case, Mitchell aroused in her a feeling of pity."

And Mitchell became very fond of the woman during the four days and four nights they spent together, said Mr. Jones.

'Afraid'

Explaining how the girl came to be at the flat, Mr. Jones said that Reginald Kray, Cowley, Donoghue and Whitehead visited the club where she worked.

Went on Mr. Jones: "Cowley ordered this young woman to join them and asked her to do him a favour. She was too afraid to refuse and too afraid even to ask what that favour was.

"She was taken to a cab by Cowley and there was Reginald Kray and Donoghue. Kray told her he wanted her to do them a big favour and that if she did it she would get the respect of everyone in London—certainly in the East End."

The girl was then taken to the Barking Road flat and Mitchell was introduced to her.

Said Mr. Jones: "She was forced to remain there. She was probably as much a prisoner as Frank Mitchell himself."

He spoke then of a conversation between Mitchell, Donaghue, Whitehead and others on :—

THE LAST DAY in the flat, Donaghue and Whitehead, said Mr Jones, wanted Mitchell to go back to prison.

But Mitchell wanted to stay out at least over Christmas—and in this he might have been influenced by the attachment he had formed for the woman, added Mr. Jones.

He said that Mitchell left the flat believing he was to be taken away and that the girl was to go with him or join him afterwards—Donaghue told him that she would follow "in an hour's time."

Apparently this satisfied Mitchell, who had earlier refused to go without the woman, and he walked out of the flat without any luggage and flanked by Donaghue and Whitehead.

Said Mr. Jones: "The woman was left in the flat with the owner and Dickson and the lights were put out."

A little later, it was alleged, Mitchell was shot, and Mr. Jones told of :—

THE MESSAGE sent over the phone by Donaghue—"The dog is dead."

Mr. Jones said that following Mitchell's departure from the flat there were four or five bangs.

He said: "Witnesses will describe them like a gun being fired. Muffled because they sounded as if they came from inside a car and the submission of the Crown is that these were the shots that killed Mitchell.

"After about five minutes, Donaghue and Whitehead came back into the flat."

Donaghue then made "The dog is dead" phone call. "That was all that was said. Donaghue put the phone down."

Mr. Jones continued that Donaghue ordered a man in the flat to remove "every trace of Mitchell."

'No prints'

Some of Mitchell's belongings were burned, including a beret and a mask, and some were taken away and disposed.

The furniture and fittings were wiped clean of fingerprints. Then having removed all traces from the flat, Donaghue and Whitehead then took the girl to another flat in Whitehead's car.

The inference, said Mr. Jones, was that Mitchell must have been shot in another car which had been used to remove him from the scene.

Went on Mr. Jones: "At this other flat the girl saw Reginald Kray and he threatened her in the most solemn terms that if ever she told anyone about this, that they would get her no matter where she went, no matter how long it took."

Reginald Kray asked her if she had taken anything belonging to Mitchell and indeed, if Mitchell had anything belonging to her.

Mr. Jones said that the girl had a calendar which had

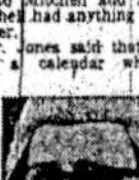

KENNETH JONES, Q.C.
Crown counsel

apparently been cut from a newspaper and which "Mitchell had kept to strike off the days as his sentence passed."

The girl, he added, was given more than £100, which she was told came from Reginald Kray.

She counted the money and spent it as quickly as possible so that she could get rid of it.

Mr. Jones then told the magistrate of :

THE TALK between Donaghue and Reginald Kray. Donaghue was overheard to say words to the effect: *"They gave him four injections in the nut. He fell on the floor and he was still moaning."*

Mr. Jones said that it was the submission of the Crown that this tied up with the bangs that were heard.

"Four injections were, in fact, four bullets in the head. That was why he fell over on the floor and was still moaning."

Mr. Jones said he would call certain evidence relating again to Reginald Kray, in which he was claimed to be saying before Christmas 1966 that "they" had sprung Mitchell.

And that Mitchell had refused to go back when told he should return to prison and that he had threatened the Krays' parents.

"Finally, Reginald Kray was saying in conversation that he intended to dispose of Mitchell and, in a later conversation, made it clear that that had been done—that Mitchell had been disposed of."

Mr. Jones also alleged that later Kray was apparently saying that the girl would "have to go."

"Apparently, she must have been entertaining some doubts of the effectiveness of the threat," added Mr. Jones.

Pointing out that there was no direct evidence that could be called proving Mitchell's death, Mr. Jones stressed: "No direct evidence in the sense of someone who has seen his dead body."

He added that Mitchell disappeared on the night of Friday, December 23, in the fullest sense of the word—"he has never been seen or heard of since that night."

Concluding his opening speech, Mr. Jones said the Crown alleged the Donaghue and Whitehead took Mitchell to his death, and were in all probability present when he was shot.

'In charge'

It was also submitted that the Kray brothers were the organisers of the whole of the conspiracy and were in charge of the operation.

Said Mr. Jones of the Krays: "As long as Mitchell would do their bidding, he was safe. When he refused, they employed henchmen to dispose of him."

Among the first witnesses called by Mr. Jones to give evidence was :—

THE GIRL who went to Dartmoor. Like the woman at the flat she was not named by Mr. Jones—"in the interests of the particular individuals," he explained.

Miss "A" told of car trips to the Moor. The first was after Patrick Connelly approached her in the Regency Club and asked her if she would like to go for a ride the next day, without saying where to or what for.

She said that along with Garelick and Connelly she went to Torquay and the following day visited Mitchell, staying with him for about two hours.

Mitchell, she said, talked a lot about "Ronnie" Kray, and said he wanted to go home. Connelly said he would be home before Christmas.

Miss A continued that about two months later she went down again with Garelick, a man called Alfie, and another girl. This time she did not go into the prison.

On the return journey, she said, they wanted to see various places near the prison, and they went around the countryside, travelling along lanes.

'A place'

Mitchell was pleased to see them and again said he wanted to come home. Miss A said that "Wally" (Garelick) said he would be coming home.

She added that later when she was with Garelick and Connelly in a night club she asked Connelly if Mitchell "would come home."

Connelly said he would. And Garelick added that "Ronnie" said he had a place for him to go to.

Miss A. complained of feeling unwell as she gave evidence and while she rested outside the courtroom the magistrate heard from :—

THE PUBLICAN on the Moor, Alfred Wise, of the Forest Inn, at Exworthy on the eastern side of Princetown.

Mr. Wise said that about the time of Mitchell's escape, three men—two of whom he recognised as Garelick and Connelly —paid two visits to his inn.

The first was on December 4, 1966. The men had lunch, and the third man, whom Mr. Wise did not recognise in court, said that they would be calling again the following Sunday.

The third man explained they would be travelling all night on their second visit, and asked if they could come early in the morning and have the use of a bathroom.

Mr. Wise said that on the following Sunday, December 11,

Continued on Page 5

Frank Mitchell . . . he was serving a life sentence

BLONDE TELLS OF LIFE WITH AXEMAN

By ARNOLD LATCHAM

IN 12 whispered words an attractive 27-year-old blonde yesterday told of her feelings for Frank Mitchell, the Mad Axeman, after four days and nights with him on his escape from Dartmoor.

"I felt very sorry for him towards the end of the period," she said in the Bow Street Court murder case hearing against the Kray brothers, Charles, Ronald, and Reginald.

The woman — a well-spoken former West End club hostess —was referred to in court as Miss C.

She wore a plain, mini-length black dress with white collar decorated with a gold chain and small medallion. A black tweed coat hung loosely over her shoulders. And dark, shell-rimmed glasses hid her eyes as she stepped into the witness-box surrounded by four detectives and two policewomen.

Five men, including the Krays, are accused of Mitchell's murder and, with four others, of plotting his escape.

'A SEARCH'

Two things Miss C disclosed about herself . . .

She had a baby at home—as she told Mitchell when they chatted for an hour or so after being introduced in an East Ham, London, flat.

And when she went there she was working at Winston's Club.

For 35 minutes she told of her life with Mitchell after arriving at the flat at 3 a.m.

She alleged that accused man Albert Donaghue (32), said: "I want you to meet a friend of mine, the Mad Axeman." And then laughed.

Miss C. said: "I was under the impression I wouldn't be able to leave that night. They told me I had to spend it with Frank Mitchell in the other room"—the main bedroom.

Only once did she leave the flat —to be driven by a man she knew as Bill to her own flat to collect underwear.

"Bill," she added, "searched my flat afterwards to see whether I had left a note."

When the court adjourned until tomorrow Miss C.—who has not completed her evidence—was hustled out of court and returned to her secret and well-guarded police hideaway.

Kray escort P.C. hurt in crash

One of the police motorcyclists escorting the Kray brothers from Bow Street Court to Brixton prison after yesterday's hearing fell from his machine on Westminster Bridge.

Constable Roger Robertson, aged 24, was taken unconscious to St. Thomas's Hospital.

Charles Kray is cleared of Axeman killing

By BRIAN McCONNELL

CHARLES Kray, 41, elder brother of twins Reginald and Ronald, was cleared of the "Mad Axeman" murder charge yesterday.

So was Cornelius Whitehead, 30, another of the five men accused of murdering "Axeman" Frank Mitchell after his escape from Dartmoor in December, 1966.

Three men were sent for trial on the charge: Reginald and Ronald Kray, 34, and Albert Donoghue, 33.

After discharging Whitehead on the murder count, Mr. Frank Milton, London's chief magistrate told him he would be committed for trial on another charge that, knowing or believing an offence had been committed he acted with intent to impede arrest or prosecution.

All nine men, before Mr. Milton at Bow-street, were sent for trial on charges of conspiring to aid Frank Mitchell's escape and of afterwards harbouring him.

The nine are: The three Kray brothers, Whitehead, Donoghue, Thomas Cowley, 32, Wallace Garelick, 26, John Dickson, 38, and Patrick Connolly, 39.

The prosecution have alleged that Frank Mitchell, after his escape, was kept for eleven days in a flat and then taken out and shot. During defence pleas yesterday, it was submitted that there was no real evidence that Mitchell was dead.

After hearing their submissions, Mr. Milton said: "I am satisfied that he is dead and that he was murdered."

Fell

Mr. Desmond Vowden, Q.C. for Charles Kray, had earlier told the magistrate: "So far as murder is concerned there is no evidence of him being concerned at all."

Mr. Lionel Thompson, for Whitehead, said the case against him fell to the ground and he was certainly not involved in any way with murder.

Of the nine men sent for trial yesterday, only Garelick was granted bail. The magistrate agreed with his counsel, Mr. Ronald Stewart, that Garelick was in a "different category" from the others.

Garelick stood in the dock as his mother, Mrs. Daisy Garelick, agreed to stand £500 bail for him.

The magistrate told Mrs. Garelick that her son must live at home, report to the police daily and not get in touch with anyone else involved in the proceedings.

Reserved

After being sent for trial, the nine men all pleaded not guilty and reserved their defence.

Before they left court, counsel raised the question of legal aid.

The magistrate observed: "Mention has been made in this case concerning affluence."

"While I hate to consider not only your clients, I must also consider the spending of public funds."

Detective Superintendent Leonard Read said a Scotland Yard detective has been deputed to look into the means of the defendants.

THE 'SECRET' NAME IS GIVEN IN HIGH COURT

By MIRROR REPORTER

A LEGAL tussle over the name of a "male person" referred to in a charge of conspiracy to murder was ended yesterday by the mention of two words: George Caruana.

Mr. Caruana was named in the High Court as being the man concerned in a charge against the Kray twins Reginald and Ronald and Thomas Cowley.

Asked

The name was given despite protests by counsel for the Director of Public Prosecutions that it should be kept secret until the charge is heard by the magistrate at Bow-street.

Counsel for the Kray twins and Cowley were told the name privately last week but wanted it made public.

Mr. Ivan Lawrence, for the accused men, told Lord Parker, the Lord Chief Justice, that the Bow-street magistrate had been asked nine times to allow questions and answers involving the name.

Each time there had been a refusal, Mr. Lawrence added.

Mr. John Leonard for the Director, said it was only a question of protecting the man himself and other witnesses.

After hearing submissions, Lord Parker said to Mr. Lawrence: "We see no reason why you should not reveal the name publicly in court today."

Mr. Lawrence then read out the charge that the Kray twins and Cowley conspired to murder George Caruana between January 1 and May 6 this year.

Lord Parker, who sat with two other judges, said: "The court has no criticism of the magistrate in the slightest."

CALL ENDS PLOT CHARGES 'SECRET'

THE Kray twins and two other accused men have been told the names of the "male person" referred to in two charges of conspiracy to murder, the High Court heard yesterday.

The four men had been given leave to seek an order against the Bow Street magistrate requiring that the information should be revealed.

Three judges were told when they granted the leave last week that the prosecution intended to keep the information secret for the time being for security reasons and the risk of interference with witnesses.

But yesterday Mr. Ivan Lawrence, appearing for the four men, said he had been given the information by prosecution counsel by telephone on Wednesday evening.

The judges—headed by Lord Parker, the Lord Chief Justice—were not told what the information was.

The first of the charges is "conspiring together with other persons to murder a male person" on dates between January and May this year. The second charge is in the same terms but relates to earlier dates.

Reginald and Ronald Kray, aged 34, and Thomas Cowley face both charges. Richard Morgan, 35, faces one charge.

Mr. Lawrence's application was adjourned.

In this bag, says QC in the Kray case, was..

'POISON GUN FOR MURDER AT THE OLD BAILEY'

By BRIAN McCONNELL

THE Kray twins were alleged yesterday to have ordered the murder of a man as he sat in court at the Old Bailey.

The weapon, a QC claimed, was to be a briefcase containing a hidden poison-filled hypodermic needle.

Mr. Kenneth Jones, Q.C., prosecuting at Bow-street, said the "fiendish idea" was foiled because the man hired for the killing decided not to go through with it.

In another alleged murder plot, said Mr. Jones, a crossbow with telescopic sights was bought to kill a man called "Greek George" —but it was decided to dynamite his car instead.

At one point in the hearing 34-year-old Reginald Kray protested: "Is James Bond going to be called as a witness? This is getting ridiculous."

Victim

The twins, Reginald and Ronald, were accused with another man of conspiring to murder an unknown man at the Old Bailey by firing hydrogen cyanide at him from the briefcase.

Two men are accused with them of conspiring to murder "Greek George" Caruana.

Mr. Jones told the court that neither intended victim was in fact killed.

He said the three accused in the first charge engaged a man called Cooper and another called Elvey because they required a man to be killed.

Mr. Jones continued: "It was a man who would not keep a meeting in an out-of-the-way place where he could be done to death.

Clips

"The final indication was that it might take place in the Central Criminal Court itself, where the man was appearing in some capacity."

Then Mr. Jones showed the court a briefcase.

In it, he said, were clips to hold a hypodermic syringe, which protruded through a hole in the case.

When a ring under the handle was pulled, springs were released and the needle was pushed out.

Mr. Jones also produced a crossbow. But, he said, Elvey may have decided it was not suitable for killing Greek George.

— Full court story—Centre Page.

Kray twin cried over 'Axeman' shooting

COURT IS TOLD

REGINALD KRAY cried on the night "Mad Axeman" Frank Mitchell was alleged to have been shot, a court was told yesterday.

A witness said Kray cried when told: "The other fellow's gone ... he had four injections in the nut and was still moaning."

This was the claim of witness William Henry Exley at Bow Street, London. He said he heard the conversation during a party at the flat of a girl called Carol in Evering Road, Hackney.

Exley, aged 45, of Woodseer Street, Stepney, is one of the men the prosecution allege "murdered" Mitchell during the 11 days he was hidden in an East London flat — four with a girl Mrs. C.— after his escape from Dartmoor on December 12, 1966.

The three Kray brothers, twins Reginald and Ronald, aged 34, and Charles, aged 42, are accused with two other men of Mitchell's murder and with four others of plotting his escape.

BAD HEALTH

Exley, serving two years for shooting with intent to murder —a sentence passed on him at the Old Bailey on June 10 last —gave his evidence with two prison warders behind him and a doctor at his side. It was said he was in bad health.

He told the court that a week after the party he asked Reginald Kray about rumours that Mitchell was dead.

Reginald Kray said: "Tell everybody we got him away abroad."

A week later, he said, he talked to Reginald Kray about the girl.

Kray said: "It looks as if you may have to go. You can do it. We're all in this together."

Exley added he told Kray: " —off. I ain't in nothing." And he said that referring to "Len"—the owner of the hideaway flat, Kray declared: "He has a weak heart. It's a pity he doesn't drop down dead."

Exley said he had known the Kray brothers about six years. He once went with Ronald Kray to visit Mitchell in Maidstone Jail.

SILLY

In October 1966 he went with Charles Kray to see Mitchell— who was serving a life sentence for "robbery with violence"—in Dartmoor.

Mitchell asked for a motor cycle to be sent down to him. Said Exley: "I said it was silly, having to worry about the tax. Have an ordinary bicycle." Charles Kray told Mitchell: "Don't worry, we'll get you something."

Exley, who said he used to drive Ronald Kray around in a mini car, then told of alleged telephone calls from Mitchell to a public house near Reginald and Ronald Kray's home in Vallance Road, Stepney.

"The first time I saw Frank Mitchell," he continued, "was at night. Charles Kray took me there by car. In a pub the three had asked me if I would look after Frank, I agreed."

WHY? I asked Mr. Kenneth Jones, Q.C., prosecuting.

Said Exley: "It was fear that something might happen to me if I didn't agree." He said

The hearing continues today.

THE KRAYS IN COURT

Charles Kray told Mitchell: "I've brought Bill to keep you company."

Exley added: "I stayed at the flat until 6 to 8 p.m. the next night, when another man— accused John Dickson, aged 33, arrived to relieve me.

"I went back to the flat the following night and this continued on alternate nights."

STAYED.

Then the girl arrived and stayed—apart from once, said Exley, when he took her back to her flat to collect clothes and leave the rent.

"The last time I saw Frank Mitchell," he said, "was when I was going out of the flat myself. I had intended to stay indoors at home but Reginald Kray insisted I should go to the party."

Exley said: "I was due to Mitchell to the flat where better-to, I told Reggie I'd rather Jack. He said they'd got someone else there that night."

It was while he continued at the party, Exley said, that accused Albert Donaghue, aged 32, arrived and told Reginald Kray: "The other fellow's gone.

The hearing continues today.

Cornell murder: Another charge

John Alex Barrie, a 31-year-old Scot, was charged yesterday with "being concerned" with Ronald Kray" in the murder of George Cornell at the Blind Beggar tavern two years ago.

Kray, aged 34, has already appeared at Bow Street magistrates' court charged with murdering Cornell. Barrie will appear at Bow Street today.

Quote *from the dock by REGINALD KRAY*

❝WILL JAMES BOND BE GIVING EVIDENCE IN THIS CASE? IT IS ALL TOO RIDICULOUS❞

'I was a US secret service man'

—SAYS WITNESS

ALAN BRUCE COOPER, 37 - year - old short, dapper - dressed American, told the Kray case hearing yesterday — that he was connected for two years with the American Secret Service.

And he claimed that he is the man who set up the plan to murder a man at the Old Bailey with a poison syringe.

At Bow Street, in the case in which Kray twins Reginald and Ronald, 34, and Thomas Cowley, 32, are accused of conspiracy to murder an unknown man, Cooper came under fire from defence counsel as being "a notorious police informer."

He said: "I was asked to get in touch with the British police by the American Secret Service."

Which department? asked Sir Lionel Thompson, appearing for Cowley.

Said Cooper: "THE Secret Service."

"The C.I.A.? The F.B.I.? The Treasury? Or the Drugs and Narcotics Bureau? Which? Sir Lionel persevered : "Just tell us what connection you have with the Secret Service."

Said Cooper: "That is my own business."

Cooper appealed to the magistrate, Mr. Kenneth Barraclough: "Surely it has no bearing on this case?"

Ask!

Sir Lionel: "It has bearing while you are being cross-examined as to your credit. The truth can be ascertained from the American Secret Service."

Cooper replied: "Then why don't you make application and find out? That is all I can say."

As the clash continued, Sir Lionel said: "I suggest the reason why you cannot give a satisfactory answer is that you are making it all up."

Cooper said: "Don't accuse me of something you can't back up. I don't think it is proper for me to answer. You are not tricking me into anything."

Sir Lionel: "So that we can make inquiries, which department of the U.S. Government should my instructing solicitor apply to for information to confirm what you say?"

Cooper then told him the head of the American Secret Service in Europe to whom he was known, he said, under his own name.

Sir Lionel: "The essence about a Secret Service man is that he should observe secrecy. You have been blaring it about that you were in the Secret Service."

Cooper: "No, because then only a fool would think of trusting me."

Sir Lionel: "You have been reading too many comics."

Cooper further denied that while on visits to America he had sought to make contact with the Mafia or that it was he who had brought in from the States the leather-briefcase fitted up with a poison syringe "gun."

He said: "Every time I come here the Customs search me, strip me down to my ankle socks. I haven't the faintest idea why. I have asked and taken legal advice but draw a blank.

Trouble

"If I'd brought that case in" —it is said by the prosecution to have been provided by ex-speedway star Split Waterman, now in jail for gold smuggling offences—"I would have been in great trouble."

Cooper further denied that he "split" on Split Waterman, and his own father-in-law recently jailed for "big" drug offences.

Cooper claims he was approached by the Krays to find someone to kill a man attending a case at the Old Bailey.

Mr. Ivan Lawrence, for Ronald Kray, cross-examined : "If your story is true, the Krays must have had reason for thinking you might be amenable to take part in a murder or find a friend who would do the job for money."

Cooper replied: "No . . . I knew I ran the risk of being arrested. Nevertheless I went ahead with the arrangements.

Why? asked Mr. Lawrence.

Said Cooper, in reply: "You've never been in a position to turn the Krays down, have you?"

Cooper added a man named Paul Elvey to ask if he would like to do the "contract." Elvey said yes.

Mr. Lawrence: "You approached him because you knew he would be a hired assassin?"

Cooper: "I did have that impression of him."

Earlier Cooper told of going with police officers on May last to a Weymouth Street nursing home in London's West End.

In bed, in pyjamas, he telephoned the Krays—while police were listening in from another room—to get an admission out of them.

Cooper said he first had contact with the police, and told them about the suitcase in the early part of this year. He was paid by Detective Chief Inspector Mooney but was never paid in cash or kind.

He made a statement to Detective Superintendent Leonard Read—in charge of inquiries into the Krays—early in May.

THE KRAYS IN COURT

Report by Arnold Latcham

he should write it down, Ronald Kray protested in a loud voice : "This hearing is open to the Press. It don't seem like it . . . you only do it when it suits yourself.

"Don't worry about his living charge. You want to keep it all quiet."

A trap?

Mr. Lawrence, at the outset of his cross-examination, said : "The police put you up to the nursing home and telephoning the Krays so they might be trapped in some way?"

Cooper replied : "So they could get some kind of admission out of them."

"A trap?" That's your word, sir."

Mr. Lawrence : "Did the police tell you they wanted to get the Krays?"

Said Cooper : "Not in those words. I understood the police would like to lay their hands on any criminal, the Krays included."

Mr. Lawrence : "Did you tell the Krays six months before you went back to America that the police were trying to fit them up?"

Cooper : "To the contrary. I told them that in my opinion if they were taken it would be from a fit-up."

Asked by the magistrate to explain a "fit-up," Cooper said : "It's British colloquialism. Have this on me."

Cooper said that when he was 16½, he was sentenced to five years by an American Army general court martial for robbery.

'Stockade'

"I was a year and two months in the stockade," he added. "The case was reviewed because I was a juvenile when it happened."

Cooper's evidence took a dramatic turn when Sir Lionel Thompson began his cross-examination.

Cooper was asked if he was Jewish and believed in God's teachings through the enunciations of Moses. He said he was not a practising Jew, but he believed in God and Moses's teachings.

An Old Testament was handed across to him which he was asked by Sir Lionel to open at Exodus, chapter 20, and read verse 13.

Cooper read out, loud : "Thou shalt not kill."

Sir Lionel : "You have said you are sensitive about your stammer. Were you not equally sensitive about breaking one of God's Holy laws?"

Cooper said : "I have not broken any of God's laws."

"You were going a long way to killing a human being," said Sir Lionel. "Aren't you sensitive about the thought that you might have been breaking one of God's Holy laws?"

"Yes I am. But I never then gave it the thought I should have done," said Cooper.

"A very great deal of what you have told the court is so far from the truth as to be unbelievable?"—No.

'Comics'

Sir Lionel then held up a copy of yesterday's Daily Express and read the headline of Reginald Kray saying from the dock : "Will James Bond be giving evidence in this case? It is all too ridiculous."

Said Sir Lionel : "Isn't that about the truth? That you have been reading a lot too much about James Bond and The Avengers and a number of comics in your American childhood?"

Cooper retorted : "I went to school in this country."

Sir Lionel : "Very well. We have comics over here of the same fashion."

Sir Lionel then asked : "What have the police got on you?"

"Nothing so far as I know," Cooper said.

Said Sir Lionel : "You have been a notorious police informer for a number of years. I suggest so notorious were you for your bravado and silly schemes that you were known throughout London as Silly B——s?

Cooper, joining in the laughter, said the nickname was news to him.

But, said Sir Lionel, didn't he one plan to abduct the Pope and hold him to ransom? Cooper laughed again.

"I could be very rude, but I won't," he said.

Also did he not plan to set up a private army and release President Tshombe? "Not me," said Cooper. "That was thought by the Krays. They put it to me. I said it was stupid."

A laugh

Also did he not talk about raising an army to assassinate Dr. Banda?

Cooper laughed again and shook his head.

Had he not boasted he was the ace Palestinian terrorist and he had parachuted in against the British? Said Cooper : "I believe you are referring to Mr. Elvey. I would be too scared to jump out of an airplane."

"Weren't you trying to impress everybody how tough you are?"—No.

"Do you know you were a laughing stock?"—Not to my knowledge.

Questioned about Split Waterman, Cooper said he knew Waterman was trafficking in gold and had an arms arsenal.

"I know because he sold three machine guns to the twins," he told Sir Lionel. "I saw the exchange take place outside the Regent Cinema, Stamford Hill, one night after dark."

The hearing continues today.

Kray twins sent for trial

Ronald Kray, aged 34, of Bunhill Road, Islington, London, and 31-year-old John Alexander Barry, of no fixed address, were at Bow Street yesterday sent for trial at the Old Bailey accused of murdering George Cornell at the Blind Beggar public house, Stepney.

Reginald Kray—twin of Ronald —was sent for trial accused of impeding the arrest of the other two men, knowing they had committed an offence. All three pleaded not guilty.

KRAYS ARE CLEARED OF OLD BAILEY DEATH PLOT

By BRIAN McCONNELL

A MURDER plot charge against Kray twins Reginald and Ronald and a third man was dismissed yesterday.

The charge had alleged that the 34-year-old twins and the other man — Thomas Cowley, 32—conspired to murder an unknown person at the Old Bailey.

All three men were sent for trial with Richard Morgan, 35, on a charge of conspiracy to murder a named person.

In the case concerning the unknown person, the prosecution alleged that the plan involved a poison syringe operated by a spring inside a briefcase.

Crossbow

On the charge concerning George, the prosecution claimed that the plot was to use a high-powered rifle, a crossbow or dynamite.

A magistrate at London's Bow-street court had been asked to send the accused men for trial.

After hearing evidence the magistrate, Mr. Kenneth Barraclough, gave his rulings yesterday.

On what he called the suitcase charge, the magistrate held that the evidence "is so confused and therefore too slender to commit before a jury."

He went on: "I want to make it quite plain that I have to look at these two

charges in an entirely separate way.

"The mere fact that I come to a conclusion on the evidence as a whole on the suitcase allegation does not affect the still vitally important issue that I must not usurp the function of a jury.

"Entirely different considerations arise on the other matter, and I have no doubt there is a case to answer."

The magistrate then said the second charge should be amended to read that the four accused men conspired with others to murder a male person named George—with no reference to a surname.

All four accused men, through their counsel, pleaded not guilty and reserved their defence.

Mr. Montague Sherborne, for Reginald Kray, said his client maintained: "I am innocent of this charge. I have a complete answer to it."

Mr. Ivan Lawrence, for Ronald Kray, said his client had declared his innocence.

The Kray twins and Thomas Cowley were sent for trial at the Old Bailey. The fourth man, Richard Morgan was allowed bail of £1,000.

I HEARD A KRAY TWIN SHOUT 'KILL HIM, REG'

By BRIAN McCONNELL

THE sound of music was turned up in a flat to set the scene for the murder of "Jack the Hat," a court heard yesterday.

The louder music was intended to drown the noise of a shot, said a prosecution witness, Ronald Joseph Hart, at Bow-street, London.

But a gun held by Reginald Kray did not go off, Hart added. Then, while twin brother Ronald Kray held "Jack the Hat" and kept saying "Kill him, Reggie," Reginald stabbed him with a knife until he was dead.

Hart made his allegations when the 34-year-old Kray twins and four other men were accused of murdering "Jack the Hat"—the nickname given to gambler Jack McVitie because he was rarely seen without a hat.

Another four men—including the Kray twins' 41-year-old brother Charles—are charged with being accessories after the fact.

Flat

Mr. Kenneth Jones, Q.C., prosecuting, told the court that McVitie had not been seen at his home in Stratford, East London, since he left it on Saturday evening, October 28, 1967, Mr. Jones added, "because that is not surprising," "in the early hours of the following morning, in a flat in Evering-road, North London, McVitie was killed deliberately and in cold blood by Reginald Kray."

The alleged scene of murder—a basement flat—was occupied by a woman known as "Blonde Carol," said Mr. Jones. She was going to hold a party that night but, when the Kray twins and others arrived, she and her guests were sent to a party elsewhere.

Mr. Jones spoke of the six men accused of murder and their alleged roles....

The Kray twins, of Braithwaite House, Clerkenwell, were alleged to have been concerned in the act of killing.

Two brothers, Christopher Lambrianou, 29, a car-wash proprietor, of Bedford House, Queensbridge-road, Hackney, and Anthony Lambrianou, 26, a driver, of Blythe-road, Bethnal Green, were said to have brought McVitie to the flat.

Ronald Bender, 29, unemployed, of Cubitt House, Cubitt Town, Poplar, was alleged to have produced the knife.

Anthony Barry, 30, a company director and part-owner of a club, of Old Nazeing-road, Broxbourne, Herts, was said to have brought the gun.

Prosecuting counsel then spoke of the four men alleged to have been accessories....

Charles Kray, of Rosefield - gardens, Birchfield Estate, Poplar, was alleged to have arranged the disposal of the body.

Frederick G. Foreman, 26, of the Prince of Wales public house, Lant - street, Southwark, and also a director of a bookmaking firm, was told to have disposed of the body.

Cornelius Whitehead, 30, of Bigland-street, Stepney, was alleged to have cleaned up the scene of the murder.

Albert Donaghue, 32, of Evans-road, Bow, was said to have "completely redecorated the flat and destroyed all traces of the murder."

Towards the end of his opening speech, Mr. Jones told the magistrate, Mr.

Party

It was arranged to go to a party in "Blonde Carol's" in Evering-road, continued Hart.

Before he left the Regency Club, Bender showed him a carving knife which he had stuck in his trousers.

In "Blonde Carol's" flat Hart continued, there were a number of people—men and women—but some of them were sent away by Ronald Kray.

"After they had gone, no women were left in the basement room at all," said Hart.

"Tony Barry came in. He spoke to Reg. I didn't hear what he said. He gave him a gun. It was a black automatic.

"After he had spoken to Reggie Kray and given him the gun, Barry left.

"Tony and Chrissy Lambrianou were sent to the Regency Club by Ronnie Kray.

"He said: 'Go to the Regency, pick Jack up and bring him back.' Ronnie Kray told me to go upstairs and look for them."

'Gun jammed and knife was used'

Geraint Rees: "To this day Reginald Kray bears upon the palm of his left hand a linear scar, which the prosecution say is the scar where he cut himself in the course of stabbing McVitie."

Prosecution witness Ronald Joseph Hart then described the alleged killing of "Jack the Hat."

Earlier that evening, said Mr. Hart, he was in the Regency Club, Stoke Newington, and went into the office with the man in charge, Tony Barry, and three other men including Reginald Kray.

"Reggie told Tony Barry that he was going to see McVitie in there that night and that he would kill him is there." Hart added: "He asked Barry if he would get him into the office for him.

"Barry said no, he would not. He said he did not want anything to happen in the club."

The scene of an alleged murder

The house in Evering-road, Stoke Newington, London, where "Jack the Hat" is alleged to have been stabbed to death by Reginald Kray

"Jack the Hat" . . . he has never been found, said a QC.

Mr. Jones: Did anyone say anything while Reggie Kray was stabbing McVitie?

Hart: Yes — Ronald Kray was telling Reggie to kill him.

Mr. Jones: What were the words?

Hart: He was saying "Kill him, Reggie." I don't know how many times he said it, but he kept repeating it.

Rasping

McVitie then fell to the floor under the window, his back on the floor and his legs bent up. He was breathing heavily and making "a rasping noise."

Hart went on: "Then Reggie stood astride him and he stuck the knife in his throat. Reggie Kray was holding the knife in both hands, pushing down."

Mr. Jones: Did you see how?

Hart: The knife went straight through and out the back. Then he pulled it out again, and put it in, and twisted it.

Mr. Jones: What happened then?

Hart: Then he just pulled it out again.

Hart went on: "Jack was making funny noises and blood was bubbling out of his throat. Ronnie told me to put something in his mouth, so I put a handkerchief in.

"When I did this, McVitie was not moving. He was already dead."

He added that Bender felt McVitie's heart and listened to it, and then said: "He is dead."

Continuing his evidence, Hart said that when the gun did not go off at first, Tony Lambrianou told Reginald Kray that he would go and get his brother Chris's gun.

Washed

When McVitie was dead, Hart added, Ronald Bender washed the knife and gun. Ronald Kray told him to give the gun to Hart, which he did.

Reginald Kray asked what was to be done with the body and Bender said leave it to him, he would take care of it.

"The twins told him to dump the body over the railway near Coral's in Cazenove - road," Hart further alleged.

He noticed that Reginald Kray had a cut on his left hand across the centre line of the palm. It was about two or three inches long and was bleeding.

'JACK TRIED TO DIVE OUT OF WINDOW'

he followed them down to the basement flat.

As they went downstairs, Chris Lambrianou said: "I didn't know it was going to be anything like this, or else I would not have had anything to do with it."

Then, said Hart, he sat down on the stairs and cried.

Asked if he knew why the music was to be turned up, Hart replied: "Ronnie

Kray brought him back and sat him by a telephone table. Hart went on.

Before this, however, Reginald Kray was trying to shoot McVitie, but the gun would not work.

While McVitie was sitting by the telephone table,

he struggled with Reginald Kray.

"But the knife was bending and would not go in his back," said Hart.

The next thing was when McVitie tried to jump through the window. "He broke the window and we pulled him back," Hart went on.

He added that by "we" he meant himself. Ronnie Kray and Reginald Kray.

Ronald Kray then got McVitie in a lock from

in front of McVitie, Bender and the Mills brothers were also in the room.

Continuing his evidence, Hart told the court of the events which followed.

"Reggie then held the gun against McVitie and

'Blonde Carol' tells of Krays' flat visit

Reg Kray in 'fat slob' uproar

A REFERENCE to his dead wife Frances sparked off a tirade from Reginald Kray at the Old Bailey yesterday.

He called murder trial prosecutor Mr. Kenneth Jones, Q.C., "a fat slob."

And he variously addressed others in court as "animals, bastards, and dirty pigs."

The outburst came as a woman giving evidence for Ronald Bender, accused of the murder of Jack (The Hat) McVitie, was asked a question about Mrs. Kray.

Immediately Kray jumped up in the dock and exploded at Mr. Jones: "You fat slob, what has this got to do with the case?"

Then he pointed to Detective Sergeant Trevor Lloyd-Hughes, sitting near the dock.

"I'll tell you something," Kray yelled. "He even followed me to the funeral and mortuary, dirty pig."

Leaning over the dock, still pointing at the detective, Kray added: "And I've got witnesses, you stinking pigs."

His anger and abuse mounting, he switched his glare back to Mr. Jones and yelled again. "Fat slob, sit down."

As warders tried to restrain him, Kray shook with rage—and turned on Mr. Justice Melford Stevenson when the judge ordered: "Take him down."

Pointing at the judge, Kray yelled: "You're biased. I have had enough of your comments. This is a murder charge."

Eventually Kray's elder brother Charles, one of the 10 men in the dock on various charges arising from two alleged murders, persuaded him to calm down.

After that the trial proceeded quietly. It continues today.

'I was a US secret service man'
—SAYS WITNESS

A LAN BRUCE COOPER, 37-year-old short, dapper-dressed American, told the Kray case hearing yesterday — that he was connected for two years with the American Secret Service.

And he claimed that he is the man who set up the plan to murder a man at the Old Bailey with a poison syringe.

At Bow Street, in the case in which Kray twins Reginald and Ronald, 34, and Thomas Cowley, 32, are accused of conspiracy to murder an unknown man, Cooper came under fire from defence counsel as being "a notorious police informer."

He said: "I was asked to get in touch with the British police by the American Secret Service."

Which department? asked Sir Lionel Thompson, appearing for Cowley.

Said Cooper: "THE Secret Service."

The C.I.A.? The F.B.I.? The Treasury? Or the Drugs and Narcotics Bureau? Which? Sir Lionel persevered: "Just tell us what connection you have with the Secret Service."

Said Cooper: "That is my own business."

Cooper appealed to the magistrate, Mr. Kenneth Barraclough: "Surely it has no bearing on this case?"

One Kray is cleared

'NO EVIDENCE' AGAINST ELDEST BROTHER IN AXEMAN MURDER CASE

By ARNOLD LATCHAM

C HARLES, at 41 the eldest of the three Kray brothers, was cleared yesterday of the murder of Mad Axeman Frank Mitchell.

But he still faces trial accused of plotting Mitchell's escape from Dartmoor in December 1966 and fraud charges.

At the end of the prosecution's case at Bow Street, counsel Mr. Desmond Vowden successfully submitted there was no evidence to link Charles Kray with the death of Mitchell—if indeed he was dead—other than the testimony of Charles Mitchell, a convicted criminal "of the worst kind."

Q.C. TELLS OF ...

MR. KENNETH JONES

- A briefcase with a poison needle
- A crossbow bought for £51 ...
- Then talk of turning to dynamite

The night Jack the Hat vanished

By RICHARD WRIGHT

RONALD KRAY held down "Jack the Hat" McVitie, while his twin Reginald brutally stabbed the 39-year-old bookmaker's clerk to death, it was alleged yesterday.

The scene: a basement flat in Evering Road, Stoke Newington, said Mr. Kenneth Jones, Q.C., opening the prosecution case at London's Bow Street court.

The time: the early hours of Sunday, October 29, last year.

Describing the alleged murder, Mr. Jones claimed that 34-year-old Reginald Kray first of all tried to shoot McVitie.

Held down

But he failed because of a faulty mechanism which stopped the gun working. Then, said Mr. Jones, Reginald Kray took a carving knife and stabbed McVitie—who was being held down on a couch—in the stomach or side.

All the time, Ronald was urging his brother Reginald to "do him." McVitie fell to the floor very seriously wounded. Then "Reginald Kray, standing over him, plunged the knife into his neck and twisted it in the wound," added Mr. Jones.

Eventually McVitie lay dead in a pool of blood.

The Kray twins, of Braithwaite House, Bunhill Row, Clerkenwell, London, are among six men accused of McVitie's murder.

The others are: Christopher Lambrianou, 29, car wash proprietor, of Bedford House, Queensbridge Road, Hackney; Anthony Lambrianou, 26, driver, of Blythe Road, Bethnal Green; Ronald Albert Bender, 30, of Cubitt House, Cubitt Town, Poplar; and Anthony Thomas Barry, 30, company director, of Old Nazing Road, Broxbourne, Herts.

Four others are accused of being accessories.

They include the Kray twins' elder brother, Charles, 41, of Thornfield House, Birchfield Estate, Poplar. He was accused of hindering the twins' arrest, knowing they had committed an indictable offence.

Also charged with being accessories are: Frederick Foreman, 36, a publican, of the Prince of Wales, Lant Street, Southwark; Cornelius John Whitehead, 30, of Bigland Street, Stepney; and Albert John Donaghue, 32, of Devons Road, Bow.

COURT IS TOLD OF MAN'S STABBING AFTER KRAY TWINS' PARTY

McVitie—body never found, court told

ENDED IN 'MRS. A's' FLAT

'Kray Twins walked in —covered in blood'

JUDGE: 'STAND BACK AND LOOK AT EVIDENCE AS A WHOLE'

Mr. Justice Melford Stevenson

KRAY JURY DECIDING

The Kray brothers—Reginald (left), Charles and Ronald.

By STUART FRIEND and MICHAEL McDONOUGH

The Krays trial jury were out this afternoon considering their verdicts.

They left the Old Bailey courtroom at 12.12 p.m. on this, the 39th day of the hearing.

Earlier there was drama as the judge neared the end of his summing-up.

Blonde Mrs. Dolly Kray collapsed in the public gallery watched by her 42-year-old husband Charles from the dock below.

Mrs. Kray, her face white against the black of her fur coat, was carried limp from the court by four police.

Carried from court

Another woman sitting with her, in the space reserved for relatives of the defendants, burst into tears.

The incidents came when Mr. Justice Melford Stevenson in his speech which he began last Thursday, summed up the Crown case against Charles Kray.

The judge's last words to the all-male jury were: "I repeat the appeal that I made to you earlier.

"Having considered the evidence in relation to each witness in this case, stand back and look at the evidence as a whole.

"And having looked at it, ask yourselves if it presents a complete and convincing picture."

As the judge approached the end of his speech, instructions were given for all doors of the court to remain closed to prevent interruptions.

The Krays and seven other men deny various charges concerning the alleged murders of John "The Hat" McVitie and George Cornell. Each faces different charges.

It's the tightest security yet

By JAMES REID

Rigid security was in operation in No. 1 Court at the Old Bailey for the jury's return in the Kray case later today.

Each of the ten defendants was being brought up to hear the verdicts separately.

No one was to enter or leave the court at this time.

The already large contingent of CID men was increased still more. Between 30 and 40 detectives, many armed, were sitting or standing around the dock.

Others were gathering in the public gallery to prevent any demonstration or speaking.

Should the guarded all-male jury continue their discussion until late tonight, arrangements were made for them to sleep in the Old Bailey. Beds have been prepared in special rooms in the building.

No juryman was to leave the building or speak to anyone until all the verdicts were returned.

THE ACCUSED AND CHARGES

The accused are: Ronald Kray, 34, his twin brother Reginald, both of Braithwaite House, Bunhill Row, Islington, and their brother, Charles, of Rosefield Gardens, Tower Hamlets.

Cornelius Whitehead, 33, of Rosefield Gardens, Tower Hamlets; Christopher Lambrianou, 29, Queensbridge Road, Hackney; Anthony Lambrianou, 26, Blythe Road, Bethnal Green; Ronald Albert Bender, 30, Cubitt Town, Poplar; Anthony Barry, 30, Old Nazeing Road, Broxbourne, Herts; Frederick Foreman, 26, Lant Street, Southwark; and John Barrie, 31, of no settled address

The Kray twins, Christopher Lambrianou, Anthony Lambrianou, Bender, and Anthony Barry all plead not guilty to the murder of Jack McVitie.

Charles Kray, Foreman and Whitehead all plead not guilty to being accessories to the murder of McVitie.

Ronald Kray and John Barrie plead not guilty to the murder of George Cornell. Reginald Kray pleads not guilty to being an accessory after the fact to the murder of Cornell.

An eleventh man, Albert Donaghue, 32, of Devons Road, Bow, has already pleaded guilty to being an accessory after the murder of McVitie.

Mrs. Charles Kray (right), who collapsed during the summing-up today. With her is Mrs. Frederick Foreman, wife of another of the accused.

FOR the second time in ten months Charles Kray was yesterday cleared of the murder of Frank (The Mad Axeman) Mitchell.

The first time was when Charles, eldest of the three East End brothers, appeared at Bow Street magistrates' court.

The charge against him was then dismissed after legal arguments. But later it was reinstated.

Yesterday, at the end of the prosecution's eight-day case at the Old Bailey, Mr. Justice Lawton held there was not sufficient evidence to "make a conviction safe" on murder charges against greying Charles Kray, 42, and his bespectacled brother Ronald, 35.

The judge said at the time of Mitchell's alleged shooting on December 23, 1966, Ronald Kray was keeping out of the way—wanted on a warrant for failing to attend court as a witness.

Wept

There was no evidence, he held, that Charles Kray, after meeting other men on the morning of Mitchell's disappearance, had anything whatever to do with subsequent events.

When the judge announced his decision Charles Kray broke down and wept. He shook hands over the ledge with his junior counsel, Mr. Patrick Pakenham, and asked for a drink of water.

As Kray's emotions deepened, his "silk," Mr. Desmond Vowden, Q.C., asked permission for him to leave the dock for the cells below.

Mr. Justice Lawton agreed.

Then, when the jury returned, after leaving court during legal arguments, they were instructed to find both Charles and Ronald Kray not guilty of murder.

Outside the court Charles Kray's blonde wife Dolly, mother of two, burst into tears when told—then smiled.

Daily Mirror

5d. Wednesday, March 5, 1969 * No. 20,276

GUILTY OF MURDER

30 YEARS

By ALLAN HALL

ON the way to the Old Bailey yesterday morning, the sun was shining. It was cold, but it was good to be walking along the pavements of London.

Inside the court, Mr. Justice Melford Stevenson said to Ronald Kray:

"*I don't propose to waste any words on you. In my view society has earned a rest from your activities.*"

He sent him to prison for 30 years.

Kray did not flinch. He turned round, quickly strode to the stairs that lead down from the dock to the cells, and made a small gesture with his right arm to a familiar face in the gallery.

There was, briefly, a smile for the friend, and then the face was grim again. A photograph would have shown no emotion on the face at all; I knew I was seeing the face of dreadful sickness.

RONALD
Face of dreadful sickness

REGINALD
He looked shattered

30 YEARS	30 YEARS	20 YEARS	20 YEARS	15 YEARS	15 YEARS	10 YEARS	10 YEARS	7 YEARS	2 YEARS
Ronald Kray	Reginald Kray	John Barrie	Ronald Bender	Anthony Lambrianou	Christopher Lambrianou	Charles Kray	Frederick Foreman	Cornelius Whitehead	Albert Donoghue

51

Ronald Kray, 35

John "Ian" Barrie, 31

Ronald Bender, 30

Reginald Kray, 35

Charles Kray, 41

Anthony Barry, 30

Christopher Lambrianou, 29

Frederick Foreman, 36

Anthony Lambrianou, 26

Cornelius Whitehead, 30

OLD BAILEY IMPRESSION BY OLIVER WILLIAMS

RONALD KRAY was the first of the other nine to be brought into the dock yesterday.

The 35-year-old twin, found guilty of two murders, was jailed for life on both counts.

He stood silent as the judge said: "I am not going to waste words on you.

"In my view society has earned a rest from your activities and I recommend you be detained for thirty years."

JOHN "IAN" BARRIE, 31, was the man who went with Kray to the shooting of Cornell at the Blind Beggar pub, Whitechapel.

He was jailed for life for murder, with a recommendation that he should serve twenty years.

The evidence was that he fired warning shots while Kray killed Cornell.

REGINALD KRAY, a widower—his wife killed herself with an "enormous overdose of drugs"—helped his brother Ronald and Barrie to escape after the Blind Beggar shooting.

He also stabbed to death McVitie and was sentenced to life imprisonment.

The judge told him: "For reasons I have already indicated in this case of your brother, Ronald, I recommend you to be imprisoned for thirty years."

CHARLES KRAY 41-year-old—brother of the twins, was convicted of being an accessory to the murder of Jack the Hat and jailed for ten years. The judge said: "It may well be that you were not a member of the Firm, but I am satisfied that you were an active and ready helper in the dreadful enterprise of concealing traces of the murder your brothers committed."

The Lambrianou brothers, Christopher and Anthony, were also jailed for life with a recommendation that they should serve fifteen years.

CHRISTOPHER LAMBRIANOU, 29, tried to hang himself in Wandsworth prison last year, said Mr. Petre Crowder, Q.C.

Mr. Crowder said: "He had said if he was not convicted on one charge he would be convicted on another."

Brother

ANTHONY LAMBRIANOU, 26, his younger brother, married with a six-year-old child, was also convicted of the murder of McVitie.

RONALD ALBERT BENDER, 30, convicted of murder, was sentenced to life with a recommendation that he be detained for twenty years.

FREDERICK FOREMAN, 36, married with three children, was sentenced to ten years as an accessory to McVitie's murder.

Last came **CORNELIUS WHITEHEAD**, 30, who was also found guilty of being an accessory. He was sentenced to seven years.

THE LAST LOOK AT FREEDOM

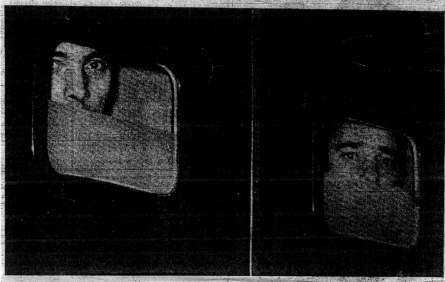

Story by TOM TULLETT
Picture by TOM KING

TWO members of the Kray Firm take their last look at freedom for a long time.

Reginald Kray, on the right, and Anthony Lambrianou peer from the windows of the prison van taking them to London's Brixton jail—and a life sentence.

Now the Home Office face a problem: Which jails should the gang members go to?

Olive Cornell, 35-year-old widow of George Cornell, the man Ronald Kray shot dead as he sat at the bar of the Blind Beggar public house, says of the Kray twins: "They are vicious, violent and dangerous men."

She might also have called them bullies and pathetic products of the East End underworld who, when they had bashed and slashed their way to criminal dominance, strove to achieve a kind of grotesque respectability to go with the £100,000 a year they are estimated to have raked in from shops, bars, clubs and pubs in the East and West End of London.

The Kray story begins in Gorsuch Street, off the Hackney Road, where, in 1928 Charles Kray was born.

His twin brothers Ronald and Reginald were born at a house in Lee Street, Shoreditch, seven years later.

A JUDGE REJECTS KRAY GANG'S BID TO APPEAL OVER KILLINGS

1970's

"Shortly after I was convicted I was given a scroll with the poem 'Desiderata' on it. Part of the passage reads: 'Avoid loud and aggressive persons for they are a vexation to the spirit.' I found this passage to be particularly true."
Reg Kray

"I believe at the end of the day, the government of England were even more corrupt and evil than they said we were."
Ron Kray

Ronald Kray: 'slight' cuts

Former London gangland leader Ronald Kray was said to be continuing normal prison routine in Durham Jail yesterday after cutting his wrists on Saturday night.

A prison spokesman said the wounds were slight. Kray had been suffering from depression over his 30-year sentence for murder.

Ronald Kray in jail shuffle

A dozen major criminals including Ronald Kray, some of the Great Train Robbers, and members of the Richardson gang, were switched to different jails yesterday.

Kray went from Durham to Parkhurst in the operation between top security prisons. The moves are designed to foil escape plots and a repetition of the Parkhurst riot in which 33 officers were hurt.

● WHEN Ronald was switched from Durham, Reginald was moved out of Parkhurst, to Leicester under a Home Office policy designed to prevent trouble building up in any one jail.

'KRAYS GUN PLOT' WAS A FRAME-UP

By GEORGE GLENTON

A MAN tried to frame a solicitor's clerk by pretending he was involved in a plot to smuggle a gun to the Kray twins in Durham Jail.

The plot was a "complete invention" by lorry driver Henry Bird, who had a grudge against the clerk's firm.

Mr. Richard Beckett, prosecuting at the Old Bailey yesterday, said that Bird told police and a journalist about the plot.

Bird, 29, of West Ferry-road, Poplar, East London, told police they would find the gun with the clerk, Ralph Haeems. Then he sent a parcel containing a gun to Mr. Haeems.

Mr. Haeems told the police at once.

Bird admitted the plot. He had a grievance against the solicitors' firm.

He told police: "I have been a fool. I wanted to leave the gun with Ralph Haeems so that he would get nicked."

Bird was jailed for nine months for unlawfully possessing a gun, and fifteen months for stealing a car and dishonestly handling stolen cars.

Punch lands Ronald Kray in 'solitary'

Express Staff Reporter

RONALD KRAY has been ordered into solitary confinement after attacking a senior prison officer during a top security wing punch-up at Parkhurst, it was learned last night.

Visiting magistrates yesterday took away all Kray's privileges and banned him from associating with other prisoners.

The fists-only attack took place on Thursday — two days after the East End gang leader was transferred to the Isle of Wight jail from Durham's security wing.

The officer was not seriously injured, but did get "painful facial injuries." He has been given several days off to recover.

Kray and his twin brother Reggie were both sentenced last year to 30 years' for murder.

Solitary confinement means a one-man punishment cell which has no bed or furniture, and only two blankets are provided.

Upset

The twins' mother, Mrs. Violet Kray, visited Ronnie in Parkhurst on Monday. Last night, just back from a visit to Reginald in Leicester Jail, she said: "I am upset about what has happened to Ronnie. I don't feel it is his fault.

"He needs a certain sedative medicine regularly and he has not been given it since he arrived in Parkhurst.

"Without the medicine Ronnie gets aggressive. He was under medical supervision in both Brixton and Durham and was no trouble at all.

"When I saw him he was very depressed. He told me he had spent four days in chokey [solitary] but he did not tell us what conditions were like."

Mrs. Kray added: "I gave Reggie the news and he was very upset too."

Lord Linley 'shadow' at school

By ALISTAIR WILSON

VISCOUNT LINLEY will have a detective bodyguard assigned to him for an indefinite period when he returns to his Sussex preparatory school today.

A watch will be kept on anyone approaching the school, on the edge of Ashdown Forest.

The tight security measures around the eight-year-old son of Princess Margaret and Lord Snowdon were ordered after telephone consultations yesterday between Clarence House, Scotland Yard, and Mr. William Williamson, joint head master of Ashdown School.

This follows reports of an alleged plot to kidnap Lord Linley and hold him to ransom for the release of jailed gang leaders Ronald and Reginald Kray.

SCOTLAND YARD was worried last night that a new kidnap ransom alert —this time involving M.P. Sir Gerald Nabarro's daughter— might unleash a spate of threats against well-known people.

"This sort of thing can snowball," a senior detective said. "Our difficulty is sorting out hoaxes from threats made in earnest. We have to take precautions —just in case."

At Sir Gerald Nabarro's home in Broadway, Worcestershire, police were on guard over his 19-year-old student daughter Sarah following an anonymous telephone warning that "arrangements" to kidnap Princess Margaret's young son Viscount Linley had been "transferred" to her.

KIDNAP GUARD ON ROYAL CHILDREN

'Plot to free Kray twins from jail'

Story of an island hideaway in plot to free Kray twins.. and £50,000 paid by 'their friends'

KRAY

RONNIE KRAY

TWINS

REGGIE KRAY

TOGETHER
IN JAIL

THE Kray twins are together again for the first time since they were given life sentences for murder two years ago.

Reginald has moved from Leicester to join Ronald at Parkhurst. Isle of Wight.

Their parents, Mr. and Mrs. Charles Kray, saw them at the weekend. "A lovely visit," said Mrs. Violet Kray

Mrs. Kray, who lives in Bishopsgate, London, said that her sons, who are 37, "had been worrying over each other."

Then "in the last few days both had the feeling that they were going to see each other soon—being twins, they get these feelings."

The twins were sentenced at the Old Bailey in March 1969 —Ronald for the murders of George Cornell and Jack McVitie, Reginald for McVitie. Mr. Justice Melford Stevenson told them: "Society has earned a rest from your activities. I recommend that you be detained for 30 years."

YARD IN NEW MAFIA CLUB PROBE

SCOTLAND YARD'S "gang buster" squad is probing allegations involving a former London magistrate, a business man and Mafia gambling club interests.

The team called in to prevent a takeover of territories formerly held by the Kray twins and the Richardson gang has sent a full report to Home Secretary Mr. Reginald Maudling.

Mr. Maudling is determined to stamp out American crime influence in London's clubland and the rest of the country.

He recently expressed concern at the abuse of the 1968 Gaming Act which demands that all gambling clubs should be licensed.

And only last week he signed an order under the Act which requires all gaming and bingo club operators to take out a £5 licence.

To get a licence they are thoroughly vetted by the Gaming Board.

Kray twin ill

Ronald Kray, one of the Kray twins serving 30 years for murder, is under observation for depression at the Parkhurst Jail sick bay on the Isle of Wight.

JAIL FOR MAN HATED BY THE KRAYS

Payne . . ." The brains"

THE man who shopped the Kray twins went to jail himself yesterday.

Leslie Payne, the Mr Fixit of London's underworld, was sent to prison for five years.

It was the end of a complicated series of trials, lasting since June, at the Old Bailey.

Mr. Justice Kilner Brown described the case as "the most amazing I have seen in my forty years on the Bench and at the Bar"

Yesterday the police officer who led the fight to jail the Krays, Commander Leonard Read, was called as a defence witness to tell how valuable Payne's evidence had been.

Payne decided to give evidence against the twins after hearing that they had

He shopped gang twins

put a price of £5,000 on his head.

He was the key informant against them, and provided the information needed for the trial which resulted in their being jailed for thirty years said Commander Read.

Payne was jailed yesterday for attempting to obstruct the course of justice in two trials involving stolen cars.

Fake

He was found guilty of persuading a key defendant in one of the cases to fake suicide so that he could not be prosecuted and could accept the blame for four other men involved.

He pleaded guilty halfway through his trial to smuggling the defendant in another case out of Britain

so that he could play a similar role, and so bring about the acquittal of another man.

The judge told Payne, 48, of The Netherlands, Coulsdon, Surrey, director of a dozen companies compulsorily liquidated over the past fifteen years. "You cannot stop trying to acquire money other than by dishonest means.

"Your involvement in these matters was motivated by greed, and I am satisfied that you were the man with the fertile brain."

With Payne in the dock was John Hutton, 47, of Walthamstow and James Moore, 48, of Pinner both accused of being involved in trying to obstruct the course of justice.

Hutton was jailed for three years, and Moore was jailed for thirty months.

Barn: Alibi woman is Kray wife

KRAYS MAY FACE JAIL ATTACK CHARGES

Pub man 'was gang boss'

A PUBLICAN was named at the Old Bailey yesterday as the "guv'nor" of an East End protection gang.

Prosecutor Mr. Michael Corkery named licensee Phillip Jacobs, of The Plough and Harrow, High Road, Leytonstone, and other pubs in Canning Town and Southwark, as the gang boss.

Jacobs who is alleged to have taken over the Kray twins territory, was said to have owned three pubs and a Rolls-Royce in which he was driven around by his henchmen.

Mr. Corkery said that the eight men sharing the dock with Jacobs were his henchmen.

Three are brothers: George Dixon, aged 32, of Morgan Street, Bow; Alan Dixon, aged 30, of Beaconsfield Road, Stratford; Brian Dixon, aged 28, of St. Stephen's Road, Stratford.

'INFAMOUS KRAYS'

With charges of conspiracy, extortion and assault involved, the shadow of the jailed gangster twins Reginald and Ronald Kray hangs over the trial, expected to last two months.

Mr. Corkery told the jury: "This is a story about the tough area of East London where the infamous Kray twins and their associates once held sway.

And he claimed that on arrest George Dixon told police: "When the twins went away I knew others would get nicked. But nobody is going to stand up against me."

But, said counsel, he was wrong. Victims had stood up against him and "The Team" and would be giving evidence of the threats, demands for money, and the terror they faced.

Mr. Corkery said, the jury would hear that one victim was told: "We have taken over where the Krays left off."

Accused with Jacobs and the Dixon brothers are: Michael Bailey, aged 32; Michael Young, aged 27; Lambert Jacobs, aged 38; Brian Taylor, aged 34 and Leon Carlton, aged 34.

The hearing continues today.

Kray twins put in the 'cooler' after jail attack

GANGSTER twins Ronald and Reginald Kray were in solitary confinement in a top security jail last night after an attack on another prisoner.

Detectives investigating the attack were told that one of the twins had held the man down while the other slashed him with a broken bottle.

The attack happened at Parkhurst Jail on the Isle of Wight. The Krays were among a number of long-term convicts locked in the top-security prison's "cooler" after the incident.

Stitches

They were all questioned by a team of police under Detective Chief Inspector Bill Durrant.

The prisoner, Royal Stuart Grantham, needed more than forty stitches for cuts to his arms and shoulders.

He has recently been moved to Parkhurst from another top security jail after a prison officer was attacked there.

Last night Grantham was in the prison hospital. A Home Office spokesman said his condition was "not dangerous."

The attack was the first flare-up at the jail since new governor Maurice Brian took over earlier this year.

There are more than 400 prisoners in the main jail at Parkhurst and about twelve in the top security wing.

JAIL ATTACK: KRAY TWINS SENTENCED

THE KRAY twins, serving life for gangland murder, have been convicted of taking part in an attack on another prisoner.

The victim was held while his shoulders and face were slashed with a sharp instrument. He needed more than forty stitches.

Visiting magistrates at Parkhurst jail have sentenced the twins, Ronald and Reginald, to 28 days' loss of earnings and privileges.

KRAY WIFE.. THE MYSTERY WITNESS

THE secret of the mystery woman in the Barn murder trial was revealed last night . . . as the wife of jailed gangland leader Charles Kray.

Charles Kray . . . jailed.

FOUR YEARS ago Dolly Kray watched her husband Charles led to the cells from the Old Bailey and declared :—

"*I never want to see a court again.*"

This week Dolly, mother of Charles Kray's two children, went back to a court . . . to reveal a secret that this time helped her man win.

But it was not husband Charles in the dock. It was George Henry Ince.

To prove that he was not the man who shot down Mrs. Muriel Patience, Ince needed to reveal Dolly's secret. She was having a love affair with Ince while her husband was in jail.

Bed

And Ince was forced to admit that he and 39-year-old Dolly — she changed her name to Mrs. Doris Gray by deed poll in 1969 —had been in bed together while a bloody night of terror was going on 40 miles away at Braintree, Essex.

To the 12 jurors Mrs. Gray was introduced as a married woman whose husband was "not around" every Saturday night. This was the night the couple met for their intimate affair at her Poplar, East London, flat.

Despite her hatred of courts, Mrs. Gray stood before the Chelmsford judge and jury on Monday and told why Ince could not have been the murderer.

"He did not leave my side," she said. The jury was not told her true identity in case it affected the result.

Many times her secret *did* almost come out.

Slip

Prosecution counsel Mr. John Leonard, Q.C., got close to revealing it by hints—even down to a slip of the tongue when he addressed her as "Mrs. Kray."

Dolly — and the Kray family—have tried to keep the affair from Charles who is in Maidstone prison and due to be freed in 18 months on parole.

But his brothers, twins Ronald and Reginald, suspected before they went to jail that their sister-in-law might have attracted Ince.

Their mother, Mrs. Violet Kray, said : "She did not want to know the Krays."

Their father, 65-year-old Charles Kray, said : "When my son gets back into circulation I reckon he will not want to know."

CHARLIE KRAY STEPS OUT

THIS was Charlie Kray's first taste of freedom in six years.

It came yesterday as he stepped through the solid oak gateway of Maidstone jail to begin four days "acclimatisation" leave.

Kray—43-year-old brother of the killer twins Ron and Reg—blinked in the bright sunshine and said: "Oh, I feel good."

Kray received a ten-year sentence for being an accessory after the murder of Jack "the Hat" McVitie.

He is staying in Kent with a couple who befriended him in jail.

He is due back in jail on Monday morning and hopes to get a full week's leave before being finally freed next January.

Meanwhile Kray is determined not to let the events of the past cast a shadow over his weekend of reunions with family and friends.

He said: "Anyone who has not been inside can never know what it is like to feel free—if only for a short while."

Pictures: Eric Piper and Peter Powell

Free! Charlie Kray steps through the gate of Maidstone Prison to be greeted by a friend's wife

'MY MARRIAGE IS FINISHED'

Kray brother goes home for the weekend after 6 years

A mother's welcome . . . Mrs. Violet Kray with Charlie at the celebration tea.

GOODBYE DOLLY! . . CHARLIE SAYS MY WIFE'S AFFAIR WITH INCE HAS ENDED MARRIAGE

Wall of silence as man is shot dead at club

A MAN was shot dead at the bar of a crowded working men's club near London's dockland area late last night.

He died when a man walked into the Comrades Club in Grays, Essex, with a double-barrelled shot gun in his hands.

The dead man, aged 28, lived in Tilbury and was unemployed.

It is understood he was associated with an attractive blonde divorcee Mrs. Stella Burnett whose name has been linked with Ronnie Kray.

She had told friends she was prepared to wait for ever for Ronnie Kray, now serving 30 years at Parkhurst on the Isle of Wight.

Detective Chief Superintendant Mitchell said: "At the moment the shooting is shrouded in mystery.

"Obviously there is more in it than meets the eye but so far we have managed to get very little from witnesses. They are all clamming up."

The dead man, not named by police last night, was rushed to Orsett hospital, in Grays, after the shooting but was found to be dead on arrival.

Police did not release the name of the victim because they were unable to trace any of his nearest relatives.

A Home Office pathologist was called to Grays to hold a post-mortem on the body.

Detectives led by Mr. Mitchell who is Essex C.I.D. chief were questioning 100 or so members at the club at the time.

The Kray twin's mother, Mrs. Violet Kray revealed two years ago that Mrs. Burnett had visited the former terror of London's gangland while he was in Durham prison before being transferred to Parkhurst.

Mrs. Kray was quoted as saying: "If Stella is willing to marry Ronnie and wait for him, I'll be happy for them both."

Later a man was helping police at Grays police station.

Ronnie Kray: Mentally ill

GANGLAND killer Ronald Kray is to be transferred from Parkhurst Prison on the Isle of Wight where he is serving a life sentence, to Broadmoor special hospital for the criminally insane.

Twin brother Reggie, also serving a life sentence for his part in London East End killings, is to stay on at Parkhurst.

The move has been arranged between the Home Office and Department of Health, and it now only remains for Home Secretary William Whitelaw to give final approval.

The twins, who are 45, have now been in prison 10 years, and for the last eight years they have been together in Parkhurst, where they are said to be "inseparable."

Ronnie Kray's mental condition has deteriorated, and he has now been diagnosed as a "paranoid schizophrenic."

During the 60s, the Krays were kings of the underworld. Their life of crime came to an end in 1969, when they were given life sentences.

Ronnie Kray was convicted of the murder of George Cornell in the Blind Beggar pub in the East End and Jack "The Hat" McVitie. Reggie was convicted of the murder of McVitie and being an accessory after the murder of Cornell. Cornell was killed in 1966, and McVitie in 1967.

It will be the first time that Ronnie Kray has been transferred from prison to a mental hospital.

In 1958 he was certified as a paranoid schizophrenic while serving a sentence at Winchester Prison and transferred to a "closed ward" at Long Grove Mental Home, Epsom.

He escaped by swopping places with identical twin Reggie on visiting day. Police took five months to catch up with him, and return him to the hospital.

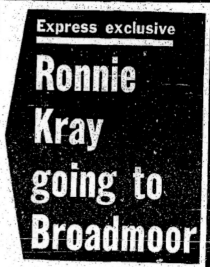

Express exclusive

Ronnie Kray going to Broadmoor

Photographs

Above: A young Fred, late 50's.

Left: Reg aged 16 in boxing pose at Robert Browning Amateur Boxing Club in 1947.

Right: Charlie, Ron, Reg, Gary and Dickie Morgan outside Vallance Road in 1955.

Two early photographs of Fred from his boxing days.

Above: Reg, early 60's.
Location unknown.

Above: A young Fred and wife Maureen in
the mid 50's. Son Greg is in his arms.

Left: Reg at the
christening of Jamie
Kensit in 1963 - Reg
was godfather.

Left: Charlie leaving the Regal in 1953.

Below: An uncomfortable looking Reg with female friends in Bethnal Green Road circa 1965.

Below: Fred and friends at the Albert Hall circa 1967.

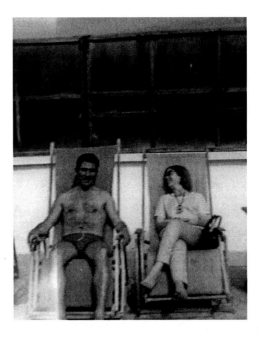

Above & Left: Reg and Francis on holiday in Spain 1964.

Above: Francis, taken by Reg on holiday in Spain, 1964.

Above: Reg, Francis and unknown.
Spain 1964.
Left: Johnny Squibb, Reg and Francis,
Spain 1964.

Above: Francis and Reg sunbathing
in Spain, 1964.

Above: The passport photos of Charlie Senior, Violet, Charlie, Ron and Reg.

Above: Charlie Kray Senior and Violet enjoy a night out with Limehouse Willy in the West End.

Above: Father and son Charlie and Gary celebrate with
Violet and Julie Dwyer at Charlie's release party in 1975.

Above: Fred in his boxing gym (the Marshall Sea) with Dave Charnley on
the punchbag. 1960's.

Above: An evening out at the Jack of Clubs in Brewer Street, W1.
Right to left Charlie, Fred, Big Pat Connelly, Francis, Reg and Dolly. Circa 1965.

Above: Fred in his own club (211 Club) with
George Raft and Scotch Jack Dickson

Above: Charlie and Susan Dwyer
taken on weekend release in 1974.

Above: Charlie Kray Senior departs
a plane in Spain circa 1965.

Above: Reg chats with associates.

Above: Reg and Ron either side of Sonny Liston at the Cambridge Rooms in 1965. Also pictured are Micky Fawcett and Big Pat Connolly.

Above: Reg, Charlie and Ron.

Above: Fred and Laurie O'Leary.

Left: Charlie, Judy Stanley, John Corbett and Gary Kray pictured outside Broadmoor after visiting Ron in 1993.

Above: Fred chats to Tom Hardy on
the set of Legend in 2015.

Above: Fred and godson Christian Simpson.

Top Left: Charlie at an event in 1992.

Top Right: Fred with daughter Danielle in 2004.

Right: Ron in a rare photo taken in Broadmoor around 1994.

1980's

"I am not an angel but have my basic principals and a code of honour, yet the media have made me and my brothers out to be something terrible. I consider myself a saint compared to the people I have known to get parole."
Reg Kray

"Believe me, insanity is a terrible sensation."
Ron Kray

KILLER KRAY SET TO WED

GANGLAND killer Reggie Kray is said to be in love and planning to wed.

His bride to be? A 28-year-old university student called Beverley.

She started to write to him in prison about a year ago.

Later she was given permission for a prison visit.

Kray, now 48 and jailed for life 13 years ago, is in Parkhurst on the Isle of Wight.

Twin Reggie falls for student of 28

The judge at his trial recommended he should serve at least 30 years.

His twin, Ronnie, who received a similar sentence, was later declared insane and is now in Broadmoor.

Their brother, Charlie, said yesterday: "Reggie has told me he is in love with Beverley and plans to marry her.

"She is a pretty young thing.

"He has several girls writing to him but she's the one he wants.

"But I can't honestly see him getting married in prison. It wouldn't be like him."

Beverley is said to be reluctant to marry until she finishes her studies.

Kray who with his twin ran an East London gangland "firm" specialising in extortion and violence, may be using marriage as a ploy to be granted parole.

The authorities could be more sympathetic to his application if he indicated he wanted to wed and settle down.

An official at Parkhurst said they had no knowledge of an official application to get married.

Kray twins mum dies

VIOLET KRAY, mother of the notorious gangland twins Ronnie and Reggie, died early on Wednesday — the day before her 73rd birthday — after a short illness.

She had devoted the past 14 years of her life to getting a better deal for her imprisoned sons.

But she passed away in St Bartholomew's Hospital, without ever fulfilling her wish to get Reggie off the dangerous prisoner list at Long Larten Jail, Leicestershire. Ronnie is in Broadmoor Hospital for the criminally insane.

Violet's sister Mrs May Fuller, who lives in Bethnal Green, told the Advertiser: "Violet had done so much running about for her sons. She never missed her weekly visit to them, come snow or rain."

She added: "She came to me a few days ago and said she didn't feel well, so I took her to see a doctor.

"It was then she was taken into St Bartholomew's. Her death has come as a shock to all her family."

Violet, who lived with her husband Charlie, 76, at their home in Bunhill Road, Islington once vowed: "I'll keep visiting my sons until the end of my days."

Yesterday her husband was too upset to talk about her death. But her eldest son Charlie, was visiting his twin brothers in prison to discuss funeral arrangements.

It is not yet known whether the twins, aged 49, will be allowed to attend the funeral. But a Home Office spokesman said they would "carefully consider any request."

Both have so far served 14 years of their 30-year sentences passed in 1969 for their gangland activities and killings.

Earlier this year, Reggie tried to commit suicide by slashing his wrists. Following the suicide attempt Violet pleaded with Home Office chiefs to "give her son something to live for."

VIOLET'S FREEDOM DREAM

AFTER Charlie was released from jail in 1975, having served seven years of a 10-year sentence for being involved in the murder of John "The Hat" McVitie, he visited Violet every day.

He said: "Mostly we talked of Ronnie and Reggie. Mum always hoped she'd live long enough to see at least one of them released. It was her life's ambition.

"When the three of us were first sent away she said, 'I hate to think of the years they'll be away in my lifetime.

"'But I want to make these years for them as happy as I can please God, while it lasts'."

● Violet . . . a local beauty.

The young Violet...

VIOLET Kray was born on August 4, 1909. As she grew up she became something of a local beauty in the East End.

She married Charlie, who was nearly four years her senior when she was just 17.

As a young woman (pictured left) she was strong-willed, romantic and possessive, and she built her life around her sons. She called her twins "my lovely boys".

The twins called her "Our Queen Mum."

She died without ever fulfilling her wish to have her son Reggie taken off the Category A dangerous prisoner list.

KRAY MUM KEPT A TRAGIC SECRET

Please don't let my sons know I'm dying

FORMER gangland boss Charlie Kray broke down and wept as he told how his mother Violet lived with a secret fear about her health for six months.

Determined to keep the truth from Charlie and his brothers, twins Ronnie and Reggie, she had confided only in his common-law wife, Diane.

His voice breaking with emotion, his blue eyes filled with tears, Charlie said: "Mum made Diane give her a solemn promise that she'd never let on to my Dad or any of us three boys how ill she really was.

"All year, apparently, she'd had a pain in her side, but she was afraid that if we knew we'd have stopped her making her long weekly journeys to visit the twins in prison."

Violet died on the eve of her 73rd birthday last week after a fortnight in hospital.

VIOLET at home with Charlie and Charles, senior. On the wall hangs a picture of the Kray brothers in their gangster heyday. "We spent evenings just chatting about the twins," says Charlie.

Reggie's tribute to a 'beloved lady'

Of all the tributes that poured in this week one held a special place — the one from Reggie.

Sent out from his cell, especially for the Advertiser it read: A TRIBUTE TO 'MUM'

Charles Boyer kissed her hand when he met her back stage, she dined with George Raft, Eddy Calvert and Billy Daniels. met Joe Louis and Sonny Liston, who kissed her when she presented £4,000 to a charity at the Cambridge Rooms Restaurant.

Edmond Purdom visited her at Vallance Road and kissed her and her friend Rose Locker. Stars like Alan Lake and Diana Dors visited her regularly. David Bailey and David Puttnam, the producer, used to have cups of tea with her and discuss the film 'Bugsy Malone' when it was just an idea. She had holidays in the South of France, Spain and Tangiers and met her friends, gangsters like Billy Hill, Albert Dimes and Mafia man, Eddy Puchi.

Ted Kidd Lewis, the fighter, was a regular visitor to her for Sunday dinner and she knew other fighters like Kid Borg, Terry Spinks, Terry Downes and Len Harvey. She drank with Lord Effingham and Tom Driberg MP. She was introduced to Frank Sinatra Junior when in London. Judy Garland was amongst her friends. She knew and mixed with people from all walks of life.

She loved and married my father.

Mrs Dora Hamilton, her friend the magistrate, was recently compiling her life story.

She was a beloved lady — Mrs Violet Kray.

KRAYS BURY DEAR MUM

—REPORT: DIANE ROBINSON—

IT WAS a sad day for the infamous East End gangsters, Ronnie and Reggie Kray.

Their first taste of freedom after 14 years behind bars, was spent in mourning.

Under heavy police escort and handcuffed they travelled to Chingford Old Church to say their final farewell to the mother that had loved and adored them, Violet Kray.

It was the first time they had been seen by the outside world since their prison sentence for gangland killings began back in 1969.

It was the first time they had been reunited as a family. And it was grief that brought them together. It was a grief that showed on the faces, of two of the toughest men the East End has ever known. It was grief almost certainly felt in their hearts.

It was a day the twins would undoubtedly never forget. And it was a day the East End would remember for a long time to come.

The brief taste of freedom . . . Ronnie Kray (above) and twin Reggie (below) — ringed by police — leaving Chingford Old Church after the service. And (inset) how they looked in their infamous gangland days.

IT was so touching, wasn't it, when those darling misunderstood boys Ronnie and Reggie leaned forward to plant a kiss on their mother's oak coffin?

It is a pity that years ago they did not feel similarly inclined.

For I do not recall the Krays kissing the coffins of their victims.

"The Kray brothers are deeply upset that neither Mr Whitelaw nor Lord Longford came to the funeral"

Kray twins' father found dead

Any request by the twins, Ronald and Reginald Kray, to attend their father's funeral would be dealt with "sympathetically", the Prison Department said yesterday.

Mr Charles Kray, aged 75, was found dead yesterday at his home in Braithwaite House, Bunhill Row, Clerkenwell, north-east London, by his grandson, who shared the flat.

Ronald Kray, who is in Broadmoor, and Reginald Kray, in Parkhurst, aged 48, were allowed to attend the funeral of their mother last August. They are both serving life sentences for murder.

The twins' brother, Charles Kray, said: "My father always said he wanted a quiet affair. He was not happy at all about the fuss made over my mother's funeral. I hope it goes quietly."

The twins' brother said he hoped to see them today but was busy with funeral arrangements. He said whether the twins came would be up to them.

'Kray attack' sparks quiz

Former East End gangster Ronnie Kray was at the centre of a security review today after it was claimed he was caught throttling a fellow patient at Broadmoor.

Staff were said to have dragged Kray off his victim. Kray, who had been depressed for several days, was provoked by the victim, who was not thought to have suffered serious injury.

"He has never done anything like that while he has been at Broadmoor. This was a one-off incident," a source at the top-security hospital said.

Krays may be freed for dad's funeral

By JAMES NICHOLSON

THE Kray twins' dad died yesterday —just seven months after their mother's funeral.

And the Home Office is being asked to free them again to say farewell to 75-year-old Charles.

Last August the twins were allowed out for the first time in 13 years to attend the extraordinary funeral of Violet Kray.

They were joined by hundreds of mourners from London's East End.

Charles, who suffered bronchial trouble for more than 30 years, looked pale and drawn as he told me then: "When I go I hope it will not be a circus like this.

Boxing

"Everybody loved Vi, but I always kept away from the limelight."

But a similar turn-out is expected at next week's ceremony for "Old Charlie".

He had many friends, especially in the boxing world.

Charles was the inspiration behind the Kray brothers. All three, including the eldest son Charles, made their names as boxers before the law caught up with them.

And through them he met all the greats of the ring, including Joe Louis, Rocky Marciano and Sonny Liston.

Yesterday Charles Kray Jnr. said: "Whatever we are supposed to have done, I wish the public would remember that it is a great shock

"Old Charlie" Kray

to lose both parents in such a short space of time."

He added that his father, who was found dead in his Clerkenwell flat, had not seen the 48-year-old twins since Violet's death.

He had been too ill to visit Ronnie in Broadmoor and Reggie in Parkhurst.

'I think the twins are now very different…in every possible way'

Parole for Krays, by their priest

FATHER RICHARD HETHERINGTON with members of the Kray family at yesterday's funeral. Earlier he had a private talk with the twins.

THE KRAY TWINS Reggie, left, and Ronald at their mother's funeral yesterday.

THE Anglican priest who conducted the funeral service for the mother of the Kray twins said he would support a call for parole for the former East End gangsters.

The twins, Ronnie and Reggie, were sentenced in 1969 to serve at least 30 years for murder.

In their heyday they brought a reign of terror to the East End with protection rackets and gangland killings.

Yesterday the twins caught their first glimpse of freedom for 13 years when they were allowed to attend the funeral service for their mother, Violet, at Chingford Old Church.

Private

The service was taken by Father Richard Hetherington, a prebendary of St Paul's Cathedral, who has known the twins since they were 10 years old and he was a parish priest in Bethnal Green.

He spent 10 minutes talking to Ronnie and Reggie in the vestry before the service.

Today Father Hetherington would not reveal what was said, saying it was entirely private, but he told The Standard: "If I was asked to support any kind of move leading up to parole I would.

"It would require excessively careful looking into, and would rest entirely with the Home Office, but I myself think that they are very different in every possible way to what they were."

Father Hetherington, aged 78, was critical of the crowds who lined the streets in Chingford yesterday to watch the arrival of the funeral party.

"I found the gawpers and the gazers very distasteful, particularly as it is the very last thing that Mrs Kray would have wanted," he said.

"I had a very high regard for her indeed — her loyalty, sincerity and love for her family through many difficulties."

Father Hetherington added that he had been distressed by scenes inside the church after the service when members of the congregation rushed forward to embrace the twins and shake their hands.

● Prisoners are usually eligible for parole after serving a third of their sentence. Lifers are usually considered after 12 years.

TIMES OF PAIN AND SUFFERING — by Reggie Kray

❝All long term prisoners go through periods of time suffering from loss of identity. This is understandable when one thinks of people such as Sir Francis Chichester who, after a year at sea on his yacht, could not converse properly on arrival home, because of a personality disorder, brought about by being in solitude as a lone yachtsman.

In fact, he wrote a book on his experiences of how he won his battle against insanity. He found the effects of close confinement frightening If one considers his 18 months in comparison to a life sentence, with a recommendation of a minimum of 30 years, one will get some idea of what I, and others are up against.

I know the effects of long term imprisonment, when one is cut off from friends and relations. In fact, the pen became the instrument of my emotions, until recently when I was moved to the main wing here at Parkhurst from the hospital wing, and have once again come into contact with many people. At the moment I am quite happy in my surroundings. I have

Astrology — why I'm studying it

come to terms with the essence of the time element, and so enjoy each day, and wish the time away.

At the moment I am studying astrology, because 15 years ago I vowed to do so, at the suggestion of my QC at my trial, the late Mr Paul Wrighton.

I have also many pen-friends across the country, which helps me to keep occupied. I have written two books that should be published around July to August time. The first is a Keep Fit book.

My plans also include a recipe and slang book being compiled by my good friend Steve and myself, which should be ready for publication by December. A percentage of these books will be donated to different charities.

Some of my views on prison life surround the parole system. The radio and the newspapers, and my own experiences tell me there is a crisis about to break in the prison system.

To solve this overcrowding problem, half remission should be brought in for all lengths of sentences, and once again the prison population would become stable. If something does not happen, as sure as night follows day, there will be a lot of trouble within prisons throughout the country.

Inmates should be personally interviewed by the parole board, instead of by faceless officials of the Home Office.

Some other views of prison life I have. There is much humour in prison as the tale of the lifer who bore a grudge against his brother, who had a beautiful garden in the suburbs. This particular lifer confessed to several murders, and said the bodies were buried in his brother's garden, under the pretext the beautiful garden was dug up, and he had evened the score with his brother, much to the dismay of the police, who only discovered flowerbeds, and roots.

Prison cells are not like luxury flats as impressed on the public. They are bare and sterile. We have to use plastic cutlery and plastic chamber pots. Some cells have compressed cardboard furniture, in case of prisoners smashing up out of frustration, but I have made my cell comfortable.

The walls are adorned with photographs. I also have a Chinese lantern.

My best friend and I have named my cell "The Blue Lagoon."❞

BROTHER RON IS SO KIND

— by Reggie Kray

"The public in general have got the wrong impression of my brother Ron. He can be very articulate, and is a kind person in many ways. Over the recent years he has done a lot for charities, which has not been advertised. My brother Charlie keeps us happy with regular visits.

During my stay at the hospital here in Parkhurst I can recall some strange experiences. One day I was walking along with my friend Mick, when I noticed him go white in the face. He then just walked away and butted a window in, which makes me think, when some of my friends write to me and complain about the weather. I wonder how they would react under similar pressures.

Dr Cooper and his staff at the hospital have always been good to me. So I have no reasons for complaint. All these memories are clear in my mind, because I have a retentive memory bank. My friend's call me Scorpio. All Scorpios are supposed to have good memories.

During my time in the hospital, I also gave a lot of thought to the young people who are within the complex world of prison society. I have come to the conclusion that the authorities could be more humane if they were to realise that these youngsters need to be given short sharp lessons, similar to those of detention centres, because one can learn, if one has any sense, within a year of any sentence, that prison life is a total waste both physically, mentally and spiritually, benefit these youngsters, in as much that if they had an initial lift on release from prison, the State would be saved huge sums of money.

I do blame the use of drugs for the increasing crime rate, especially in the juvenile age group, who are not aware of the consequences.

Life with notorious killers

One does not have to suffer sentences of six years or four years to have this lesson impressed upon your mind.

I also feel the more practical help in the way of financial assistance would benefit these youngsters talk from the top of their heads, and lack tact, diplomacy and respect, which can lead them into trouble, especially so among themselves. They would have been in serious trouble had they lived in an area like the East End of London in the 1960s.

Unlike many of these youngsters, I am very tolerant towards my fellow inmates, because I have been through paranoia, where one thinks he is friendless.

So I look upon the bright side of people's personalities and make-ups.

Apart from the trouble caused by my illness sometime back, I am a stable person with a calm personality. I have studied, for mental progress over the years, and have also kept physically fit by different methods of training.

Sometimes in the quiet of the night when everyone is locked up, I theorise about the occupants of the different cells to my left and right. Locked up with their dreams and frustrations in this human zoo.

Prison life has given me a good insight into human nature. I have mixed with all the most notorious criminals in the country. Such as Harry Roberts, the police killer who adores his mother. I watched John Duddy the triple police killer die from the effects of a stroke. Seen the pathetic ways of the baby killer John Straffen. Was aware of the evil eyes of Brady the moors murderer, and I have come across many good people in prison.

I go up for my Category A review in october, which is also the month of my 50th birthday. This interview could hinder my chances of coming off the status of Category A, but to my way of thinking it should not do so, because no truth is ever a lie. I am also up for a lifer's review in July. I hope that one day the parole board will consider this proverb.

One will never learn to swim unless one goes into the water.

As I will not be able to adapt again to society unless given a chance to do so."

THE CRAZY WORLD OF RONNIE KRAY

RONNIE KRAY will have smoked salmon for his supper tonight, with thinly-sliced brown bread and Normandy butter — all delivered specially from Harrods, the top people's store.

The only thing missing will be a bottle of chilled white wine, because at Broadmoor hospital for the criminally insane they are funny about allowing alcohol.

And when he says his prayers — as he does every night — one more meaningless day will be almost over in his empty life. And yet, despite it all, Ronnie Kray is one of the most cheerful and caring men I have ever known.

Ninety miles away, behind a 30ft. wall, his twin brother Reggie sits alone in his cell at Parkhurst Prison on the Isle of Wight.

In the old days the two virtually ruled London. There wasn't a casino that didn't spin a wheel for them. Not an East End night club opened without the Krays being there as silent partners.

And their name represented just about the best insurance policy against gangland harassment an East End bookmaker could ever have.

YARD HUNT £7M TOFF!

- **Gang of 14 called their boss Paddy One**
- **He was a military type with posh accent**

By MICHAEL FIELDER and STUART HIGGINS

A GANG of 14 supercrooks—led by a "toff" with a posh accent—carried out the £7million Great Banknote Robbery.

The exclusive information was revealed last night to The Sun by one of the security guards held up at gunpoint by the raiders.

The guard said the team who used phoney Irish accents—acted with military precision.

They knew every detail of the vaults and even the names of staff before they raided the Security Express HQ in Curtain Road, Shoreditch, East London, on Easter Monday.

CONTACT

The guard, who asked not to be named, told The Sun how the toff called himself Paddy One.

And in a dramatic development last night an underworld contact gave what is believed to be the real name of The Toff and his alleged lieutenant to The Sun.

The contact told us: "He's so posh, he could have been through military school."

The Sun immediately passed the names to Scotland Yard.

Robbery squad boss Commander Frank Cater said: "This information is extremely interesting.

"We shall be following it up straight away."

The Toff was said to be a middle-aged man who lived in the Canning Town area of East London until he mysteriously vanished three months ago.

He is thought to have a

Continued on Page Four

MOVE AND WE BLOW YOU AWAY
—Pages 4 and 5

Gang donned security guard disguises

The gang who came and went without causing a ripple to the quiet Easter Monday in Curtain Road probably did so by disguising themselves as Security Express staff.

Police believe that their vehicle also bore the bonafide green and yellow colours of the company.

Commander Cater said: "There are indications that those responsible were dressed in uniforms and helmets identical or similar to those worn by Security Express employees."

Commander Cater said he believed the masked gang numbers between six and 10 and that they drove the five tons of loot away in one large lorry or two smaller ones.

"It is possible that those vehicles may have been disguised to represent legitimate security vehicles and may even have had "Security Express" written on the side," he added.

The vans should have been noticeable in London that day as no other Security Express vans were on the road.

All quiet in Curtain Road

RESIDENTS and workers from Curtain Road were oblivious that Britain's biggest cash robbery had taken place on their doorstep — until after it was all over.

Shops, pubs and cafes were closed for the Easter holidays and the whole area was deserted.

Owners of the Acron Café — where many Security Express guards go for their meals — were in their flat above the café but saw and heard nothing.

The woman who runs the café told the Advertiser: "I was indoors on Monday but I never saw anything. All the businesses here were closed and there was nobody about. The first I knew of it was when I heard it on the news."

An office worker from next door Cargo House

said: "I didn't even know Security Express was so close to us. It's amazing that a thing like this should happen with so much money involved."

The Chevron Petrol station at the end of Curtain Road was also closed but a pump attendant said: "Who would believe there was so much money kept in a little back street like this?"

Help me nab 'em plea by top cop

PLOT TO KILL THE RIPPER

By MICHAEL PARKER

A CHILLING contract on the life of Yorkshire Ripper Peter Sutcliffe has been put out by Britain's most notorious prison godfathers.

"Sutcliffe is a dead man," the News of the World was told.

The plot was revealed by an ex-inmate of Parkhurst, the powder-keg jail where the mass murderer is held.

He said the prison's crime czars planned to offer a £100,000 reward to the family of the man who "executed" 37-year-old Sutcliffe—but this had been scrapped.

Instead, the godfathers have decreed that the death of the man who killed 13 women is every prisoner's, "moral duty" and "a matter of honour."

We were also told that open revolt is simmering behind Parkhurst's fortress walls as the desperate inmates' parole hopes recede.

IRA prisoners are said to be teaching others how to make bombs for the riot they regard as "inevitable."

Our informant, an armed robber who was in Parkhurst's top-security C Wing with gang bosses Reggie Kray and Charlie Richardson and other infamous danger men, revealed that Sutcliffe is well protected.

He claimed the Ripper had bribed two orderlies to guard him in the jail hospital wing, where he may soon be joined by crazed Horror House killer Dennis Nilsen.

Outside the wing, Sutcliffe is shadowed by up to six warders when he acts as altar boy in Parkhurst's Catholic Chapel.

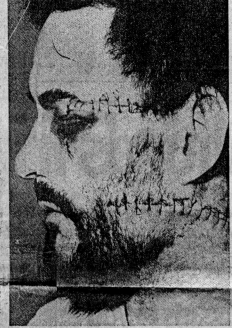

SCARRED: The Ripper after Costello's coffee-jar attack

PLEASURE

But the robber, who has just been transferred from the Isle of Wight jail to one in England, declared: "Sutcliffe should consider every day he lives a bonus.

"Every man in the prison would happily serve an extra 30 years for the pleasure of killing him."

The startling disclosures follow last week's five-year sentence on Glasgow thug Jimmy Costello for a coffee-jar stabbing attack on the Ripper at Parkhurst.

When I visited our informant at his present jail, he told me:

Costello made just one mistake — he didn't finish the job.

The real shame is that it wasn't one of the C Wing professionals who had his opportunity.

When Sutcliffe goes, it will be at the end of a knife — there are plenty about in that prison.

It won't be quick and easy. Whoever gets the job will make it as slow as Sutcliffe made it for the women he killed.

I've never known anyone be hated so much.

That's why the leaders of C Wing decided the Ripper's death was the moral duty of every prisoner.

One scheme to get him in the chapel recently was foiled. He was tipped off by one of the orderlies he has managed to bribe.

The incredible thing is that he doesn't seem to want to help himself.

He taunts other prisoners about their wives, saying things like: "She's next on my list."

He's wound everyone up so much that someone even suggested a man should be hired to kneecap his wife Sonia.

But we finally agreed we couldn't have that on our consciences.

REVULSION

Sonia upsets our visiting wives and relatives. She often comes looking like a schoolgirl, wearing knee-socks and the whole outfit.

She's always clutching a Bible or some religious book.

As well as Kray and Richardson, Parkhurst's C Wing inmates include such men as police killer Fred Saul, axeman John "Ginger" Bowden and IRA bomber Billy Armstrong.

Said our informant, who has not been paid by the News of the World: "Everyone in that jail has a deep sense of revulsion at what the Ripper did.

"Even the IRA prisoners want him dead. In fact, they reckon if one of their men gets him, it will be a good propaganda coup.

"Whoever kills Sutcliffe will be the criminal world's biggest hero.

"Despite the fact that the £100,000 contract was called off, that man's family will be set up for life with cash from his friends.

"There are millionaires behind bars in C Wing. But the money doesn't matter.

"It has become a point of principle — the Ripper must die.

"Even if I had only half-an-hour of my sentence left and I got the chance to do that bastard, I'd happily take it."

BAN FOR KRAYS AT DI'S BURIAL

Jail chiefs say no

By MICHAEL FIELDER and TONY SNOW

THE notorious Kray twins were yesterday banned by prison chiefs from going to the funeral of Diana Dors.

Sex symbol Diana knew the East End gangsters well and was among the mourners when their mother Violet was buried two years ago.

Diana also visited Ronnie Kray in Broadmoor where he is serving his life sentence.

SHATTERED

Reggie, also doing life, is in Parkhurst Prison on the Isle of Wight.

The 49-year-old brothers—said to be shattered by Diana's death on Friday—made it clear that they desperately wanted to

Diana . . . brave star

Continued on Page Two

KRAY TWIN RONNIE TO WED

He loves Elaine, 28

By MERVYN EDGECOMBE

NOTORIOUS gangster Ronnie Kray plans to marry a divorcee nearly half his age.

And last night mother-of-two Elaine Mildener, 28, talked about her amazing romance with the 51-year-old double-killer.

Elaine, who has visited Ronnie in Broadmoor top-security mental hospital every week for the past two years, said:

"We're very much in love and extremely happy."

Elaine, of Islington, North London, called Ronnie "a perfect gentleman" and added: "We'll be good for one another . . . nothing can put us off."

East End mobster Ronnie and twin Reggie have served

EXCLUSIVE

15 years of 30-year sentences for murder.

Ronnie has asked permission to marry Elaine as soon as possible.

He said: "Elaine is the best thing ever to have happened to me. Now I just can't wait for the wedding."

Ronnie, who has previously admitted homosexual tendencies, added: "That's all in the past."

Elaine . . . clutching a photo of the Krays
Picture: ARTHUR STEEL

Ronnie . . . double-killer

SHE VISITS TWIN REGGIE IN JAIL

ELAINE has been devoted to Reggie as well as twin brother Ronnie.

Every fortnight she has made the long trek to Parkhurst Prison, on the Isle Of Wight, to see Reggie.

"At times it's like visiting the same man because they're so alike," Elaine says, "Their telepathy and understanding between one another, is quite unbelievable."

Could Reggie become jealous? Elaine says: "I know they have a unique closeness but there's no chance of it happening. I've too much respect for them both to let it happen."

Already, Reggie has given the couple his blessing — inviting Elaine to visit him in Parkhurst so that he could tell her personally how much he approved of the wedding plans.

"I think you will make a terrific couple and I'm delighted for you both.

"It's the best news we have had for years, and I've said the same to Ronnie," Reggie told her.

Reggie doesn't expect to get permission to attend the wedding ceremony, but he has told Ronnie by letter that it will make no difference.

"I couldn't ask for a better sister-in-law and friend," wrote Reggie, whose own marriage ended in grief when his wife committed suicide.

STRONG

Charlie Kray, the twins' older brother, is also delighted with the news

"Elaine is a strong, solid upright girl who is perfect, for Ron," says Charlie, who lives near Elaine.

"She will give him stability and a purpose in life."

REGGIE: Delighted

86

MINDERS!

JAILED gangland killers Ron and Reg Kray are the sleeping partners in a new firm offering protection to celebrities.

The East End organisation offers film stars and rich Arabs round-the-clock protection by a personal minder and the use of a chauffeur-driven Rolls Royce or Mercedes.

The wealthy and the famous should be in safe hands if they get burly minder-to-the-stars Paul Goodridge as their bodyguard.

Paul, 34, who is six-foot tall and weighs 15 stone, numbers Richard Harris among his clients as well as former customers like Elizabeth Taylor and Richard Burton.

He runs the protection side of Krayleigh and Budrill Enterprises of Cleveland Way, Stepney, launched amid popping champagne corks on Wednesday,

The directors of the company are Ron and Reg Kray, both serving life sentences for murder, elder brother Charlie, and businessman Jack Leigh.

Also involved is millionaire businessman Thomas Pollock who provides the exclusive transport.

Jack Leigh, 52, who runs an antique and furs business in Roman Road, Bow, said: "We've hardly opened and people are already interested in our services."

Paul added: "Famous people need us. Just look what happened to John Lennon.

And he warned: "This country is going the same way as New York — there's more and more armed violence — anyone famous, anyone with money is a possible target."

"I'll tell you this too,' he said, "I give this job 100 per cent and I've never lost any-

one. And I don't intend to start now."

Backer Thomas Pollock chipped in: "You have to be streetwise to do this job properly, you've got to sense trouble before it happens — then steer clear of it."

Paul revealed that Richard Harris is to be Krayleigh Enterprises' first client, but he refused to say when the star would be coming to Britain "for security reasons."

Charlie Kray, 58, said: "I'm looking forward to this new business venture. My job will be to provide the celebrities through their connections with Ron and Reg.

"The twins are well pleased about this getting off the ground. It'll give them something to look forward to when they come out."

Elaine Kray, 29, who married Ronnie in Broadmoor Hospital last year, said: "I've just visited Ron and he is in great shape and glad to have something to come out to."

The family : Charlie Kray with " official " T-shirt

Parole bid by gang killer Reggie Kray

JAILED gangland boss Reggie Kray, the younger of the infamous Kray twins, is in line for release after serving 18 years of a life sentence for murder.

Details of Reggie's case are being reviewed by a local parole committee before being sent on to the full Parole Board. He has already been interviewed.

Hospital

If he wins his plea, Reggie, 52 —who was jailed in 1969 and recommended to serve at least 30 years for the murder of Jack " The Hat " McVitie—could be free by Christmas.

He has already made plans for the future. He has written a book now being considered by publishers Sidgwick and Jackson.

Ten days ago, I can reveal, he was visited in Parkhurst Prison on the Isle of Wight by Sidgwick and Jackson managing director William

Armstrong and his deputy editorial director, Miss Susan Hill.

Rumours of Reggie's possible release were further fuelled by a visit last Wednesday from Lord Longford, who is also a veteran campaigner for parole for Myra Hindley.

A Home Office spokesman said : " Mr Kray was told at the beginning of June his case was going to be reviewed."

" It is still in the early stages."

Reggie's twin, Ronnie, is serving a life term in Broadmoor maximum security hospital. He is considered less suitable as a candidate for parole.

The Kray twins were the leaders of the notorious " firm " which ruled London's East End by terror in the 'sixties.

Criminals

Last week, their elder brother Charlie, who served six and a half years for his part in the murder of gangland thug McVitie, appealed for Reggie's release.

" We are just waiting and hoping something will happen," he told me.

" No one could say the public wouldn't be safe if they were let free. They have done their time now.

" I didn't want to defend what they did. It was wrong and they know it. But they are now into their 19th year. It is a long time.

" The twins have never harmed anyone but criminals." If they come out, the kids and the women will be

Charlie believes his brother would not want to return to his old East End haunts.

He said : " I don't think he would live in London. It would be too claustrophobic here and the twins always liked the country.

" He has said that when he comes home he would like to get into writing. It would give him something to do and I think people are interested in his writing, aren't they ? "

Publisher Mr Armstrong was stunned that news of his Parkhurst visit had leaked out.

Coincidence

He refused to give details of Reggie's book but added : " We are looking at something he has done and it has got no further than that."

Lord Longford also refused to be drawn on the subject.

He said : " It really is a genuine coincidence that I visted him just a week after William Armstrong.

" I hadn't seen Reg for two years and I thought he looked incredibly well. He trains for three quarters of an hour every day in the gym and is looking very fit."

Angry

Charlie said he last visited Reggie, who has been considered for parole before, on Tuesday and found him in good spirits.

" professionals of violence."

Charlie said : " Someone showed me the T-shirts three months ago and I thought they were a *bit strong*.

" So I did a bit of investigating and eventually found out who was doing it. Then I phoned up and said : ' If you carry on doing this, I am going to take you to court.'

" I decided to do it all legally. I have no heavy people around me. It seemed to work because they all stopped.

" Then I decided to do some T-shirts with a friend and we put the twins' signatures on them to authorise them.

" But all this rubbish about the *twins making money out of it really* annoyed me. My brothers never had a penny out of it. They heard about it and were furious."

> ❛ The twins have never harmed anyone but criminals ❜

Kray wife in plea to Queen

No love for Ronnie leads to prison divorce move

THE wife of gangland killer Ronnie Kray has made a desperate plea to the Queen to save their marriage.

Elaine Mildener, 32, wrote to Buckingham Palace in a last-ditch bid to keep the two-year partnership going.

But her appeals have drawn a blank and Elaine is to divorce Ronnie, currently serving a 30 year sentence in Broadmoor.

The mother-of-two wanted another child ... but prison officers have ruled that she cannot see her husband in private and is, therefore, unable to consummate the marriage.

Now friends of the convicted murderer, who said on his wedding day that he had put his homosexual past behind him, fear for his safety.

"I think the marriage made him very stable," said friend of the couple Maureen Flanagan, of Hackney.

"I just hope this latest news does not unbalance him in anyway. Let's hope it does not upset him too much."

"The last time I spoke to Elaine she was very sad. She had a lot of affection for Ronnie and has been very good to him. No one has done more."

Elaine, of Islington, would regularly travel to Broadmoor but will be cutting down her visits from once a week to once a month.

"She will be going there just as a friend from now on. But she will always help with the campaign to get parole for the twins," said Maureen Flanagan.

REGGIE'S WAY

I would like to point out that having come to terms with the time element I enjoy each day and no longer wish the time away. How can I not be happy when I have the support of my brothers Ron, Charlie, and 25-year-old Steve who is as close as a brother. My best wishes to all in the East End.

REGGIE KRAY

H.M. Prison,
Parkhurst,
Isle of Wight

New bid to free Reggie

CHARLIE Kray, brother of jailed gangland bosses Ron and Reg, is planning a nationwide petition in the New Year, calling for the release of the Twins.

It will be aimed to coincide with the 20th anniversary of their imprisonment. Ron is in a psychiatric hospital at Broadmoor and Reg was moved to Gartree Prison, Leicester, 18 months ago.

A national newspaper claimed that Charlie, 58, was organising a travelling roadshow to get signatures supporting the twins' release but Charlie told the Advertiser: "I haven't yet decided what the campaign will be but something will be happening."

He added: "I feel there is a lot of support for their release not just in the East End but nationwide and a petition will definitely form part of the campaign.

"On May 8 next year Ron and Reg will have been behind bars for 20 years of their 30 year sentence which I think is unfair when IRA killers and mass murderers like Dennis Nielsen get sentences of 25 years.

But Charlie is facing an uphill battle because Reg has already been turned down by the parole board earlier this year. That effectively means he must wait another four years for a review of his case.

The Twins were recommended to serve at least 30 years for the murder of George Cornell at the Blind Beggar pub, Whitechapel Road, and the shooting of Jack 'the Hat' McVitie.

THE BOY REGGIE KRAY LIVES FOR

GANGLAND terror boss Reggie Kray has been tamed . . . by the friendship of a handsome young body-builder. What began as a casual encounter in Parkhurst Prison has developed into what Kray himself describes as his "magnificent obsession".

Now free after serving four years for armed robbery, 28-year-old Peter Gillett has told how he defied the "gay" taunts of fellow prisoners to pursue his remarkable relationship with one of the most feared men in British criminal history.

I bedded busty Babs says Charlie...

LIFE STORY... how Charlie reveals all

BUDDIES: Peter gives Kray a hand with the weights in the prison gym

Love and kisses of The Godfather

FREE MAN
Freed jailbird Peter Gillett, who claims Kray took an instant liking to him in prison and now regards him as his son.

REGGIE KRAY

AT 53

● REGGIE KRAY, the gangland boss who once ruled London's underworld with an iron hand is now 53 and keeps fit by daily bouts in the prison gym . . pumping iron.

After 20 years inside Britain's most evil villain confesses

RONNIE: 'I believe I'll never leave Broadmoor'

RONNIE KRAY: I'M STILL GAY AND MAD

FRANKLIN

REGGIE KRAY GOES GAY!

" D'YOU THINK HE'LL LIKE THE LILAC BARS WITH THE PINK CURTAINS? "

THE KEMPS: Martin (left) and Gary are ready for their movie debut

POP BROTHERS TO PLAY THE KRAYS

POP idol brothers Gary and Martin Kemp are to make their film debuts—playing the gangland Kray twins.

The Spandau Ballet heart-throbs will put the clock back 30 years as Reggie and Ronnie, the hoodlums who terrorised the East End.

Their manager Steve Dagger said: "The boys have a background in acting. They're the right age and even look like the young Krays."

Six-foot hunk Martin, 26—engaged to gorgeous blonde Shirlie Holliman of the hit duo Pepsi and Shirlie—appeared on television as a child in Jackanory and the Glittering Prizes.

Gary, 28, who plays Reggie, said: "It was around the part of

THE KRAYS: Ronnie (left) and Reggie

By MICK HAMILTON

London where I come from that the Krays reigned.

"I've probably got relatives who were in their gangs!"

The brothers—who have clocked up 18 hits in the Top Forty—beat several established stars for the roles.

The Krays, now 54, were both jailed for life in 1969 for murder ending their reign of terror.

LIFE
AND TIMES OF A GANGSTER

Fit — boxing twins Reggie and Ronnie in the Fifties.

GANGSTER Reggie Kray's secret life in prison is revealed today in a series of remarkable photographs.

They show that despite 20 years behind bars, the 53-year-old killer is still fighting fit.

These exclusive pictures are the world's first glimpse of Kray's battle against old age.

Last week his hopes of an early parole were dashed. But the struggle to stay in shape in jail goes on.

THE man who once ruled London's underworld with a fist of iron now pumps iron five nights a week in the gym at Leicester's top-security Gartree prison.

For an hour each time he grunts and sweats his way through a series of gruelling weight-lifting exercises—"getting fit on Porridge," according to an old lag's joke.

The spectre of his twin, Ronnie, is always there to haunt him.

The brothers—both keen boxers—were jailed for life for the murder of Jack "The Hat" McVitie in 1967.

Now Ronnie is locked up with the criminally insane at Broadmoor. And Reggie is determined it won't happen to him.

His other brother Charlie says "Reggie has to discipline his mind and body to keep going, otherwise you'a just go mad.

"He's in fantastic shape. If it wasn't for the food he'd be in better shape now than he was when he went inside."

WEIGHT-training is the highlight of Kray's life behind bars.

Every day he is woken at 7am to slop out before eating breakfast alone in his cell.

Then he has to pass the time until his evening work-out in the gym.

Reading and writing are his main interests.

He has 800 names on his correspondence list—with Ronnie at the top.

Reggie—who the judge recommended should serve at least 30 years—has told friends:

"When you have no definite sentence you don't equate with time.

"On a fixed sentence you worry about the days and months. I don't even worry about the years."

HE still dreams of life on the outside as he does his work-out, a life away from big cities and memories of his evil past.

He has said: "Much as I like London I would seek a quieter way of life.

"I just want a bit of peace and solitude."

His next chance of freedom comes in four years when his case comes before the parole board again.

Meanwhile he just keeps pumping iron . . .

THAT BASTARD INCE WAS MY GIRL'S REAL DAD

ME AND MY BROTHERS By Charlie Kray

CHARLIE KRAY'S marriage to blonde Dorothy Moore was foundering long before he was jailed in 1969.

For he had discovered that his precious daughter Nancy was not his child. Her real father was "that bastard George Ince."

In his soon-to-be published book, Me and My Brothers, Charlie says:

"Dolly told me about it during a row when Nancy was two.

"It wasn't easy to accept, and for a long time I refused to believe it. Not mine!

"That laughing, giggling, squealing little ball of wide-eyed innocence, that cart-wheeling bundle of energy, that adorable impish little girl? Not mine!

"Dolly, later took it back and said it was a lie she had dreamed up in the heat of the moment.

"But it was too late. She had sowed the seed of doubt in my mind and it was to grow and grow."

Retrial

The bombshell finally hit Charlie when he was in jail.

Gangster George Ince appeared at Chelmsford Crown Court in May 1973, accused of murdering Muriel Patience at the Barn restaurant in Braintree, Essex.

Seven days later the jury could not agree on a verdict and a retrial was ordered.

It began on May 14 and a mystery witness was mentioned.

"I knew immediately it was Dolly, but when she visited me I didn't say a word. Nor did she.

"Then the papers started referring to Doris Gray, the name which Dolly had adopted by deed poll when I was sent to jail—and I knew for certain I was right.

"The mystery woman was going into the witness box to say George Ince could not have been at the Barn Restaurant that night —because he had been in bed with her.

"My stomach knotted in fury and I paced up and down my cell.

"Agonising thoughts kept invading my mind ...

"How often had that bastard Ince been to the house? Had little Nancy been encouraged to call him daddy? Did he walk about the house half-naked like I'd done. Did she see her mother making love with Ince in my bed?"

Dolly eventually visited Charlie and confessed she and Ince were lovers.

She did give evidence and Ince walked out of Chelmsford Crown Court a free man ... and later they married.

Charlie says: "I hated the idea of seeing Dolly again but I had to because of the children. We needed to talk about what was going to happen to them after the divorce.

"On her next visit I told her we were finished, but she refused to accept it ... but it was all over."

THE OTHER MAN ... George Ince was Dolly's lover

From ME AND MY BROTHERS by Charles Kray with Robin McGibbon, to be published by Grafton Books on November 17, 1988. Price £3.50. © Charles Kray, 1988.

Reign of terror? It never existed

I'VE never been able to understand all the talk of terror—and neither have Ronnie and Reggie.

The East End locals welcomed them with open arms because they were respectful, generous and spent a lot of money.

If there was a "reign of terror" is it not fair to assume that a few of the supposedly terrified working people would have been queuing at the Old Bailey to drive a nail into their persecutors' coffin?

The fact that not one such person made a statement against either Ronnie or Reggie speaks for itself.

Quite simply, no one could say anything because there wasn't anything to say.

Ronnie and Reggie carried the can for certain members of their Firm who grassed them to the police.

Hard though it is for me to accept, I feel I may be the guilty one in the Kray story.

Attitude

I was the one who made them aware their fists were lethal weapons. I was the one who persuaded them to turn pro, then trained and sparred with them.

I was the one who made them believe they were invincible.

I don't want to apologise for what I did. My attitude to the twins was motivated by the best of intentions.

But in the light of what happened, I wonder if it would all have been different if I'd have bought the twins a football instead of boxing gloves.

THE FAMILY MAN ... Charlie with his mum and son

How we freed Axeman

THE most brilliant stunt we pulled was in 1966 when we freed a con known as the Mad Axeman from Dartmoor.

His name was Frank Mitchell and he was extraordinary—6ft 3in, with a dagger tattooed on his arm, a huge physique and great boxing skills.

He got his nickname when he threatened some people with an axe to get money. But he was really a gentle giant—he wouldn't have hurt a fly.

Reg and I felt sorry for Frank. His crimes weren't serious yet he was in Dartmoor, Britain's most primitive jail, with no release date. I promised him we would free him, though I never thought he'd take me up on it. Then he wrote to us saying how desperate he was.

Two of our top men drove to Dartmoor on a morning when we knew Frank would be on an outside working party.

Booze

He slipped away and when Albert and Teddy found him he was contentedly feeding moor ponies. They bundled him into a car and raced to London.

But there was no need to panic—it was SIX HOURS before he was missed!

The landlord of a pub six miles from Dartmoor revealed that Frank had often been in to buy bottles of booze.

He also used to go shopping by taxi to Okehampton, where he would buy budgies for other prisoners.

And most amazing, he had a couple of girlfriends on the moor and he would nip off for romps in the heather!

The warders seemed to think Frank would be no bother if he was just kept happy.

We took him to a farm in Suffolk we had used and then to Europe. I doubt if he will ever be found. It's amazing what a new passport and plastic surgery can do.

FRANK MITCHELL He was never recaptured

91

I HAD TO KILL JACK THE HAT BEFORE HE GOT ME!

says Reggie Kray

McVITIE . . . gangland heavy

YES, I killed Jack McVitie. I denied it at my trial and I've wished ever since that I hadn't. You see, I'm not ashamed of having killed him. I don't believe I had a choice.

It was either him or me. In my book, I had to kill McVitie. He was killed for several reasons. He cheated us more than once.

He had said publicly that he wanted to kill me and I had good reason to believe that it was no idle threat. He had become crazy, his mind demented by a combination of booze and drugs. So in October 1967, I killed him.

I did not regret it at the time and I don't regret it now, even though the extermination of a man no better than a sewer rat has cost me my freedom for the best part of my life.

I felt bad afterwards. I had a lot of nightmares. Not because I'd killed McVitie—one of the nastiest villains I have ever met—but because sticking a knife into anyone is not a pleasant thing to do.

Unless you're a psychopath—and I'm not—it's not an enjoyable feeling. It's a bloody awful one.

And the panic afterwards when you realise what you've done.

But you can't turn the clock back. What's done is done and you have to pay the price. I think I've paid all right—it's cost me nearly half my life.

McVitie was a slag.

I am still top man in here, they all call me Colonel!

Truce with old rivals

AMAZINGLY enough, Reggie and I later became friends with Charlie and Eddie Richardson.

In 1969, Eddie and Reg were both in the special security block at Parkhurst.

At one time Eddie went on hunger strike with the intention of bringing various complaints he had to the attention of the Press.

However, though he was officially on hunger strike, he didn't really want to starve.

So Reg used to leave hard-boiled eggs for him behind the toilet seats to help stave off his hunger pains.

And to think that only a few years earlier they had been such deadly enemies.

What might have happened if we could have settled our differences and got together? We could have ruled Europe.

CHARLIE RICHARDSON
We became friends

What a knock-out!

WHEN the Kray twins gave former world heavyweight boxing champion Joe Louis a helping hand they were KO'd —by the law.

Charlie explains: " Joe needed a bit of work, so Reggie and Ronnie organised a promotional tour of clubs in Newcastle.

" But when they got there the police pounced. They labelled the twins " The London Mob " and put them on the next train back to London.

" Poor old Joe was bewildered. He told the police the twins were only trying to help him.

" Later, he apologised to them both . . . for getting them into trouble."

Another world champion, Sonny Liston, no stranger to the underworld himself—met the twins.

And afterwards he confessed he was terrified of Reggie !

It wasn't for Ron

BOOKS and newspapers have said that I killed McVitie because I was under the influence of my brother Ron.

They also said it was because I was frightened of him, because I was trying to prove that I was as tough as he was, because he had killed.

Madness

But none of it is true. I was not under Ron's influence.

I am sick to death of people saying Ron was the bad one, the evil one, and I was the nice one, the weak one, who was led astray by him.

I was every bit as bad—if that's the word to use—as my brother. He didn't frighten me.

Even in his black moods, when depressions hit him hard and the madness started to set in, I was never frightened of Ron. Why should I have been?

Apart from Charlie and our mother, I was the one person in the world he would never have hurt, the one person he trusted.

I never felt I had got to prove myself to Ron by killing another man. He never tried to goad me into it.

92

I FELT MARVELLOUS AFTER KILLING GANGSTER GEORGE

I KNEW from a very early age that I was going to kill someone. It was part of my destiny. And I always had this love of guns. I loved the feel of them, the touch of them and the sound they made when you fired them.

I, Ronnie Kray, had shot one or two other men before I shot George Cornell. With the others, though, it was always business and not personal. I always aimed to maim, not to kill.

With Cornell, though, it was different. It had become personal as well as business, and—I make no bones about it—I intended to kill him.

I had known Cornell for a very long time, right from when we were both tearaways in East London. In those days he went under his real name of Myers.

He probably changed it later to confuse the police.

Even in those early days he was a loner and a really mean bastard. But he left us well alone and we left him alone.

There was no point in looking for trouble, especially with someone you knew could look after himself.

Living

Cornell really began to be a problem for us when he moved south of the river and joined forces with the Richardson gang.

This was run by two brothers, Charlie and Eddie Richardson, in conjunction with a man known as Mad Frankie Fraser.

The Richardsons ran a successful scrapyard in Brixton. They made a really good living from it.

But Charlie and Eddie were always fascinated by the low life, by doing deals, by making money, by cheating the system.

So they began to put together an army of crooks and hardmen.

They were a mightily powerful and feared organisation. Feared because if anyone crossed them the Richardsons were ruthless in their retribution.

Some of the techniques used by the Richardson gang made the Kray twins look like Methodist lay peachers.

Reg and I believed that a thick ear or a punch on the jaw would persuade most people around to our way of thinking. The Richardsons, it was claimed, believed in torture and would torture anyone who got in their way or was even suspected of being disloyal.

Even our guys were scared stiff that they'd fall into the Richardsons' hands.

There was a sort of truce between us and the Richardsons, based on the understanding that we each stayed on our own patch.

But it was always an uneasy truce and I had a gut feeling that something or someone would force us into a full-scale war. That someone turned out to be Cornell.

He moved south and became the Richardsons' chief hatchet man and torturer.

He was extremely well qualified for the job.

Spies

We had spies in the Richardson camp and it wasn't long before we started hearing stories that Cornell was stirring things up for us.

He kept on at the Richardsons to move into our territory and wipe us out.

That would have made the Richardson gang the kings of London. It was a situation we could not tolerate. It was beginning to affect our business affairs.

We were in the early stages of negotiations with the American Mafia, and they got uneasy because they could smell trouble in London.

The trouble might have been avoided, but then Cornell did the most stu-pid thing he'd ever done in his life.

In front of a table full of villains he called me, Ronnie Kray, a "fat poof." He virtually signed his own death warrant.

It happened just before Christmas, 1965. We decided to call a meeting with the Richardsons to work out a deal to avoid a full-scale gang war.

We all turned up at the Astor Club, off Berkeley Square, and it soon developed into a very stormy meeting, mainly over how much of the action the Richardsons were going to get in our dealings with the Americans.

Stupid

We didn't want them to have any but knew we might have to compromise to avoid bloodshed.

Cornell, of course, couldn't resist sticking his oar in, time and time again, even though it was strictly none of his business.

The negotiations were actually between the Krays and the Richardsons—others were there merely for protection. But Cornell was doing his best to stir things up.

He said we were talking a load of rubbish. Then he did that very stupid thing.

In front of all those people—our own men and top men from the other side—he said: "Take no notice of Ron Kray. He's just a big, fat poof."

From the moment he said it, he was dead.

After that meeting the troubles and the aggro really began. It was sud-denly all about who were the top dogs in London—who were the real kings of the underworld.

And do you know what? I was loving it. This, to me, was what being a gangster was all about. Fighting, scrapping, battling—that's what I'd come into it for in the first place.

Don't get me wrong. I didn't want to kill people—I just wanted a bloody good scrap.

But in March, 1966, the Richardsons spoiled it all. They launched a full-scale attack, guns blazing, on a club called Mr Smith's, in Catford, South London. Nobody really knows why.

One member of our firm was there at the time—a young guy called Richard Hart, who was having a quiet drink.

He was an extremely nice fellow, with a wife and little kids, but they shot him dead.

As it happened, the Richardsons, Cornell and the rest of them, got more than they bargained for that night.

Mr Smith's was full of gangsters who could look after themselves, and when the Richardsons burst in with knives and shooters these guys hit back.

There was an almighty battle and Eddie Richardson was badly wounded. He was also arrested, along with Charlie Richardson.

Typically, the one who slipped through the police net, the snake who slithered away through the grass, was Cornell.

Hart had to be avenged. Nobody could kill a member of the Kray gang and expect to get away with it.

The Richardsons were both in custody. That left Cornell. He would have to be the one to pay the price. And, let's face it, who better? All I had to do was find him.

The next night, March 9, I got the answer. He was

> ❝The jukebox played The Sun Ain't Gonna Shine Any More—for George Cornell that was certainly true.❞

drinking in the Blind Beggar. Typical of the yobbo mentality of the man.

Less than 24 hours after the Catford killing, and here he was, drinking in a pub that was officially on our patch. It was as though he wanted to be killed.

I unpacked my 9mm Mauser automatic and a shoulder holster. I called Scotch Jack Dickson and told him to bring the car round to my flat and to contact Ian Barrie, a big Scot, and to collect him on the way.

As we drove towards the Blind Beggar I checked that Barrie was carrying a weapon, just in case.

At 8.30pm precisely we arrived at the pub and quickly looked around to make sure that this was not an ambush.

I told Dickson to wait in the car with the engine running, then Barrie and I walked into the Blind Beggar.

I could not have felt calmer. It was very quiet and gloomy inside the pub. There was an old bloke sitting by himself in the public bar and three people in the saloon bar—two blokes at a table and Cornell sitting alone on a stool.

As we walked in, the barmaid was putting on a record. It was the Walker Brothers singing The Sun Ain't Gonna Shine Any More. For Cornell that was certainly true.

As we walked towards him he turned round and a sort of sneer came over his face. "Well, look who's here," he said.

I never said anything. I just felt hatred for this sneering man.

I took out my gun and held it towards his face. Nothing was said, but his eyes told me that he thought the whole thing was a bluff.

I shot him in the forehead. He fell forward on to the bar. There was some blood on the counter.

That's all that happened. Nothing more. Despite any other account you may have read about this incident, that was what happened.

It was over very quickly, then there was silence.

Everyone had disappeared—the barmaid, the old man in the public and the blokes in the saloon bar. It was like a ghost pub.

*I felt ****ing marvellous.*

I have never felt so good, so bloody alive, before or since. Twenty years on and I can recall every second of the killing of Cornell.

I have replayed it in my mind millions of times.

After a couple of minutes we walked out, got into the car and set out for a pub in the East End. On the way we could hear the screaming of the police car sirens.

I gave my gun to a trusted friend we used to call The Cat and told him to get rid of it. I suddenly noticed my hands were covered in gunpowder burns, so I scrubbed them in the washroom.

Drinks

I showered and put on fresh clothing. All my old gear was taken away to be burned.

Upstairs in a private room, I had a few drinks with some of the top members of the firm—Reg and others.

We listened to the radio and heard that a man had been shot in the East End.

As the news was announced I could feel everyone in the room, including Reg, looking at me with a new respect.

I had killed a man and was someone to be feared. I was now the Colonel.

Cornell was dead, the Richardsons were locked up and the Krays ruled London. Nothing at that stage could stop us.

Everyone seemed frightened of us—people were actually ringing up begging to pay protection money.

Reg and Ron are friends once again

WITH Ronnie Kray's wedding just around the corner and brother Reg's book on slang due for release, the Twins have decided to settle their differences.

In recent weeks the pair have had cross words over Ron's pending nuptials to former kiss-a-gram girl Kate Howard.

Ronnie, who is serving his sentence for murder in Broadmoor, was said to be furious over saucy claims that his blonde bride-to-be was involved in a sex romp with Reg's former cellmate Pete Gillett.

But in an exclusive letter to the Advertiser Reg says: "I am due to see Ron soon and we are friends again.

"Ron told me in a letter that he wishes to withdraw all personal remarks against Pete. They were only made in anger," adds Reg, who is in Lewes Prison, Sussex.

However, with the wedding on the cards for some time, in the next few weeks and the publication of Reg Kray's Book of Cockney Rhyming Slang on November 2, the Krays are mates again.

KRAYS Inc

Ron and Reg make £1.25m a year—and it's all legit!

MILLIONAIRES... Ronnie and Reggie are raking it in from their "offices" behind bars

OUR WEDDING KRAY

Bride Kate tells how she got Ron smart in £500 suit

UNITED . . . *Happy moments before the parting*

By SUE TOMPSETT

RONNIE KRAY'S bride of nine days told last night how she borrowed a gag from Hale And Pace to liven up her wedding.

Bubbly Kate Kray, 33, said that the 56-year-old gang boss—wearing a £500 tailored suit, tinted glasses and crocodile shoes—gave a quiet "I do" when asked to deliver the traditional marriage vow.

But when she was asked: "Do you take this man to be your lawful wedded husband?" she chirped loudly: "I do, Ron, Ron, I do."

Laugh

The 25 guests in a small room at Broadmoor, which had been set aside for the wedding, burst out laughing.

"I had to do something," said Kate. "It was so quiet it was as if someone was being buried. My little joke certainly livened things up."

So did Kate's choice of music to kick off the post-wedding celebration.

As guests sipped champagne and tucked into salmon, lobster and caviar laid between two blue dolphins carved from ice, Kate switched on a tape. It was Elvis Presley singing JAILHOUSE ROCK!

She said: "Ron looked at me disbelievingly but saw the irony. 'You're mad,' he teased.

"Ron likes ballads and wanted Joe Longthorne. But I said we weren't having him on our wedding day. "'Why not?' Ron asked. " 'Because he gives me a bloody headache,' I said."

Kate, who divorced her first husband, is the most unlikely gangster's moll.

picture special

She doesn't smoke, drink or take drugs, and rarely swears. She runs three companies—a strippagram service, a car hire firm and a property business.

She admits she tried to change Ron's appearance for the big day. She said: "He was going to wear his usual heavy-rimmed spectacles.

"But I said they looked like an old man's glasses and insisted he wore tinted ones. He also allowed me to buy him some crocodile shoes.

Heavy

"He had his own way with his wedding suit, though. I arranged for a tailor to measure Ron in Broadmoor and we ordered four £500 suits.

"I urged him not to wear a light suit because of his pale complexion but to go for a dark grey, double-breasted cashmere. But on the big day he was wearing a light grey Prince of Wales check I had taken to him three days before. And he had opted for a blue tie.

94

Reggie Kray leaves top security jail

S. Exp. 30 IV 89

by
OONAGH BLACKMAN

NOTORIOUS gangland killer Reggie Kray has been moved secretly out of a maximum security jail.

He was transferred quietly from the tough Category A Gartree Prison in Leicestershire to the less strict Category B regime at Lewes Prison, Sussex.

The move is being seen as the first major step towards the 55-year-old Kray twin's eventual freedom.

It will mean a sharp reduction in supervision during prison visits and longer periods of mixing socially with other prisoners.

Reggie and his brother Ronnie were sentenced to a minimum of 30 years by an Old Bailey judge on March 8, 1969,

Reggie in his heyday

for the gangland murders of George Cornell and Jack (The Hat) McVitie.

The Home Office last night refused to discuss Reggie's transfer or a possible release date, but it has been made clear in the past that 1991 is the earliest his case could be reviewed by the Parole Board.

Ronnie, diagnosed as a chronic paranoid schizophrenic, is not expected to be released from Broadmoor mental hospital, his home for the past 16 years.

News of Reggie's dramatic switch to Lewes Prison spread quickly among his family and friends.

Elder brother Charlie said last night: "It's a good move, and about time too. He has been in Gartree long enough.

"I found out from a friend who spoke to him recently and I'm sure this a step towards his release, although nobody knows when that will be."

Reggie's transfer means he is not now considered an inmate whose escape would be dangerous to the public. If he continues to behave like a model prisoner in Lewes eventually he could be moved to an open prison prior to freedom.

Bitter

A £5 million film is about to be made starring Spandau Ballet brothers Gary and Martin Kemp as the violent East End overlords.

If Reggie does get parole in 1991 he could get a front seat to see the gangland epic. Production company Fugitive Features of Notting Hill Gate, London, has been hit by delays—but if the filming schedule is met, both Reggie and the movie could be released together.

In the Kray twins' sentimental and at times bitter biography Our Story, published last year, Reggie wrote: "All we want now is the chance to enjoy some peace, quiet and solitude".

He also said he would not feel safe any longer on his old territory in London: "We'd be eaten alive by the new young men who now control British crime".

COSTA CRUNCH

Continued from Page C.1

Marbella flat by armed Spanish police PUNCHED, KICKED and SPAT AT the men escorting him.

Foreman, handcuffed to two of the cops, was finally chained into a seat on Iberia Flight 610 for the 1 hour 45 minute flight.

He was the only passenger in the plane's first-class section.

An eye-witness at Malaga airport said: "He went absolutely berserk. He was desperate not to be put on the plane.

"When they finally got him aboard his shirt was torn and he looked a real mess.

"There was a battle royal in the airport police station and another on the steps of the plane."

A senior Spanish police officer said "This man is an animal. We are glad to see the back of him."

Foreman was met at Heathrow by Flying Squad detectives who want to quiz him about the raid on security vaults in Shoreditch, East London, in Easter 1983.

Flying Squad chief Commander John O'Connor said last night: "This is an important breakthrough."

He said Foreman would be taken to Leman Street police station in East London.

Scotland Yard is seeking the expulsion of three other Londoners in connection with the robbery.

They are publican Cliff Saxe, Ronald Everett and Ronald Mason.

Foreman's arrest signals the start of tough new moves against fugitives promised to Home Secretary Douglas Hurd by Spain last year.

1990's

"Ron had great humour, a vicious temper, was kind and generous. He did it all his way, but above all he was a man."
Reg Kray

"How can you ask me to pay tax? I'm a madman."
Ron Kray

"Obviously I wish we'd got a share of the profits but I really didn't expect the film to be that successful. It's one of those things, you can't cry about it afterwards."
Charlie Kray

RUTHLESS HENCHMAN TO KRAY TWINS

PARTNER: Ronnie Kray

PARTNER: Reggie Kray

The Star - 5 IV 90

FREDDIE Foreman learned his criminal craft as a hitman for the Kray twins.

During London's lawless Sixties, the former publican and streetfighter built a fearsome reputation as one of the hardest men in Britain.

His nickname in the criminal underworld was The Mean Machine.

British courts first heard of Foreman in 1969 when he was convicted of taking part in two murders with the Krays.

He served six years of a ten-year sentence for helping to dispose of the body of Jack "The Hat" McVitie, who is believed to be buried in the foundations of a block of flats.

But Foreman was later cleared of shooting dead Frank "Mad Axeman"

STAR REPORTER

Mitchell, despite evidence that he pumped four bullets into him.

In 1975, he was charged with murdering small-time crook Thomas "Ginger" Marks — and was again cleared.

In 1983, he was named as a suspect in the £6 million Security Express raid. Police also wanted to quiz him about the

Brink's Mat bullion raid. But Foreman fled to Spain's Costa De Sol where he bought a villa.

It took Scotland Yard almost six years to get legal clearance to bring Foreman home to trial.

Even so, Madrid's Supreme Court only agreed last July that he was an "undesirable".

But the Krays' sidekick didn't go without a fight . . . and went berserk at the airport.

Sightseers book for Kray trip

A GANGLAND coach tour of Reg and Ronnie Kray's old East End haunts is being organised to celebrate the killers' 60th birthday.

The October weekend break will take in the Blind Beggar pub in Whitechapel where Ron gunned down George Cornell, and the flat where Reg knifed to death Jack "The Hat" McVitie.

Included in the £8 trip is a commentary by a childhood pal of the Krays, Laurie O'Leary.

Laurie said: "It would be nice if the Krays were able to celebrate the day with us."

WHAT A KRAZY WORLD

AFTER 23 years behind bars for killing one villain, Reggie Kray has been told his case for parole won't be heard again until 1995.

He says he doesn't mind, as he's content in himself. I say it's diabolical. The average sentence for murder is eight years. The perverted vermin who slaughtered little Jason Swift got 15 years.

I am against lenient jail sentences. I would prefer to see killers dangling from the end of a rope.

But if leniency is the order of the day, it should be applied across the board.

Is there one logical reason why Kray shouldn't be released tomorrow?

CUE HERE FOR KRAY T-SHIRTS

THE notorious Kray twins are trying to set up a string of snooker clubs—to sell Kray souvenirs.

Reggie and Ronnie, serving life for gangland killings, have a cult following who collect valuable Kray memorabilia like T-shirts.

But the twins are fed up with rivals ripping them off and want to cash in by selling their own merchandise from snooker clubs across the country.

Negotiations involving the twins' Jersey-based company are under way for the first club in Swansea—but it faces local opposition.

97

ACTION RE-KRAY!

EVIL TWINS: Reggie and Ronnie Kray ruled by fear

Charlie Kray gives Martin the lowdown on his brothers

HEART-THROBS: Gary and Martin as Spandau fans know them

GUN LAW: Gary Kemp (left) and brother Martin step out as gun-toting gangsters Reggie and Ronnie Kray in the new movie

By SANDIE LAMING

POP hunks Gary and Martin Kemp look a real mean machine as they take to the streets as gun-toting gangsters Reggie and Ronnie Kray.

The Spandau Ballet stars have made themselves **WALK, TALK** and even **LOOK** like the evil twins in a chilling movie portrayal of the Sixties mobsters.

Their performance is so frighteningly realistic that even the Krays' big brother Charlie feels a shiver run up his spine as he watches them on the set of the £5 million film.

The singing duo have gone to extraordinary lengths to perfect their role as the killers who once ruled the East End.

The chartbusting brothers even visited the Krays in jail to study their mannerisms.

And they called in ex-boxing champ John H. Stracey to help them build up their mus-

cles so they would look convincing as they re-enacted the Krays' bloody past.

But the effort has been worth it.

For when the Kemp brothers step in front of the camera they **ARE** the Krays.

Martin, 29, looks like Reggie's double as he struts about with the gangster's fam-

ous macho scowl—and 30-year-old Gary is every inch a backstreet hard man like Ronnie.

Even the suits the boys wear are made by the same East End tailor that the Krays used in the days when they swaggered around their Cockney kingdom.

Charlie Kray—a consultant on the movie—gasps in shock

Pop stars are double of Sixties gangster twins

NEWS OF THE WORLD PICTURE SPECIAL

when he watches Gary and Martin in action.

An insider said: "Charlie looks haunted by the incredible likeness of the Kemp brothers to Reggie and Ronnie.

"He's absolutely astounded by the boys' performance and stands there open-mouthed in amazement."

Fans

The brothers are determined to prove they can act.

Gary told a pal: "We're taking this film deadly seriously."

The boys already have two fans . . . Reggie and Ronnie themselves.

Charlie said: "They think the world of Martin and Gary."

98

9 YEARS? FREDDIE CAN DO IT STANDING ON HIS HEAD

Crook dodges £412,000 bill

By JAMES LEWTHWAITE

GANGSTER Freddie Foreman started a nine-year jail term yesterday — and a relative said: "He can do that standing on his head."

Hardman Foreman, 58, showed no emotion as he was sentenced for handling a fortune in loot from the £8 million Security Express robbery.

The Cockney villain was told he will **NOT** have to pay £412,000 — the £362,000 he stashed from the ruthless raid plus £50,000 costs.

Judge Stephen Mitchell, QC, turned down a prosecution plea for Foreman to be ordered to fork out the compensation.

The judge said at the Old Bailey: "I don't have a shred of evidence that he can pay."

Foreman — dragged back to face British justice last year after seven years of high living on Spain's Costa Del Crime —claimed he was **BROKE.**

He said his share of the robbery haul, stashed away in used notes in Spanish banks, had gone on lawyers' fees and medical bills for his wife Maureen.

Villain . . . Freddie Foreman

Career of crime . . . from The Sun yesterday

Justice

The former Kray gang enforcer, who lavished money on wine, food and women on the Costa, now seems to have only his old age pension to look forward to after release.

Foreman, immaculate in dark City suit and tie, merely raised his eyebrows at members of his family in the public gallery as he was jailed.

The judge told him: "I disregard the fact that, due to your resourcefulness, you were able to escape justice for so long and were able to enjoy a life of relative ease and security in Spain."

Foreman, from Bermondsey, South London, was found guilty on Wednesday of the handling charge and a passport offence.

Assets

He was cleared of taking part in the 1983 Security Express raid in Shoreditch, East London.

Foreman had evaded several attempts by British police to bring him back from his Costa hideaway.

He was finally bundled out, kicking and screaming, as seven burly Spanish policemen put him on a London-bound plane. Scotland Yard officers arrested him at Heathrow.

Security Express boss Terry Connell hit out last night at the refusal to order Foreman to pay back the loot.

He said: "Foreman should have been forced to prove in court that he did not have the means to repay the money."

Courts now have the power to seize the assets of big-time villains. But first police must find the property or cash.

A legal expert said last night: "If Foreman has no property here or in Spain and if no cash or valuables can be linked with him, how can the court extract compensation?"

One detective said: "If Foreman has money stashed away he has done it very carefully.

"We cannot get our hands on it."

But Flying Squad chiefs are taking seriously a tip-off that Foreman offered £1 million to the underworld to spring him.

BARMY REG THOUGHT A ROBIN WAS HIS DEAD WIFE

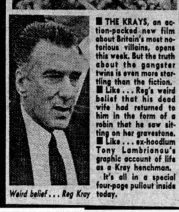

Weird belief . . . Reg Kray

■ THE KRAYS, an action-packed new film about Britain's most notorious villains, opens this week. But the truth about the gangster twins is even more startling than the fiction.
■ Like . . . Reg's weird belief that his dead wife had returned to him in the form of a robin that he saw sitting on her gravestone.
■ Like . . . ex-hoodlum Tony Lambrianou's graphic account of life as a Kray henchman.

It's all in a special four-page pullout inside today.

March in bid to free Krays

Supporters of the Kray twins plan to march to No 10 Downing Street to campaign for the killers' release.

Hundreds of supporters of the gangland duo, who terrorised London's East End in the sixties, are expected to march from Hyde Park Corner to Downing Street on October 9.

The march will mark the 60th birthday of the Krays and will end with supporters handing a petition to John Major.

The Krays were jailed in 1969 for the murders of Jack "The Hat" McVitie and George Cornell. The judge recommended they serve at least 30 years.

99

GIVE US THE READIES FREDDIE

Gotcha . . . Foreman back in Britain after his arrest

GANGSTER Freddie Foreman may be ordered today to PAY BACK the fortune he collected from a huge robbery haul.

He faces a £412,000 demand after being found guilty yesterday of handling loot from the £6 million Security Express raid.

Prosecutor Michael Worsley, QC, asked the judge to order Foreman to pay compensation

By MICHAEL FIELDER

for the £362,000 he stashed — PLUS £50,000 costs.

But the Cockney villain's defence lawyer claimed Foreman, 58, was nearly BROKE.

Mr John Mathew, QC, told the Old Bailey: "There is no money left to pay compensation."

Mr Justice Stephen Mitchell will announce his decision today when he sentences Foreman — who was last year

deported kicking and screaming from Spain's Costa Del Crime.

Foreman, who stashed his fortune in used notes in Costa banks after the robbery, claims that huge fees from Spanish lawyers swallowed up much of the cash.

His QC told the judge that Foreman's wife Maureen was still in Spain, where she needs urgent medical treatment for a liver condition.

Formidable Foreman just shrugged his shoulders when he was found guilty after the jury returned. They were out for 13 hours.

Relatives and friends in the public gallery looked on in stunned silence.

VAULTS

The verdict came seven years to the day after armed robbers pounced on the Security Express vaults in Shoreditch, East London.

Gangland godfather Foreman, once an enforcer for the Kray Twins, was cleared of

Continued on Page Five

Order guilty Foreman to repay £412,000 says QC

'Krays' £½m rural retreat

D. Mail 25 I 90

Gangland twins plan 'peaceful' retirement when they leave jail

The Krays' future home: 'People shouldn't worry — they won't rob the post office'

Continued from Page One

taking part in the robbery. He was found guilty of making a false passport application.

The jury heard that Foreman fled to Spain shortly after the ruthless robbery in 1983.

He built up a property empire in the Costa del Sol playground of Puerto Banus, near Marbella.

Foreman also owned a nightclub and restaurant.

ARMED

His pay-off from the crime — Britain's biggest cash robbery — was to be Foreman's "pension" after a lifetime of villainy.

He was said to have only £75 in the bank before the raid.

Throughout the three-week trial, the court-

Vanished . . . Mitchell

room was guarded by armed policemen.

Flying Squad chiefs received a tip-off that Foreman was offering £1million to gangland associates to spring him from jail.

Police also feared attempts would be made to nobble the jury.

The trial was halted when a man on the jury reported a nobbling attempt.

But detectives ruled

Vanished . . . Ginger Marks

out a bribery bid after discovering the man had been drinking heavily. He was kicked off the jury.

Foreman's reputation as an underworld hardman was well earned.

He was sentenced to ten years in jail in 1969 for disposing of Jack "The Hat" McVitie's body for the Krays.

He walked free from two murder charges —

involving Frank "Mad Axeman" Mitchell and Thomas "Ginger" Marks.

Both men vanished without trace from the streets of East London.

Foreman's actor son Jamie starred in TV's London Burning.

Jamie, who regularly flew out to see his parents in Marbella, said recently: "I thank them for showing me life and I love them to the end

"I have seen as much violence as anybody brought up in South London.

"But in certain areas you can't escape the fact that violence is the only answer a lot of the time.

"It's their own kind of justice. People have not got the money to buy themselves out of trouble, so they set their own laws and own standards."

100

FROM BLAGS TO RICHES

END OF THE COSTA CRIME KING

1966 Mine host . . . Foreman and his wife with actor George Raft, far left, and villain Ronnie Kray

1983 Raid scene . . . security warehouse where £6million was snatched in Britain's biggest cash raid

THE jury's guilty verdict on loudmouth Freddie Foreman yesterday spelled an end to his reign as the Godfather of the Costa del Crime.

Fearsome Freddie — one-time enforcer for the notorious Kray twins and a Mafia link man — played host to every villain worth his stripes in his Eagles Country Club outside Marbella.

For seven years, he lived a luxury lifestyle of sex, sunshine and sangria in his Spanish hideaway.

It was all built on London's biggest cash "blag" — the £6million Security Express robbery exactly seven years ago yesterday.

But the 58-year-old they nicknamed the Mean Machine couldn't keep his mouth shut. Believing he was safe from extradition, he bragged to Spanish police that he was one of the gang who pulled off the raid in Shoreditch, North London.

He told them: "Me and Ronnie Knight did the Big Job."

And he added with pride "It was a clean job — no one got hurt."

By MICHAEL FIELDER

Wife

Those few words, spoken in the bar of a five-star hotel near Marbella, finally sealed his fate.

Foreman fled to Spain after the raid with his wife and family — and at least £350,000 of the loot. And he set up a powerful new crime empire.

He splashed out £90,000 on three luxury flats in the up-market development of El Alcazaba in Puerto Banus, jet-set playground of the world's biggest villains.

He used one as a stylish home for his family. The other two were let as holiday flats.

All were registered in the bogus name of Ultra Marine Ventures of Panama and are now worth more than £250,000.

It was a far cry from the council flat in Starkleigh Way, Bermondsey, South London, where he lived before the raid.

Foreman had been so broke there that his rent was reduced to only £7.75 a week.

Even after the 1986 extradition treaty with Spain was signed, Foreman and his cronies considered themselves safe because the law could not be backdated.

But the British police were becoming increasingly alarmed at the frightening power base being built up on the Costa by British villains

Crooks

Top-level approach to the Spanish authorities finally jerked them into an all-out campaign against the Costa crooks

Foreman fought repeated attempts in the Spanish courts to keep him out.

But just in case, he set up a bolthole in Morocco, North Africa which has no extradition agreement with Britain. And he arranged for a powerboat to be on stand-by in Puerto Banus harbour in case he had to flee from Spain suddenly.

The end of Foreman's reign came out of the blue last July as he was leaving the home of his mistress Janice King.

As he strolled to his car after a night of passion with Janice, armed Spanish detectives surged from the undergrowth and grabbed him.

Foreman was taken to Marbella police station and told he was being expelled.

Cursed

He just smirked. He had been down that road before and his powerful connections had always come to his rescue.

It was only when he was bundled into a police car and driven, with sirens blaring, to Malaga airport, that he realised this time it was for real.

Fighting Foreman went berserk. As the police car screeched to a halt beside the daily Malaga to London flight, he launched into a last desperate bid to keep his freedom.

It took **SEVEN** burly Spanish policemen to manhandle him up the gangway as he kicked and cursed.

"It's a kidnap, it's a kidnap" he yelled at startled British passengers on the flight.

Judge

As two of the battered Spanish officers went to hospital for treatment, two others stayed on the plane to escort handcuffed Foreman home.

The villain who sneered at Scotland Yard for seven years from his Spanish bolthole was met at Heathrow Airport by two Yard detectives with an arrest warrant.

At the Old Bailey,

Foreman put on the act of a lifetime in a bid to convince the jury he was Mr Nice Guy.

He appeared each day immaculately dressed in dark suit and tie.

Grey-haired and balding, he looked like a City stockbroker.

He bowed courteously to the judge.

But the jury did not swallow his story that his bank account of less than £75 before the robbery · dramatically swelled to £362,000 afterwards through selling up his business assets.

TODAY wins backing for Kray boycott

TODAY's campaign against the film which will make £250,000 for the evil Kray twins was backed by MPs last night.

And Home Secretary David Waddington is to study a plan to ban deals between film companies and criminals.

The film, in which the killers are played by pop stars Gary and Martin Kemp, above, is now the target of a major public outcry. Tory

by JON CRAIG

MPs are urging a mass boycott and demanding a full-scale Commons debate.

Andrew Mackay, whose East Berkshire constituency covers Broadmoor hospital where Ronnie Kray is held, said: "It is quite wrong that these two evil murderers should profit by a single penny."

The twins and
Turn to Page 4

The secret 'son' of Reggie Kray

A YOUNG schoolboy today reveals his astonishing bond with notorious gangland killer Reggie Kray... the man he calls "Dad".

The former East End gangster has written to 11-year-old Brad Lane an incredible 443 times in two years, and tells friends that Brad is his "adopted" son.

Brad regularly makes the 600-mile round trip from his home in Dunscroft, Doncaster, to visit Kray at Lewes Prison, Sussex. He writes to him every day.

Today, Father's Day, Britain's most infamous twin will have a present and card from Brad waiting for him in his cell.

KRAY, 56, serving life for murder along with twin brother Ronnie, wants Brad to live with him if he is freed from prison.

He has showered the schoolboy with presents including his own paintings, teddy bears, and a golden cross and chain.

And in one emotional letter Kray tells Brad:

EXCLUSIVE by JOHN KELLY

"Always remember I am your Dad and always will be. Never let anyone tell you different."

The bizarre relationship began because Brad, missing his real father after his parents parted, began writing to celebrities.

"Most people replied with a signed photo but Reg wrote me a letter," he said. "I wrote back and things just went on from there.

"Reg is my proper Dad. He tells me I am the best son in the world.

"When Reg gets released he has told me we will do all the things a father and son do together, like playing football or going fishing."

Kray insists that Brad stays with him throughout his two-hour monthly visits, no matter who else turns up.

I SIT on his knee and he cuddles me and tells me how much he has been missing me," said Brad, talking with his mother by his side.

"He loves to make me laugh by doing impersonations of famous people.

"We never talk about his past and I don't want to know about it."

Kray – who has served 22 years of a 30-year sentence - has told Brad he wants to adopt him.

He has given the youngster an astonishing number of presents. Brad's bedroom is a shrine to the Kray twin, with every wall devoted to gifts and pictures.

His mother Kim, 33,

Killer dotes on little Brad, 11

says she has no misgivings about her son's relationship with the killer once described as Britain's most evil man.

"We all mellow as we get older and I think Reggie has. What happens between him and Brad is up to them.

"I would have thought that by the time Reggie gets out, Brad will be old enough to know what he is doing.

"If he wants to go and live with Reggie, so be it. Brad really loves Reggie and nothing will part them."

Killer – Reggie Kray

Costa Godfather .. Freddie Foreman's reign is over

Property big-time SHREWD Foreman bought these three flats at Puerto Banus for £90,000 – now worth a cool £250,000. He also bought the Eagles Country Club, below –and business boomed

FESTIVE CHEER ... Ronnie's card

A KRAY-ZY CARD!

MEMO to all Bizarre readers who have sent me abusive letters this year: take a good look at this cheery Christmas card.

Yes... it **IS** signed by Ronald Kray!

My thanks to Ronnie—a loyal fan of The Sun—the first to wish me merry Christmas.

And a tip to disgruntled readers: all complaints are being redirected to a certain cell in Broadmoor.

Kray tribute as charity kid dies

A BOXING extravangaza supported by the Kray Twins to raise cash for a paralysed youngster was tinged with tragedy following the shock announcement that the little lad had died suddenly.

The gala fund-raising event fell silent when former gangland boss Reggie Kray paid tribute to battling Jamie Fallon in a message recorded in the evening.

ACCIDENT

Young Jamie touched the infamous East End brothers' hearts after they heard the sad story of how the 10-year-old became paralysed following a horrific road accident in South Africa.

Jamie's parents had planned to return to England but doctors advised against the move as the little boy was too ill to be moved.

Fund-raising efforts fell on stoney ground because charity organisations were reluctant to get involved because of the South Africa connection.

Message from Reg tells of Jamie tragedy

Tragic Jamie Fallon who lost his brave battle for life.

STORY: BEVERLEY TAYLOR
PHOTOS: RAY COLLINS

It was then that Reggie and Ronnie stepped in with generous offers of help for the Fallon family.

And on Friday night the Twins' brother Charlie, Ronnie's wife Kate, former model Flanagan and the Lambrianou brothers — who were sent down with the Twins for their part in the murder of Jack McVitie — gathered with 200 diners to raise funds for the Fallon family.

AUCTION

Famous faces included TV stars Glen Murphy and Ray Winstone who helped boost funds by bidding for some of the items that went under the hammer at the star auction.

A signed copy of Tina Turner's raunchy autobiography went for £70 while an early Who album and a signed copy of U2's album hit the £300 mark.

Former Page Three lovely Flanagan did the honours as she toured the boxing ring getting the bidding going.

Generous bidding at the Prince Regent Hotel, Chigwell, raised £15,000 which the Twins have decided will go to the heartbroken family of Jamie.

Family friend Bernard King told the Advertiser: "The evening went off very well indeed but obviously our thoughts were with the Fallon family.

"I have spoken to Ronnie and he is very upset. Reggie remarked on Jamie's courage in his message to everyone. They are both very sad," he added.

During the evening budding boxers from West Ham and Newham boxing clubs were presented with their trophies by Charlie Kray, Tony and Chris Lambrianou and bubbly blonde Katie Kray.

Stunning smile from Katie Kray.

Tony Lambrianou, Flanagan, and Charlie.

REG ON THE MOVE AGAIN

'He should change his name to Saunders'

EAST End gangland killer Reg Kray looks set to spend Christmas in a top security jail after being moved back to his old cell at Gartree Prison in Leicestershire.

The 57-year-old murderer of Jack 'The Hat' McVitie began touring Britain's jails last week with a move to Nottingham's category-B prison under heavy police guard from Lewes Prison, in Sussex.

Mystery surrounded the move, which was seen as a possible preparation for Reg's parole.

Unconfirmed reports claimed that Reg, caged for the last 22 years, was being punished for smuggling letters in and out of the jail.

But Kate Kray - wife of Reg's twin Ron - spoke to her brother-in-law on Tuesday: "He was ever so upset at first, but he'll soon go back to a B

prison and hopefully that will be Nottingham, because he liked it there.

"I think this is a temporary measure because there some trouble in Lewes -it was nothing to do with Reggie - but because he has a high profile they moved him out."

And Kate said Ron and her hoped Reg would be transfered to Ford open prison prior to going before the parole board in February.

A close friend of Reg's told the Advertiser that "things had been looking up at first" because security is more relaxed at Nottingham.

"Now he has been moved to Gartree it is terrible and I am sure that Reg is probably very upset," said the friend.

"He certainly hasn't done anything wrong, in fact he has been a model prisoner," she added.

"Perhaps if he changed his name to Saunders then he might be treated differently he might even be put in an open prison," she said.

REGGIE KRAY MOVED FROM GUN FIND JAIL

Killer's fury at sudden switch

By MICHAEL FIELDER

Reg Kray . . . police escort

JAILED gangland killer Reggie Kray was moved to a new prison yesterday — after a GUN was found in a remand wing.

Lifer Kray and seven other inmates were taken from Lewes jail, Sussex, to Nottingham prison under police escort.

Staff at Lewes believe the gun, possibly a replica, was intended for use in an escape plot.

But a friend of Kray, 56, whose twin Ronnie is in Broadmoor, said: "I am certain Reg had nothing to do with it.

"The bosses at Lewes just got panicky. I think the govenor took the easy way out and got rid of anyone who might cause bother."

Kray, who was sentenced to 30 years in 1969 for killing Jack "The Hat" McVitie, is said to be furious at the move.

His pal added: "Reg thinks it will be very damaging to his parole application in February."

Another inmate moved was 42-year-old David Fraser —son of the Krays' former henchman, Mad Frankie Fraser.

Security

Fraser is serving 11 years for conspiracy to rob and posessing a firearm.

Prison sources said it was "not unusual" for long-term inmates to be moved suddenly.

Send kid killers to gallows, say Krays

By NICK CONSTABLE

BRITAIN'S most notorious gangland murderers want the return of the rope . . . though not for themselves.

Ronnie and Reggie Kray have told friends that child killers should be hanged.

They argue that their own killings and torturings are "lesser crimes" because they picked only on other underworld villains.

Last night one source close to the family said: "Convicts have their own moral code, however strange it may seem to some. That code says child murderers should go to the gallows. And both the Krays would welcome that happening.

"But scum who kill kids will probably wish they are dead after a few months inside anyway. They are marked men."

The twins, 56, have each served more than 20 years.

Backed

Reggie was convicted for the murder of Jack "The Hat" McVitie. Ronnie was sentenced for the killing of George Cornell.

At their trial in 1969, Mr Justice Melford Stevenson recommended they serve at least 30 years.

ROPE

"The trouble with abolishing capital punishment and replacing it with life sentences is that the life sentence is often reduced and the killer is allowed to go free.

"With hanging the community is satisfied. The criminal cannot repeat the outrage."

He went on: "I have long thought there should be capital punishment for murder most foul.

DIANA: First Royal visitor

Princess Di meets killer in hospital

By IAN TRUEMAN

PRINCESS Di came face to face with a convicted killer during a tour of Broadmoor yesterday.

She is the first member of the Royal Family to visit the top-security mental hospital which houses gangster Ronnie Kray and Yorkshire Ripper Peter Sutcliffe.

Kray twin turns to God

REG Kray, who is serving a life sentence for the murder of Jack "The Hat" McVitie, has become a born-again Christian. From now on, he says, he will be a "vehicle for God."

ANGER GROWS OVER SCREEN PORTRAYAL OF THE EVIL KILLERS WHO RULED BY FEAR

THE big screen image of the evil Kray twins as glamorous kings of the underworld was under fire yesterday — as protests mounted over their £255,000 'fee'.

The Krays, which has its première in the West End on Thursday, stars Martin and Gary Kemp of the pop group Spandau Ballet.

The 119-minute film depicts explicit and horrifying scenes of murder and torture at the hands of the Savile Row-suited twins.

Violent enforcer: Gary Kemp as Ronnie

AMAZIN' THROUGH THE CELL KEYHOLE PICTURE...

REGGIE'S NOT SO KRAY-ZY ABOUT HIS CHANCES OF GOING FREE 'COS OF MONSTER IMAGE

BLOCKBUSTER KRAY MOVIE BACKFIRES ON REGGIE

JAILHOUSE COCK-UP... EXCLUSIVE

■ MOB bosses Reggie and Ronnie Kray ruled London's biggest crime syndicate through illegal gambling, protection rackets and moody clubs in the 60's

■ They were later jailed for murdering petty crook Jack "the hat" McVitie and George Cornell.

■ Now, after 21 years as a dangerous category 'A' prisoners in top-security nicks like Gartree and Parkhurst, Reggie Kray has been down-graded to "C" at softer Lewes Prison.

■ His psycopathic bi-sexual brother Ronnie is banged up in Broadmoor psychiatric hospital after being judged insane.

ANOTHER CRIMEBUSTIN' EXPLOSIVE, EXCLUSIVE...

GANGLAND boss Reggie Kray is terrified he'll rot in jail FOREVER because of sicko violence in the hit movie of his life.

Speaking from his cell — where this exclusive picture was taken — the former East End crime king. serving life for murder with a recommendation of 30 years, said he believes the dramatisation has backfired for being TOO gory.

Both he and twin brother Ronnie are FURIOUS with film bosses for portraying their late mum Violet as a foul-mouthed Cockney.

And now Reggie has confided in his pop star son Pete Gillet — whose new record comes out tomorrow — that he believes the Krays have lost ALL public sympathy after being cast as vicious thugs.

Sunday Sport led the campaign for Reggie's release — but since the movie opened, the twins are convinced they've been re-branded evil nutters.

Evil

"No Home Secretary in his right mind would put his career on the line to release the Krays after seeing this film," fumed Gillet.

"Reggie told me the film will seriously hinder his chances of being freed when his 30 year recommendation runs out in 1997.

"He knows the authorities will still be able to keep him inside and he believes they won't parole him.

"In the film they kill

■ FROM being Britain's Public Enemy Number One, the 56-year-old jailbird is now making a bid for pop stardom from his prison cell.

■ He's already helped pen a series of songs for an album to be released later this year.

■ And his voice appears on Pete Gillet's new record — I Began To Notice — which was written by former gang boss Reggie in top security Gartree and Lewis Jails.

■ Hear Pete and Reggie's record on our special call line 0898 122 936 (Calls charged at 25p per minute cheap rate and 38p at all other times).

LOCKED away Reggie Kray poses for this exclusive picture in his cell...but he's not so pleased with his screen portrayal.

Jack "the hat" McVitie and George Cornell in one night. It's like, 'let's get out and clear up... shut the shop and do some killing.'

"Reggie has called me and written to me saying the film has provoked an adverse reaction.

Speedy

"And he thinks his mother being portrayed the way she has is absolutely disgusting," he added.

Gillet — who has been spearheading the 'Free The Krays' campaign for the past two years — hoped the film would bring about their speedy release.

But he CRIED after the film's glittering London premiere because it contained so much brutality.

In the movie — which is breaking box office records across Britain — Ronnie Kray is seen pushing a sword into a rival's mouth.

And in another sick scene, Reggie brutally batters two men for

talking to his wife. Ironically one of his victims was played by Gillet — who was adopted by Reggie after they shared a cell in Parkhurst.

"I'm supposed to be a tough-guy, but after seeing the film I broke down and cried. The tears just came down," Gillet, 30, admitted.

"That scene where I get beaten up was the ultimate insult. I only agreed to do it because I thought that would have been Reggie's natural protective instinct towards Frances."

Harmed

The twins' brother Charlie — listed as technical advisor in the credits — is also unhappy about the movie.

"Of course it's harmed them. The twins never went running around with machine guns like they do in the film. Obviously they weren't very happy about that," he told Sunday Sport.

"The twins have become scapegoats for society."

UP in arms son Peter Gillet

KRAY FILM FACT FILE

■ It's grossed TWO MILLION quid since release two weeks ago.........

■ Spandau Ballet stars Gary and Martin Kemp play the vicious twins.............

■ MPs criticised it for glorifying crime and the Royal Family boycotted it........

■ Commons questioned royalties of £225,000 for twins...............

■ Reggie and Ronnie have still NOT SEEN the film.............

■ Comics Hale and Pace were barred from the premiere 'cos Reggie hates their Two Rons send-ups.............

KRAY FILM'S KNOCKIN' 'EM DEAD...

FORMER GANG BOSS SPEAKS FROM PRISON...

WHAT A CHARLIE!

Krays blast brother on cash from movie

GANGLAND killer Ronnie Kray has launched an amazing attack on his elder brother Charlie – claiming that he's cost him and his twin Reggie a fortune from the blockbuster film about their life.

The People exclusively revealed in April how the three brothers were paid a total of £255,000 for co-operating in *The Krays* movie.

But profits from film, video and TV sales throughout the world are now expected to top a staggering £7 MILLION.

And 56-year-old Ronnie reckons Charlie, 63, who acted as one of the chief negotiators, let them down badly.

If he hadn't sold out their existing rights to ten per cent of the profits, he says, they would now be cleaning up with £555,000 more than they got.

As it is, they won't receive a penny extra.

Forgot

In a letter to The People from Broadmoor – where he is serving life for murder – Ronnie says: "Our own brother Charlie has let us down.

"He looked after himself and forgot Reg and me completely.

"Charlie hasn't even visited me for 12 months and he's not seen Reggie for five years."

● Charlie and friend celebrate the launch of the film while twins Reggie and Ron (left) languish behind bars

FINALLY . .

MY mate Chalkie down at The York was telling us that he went for a meal at this very tough East End restaurant where the Kray brothers used to eat. Dish of the day was broken leg of lamb.

KRAYS II

Smart . . . Lindsay (left) and Leighton Frayne in Kray-style suits

Gangsters . . . the Kray twins with a pal (centre) before they were jailed

Court told how brothers acted out lives of 'heroes'

TWO would-be gangsters staged an amazing bid to model themselves on the notorious Kray twins, a court heard yesterday.

The Frayne brothers dressed in dark suits, wore red ties and had swept-back hair.

Lindsay, 25, and Leighton, 31, visited Reggie and Ronnie Kray's old East End haunts, a jury was told.

They befriended former associates of the Krays, then got guns and tried to form a gang like their heroes, it was alleged.

But their ambitious plans for a full-scale crime assault on London came unstuck when they staged a Continued on Page Nine

I'M READY TO ROT IN JAIL, SAYS REGGIE

'My years inside have been so good'

By MIKE KNAPP

FORMER gangland boss Reggie Kray is ready to spend the rest of his life in prison.

The former crime lord of London's East End admits his 23 years so far behind bars have been **GOOD** for him.

For Reggie says without his long sentence he would never have discovered his real talent as a serious writer.

His autobiography Born Fighter is in the top 10 best sellers list and he has another ready for the market called Thoughts.

Reggie opened his heart to the Daily Star after ending the long-running feud with older brother Charlie.

And he invited us along to their their first meeting for more than two years, inside the walls of Lewes Prison, Sussex.

Reggie and Charlie hugged and kissed before sitting down to discuss family business for more than an hour.

Reggie's first chance of freedom comes next January, when there is a first-stage local review of his parole.

Glorious

But he doesn't hold much hope of getting out. Reggie says: "I don't think about that any more.

"Obviously I'd rather be on the outside, but I don't like to dwell on it. There's no point sitting around moping."

Reggie has no regrets about the life of crime that led him and Ron to their long prison terms.

He says: "I don't look back on the Sixties as the bad old days. They were the good old days!

"They were comparable to the Twenties. It was a glorious age.

"I've come to terms with my sentence. It's best to go along with the tide rather than try to swim against it.

"And I wouldn't change my sentence, even if I had the chance to do so.

"I wouldn't have been a writer on the outside, because I wouldn't have had time to do it."

PALS AGAIN: Charlie Kray now backs his brothers Ronnie and Reggie

REGGIE: 'I don't think about being free again'

Foreman .. handled cash

Kray man in jail KO

A **GANGSTER** jailed over the £6million Security Express robbery yesterday lost an appeal against a nine-year prison term.

Frederick Foreman, a former Kray gang member, was jailed last year for handling cash from the 1983 raid — Britain's biggest cash raid.

He was acquitted of robbery, but London appeal judges yesterday ruled his sentence for handling the proceeds was "proper."

Foreman, 59, of Rotherhithe, South East London, was jailed in 1969 for helping dispose of the body of Jack "The Hat" McVitie.

POETIC JUSTICE PLEADS REGGIE

POEMS: Reggie

JAILED gangland killer Reggie Kray has written a book of poems in a bizarre attempt to win his freedom before he dies.

The former East End mobster – sentenced to life with twin brother Ronnie in 1969 – says in the foreword: "I never considered myself a bad person." It took Reggie, 58, just nine hours to write the book.

One poem says: "Free Reggie Kray, He has served his time, Retribution is out of line, Let him have Peace at his age, He has paid the wage of his crime, Over 20 years is the gauge of time."

Reggie Kray talks his way to £100,000

by JAMES MURRAY

JAILED gangland killer Reggie Kray could soon be freed — to start a new career as a £100,000-a-year after-dinner speaker.

The notorious East End mobster was yesterday transferred from maximum security Gartree jail in Leicestershire to the lower category Nottingham.

And it is expected he will soon be moved to an open prison to prepare him for his release.

According to his brother, Charlie, it means he may soon be available for functions — at £2,000 a time.

"I'm sure there will be a lot of offers for him to speak," Charlie said yesterday.

"And knowing Reggie he would love to do it.

"I think people would be fascinated to hear what he has to say. He is a good speaker so it would be no problem for him."

Reggie, 57, and his twin brother, Ronnie, were jailed for life in 1969 for the murder of Jack "The Hat" McVitie.

The judge recommended they serve at least 30 years. During his time inside.

RICHES: Reggie Kray

Reggie is said to have become a born again Christian and a keen writer.

He is allegedly planning a book — probably about his 23 years behind bars — which could net him a futher £100,000.

Charlie said: "Reggie loves to write. He gets up at three in the morning to jot down his thoughts.

Parole

"Writing is his passion in life now. I think he will want to write a book as soon as he gets out and then carry on writing. That's what he enjoys most."

Kray may also have plans to get married and start a family.

"He's in his fifties now, so it is not too late for him," Charlie said.

"He likes kids, and has sort of adopted a boy from up North who goes to see him with his mother. As far

as I know he does not intend to marry, but you never know what might happen with Reggie."

Charlie denied that his brother would be emerging to a £50,000 nest egg.

"He doesn't have any money," he said. "As soon as he gets any money he spends it.

"He and Ronnie have always been the same. They are not what you might call savers."

Reggie was moved to Gartree, which houses dangerous category A and B criminals, including murderers, rapists and violent armed robbers, from Lewes jail in Sussex.

A replica gun had been found at Lewes and, although he was cleared of any involvement, he later said: "I'm convinced it was a deliberate ploy by someone to ruin my chances of parole."

Nottingham accommodates category B and C criminals and security is less tight than at Gartree.

Prisoners go there for training and can learn anything from motor mechanics to languages.

Prison governor David Walmsley said he would not comment on any individual prisoner.

The Home Office refused to say what training Kray would be doing, or what category he is.

JAILED: Foreman

Appeal fails for Freddie

A FORMER member of the Kray Gang yesterday lost his appeal against a nine-year jail sentence for receiving money from the £6 million Security Express robbery.

Freddie Foreman, 60, was convicted at the Old Bailey last April after being extradited from Spain.

He had fled to Marbella with his wife Maureen the year after the 1983 Security Express raid in Shoreditch, east London — Britain's biggest currency robbery.

He had allegedly boasted to Spanish police about his involvement in the crime.

Kray twins film scoops British 'Oscars'

A CONTROVERSIAL feature-length movie about gangland killers the Kray twins last night received top prizes at an award ceremony.

The Krays, starring Spandau Ballet pop group brothers Martin and Gary Kemp, was one of the biggest hits of any British film last year.

But it caused a storm of protest when it was disclosed that the infamous East End mobsters, now serving life sentences for their crimes, received a six-figure sum for the rights to their life story.

Last night it was named the best film of the year and 29-year-old artist turned

screen writer Philip Ridley the most promising newcomer in a star-studded Evening Standard Film Awards ceremony at London's Savoy Hotel.

The Duchess of Kent was guest of honour at the celebrity dinner, which was attended by some of Britain's best-loved film stars, including Sir John Mills, Dirk Bogarde, Lynn Redgrave, Jenny Agutter, Cherie Lunghi and Nigel Havers.

Producer Jeremy Thomas, responsible for The Last Emperor, starring Peter O'Toole, which won nine Oscars in 1988, received a special award from the Duchess.

The prestigious awards are looked on in showbusiness as the "British Oscars".

Other awards included:

Best screen play — Michael Eaton for Fellow Travellers; The Peter Sellers award for comedy: Robbie Coltrane; Best technical achievement: David Watkin for Memphis Belle; Best Actress: Natasha Richardson for The Comfort of Strangers and The Handmaids Tale; Best Actor: Iain Glen for Mountains of the Moon, Fools of Fortune and Silent Screen.

The ceremony is to be screened nationwide by Thames Televison tonight.

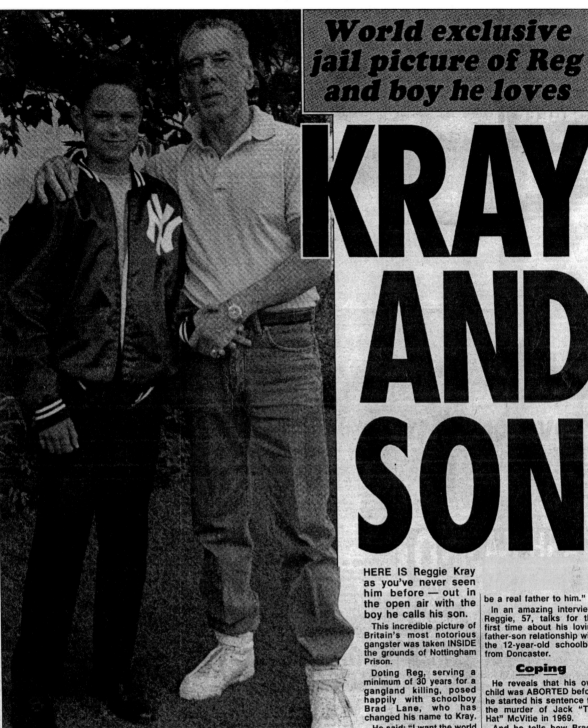

KRAY AND SON

HERE IS Reggie Kray as you've never seen him before — out in the open air with the boy he calls his son.

This incredible picture of Britain's most notorious gangster was taken INSIDE the grounds of Nottingham Prison.

Doting Reg, serving a minimum of 30 years for a gangland killing, posed happily with schoolboy Brad Lane, who has changed his name to Kray.

He said: "I want the world to see these pictures of me and my son.

"Brad has made an enormous difference to my life. And when I get out, I will be a real father to him."

In an amazing interview, Reggie, 57, talks for the first time about his loving father-son relationship with the 12-year-old schoolboy from Doncaster.

Coping

He reveals that his own child was ABORTED before he started his sentence for the murder of Jack "The Hat" McVitie in 1969.

And he tells how Brad's love helps him cope with life behind bars — and the prison authorities' decision to postpone his next parole hearing until 1995.

THAT'S MY LAD: Jailed gangster Reggie Kray with his 12-year-old "son," Brad

BRAD KRAY, 12

Boy changes his name so evil villain Reggie can become his official dad

I DON'T PAY TAX I'M MAD

Ronnie . . . owes taxman £12,500

Reggie . . . has promised to pay up

EXCLUSIVE by JOHN KAY

Jailed Kray twins in fury over £25,000 demand

TAXMEN have gone behind bars to demand £25,000 from the Kray twins.

But when Inland Revenue officials visited Ronnie Kray in top security Broadmoor Hospital he told them: "I don't have to pay — I'm mad."

Tax chiefs say the brothers each owe £12,500 on income from a film and books about their violent lives.

The Inland Revenue estimates the 58-year-old twins have raked in more than £280,000, including:

● £84,000 each in royalties from the film The Krays starring Spandau Ballet brothers Martin and Gary Kemp as the twins.

● £36,260 between them from hard-back sales of their book Our Story published in 1988.

● £14,175 from the paper-back version published a year later.

● £63,000 from newspaper serialisation rights.

Both brothers told inspectors they no longer have the money and cannot pay.

And Ronnie, who boasts he has never paid a penny of tax in his life, told officials he was not obliged to pay because he is insane.

INSANE

He is reported to have told them: "How can you ask me to pay any tax — I am a madman."

But a spokesman for the Inland Revenue said yesterday: "Claiming to be insane or being certified as such is not an excuse for not paying income tax.

"Insane people are definitely chargeable for income tax."

Two senior tax officials visited Reggie at Blundeston Prison in Lowestoft, Suffolk.

Reggie, who hopes to be freed soon on parole, told them he had no money but promised to try to pay the demand in instalments after he is released.

He also received a £25,000 advance from his autobiography Born Fighter.

This money is not part of the tax demand.

Tax bosses have been battling to recover the demand from the twins for two years.

They thought a deal had been clinched when they agreed to scale down the assessment to £25,000.

But the Krays now say they have given away all the cash to friends and underworld hangers-on.

The Inland Revenue is considering filing papers to have the twins declared bankrupt.

A close friend of the Krays last night backed up their claim that they are broke.

"Ronnie and Reggie

Continued on Page Eleven

KRAY AS YOU EARN

Born Fighter . . Reggie's own story

Screen tough-guys . . . Martin and Gary Kemp as The Krays

Our Story . . . their lives of crime

Kray gets keyed up

GANG boss Reggie Kray has got the key to the door — of his cell.

Friends who have visited him at Blundeston prison in Suffolk say he is proudly wearing the key on a chain round his neck.

It is seen as a step towards him being given parole next year.

Lisa is Kraysy on cats

★ HOOD have thought it? Lovely Lisa Forward has named her kittens Ronnie and Reggie after the twin villains.

★ It's bound to start a Krays once fellas hear about the 20-year-old Essex beauty's naughty pair. After all, she's often mobbed by lads who want to be in her gang.

Picture: BEVERLEY GOODWAY

ATTACKED: Reggie

MPs rap Reggie on 'son'

ANGRY MPs yesterday attacked jailed gangster Reggie Kray's plan to adopt a boy of 12 from a broken home.

Tory Terry Dicks said: "It's obscene. It sounds to me like the boy needs counselling.

"You wouldn't put a sick donkey within five miles of either of the Kray twins."

And he said of Reggie's designer clothes: "Prisons are like Butlin's holiday camps.

Sir Teddy Taylor also slammed the sight of Reggie, 57, in trendy clothes, calling it "a bit sick".

Mr Smiths has gone Kray-zy!

☆ ECCENTRIC star Morrissey is launching a solo campaign to get gangland killers Ron and Reggie Kray released from prison.

The 31-year-old former lead singer of The Smiths has scratched a message into the grooves of his new single, Our Frank, which reads: "Free Reg, Free Ron".

A spokesman for Morrissey says: "He has spoken about the Kray twins on many occasions and is very interested in them.

"But we don't know whether he has been to visit them in prison."

REG MUST GO FREE

THE people who write to your paper and have a go at the Krays must have short memories.

When the Twins were about, we had very few muggings. When I lived in the East End, while the Twins were inside, I'd been mugged three times.

Yes they can say the Krays were killers, but who did they kill? Only there own kind.

Some men have done more than the Krays they've been in and out of prison, while the Krays are still rotting away.

Okay, we know Ronnie will never get out, but what about Reggie? He's old before his time. Let the man out and let him live out what life he's got left in peace.

Bill Calderwood, HM Prison Blundeston, Lowestoft.

DEATH WISH OF BOY GUN RAIDER

He idolised the Krays

THE teenage bandit shot dead raiding a gun shop had a bizarre death wish, it was revealed yesterday.

Spikey-haired Colin Budd – who had mugshots of the Kray twins tattooed on his arms – told friends

he was "planning a job" with his 12-bore sawn-off shotgun.

And the 19-year-old petty criminal boasted that he would "go out in a blaze of glory".

Hours later unemployed Budd burst into the gunsmiths in North Station Road, Colchester.

He forced a terrified customer to lie on the floor, then ordered manager Peter Lamb to hand over cash and guns.

REGGIE KRAY GOES TO A JAIL BY THE SEASIDE

'DEATH THREAT TO KRAY WIFE'

By DICK DURHAM

THE wife of jailed East End hood Ronnie Kray was threatened with death in a drunken phone call from one of her hubby's Broadmoor pals, it was claimed yesterday.

The alleged threat to Kate Kray, 35, came from 66-year-old lag Kenneth Shoane — freed last year. Blonde Kate, of Headcorn, Kent, said Ronnie had asked her to get tickets for Shoane and his wife to go to the premiere of The Krays movie.

It stars Spandau Ballet brothers Martin and Gary Kemp as Ronnie and Reg.

Kate said she enclosed her phone number with the tickets.

Call

Prosecutor Martin Griffiths said that Shoane, in a call answered by Woman Det Sgt Pat Geary on December 27 last year, had threatened to kill Kate.

Shoane, from Hanley, Staffs, who kept in touch with bisexual, 58-year-old Ronnie after leaving Broadmoor, appeared for a two-minute hearing at

KATE KRAY: Sent tickets

Maidstone Crown Court, Kent.

He denied threatening to kill Kate on December 27 last year.

Judge Anthony Balston bound Shoane over to keep the peace for two years and said he risked a fine of at least £100 if he breached the order.

RONNIE: Secret trip

Ronnie Kray op

● KILLER Ronnie Kray was sneaked out of Broadmoor yesterday for a hernia operation.

He was driven from the top security hospital before 7am in a civilian car flanked by two male nurses.

● Kray was taken a few miles from Crowthorne, Berks, to an Ascot hospital.

The murderer was kept under guard in a side room away from main wards.

'Son' of Kray in bust-up

REGGIE Kray's "adopted" son was banned from his home town yesterday after he was arrested by armed police.

Budding actor Peter Gillette, a former cellmate of the gangland boss, was charged with making threats to kill.

Gillette, 31, who had a part in the film The Krays, was held after a bust-up at the home of his estranged wife Geraldine's boyfriend.

Magistrates in Crawley, Sussex, granted Gillette bail on condition that he kept out of the town.

Reggie goes off to war

GANGLAND killer Reggie Kray sent morale-boosting letters to a young soldier during the Gulf War.

Desert Rat Brent Kerry, 19, and the ex-gang boss began writing to each other after a soldier pal got a note from Reggie.

During the five months Brent served in the front line with the 7th Armoured Brigade he got more than 20 letters from Kray, who is now in Nottingham Jail.

Now Brent, from Sutton, Notts, hopes to visit him there.

Secret move to prepare for parole

By PETER KANE

GANGLAND killer Reggie Kray could soon be freed – after a secret move to a seaside prison.

Kray, 58, was transferred last week to Blundeston jail near Lowestoft, Suffolk – which trains "lifers" ready for parole – it was revealed yesterday.

He and twin brother Ronnie were jailed in 1969 for the murder of Jack "The Hat" McVitie with a recommended 30-year minimum.

A Home Office spokesman said: "Blundeston has a range of educational facilities to prepare inmates for re-entry to the outside world."

He refused to confirm Kray was there.

Governor Josephine Fowler was unavailable for comment.

But an insider said prisoners had lined up to pay homage to Kray.

Honeypot

And Prison Officers Association secretary Pat Brannigan said: "They have been like bees round a honeypot."

A prison source said Kray could be there some time before he was ready for parole.

Kray claims he became a Christian in jail and has written his life story.

Brother Ronnie is held at Broadmoor hospital.

KILLER: Kray

SORRY PETER GILLETT

ON October 8, 1989, we published an article headed "Ron Kray Fury at Sex Slur on Bride" which quoted Ronnie Kray's reaction to an earlier Sunday newspaper story.

Mr Peter Gillett was described in the article as being a liar, a ponce and gay. We now recognise that these allegations are untrue. He is neither a liar, a ponce nor gay. There was also a suggestion that Mr Gillett had betrayed a friend by fabricating a slur about his fiancee. This allegation is also untrue.

We are pleased to make the above clear and to apologise to Mr Gillett for the embarassment the allegations have caused him.

THE KRAYS.. YOU'VE READ THE BOOK, SEEN THE MOVIE, NOW PLAY THE COMPUTER GAME!

KILLERS: The Krays when they ruled by fear

EXCLUSIVE

By SAMUEL JAMES

JAILED gangsters Reg and Ronnie Kray are all set to rule the East End again – in a kids' computer game.

From behind bars, the notorious twins – already the subject of books and a film – have commissioned a firm to create a game based on their Sixties reign of terror in Bethnal Green.

Just like the bad old days, the idea is to get the brothers to take over as many places as possible. There will be police chases round their old haunts, including the Blind Beggar pub in Whitechapel where Ronnie shot George Cornell between the eyes.

But the Krays' victims will NOT be featured.

Nor will the East End map show the Stoke Newington house where Jack 'The Hat' McVitie was stabbed to death by Reggie through the eye, neck and stomach.

The brothers' business partner, Richard Driscoll, said: "All the Kray gang will be there. Kids will be able to be Reg and Ron or whoever they want.

Crime

"We've spent thousands on the project and every Kray fan will want one for Christmas.

"But neither Reg or Ron would ever condone crime and they are not trying to influence kids."

A spokesman for Richard Branson's Virgin Games Store in London's Oxford Street said: "I can't see it taking off.

"I don't think people are interested in the Krays anymore."

The brothers, now 58, were jailed for life in 1969.

Reggie is in Blundeston jail, Suffolk, and could soon be free. Ronnie, a paranoid schizophrenic, is held in Broadmoor and may never be released.

Shun this rogues gallery

I DIDN'T think there could be anything tackier than the pornographic photo album produced by Madonna, the queen of sex-ploitation.

However, the grisly Kray brothers have proved me wrong.

These violent rogues have come up with a wonderful wheeze for raking in a nice little nest-egg of £200,000.

They are putting together an up-market photo album of their ghastly family. It will be a limited edition of 1,000 and each will take the form of a hand-sewn portfolio selling at £250 a time.

The 59-year-old twins plans to use the cash to pay off a £25,000 tax debt and live on the rest if and when they get out of jail.

Apparently, the lads who were so loved by their dear old mum don't mind serving time for some of the most violent crimes of modern times. However, they can't bear the shame of being made bankrupt by the Inland Revenue!

I hope their scheme is a miserable flop. After a feature film and countless books, these men have acquired the status of folk heroes.

In fact, they are a couple of thoroughly nasty specimens.

RON KRAY WIFE ON SHOPPING CARD RAP

By SHAN LANCASTER

THE wife of gangster Ronnie Kray was yesterday charged with six credit card offences after being arrested on a shopping trip.

Kate Kray, a former kissogram girl who married Ronnie in Broadmoor in 1989, was bailed to appear in court later this month.

She was held in June when staff at a Debenhams store in a shopping centre at West Thurrock, Essex, called police after checking on a card.

Kate, 35, was questioned at Grays police station then freed on bail until yesterday.

She was charged with handling a stolen credit card, four offences of deception and one of attempted deception.

Kate, of Headcorn, Kent, will face magistrates at Grays.

She was arrested under her former name of

Kate Kray . . . bailed

Kathleen Anne Howard.

Ronnie, 58, and his twin Reggie were jailed for life in 1969 for two gangland murders in London's East End.

Kate wrote a book called Married to the Krays. She said at its launch in February: "I wanted to show what Ron is really like — a kind, gentle, nice man."

Jail bosses 'nick' Reg's tape

PRISON bosses have confiscated Reg Kray's tape recorder after a probe about his new phone line.

But no action has been taken against the 0336 phone line which was launched last week.

The Governor of Blundestone jail in Suffolk, where Reg is banged up, has carried out an investigation into the line as prison rules bar inmates from being paid for broadcasts.

But Reggie's friend, Stephanie King, who set up the line, said all profits will fund a new Krays' Supporters Club.

A Home Office spokeswoman said Reg "admitted he made a tape recording and sent it out of prison.

"He no longer has a tape recorder and any future application for a cassette recorder will be considered in the light of what has happened," she added.

On the line Reg chats freely about his life as an underworld boss.

WE'RE ADDICTED TO THE KRAY TWINS

IDENTI-KILL TWINS . . . Mike and Dave Clark in the bedroom they have turned into a Kray Twins shrine

TWINS Dave and Mike Clark share a sinister hobby. They collect memorabilia about another set of twins . . . the Krays.

The 21-year-old brothers idolise Ronnie and Reggie Kray, the gangland killers who were sent to prison in 1969 before the Clarks were even born.

Dave and Mike have spent years building their vast collection of photos, posters, newspaper clippings and books.

And when Ronnie Kray wrote from his prison cell urging them to steer clear of crime, the boys, who had been in trouble for fighting, pledged: "We'll stay clean."

Hannibal Kray

★ NOTORIOUS old lag Dr Hannibal Lecter, alias award-winning actor Anthony Hopkins, has been approached to play one of the Kray twins in a movie about their life behind bars.

Gangland twins Ronnie and Reggie are said to have been unimpressed a couple of years ago by the hit movie about them, starring Martin and Gary Kemp. They saw it on video in the nick.

Now Ron and Reg, serving 30 years for the murders of George Cornell and Jack "The Hat" McVitie, want to present their own screen version of their "colourful" life story.

So who better to chill cinema-goers than the people-eating *Silence Of The Lambs* killer?

PIECE OF THE ACTION: The TV Crow Twins muscle in. Picture: BILL KENNEDY

OH KRAY YOU GUYS . .

CAN YOU clock the connection between the upstarts above and the baddies on the left?

Here's a clue. The boys trying to muscle in on the act are the CROW Twins. And the notorious pair on the left are currently doing BIRD in Her Majesty's prisons.

If the Kray twins switch on the telly on March 16, they'll be able to give the young pretenders the once-over.

But they might not be too amused when they see the two lookalikes playing STUPID gangsters.

The Crow Twins – first names Ronnie and Reggie – are from the same firm that makes the rubbery Spitting Image puppets.

They'll be starring in a new series from Central TV called the Winjin' Pom.

The show, featuring five Aussie characters in England, is aimed at both kids and grown-ups.

Including the REAL Ronnie and Reggie . . .

Exam kid in plea to the Krays

By ALASTAIR TAYLOR

A SCHOOLBOY yesterday begged notorious gang bosses the Kray twins: "Help me pass my exams."

Andrew Ball is studying the East End killers' lives for a GCSE project.

He has written to lifers Ronnie and Reggie seeking their aid in probing mob warfare.

And the 16-year-old even wants to visit the twins in jail.

Andrew said: "I hope to see one or both of them. They are a fascinating subject."

He needed permission from teachers at Millfield High School, Cleveleys, to start the project.

A school spokesman said: "It is a legitimate matter for someone to tackle in a serious manner."

The twins ran a reign of terror before they were jailed 24 years ago.

RONNIE KRAY CHOKES NUTTER

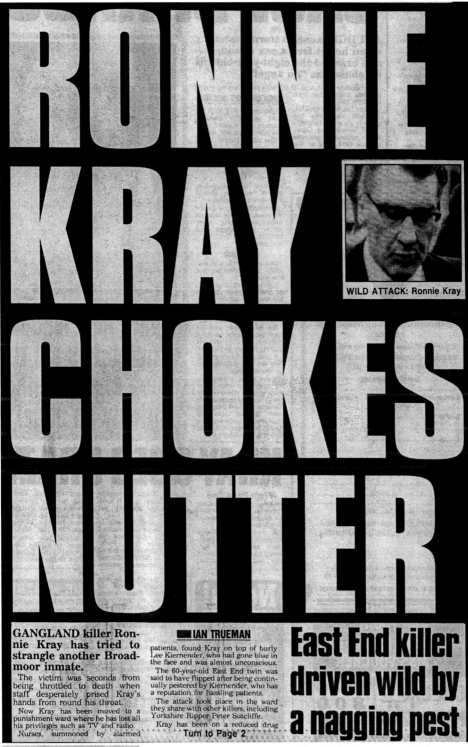

WILD ATTACK: Ronnie Kray

East End killer driven wild by a nagging pest

GANGLAND killer Ronnie Kray has tried to strangle another Broadmoor inmate.

The victim was seconds from being throttled to death when staff desperately prised Kray's hands from round his throat.

Now Kray has been moved to a punishment ward where he has lost all his privileges such as TV and radio.

Nurses, summoned by alarmed

■ IAN TRUEMAN

patients, found Kray on top of burly Lee Kiernender, who had gone blue in the face and was almost unconscious.

The 60-year-old East End twin was said to have flipped after being continually pestered by Kiernender, who has a reputation for hassling patients.

The attack took place in the ward they share with other killers, including Yorkshire Ripper Peter Sutcliffe.

Kray has been on a reduced drug

Turn to Page 2

Kray curse on judge

A GIPSY curse was put on judge Melford Stevenson after he jailed the Kray twins for 30 years.

"I got a Romany friend to put a curse on him," says Ron Kray, who claims the late judge went blind as a result.

Ron complains in his new autobiography, My Story: "He showed us no respect, no dignity. He treated us worse than animals. But he lived to regret it. He paid for it with his sight."

You say let Krays out

SUN readers yesterday voted ten to one to let the Kray twins go free.

Our You The Jury hotline took 4,378 calls saying Reg and Ron should be released — 25 years after being jailed for murder. Just 416 disagreed.

PETE REJECTS A KRAY-ZY DEAL

PETER Cook defied a protection racket by the Kray twins when he ran a London club in the Sixties. He says: "They said unruly elements might break up the place.

"Then they offered their services for £500 a week. I said, 'Thanks but the police are just down the road,' and they never came back."

Kray . . salesman

Would YOU buy a second hand motor off this man?

JAILED killer Reggie Kray has gone into business from his cell — as a used car salesman.

Kray, 59, works on commission for a dealer, flogging cars to ex-cons and some of his pen pals.

He gets them to ring Nottingham housewife Stephanie King who is his go-between with the S & B Motor Company of Rainham, Essex.

Mrs King, 36, said: "It's 100 per cent straight. Reg is all right, honestly. He's a really nice man."

Nigel Holland, 28, sales manager for "Mercedes and BMW specialists" S & B, said his involvement with Kray came about "by a fluke."

He added: "I'm not at liberty to say if he gets paid for it."

Kray is in Blundeston jail, Suffolk, serving life for murdering Jack 'The Hat' McVitie.

The Home Office says prisoners cannot receive money from businesses on the outside while they are in jail.

But an inmate said: "Reg's doing good business. The joke going round is: Would you buy a used car from this man?"

Reg's 0336 cell phone line!

PRISON bosses could pull the plug on a Reg Kray phone line launched this week.

The line features the jailed gangland boss on the blower chatting about his life and the twins' past capers.

The Governor of Blundeston jail in Suffolk, where Reg is banged up, has carried out a probe as prison rules bar inmates from being paid for broadcasts.

But the organiser of the phone line, Stephanie King, said: "Reggie isn't making a penny from the line."

She said the line was her idea and was set up to generate cash to fund a planned Krays' Sup-

BY DAVE KEEN

porters Club.

The club will be run by her son Phillip, 24, who will issue regular newsletters and offer discounts on Krays' merchandise.

On the line Reg, 59, thanks all his supporters for their continued loyalty.

He says: "I hope in the future when I get out you will be able to come to a big party that we will all enjoy."

The phone line, which will be regularly updated, will keep supporters in touch with Reg as he is unable to answer all the thousands of letters he receives.

Reg and Ron were jailed in 1969 for the killings of Jack 'The Hat' McVitie and gangster George Cornell.

The number is 0336 420516. Charges are 36p per minute off-peak, 48p a minute peak.

THE KRAYS

STORIES WE CAN TELL...

Grey-haired and thin-faced, Reggie is pictured in the audience for Macbeth at Blundeston jail

Star has double role

ACTOR Ray Winstone is to star as gangster twins Ronnie and Reggie Kray — in the same film.

Computer wizardry will let screen tough guy Ray, 46, take roles he has always wanted to play.

Bob Hoskins, 60, will play the cop who catches the twins (right), who ran a vicious crime empire in London's East End in the 1950s and '60s before being jailed for life.

Ronnie died in 1995 aged 61 and Reg died three years ago.

Writer-director Ray Burdis, who produced the 1990 film The Krays, said the new movie will tell the "real" story now the twins are dead.

He said: "I want to dispel the legend that the East End was safer when they were around. That's a load of cobblers."

It's 24 years since we banged up Reggie..
Have we thrown away the key?

How time has taken toll on Kray twin

HIS face is pale and gaunt. It is hard to believe that this man once held a terror grip on East London.

But this is Reggie Kray, the gangland villain who ruled the underworld with his twin brother Ronnie.

It is 24 years since the pair were jailed. And this amazing picture from inside shows time has taken its toll.

When the Krays were sent down in March 1969, the Vietnam War was at its height, Concorde had yet to make its maiden flight and Harold Wilson was in Number 10. Now aged 60, Reggie

still has another five years before release. Both twins were sentenced to life for murder with a recommended minimum of 30 years.

But nearly a quarter of a century after they went inside, many are asking why they cannot be freed now.

The Krays ran nightclubs in the 50s and 60s and helped themselves to a tidy share of the proceeds of various underworld "firms".

If there was a "blag" going down on their patch, the Krays wanted a piece of

it. Any villain who questioned their brutal authority was a dead man.

Two victims were George Cornell, shot dead by Ronnie in the Blind Beggar pub, and Jack "The Hat" McVitie, who was despatched by Reggie.

Recently, a campaign to win an early release for the twins has been backed by showbiz stars from Patsy Kensit to Barbara Windsor. EastEnders actor and comic Mike Reid also joined in. He says London would have been a safer place if the Krays had remained at large, and claims there were no mug-

gings in their East End "manor" during their reign.

But how many muggings were there anywhere in the 1960s?

Author John Pearson, who has written the definitive biography of the Krays, The Profession of Violence, believes too romantic a picture has been created of the twins.

He said: "They weren't a benevolent society, they were gangsters. Sentimentalising about them doesn't do them any good at all." The twins have discov-

ered the art of self-publicity since they went behind bars. They made over £250,000 from the film rights of The Krays movie alone.

While Ronnie waits in Broadmoor for doctors to certify he is sane, Reggie has been mugging up on the Bard at Blundeston Prison, Suffolk.

He was in the audience at the jail for a production of Macbeth with inmate Simon Melia in the title role and actress Lady Alice Douglas as Lady Macbeth.

The show, by the Inside Knowledge Theatre Company, runs for three nights, but is by invitation only.

Barring a sudden change of heart, Reggie looks set to stay on the jail's guest list for a few years yet.

Why are the stars still dazzled by the Krays?

GOD protect me from my friends,' was the last cry of an over-glamorised gangster, the Mafia's own Giuliano, before they gunned him down. Today that cry could hardly be made by the Kray twins.

On Saturday a protest march on the brothers' behalf and marking their 60th birthday will be staged in London. Among its supporters are Barbara Windsor, the rock star Roger Daltrey and Patsy Kensit, but otherwise the Krays' usual following of publicity-seekers and crime-freaks.

It is through their efforts — and the sepia-tinted passage of the years — that the Krays' cause is being espoused by people who choose to see them as some kind of East End benevolent society which existed to keep muggers away and help old ladies across the street.

This is an insult to the intelligence of anyone who sat through their Old Bailey trial. For they were highly effective and intelligent organising gangsters who ruled by fear and turned parts of London into virtual police no-go areas.

At the height of their power in the mid-Sixties, they were running West End protection, co-operating with the Mafia, and co-ordinating country-wide crime. They masterminded a network of swindles and rackets — and they murdered people.

'But, ah!' say their supporters, 'they only killed other criminals,' as if criminals were a lesser species to be casually disposed of. The truth is that the current Kray campaign is about the oxygen of publicity — the very commodity on which the brothers' empire was built.

It was as young tearaways and boxers in post-war Bethnal Green that the Krays first decided to be 'somebodies'. Descendants of gipsy pugilists and circus people, they had inherited a flair for self-publicity — as well as for violence.

As they organised their East End gangs and ousted old-time villains like Billie Hill and Jack 'Spot' Comer from their swindles and protection rackets, they were always careful to maintain their image as criminal 'celebrities'. In the late Fifties, at their club The Double R, they acted as a focus not just for the underworld but for any theatrical and political celebrities they could lure to the east of Tubby Isaacs's whelk stall in Commercial Road.

Supporters to march to mark Ron and Reg's 60th birthdays

SUPPORTERS of the Kray twins plan to march on 10 Downing Street in a bid to free Reg Kray.

Hundreds of fans of the jailed gangland bosses may take part in the protest walk from Hyde Park on Saturday, October 9.

The protesters plan to hand in a petition to Prime Minister John Major calling for Reg to be set free.

KRAY THERE! TV MIKE IS OFF TO VISIT PAL REGGIE

EXCLUSIVE by DAN COLLINS

EASTENDERS star Mike Reid has paid a secret visit to jailed killer Reggie Kray.

Mike and London's Burning actress Helen Keating spent two hours chatting and joking with their old friend, who was banged up with twin brother Ronnie 24 years ago for murder. An inmate at Blundeston prison in Lowestoft, Suffolk, said: "Reggie was cheered up no end.

"They took him letters and Mike was cracking jokes. He had Reggie and Helen in stitches."

The stars arrived in separate cars for their weekend visit.

Both have backed calls for 59-year-old Reggie to be released. Schizophrenic Ronnie is in Broadmoor.

Mike, 52, who plays Frank Butcher in the Cockney soap, has claimed the twins "did a lot of good" for poor people in the London's East End.

Helen, 49, who plays George Green's mother-in-law in London's Burning, grew up in the same road as Reggie and Ron.

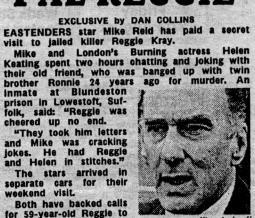

Reggie .. was "in stitches"

Helen .. childhood friend

Should we free the Krays?

NO doubt after John Pearson's 'Why are the stars still dazzled by the Krays?' the twins could be forgiven for thinking 'God protect me from my friends'.

Pearson was assisted by the Kray family and friends in research for his book The Profession Of Violence and made a considerable sum from it. Despite doubting if he would recoup his expenses, he succeeded in making a handsome profit over 25 years while getting several things wrong. No Kray film sequel is planned because the twins didn't like the inaccurate portrayal of their mother and family in the first film.

The Krays have been in prison for 25 years. Their supporters, famous or otherwise, aren't influenced by the so-called glamour, but because they have bothered to get in touch with the Krays and understand they are no longer a threat to the public. Reggie, at least, deserves a date for his release. Pearson's article was as dated as his memory of the Sixties.

LAURIE O'LEARY, London E2.

I WONDER if all the people currently supporting the Krays would be so vocal if they had suffered through their activities. The Krays started their violence when they were 16. They beat my nephew with a bicycle chain because he danced with one of their girlfriends. They were prosecuted but got away with it.

E. WALKER, Dunmow, Essex.

HARDLY a major criminal behind bars doesn't have a fashionable following baying for his release. No wonder the courts are reluctant to imprison: it can't help a judge's self-esteem to know he has just banged up a man who will soon be lionised by Hampstead intellectuals. The Krays are an embarrassment because they are a reminder of the times when malicious malefactors were dealt with severely by a confident judiciary. It has taken a long time for the fashionably merciful to take up their case because there were so many more deserving criminals to 'spring' first.

ROSEMARY OLDHAM, Gerrards Cross, Bucks.

REGGIE LEGS IT

PICTURE EXCLUSIVE

REGGIE Kray steps out with a purposeful stride across the green, green grass of jail.

After 24 years inside, this is his idea of escape ... the wide open spaces of the prison football fields on a glorious summer's day.

The unique picture of the ex-gangland killer was taken by a fellow inmate with a tiny camera smuggled into Blundeston prison near Lowestoft, Suffolk.

Confidence

It shows Reggie still lean and fit at 59 — and hungry to enjoy the exercise period which breaks the boring jail routine.

"He's always out on the field doing sit-ups and exercises," said one ex-con. "Reg keeps himself in trim

By ANTHONY HARWOOD

all the time. There's a strong air of confidence about him. But he never throws his weight around."

It was different a quarter of a century ago. Reggie and twin brother Ronnie, who ran a terror empire in London's East End, got life in 1969 for two murders.

Now Reggie, despite his fitness, is partially deaf, ageing and seemingly no longer a threat to anyone.

He is hoping to win parole shortly. The ex-con, who does not wish to be identified, said: "Some murderers have got less than Reg.

"I think it's time they let him out. And a lot of people — including some prison officers — agree."

Is it time to free the Krays?

REGGIE Kray was pictured in yesterday's Daily Mirror, exercising at Blundeston Prison near Lowestoft. He's 59 now and has been in prison for 24 years for murdering two other criminals, Jack "The Hat" McVitie and George Cornell. The judge recommended that Reggie and his brother Ron serve 30 years.

I don't suppose many people agree, but I wonder if they haven't been in long enough now. I mean no disrespect to the relatives of Mr McVitie or Mr Cornell, but 30 years now seems a bit steep for gangland killings.

The Krays were sentenced as much for what they seemed to represent — dangerous gangsters threatening to take over London — than for their actual crimes. This

TIME TO BE MERCIFUL?

EVIL sadistic killers or men who have paid their debt to society? Convicted murderers Ronnie and Reggie Kray celebrated their 60th birthday last Friday - and stirred up a hornet's nest in the process.

HAPPY KRAYS ARE HERE AGAIN FOR FREDDIE

He leaves jail for trip to pub

KRAYZY: Ronnie and Freddie

NEWS OF THE WORLD EXCLUSIVE

By DAN COLLINS

KRAY gangster Freddie Foreman is being let out of prison each day—so he can pop to the pub.

The henchman, nicknamed the Mean Machine by underworld rivals, is halfway through a nine-year stretch.

He was jailed for handling cash from the vicious Security Express raid in 1983.

Freddie, 63, spent seven years on the run in Marbella before being brought back to face justice.

But prison bosses are so pleased with his good behaviour they now let him out daily.

And this week News of the World investigators watched as he enjoyed a few moments at an upmarket pub in the posh London suburb of Hampstead.

He popped into the Old Bull and Bush and emerged moments later with a blonde woman.

Relaxed and wearing a casual green checked shirt, he chatted happily with her in the car park before they left. Earlier, he had driven alone to a house in Cricklewood, North London—believed to be a pal's home.

Most days, however, Freddie is believed to work at an old people's home near low-security Latchmere House Prison in Richmond, Surrey.

He drives there alone in a maroon Vauxhall Cavalier and is understood to look after residents as part of a job placement scheme.

It is a far cry from his past as an enforcer for twins Ronnie and Reggie Kray, who ruled London's East End in the '60s.

Freddie served ten years for disposing of murdered Jack 'The Hat' McVitie's body after Reggie shot him in a pub.

Freddie also faced trial for the killing of 'Mad Axeman' Frank Mitchell, but was cleared.

Respect

A pal said of new-look Freddie: "There's been an amazing change from the days when he was living in Spain.

"Then he was tanned, fit-looking and a really strong guy—full of beans.

"Now he really looks his age. He's greying and has put on weight.

"But when he talks he's the same old Freddie. He's still got that voice which commanded so much respect from villains.

"Everybody listens to him, believe me. He's got that aura about him even now.

"He always was known as a very bright guy, a real shrewd thinker, and he is full of optimism and ideas for the future.

"Mentally, he's tougher than ever. He hasn't allowed prison to get him down. He's done 4½ years

I'M OFF: Freddie nips out for his day job

DOING BIRD He chats to blonde pal after meeting up at pub

BEHIND BARS Old Bull and Bush gave Freddie a grin 'n tonic

so why shouldn't he be let out occasionally?"

Freddie fled to Marbella in Spain after the Security Express raid in Shoreditch, East London.

He pocketed at least £350,000 and headed for the Costa del Sol with wife Maureen, 61.

Freddie soon became the toast of the town's expat British set. He hosted lavish parties at his white apartment overlooking the Mediterranean and loved to regale guests with tales from his past.

He wore silk suits and dark glasses and invested £90,000 in three luxury flats. Today they are worth £200,000.

But after seven years on the run he was finally sent home to face the music in England.

Much of his loot went on medical bills for his ailing wife and legal fees to fight his extradition.

Freddie—who boasts that Bob Hoskins' gangland film The Long Good Friday was based on him—was jailed in 1990.

He is due to be released before Christmas.

❝The guy is tougher than ever❞

Violence .. Martin and Gary

Pop duo film The Krays sequel

EXCLUSIVE
by KAREN HOCKNEY

SPANDAU Ballet twins Gary and Martin Kemp are to make a sequel to their hit movie The Krays, it was revealed last night.

The pop stars have signed up to play Ronnie and Reggie Kray in Conspiracy Of Silence.

The £5million movie will also star rocker Roger Daltrey as the twins' right-hand man.

Thrilled

The film is based on the police investigation into the East End gangland bosses after the murders of Jack 'The Hat' McVitie and George Cornell.

Producer Ray Burdis, said the sequel will be more violent than The Krays. He added: "Underworld figures said The Krays was too arty.

"We are still negotiating contracts but Gary, Martin and Roger are thrilled to be involved."

Ronnie Kray has has heart attack after row with wife over book

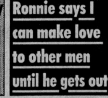

GANGSTER Ronnie Kray had a heart attack after a row with his wife over her tell-all book. The 60-year-old killer worked himself into a fury after reading Kate's sexy confessions serialised in The Sun last week.

Ronnie, who smokes 100 cigarettes a day, collapsed with chest pains at top-security Broadmoor Hospital. Last night he was "stable" and under guard.

Pals say he went berserk after reading The Sun story which revealed how he had given Kate permission to have affairs with other men. One friend said: "Ronnie ripped the paper to pieces when he saw that bit."

An associate said last night: "Kate visited Ron at the hospital on Tuesday. He had spent the whole weekend brooding over the book and was furious. He wanted to have it out with her. Ron thinks what she said made her look a tart and him a fool. They had what you might call a full and frank discussion."

Nurses at the Berkshire hospital raised the alarm at 7.30pm when they went to give Ron his regular medication. He complained of shooting pains in his chest and arms.

A doctor summoned a private ambulance which took him under escort to Heatherwood Hospital in nearby Ascot.

Ronnie, who was jailed for life with his twin Reggie in 1969 for the murder of George Cornell and Jack 'The Hat' McVitie, has become increasingly sick.

Drugs

His weight has plummeted from 14st to a gaunt 9st and he refuses to take any exercise or eat healthy food.

He has suffered heart problems at least twice before and had been warned to cut down on smoking. A year ago he underwent hospital tests after complaining of palpitations.

Four years ago he had an operation to remove a growth from inside his ear and was warned that further surgery might kill him.

It was also four years ago

HE RAGES AT SEXY SECRETS

that he married 37-year-old Kate but the couple have never been allowed to make love.

Kate revealed in her book Murder, Marriage and Madness that Ronnie gave her permission to take lovers.

On a visit to Broadmoor, she confessed to her first fling with a half-Spanish stud—and Ronnie laughed.

She wrote: "Ron was happy for me. He knew it was a good thing for me. We understand each other totally.

"I have always liked sex. I was an early starter, losing my virginity at 13 on the pool table at the local youth club."

Kate said Ronnie's main concern was that Reg never found out about the sex pact. She said: "He felt that Reg wouldn't understand."

But with the exclusive serial-

Ron gets 50 sexy letters a day, I could strangle the women who write them

isation of her book in The Sun it was only a matter of time before Reggie knew.

Ronnie's pal said: "The twins are so fired up over the book now there is even talk of Ronnie divorcing Kate."

Another close friend claims Ronnie has become so depressed over the thought that he will never be released that he has lost the will to live.

Ronnie says I can make love to other men until he gets out

EXCLUSIVE . . . our serialisation of Kate's amazing story

He said: "Ron has been suffering chronic depression for several years.

"He is on a cocktail of drugs to combat his paranoid schizophrenia but they don't seem to alleviate his terrible moods.

"In the last year he seems to have completely lost the will to live. He is down all the time and sees no point carrying on.

"In his worst moments he

has even talked of suicide."

Broadmoor insiders say Ronnie spends most of his time watching TV and chain-smoking roll-up cigarettes.

One added: "He sits in his room all day, watching a bit of TV and smoking cigarettes.

"He sits alongside his bed and rolls ten or 12 cigarettes at a time. He then smokes them and rolls up another dozen."

Strangle

Ronnie has been in Broadmoor's intensive care ward since he attempted to strangle another patient in June.

The victim—who had annoyed Ron by singing—was close to death when nurses found him.

At Broadmoor, intensive care means round-the-clock nursing—and tighter security.

The hospital insider added: "There are at least 15 staff on duty on Abingdon Ward at any one time. It's the most secure place in Broadmoor.

"He has been there since the attack on the other patient and is likely to remain there."

Friends say Ronnie's health was showing signs of improving before he was placed under intensive care.

The pal said: "Just when he seemed to be getting better this has to happen."

Give me a big send-off

RONNIE has given Kate strict instructions for his funeral.

She says: "He wants a carriage drawn by two black horses wearing big black plumes to pull him through the East End. He'll be buried next to his mum in Bethnal Green

cemetery and wants a big wreath of white chrysanthemums spelling out his nickname, The Colonel.

"I tell him I'll put on the headstone, 'Here lies Ronnie Kray—the Ruthless B*****d!'"

KATE: "glowing" after session

SEX RAGE KO'S KRAY

Wife's bonk gives Ron heart attack

GANGLAND killer Ronnie Kray had a heart attack yesterday . . . after reading how his wife bonked a mystery lover.

Kray, 59, went berserk when former strippagram girl Kate publicly revealed her lust for other men.

A Broadmoor insider said that Ronnie had read a newspaper adaptation of Kate's book, Murder, Madness and Marriage.

The insider added: "Kate claimed they had a sex pact so she could have affairs with other men and Ronnie just ripped the paper to pieces.

"He was fuming all weekend."

Ronnie — a 100-a-day cigs smoker — was rushed to Heatherwood Hospital, Ascot, Berks,

Krays sickened by Major's crime 'slur'

THE Kray twins, who dominated the London underworld during the 1960s, have attacked the Prime Minister for reportedly saying that he was worried about juvenile criminals becoming the "Krays of the future".

The gangsters, who were jailed for life in 1969 for gangland murders, told a friend they were angry at being compared to teenagers who mug pensioners or molest children.

They told Mr Steve Wraith, who plans to publish a book of Reggie Kray's poetry, they were sickened by the comparison.

In a statement released by Mr Wraith, of Gateshead, Tyne and Wear, they said: "In reponse to Mr Major's speech we would like to say that in our day no one would dream of mugging and battering old ladies, stealing from their next door neighbours or molesting and killing innocent women and children.

"The people of our day would not tolerate any such behaviour. To be compared with people like that by our own Prime Minister saddens and hurts us deeply."

Mr Wraith added: "Ronnie and Reggie are very upset by the speech and want to put their side of the case.

"Reg feels that Mr Major has tried to kill two birds with one stone by criticising juvenile criminals and keeping the Kray name in the public eye to ruin any chances he might have this year of gaining parole."

Mr Major reportedly told MPs at a dinner last month that he feared juvenile criminals were threatening to create a new generation of Kray twins.

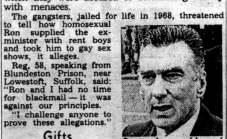

REG KRAY: WE NEVER TOOK CASH FROM PEER

By GARRY BUSHELL

FURIOUS Reggie Kray yesterday denied allegations that he and brother Ron had blackmailed a Tory peer.

A Sunday Times report claimed they made bisexual Lord Boothby pay for top lawyers when they were accused of demanding money with menaces.

The gangsters, jailed for life in 1968, threatened to tell how homosexual Ron supplied the ex-minister with rent boys and took him to gay sex shows, it alleges.

Reg, 58, speaking from Blundeston Prison, near Lowestoft, Suffolk, said: "Ron and I had no time for blackmail — it was against our principles.

"I challenge anyone to prove these allegations."

Gifts

The claims came in a Sunday Times series by John Pearson, author of Krays biography Profession Of Violence.

He said Baron Robert Boothby, KBE, entertained Ron Kray at the House of Lords and at West End clubs.

Ron gave him many gifts — and suggested they swap boy lovers.

Ron is not annoyed about revelations of his brother's relationship with Boothby — who died in 1986.

But he is furious that Pearson claims the twins blackmailed Boothby into supplying expensive barristers and a private eye during the 1965 trial.

A pal of the Krays said: "They saw themselves as men of honour.

"Their main prey were other villains. To them blackmail was cowardly and contemptible."

Reg was jailed for murdering Jack "The Hat"

Reg . . . 'a man of honour'

Boothby . . . Ron's gay pal

McVitie, Ron for killing George Cornell in the Blind Beggar pub in Bethnal Green, East London.

Ron, a schizophrenic, will never be released from Broadmoor. But a campaign backed by stars like Barbara Windsor, Glen Murphy and Mike Reid was launched this year to free Reg.

More than 10,000 have signed petitions and a march from Hyde Park to Trafalgar Square is planned in October.

Mills: no new evidence

The case of Freddie Mills, the former world light-heavyweight champion found shot dead in his car in the "gangster dominated" '60s, was reopened by ITV's "In Suspicious Circumstances" series last month, but the verdict was the same as ever - no-one knows what actually transpired that evening, and no new facts came to light.

The gutsy Mills had gone into club management after a brief show business stint following his boxing career, and one viewpoint was that either the Kray or Richardson gangs, dominant at that time, had disposed of him for some reason.

He was also said to have been a homosexual who had killed himself on the verge of his secret being discovered, or because of the death of a male lover.

MILLS: death still a mystery

Mills was also said to have been a police suspect in the investigations surrounding the death of some prostitutes in Hammersmith, west London - "The Toe-Path Murders", as those crimes became known.

But these are all well-known theories about the former champion's demise, and all ITV's programme did was re-present them to a (partly) new audience - re-hashing the old stories.

The programme, narrated by "Callan" and "The Equaliser" star Edward Woodward, was shallow and confused, but served one purpose: It reminded us all that there's a helluva good film still to made on the subject of the death of Freddie Mills.

★ BRAVEST villain of the week has to be the thief who broke into a car belonging to record producer Dave Courtney in Woolwich, South East London, and nicked all the promotional material for his successful club duo The Courtney Twins. Why brave? Because Dave is best mates with the Krays—and was actually away visiting Reggie in Blundeston Prison, Suffolk, at the time of the theft.

KRAY'S SOFTER CELL

GANGLAND killer Reggie Kray's plans to carpet his prison cell have been thwarted. Kray wanted to carpet his 10ft by 7ft room at Blundeston Prison near Lowestoft, Suffolk, in yellow. But yesterday the Home Office banned the 60-year-old, who was jailed for life with his twin brother Ronnie in 1969, from doing so. It said he could have a rug instead.

Kray away day

GANGSTER Ronnie Kray got a full police escort yesterday as he was transferred between hospitals.

Kray, 59, needed tests after his collapse with heart trouble at Broadmoor top security hospital last week.

He was taken by ambulance from his ward at Heatherwood Hospital in Ascot, Berkshire, to Wexham Park Hospital in Slough.

Blood samples were taken before he returned to the Ascot hospital, where he is expected to stay until Monday.

Kray, who was jailed for life in 1969 for murder, was rushed to Heatherwood from Broadmoor on Wednesday after a medical officer diagnosed a mild heart attack.

His condition was monitored and tests later revealed a high level of potassium in his blood and tissue.

Kray, who has had 20 visitors in hospital, was "comfortable" last night.

LIGHTING UP: Gangster Ronnie Kray has a cigarette in the ambulance transferring him for tests yesterday

SAY SORRY OR DIE IN JAIL REG

Shattered . . Reggie Kray had plea rejected

EXCLUSIVE by ANTONELLA LAZZERI

JAILED mobster Reggie Kray has been told he may never be freed — unless he says sorry for killing a gangland hoodlum.

Reggie, serving life for murdering Jack "The Hat" McVitie, asked for parole after 25 years inside.

But prison chiefs told him he will almost certainly have to serve the 30 years recommended at his trial — and may die in jail unless he shows remorse.

Shattered Reggie, 59, sent a copy of the parole report to sister-in-law Katy Kray from Blundestone jail, Suffolk.

Katy, married to Reggie's twin Ron, said yesterday: "He will never say sorry. McVitie was a gangster and it was kill or be killed.

"Reg doesn't feel remorse but reckons he has done his time.

"Both Reg and Ron have spent 25 years watching IRA terrorists and child-killers getting life, then waltzing out of prison five years later."

EastEnder Reggie was opposed to publication of any part of the report and his lawyers have been fighting to prevent the story appearing.

Ron, who is in Broadmoor, will only be freed with doctors' consent.

Killer Kray's parole snub

Kray digs his garden

JAILED killer Ronnie Kray has been given a garden as "therapy."

Kray, 59, tends his plot at top security Broadmoor Hospital, Berks, while wearing expensive Gucci shoes and hand-made suits.

A pal said: "He loves his plants and talks to them."

Ronnie, jailed for life with twin Reg for murder in 1969, hopes to grow fruit and veg when he gets out.

WE NEED A RETURN TO KRAY FAMILY VALUES.

HAPPY BIRTHDAY REG AND RON

'ere Mrs Kray! Did you know that Ronnie's divorcing you?

EXCLUSIVE
by IAN TRUEMAN

THE Daily Star yesterday broke the shock news to Ronnie Kray's wife that the gangland killer was divorcing her.

Stunned former kissogram girl Kate Howard, 37, said: "I know nothing at all about this.

"I don't believe it. It's another rumour — they have been going round for ages."

But she choked on her words when we read her an official statement announcing her bizarre marriage to the 60-year-old East End gangster was over.

Ronnie, who was jailed for life in 1969 with twin brother Reggie, has instructed solicitors to petition for a divorce on the grounds of "unreasonable behaviour".

At her home in Headcorn, Kent, Kate said: "I think I had better talk to these solicitors myself and then have a word with my Ron.

"This is all news to me. There has been a lot of gossip about us getting divorced, but it has all been untrue.

"If this petition is true I don't want to talk about it until I have seen it myself and talked to Ron about it.

"I don't really know what to say — this has all come out of the blue." The couple met inside Broadmoor and wed in 1989. They have never been able to consummate their marriage.

Last year Kray was furious at the publication of Kate's autobiography, in which she claimed they had a pact which allowed her to have sex with other men.

Happy

He told close friends she had betrayed his trust and made a fool of him, and that he was considering a divorce.

RONNIE: Wants to end marriage

STUNNED: Former kissogram girl Kate Howard did not know

Kray brothers' car is back in triumph

A CAR which once belonged to the Kray twins has been rescued from a scrapyard and turned into a wedding limousine.

The 1952 Triumph Renown was given to gangland killers Ronnie and Reggie as a 30th birthday gift.

It was found rusting by classic car buff Roy Smith, of Chatham, Kent, who spent six months renovating it. 'It was originally grey. But I thought this would not be a suitable colour for wedding transport so opted for cream instead,' Mr Smith, 55, said yesterday.

The Renown, which still has its original radio, is thought to be one of only 300 left. It is worth about £5,000.

Inside story on Reg and Ron

Reg Kray: shareholder?

PLEASE, please, stop putting in stories of the Krays.

Almost every week, your paper mentions something about them, why? Are they shareholders? Or are you under some threat?

Surely you don't admire their wicked behaviour. At the height of their infamous glory years, one would not answer them back or even give them a dirty look.

They are gangsters, who would kill anyone who crossed them. Yet your paper has assisted in publicity stunts, and getting signatures for their release.

Personally, I want them to do their 30 years. There was no reason, at the time, for them not being hung, and now everyone makes heroes out of them.

They held the East End in terror for a four years, they went north, Liverpool I'm told, to try and take-over crooked night clubs, but they found them people too tough so retired to London.

The way they are both treated inside, why do they want to come out?

J. W. Webber, address withheld.

RONNIE KRAY IN NEW HEART SCARE

FRAIL: Ron Kray goes for tests

JIM STEVENS

GANGLAND killer Ronnie Kray looked frail and gaunt yesterday as he arrived in hospital for tests in a new heart scare.

Kray, 59, said to be on his "last legs" after heart tremors at Christmas, was whisked from Broadmoor top security hospital under police escort.

He sat in an L-reg minibus flanked by four nurses. Kray is a permanent patient in Broadmoor's infirmary.

There was no sign of 100-a-day Kray's favourite roll-ups. Broadmoor managers had to delay the 20-mile journey after staff demanded police outriders.

Bespectacled Kray was handcuffed to a nurse as he entered the main entrance of Slough's Wexham Park Hospital.

Relapse

He spent 30 minutes undergoing tests in the cardiology unit watched by his escorts, before being ushered from a side entrance.

A Broadmoor source revealed later Kray had had a relapse.

His problems started last September when he collapsed with crippling chest pains.

☐ NO wonder Ronnie Kray is suffering from chest pains if he can afford to smoke 100 cigarettes a day. Prison life can't be that bad.

**ANN COPLAND,
Oldmeldrum, Aberdeenshire.**

Reggie on the lecture circuit?

■ GUESS what Reggie Kray, the former gangland killer, wants to be if his application for parole next year is successful? The cockney who has so far served 26 years for the murder of Jack 'The Hat' McVitie apparently foresees a future as a visiting university lecturer.

'He wants to do a university tour to tell young people not to get involved in crime,' says his former henchman Tony Lambrianou, who himself served 16 years for his part in McVitie's murder. He is a regular visitor to Reggie at Maidstone Prison and has written a book on those dark days called Inside The Firm.

'He wants to live in Kent,' adds Mr Lambrianou, who is convinced Reggie is a changed man. 'It's time he was released. When you think of what he has done it's ridiculous. We never hurt anyone who wasn't a villain like us.'

Kray release moves closer

REGGIE: Moving

GANGLAND killer Reggie Kray, 60, is being moved to a 'softer' jail in preparation for his eventual release.

He will be transferred from Blundeston, near Lowestoft, Suffolk, to Maidstone Prison in Kent—known for its relaxed regime—by the end of the month.

Kray and his twin, Ronnie, were both given life for murder in 1969 and the judge recommended they serve a minimum of 30 years.

Reggie Kray can next apply for parole in 1996, and the Home Office has advised him to keep a low profile.

He had been warned that a stars' campaign for his release was harming his chances.

Ron ♥ Cliff

Ronnie . . . gang boss   Young Cliff . . . in '68

Gay mobster Kray wanted to date fresh-faced star

GAY gangster Ronnie Kray fancied the young Cliff Richard and tried to arrange a date with him, a former henchman has revealed.

Ronnie spotted clean-cut Cliff in a Chinese restaurant and took an immediate shine to him. Albert Donaghue, who was the Kray twins' paymaster, said: "He was sitting there with his shades on and Ronnie said: 'Ooh, I'd like to meet him.' Straight away there's a warrant out on him — a bonus if anyone can get him to a meet."

But Ronnie, now serving life for murder, never met Cliff, Donaghue tells ITV crime show Gangsters. It is screened next month.

GARY 'NO' TO KRAYS 2

GARY KEMP has pulled out of the sequel to the hit movie The Krays—throwing the £5million project into chaos.

The former Spandau Ballet star was to have starred with brother Martin as gangsters Ronnie and Reggie in Conspiracy Of Silence.

The film is based on the police probe into the murder of Jack 'The Hat' McVitie and George Cornell.

Filming was due to start this summer, but Gary, 32, is now working on a solo album.

CHARLIE KRAY IN MURDER PROBE

EXCLUSIVE
by IAN HEPBURN

THE OLDER brother of the Kray twins was arrested yesterday over the execution of property tycoon Donald Urquhart.

Charlie Kray, 67, was quizzed for 90 minutes after informants linked him to the case.

Urquhart, 55, was gunned down a year ago as he strolled with his Thai girlfriend in Marylebone, Central London.

It is believed two men separately named Kray as a link between the assassin and the Mr Big who ordered the killing.

Kray was freed without charge by police in Peckham, South London.

A Scotland Yard source said: "He could be interviewed again."

Charlie Kray was jailed for ten years in 1969 for disposing of the body of London mobster Jack "The Hat" McVitie.

Two men — the alleged gunman and getaway driver — have been sent for trial over the Urquhart case.

CROOK'S CUSHY LIFE GETS CHOP

By GARY JONES
Chief Crime Reporter

KRAY gangster Freddie Foreman, who was spotted by the News of the World when he popped out of his open prison for a drink, has been moved to a tougher jail.

He has been kicked out of cushy Latchmere House prison, in Richmond, Surrey, for having too much loot in his cell.

The villain, once nicknamed the Mean Machine, had been let out to work at an old people's home in preparation for release in May.

But last October we spotted him enjoying a drink with a blonde in a pub in London's posh Hampstead.

Prison staff were angry that he had taken advantage of their trust and kept a close watch on him. A spot check then revealed that he had £350 in his cell. "Freddie had been hoping to have an easy ride, but he's now come unstuck," I was told.

"There's no way he should have had all that cash in his cell.

"It was silly to think he could do as he liked."

The Kray henchman is now in Maidstone Prison, in Kent—where he has teamed up with Reggie Kray. Foreman, 63, is serving a nine-year sentence for handling cash from the £6 million Security Express raid in London's Shoreditch in 1983.

He pocketed at least £350,000 and spent years living it up on Spain's Costa Del Crime before being extradited.

Foreman boasts that the Bob Hoskins gangland film, The Long Good Friday, was based on him.

A prison source said: "Freddie is none too happy about being moved to Maidstone.

"He blames the News of the World for making life difficult for him."

IT'S REG E KRAY!

EXCLUSIVE By GARY JONES Chief Crime Reporter

GANGLAND killer Reggie Kray has become addicted to the deadly drug Ecstasy in jail.

Underworld cronies smuggle him in a regular supply of the tiny white tablets—known as 'E'—at visiting time.

Now the super-crook—who once prided himself on keeping in shape—is said to have become a "haggard" shadow of his former self.

But he says of the tablets that are destroying his health: "They're ****ing marvellous!"

Reggie, 60—who once ruled London's gangland with his crazed twin Ronnie—even uses his own headed notepaper to put in his drugs orders.

The arrogant villain's letterhead bears his name in huge type, the address of Maidstone jail, and a flattering picture of himself taken 30 years ago.

Smuggle

In his barely legible scrawl he tells his mates how to smuggle drugs. One letter says: "If you can get some puff (jail slang for cannabis) between you I will appreciate it."

In another message Reggie tells a friend how to disguise the smuggled drug in this way: "If you get any puff will you put it in a condom and shape it like a cigar."

Sometimes he rings friends and orders Ecstasy, using a secret codeword to dupe warders.

Reggie—serving life for the murder of gangster Jack "The Hat" McVitie—calls the tablets "birds", because they are printed with a dove logo.

He asks pals: "Did you get them birds you were looking for?"

And he jokingly tells his mates: "When I'm out of my head I ring up all my old enemies asking how they are."

One friend revealed: "Reggie is a big fan of puff, but now he loves his 'E's as well. They make him feel good.

"There's quite a few of his mates who take them in. It's not difficult to hand them over 'cos they're so small."

Half-a-million youngsters are said to be regular users of Ecstasy. The drug stimulates bursts of seemingly limitless energy and feelings of general well-be-ing. But it's side-effects—a rapid increase in blood pressure and heart-rate—can kill.

Reggie is also an old hand at getting booze smuggled into prison.

Pals fill Coke bottles with whisky and brandy, being careful to use those with plastic tops to avoid the prison metal detector.

Whisky

Then, during a visit, someone will buy Reggie a Coke, and top it up from the illicit supply.

"Reggie doesn't mind what whisky he gets," said a friend.

"But he likes his Napoleon brandy. Reggie gets other inmates to use their visiting orders to bring in a crowd of his mates. There's often as many as twelve of them sitting at tables around Reggie. There's a real party atmosphere.

"And the screws have no idea he's laughing and joking because he's knocking back the booze."

Reggie has a huge circle of friends on the outside. He has already started sending out the first batches of the 2,000 Christmas cards he will post.

The veteran villain is hoping to be paroled next year, and has already made plans to move to a genteel Yorkshire spa town.

He has told friends he wants to settle in posh Harrogate. "He fancies seeing his life out in a more sedate environment," said one pal.

Junkie in jail

Reggie Kray

POSER: Reggie's paper with personal letter-head

VISITING CRIMES: Drugs get into Maidstone jail

LOSER: Ecstasy has turned Reggie into a junkie

MY FREEDOM POEM FOR REGGIE KRAY

The poem Ray Cann sent to the Prime Minister

MY FRIEND

My friend is in prison today,
That's something I can't forget.
He's been there for 26 years
It will have changed him I would bet.
He's paid his dues and he's done his time
And I'm proud that he's a friend of mine.
Home Office, politicians, can't you see
It's time to let my friend go free.
I know that in the past
My friend was a villain. It didn't last.
He got 'life' with a 30-year recommendation
A soldier shoots another, he'll get commendation.
My friend was top of the underworld at the time
One of his soldiers stepped out of line,
He could have killed my friend at any time.
During his long time away
He's changed so much, even turned grey.
He helps people with troubles all over this land
And people like me lend him a hand.
I've never met this friend of mine
Nor spoken to him on the telephone line.
But there are thousands like me who hope one day
That they will shake the hand of Reggie Kray.
Thise year we hope that compassion will be shown
And soon our friend will be coming home.
God Bless you, Reggie Kray.

Reggie Kray: He's served 27 of his 30 years.

Ray Cann — will poetry power free Reggie Kray?

LIFEGUARD Ray Cann is using poetry power in a bid to win freedom for notorious gangster and murderer Reggie Kray.

Ray, 34, from Dunston is campaigning for the early release of Kray, 61, who has three more years of his 30-year jail term to serve at Maidstone Prison.

Ray has written a poem, My Friend, in an attempt to persuade Prime Minister John Major and Home Secretary Michael Howard that Reggie Kray, who with his brother Ronnie terrorised London's East End in the 1960s, is a reformed character.

Ray, of Ravensworth Road, a lifeguard a Dunston Pool, received an acknowledgement from John Major on Monday.

Reggie Kray has written to Ray and thanked him for his efforts.

Obsessed

Ray said: "I must confess that I am obsessed with what I and thousands of others believe to be an unjust sentence.

"The judge ordered him to serve the full 30 years. But I have an unexplainable urge to help him in his plight"

Ray wrote to Kray after reading his autobiography, Born Fighter. "I still can't explain exactly why I decided to write to him but I am glad I did.

"He's a changed person now and devotes most of his time to helping other people inside and outside prison.

"Just one example is young Paul Stapleton, from Nottingham, who suffers from muscular dystrophy.

"Reg has used his notoriety and the help of the many people who write to him regularly to raise thousands of pounds to buy special equipment which the NHS cannot afford and to generally make Paul and his family's life more comfortable.

Auction

"I have helped to raise money for Paul through sponsored swims and charity auctions and have been helped by members of Paul Gascoigne's family who have donated gifts of Gazza memorabilia and autographed souvenirs for auction or raffle."

Ray believes that Reggie Kray has turned to charity work because he genuinely wants to — and not because he thinks it might have a favourable effect on his sentence.

"He is now coming up to his 27th year in prison and the vast majority of people know in their hearts that his release is long overdue.

"There are those who disagree and, believe me, I take some stick at times. But they have a right to voice their own opinions too."

Ray decided to put his thoughts about Reggie Kray into verse to draw attention to what he feels is society's unfair tretament of the one-time gangland king.

Replies

Ray writes once or twice a month to Kray and has received nine replies from him, expressing gratitude for his support and recommending charitable causes.

"I recently heard that I will be able to visit Reggie in the New Year and I'm looking forward to that. I will continue to help the campaign for Reggie Kray's release and to help him with his charity work whenever I can.

"Reggie is the first to admit that he committed hideous crimes, but it is time for the man to be judged on the way he is now, not on what he once was."

CUE HERE FOR KRAY T-SHIRTS

THE notorious Kray twins are trying to set up a string of snooker clubs—to sell Kray souvenirs.

Reggie and Ronnie, serving life for gangland killings, have a cult following who collect valuable Kray memorabilia like T-shirts.

But the twins are fed up with rivals ripping them off and want to cash in by selling their own merchandise from snooker clubs across the country.

Negotiations involving the twins' Jersey-based company are under way for the first club in Swansea—but it faces local opposition.

KILLERS CAN ENTER

KRAY: He could win   RIPPER: Jackpot hope

DERANGED Broadmoor inmates could become Lottery millionaires after management agreed they can join the fun.

All 550 patients at the top security hospital, including Yorkshire Ripper Peter Sutcliffe and gangland killer Ronnie Kray, are eligible to play.

They will have tickets bought for them by relatives and friends outside. One nurse said: "There's a lot of excitement here. But we don't know what we'll do if a patient wins a million —they're not allowed to handle cash."

I WAS FRIEND TO THE KRAYS

ONE of London's most feared hardcase gangsters and close friend of the Krays, Eric Mason, has set up home with his wife and family in the gentle Victorian spa town of Harrogate.

Eric Mason, an armed bank robber the Kray twins walked carefully around, is quietly working for a local charity which helps the homeless.

For 30 years the ex-boxer stalked the East End of London. Despite his fierce reputation he was regarded as a gentleman, if not a gentle man.

The last man in Britain to receive the *cat of nine tails* forty years ago, he is now at peace with a world he terrorised.

Steely-haired Eric is 63. He lives in Bilton, a suburb of Harrogate with his Northern Ireland born wife Carole, 42, and the two young loves of his life eight-year-old Michael and three-year-old Sarah.

ROBBED

But, in the Fifties, Sixties and Seventies he was the criminal innovator of the smash and grab raid, robbed banks around Britain brandishing a sawn-off shotgun, and dealt out his own social justice against such notorious criminals as the East End's Richardson brothers.

He still regularly visits his friend Reggie Kray in Blundellstone Prison, and a book written by Reggie is dedicated to him.

Eric has not been in trouble with the law for 17 years and has no intention ever again of falling into the hands of courts which sent him to approved school, borstal and, during two long terms of imprisonment, most of the country's top security jails.

"I was a rebel and a criminal, but I like to think I had a conscience. I would never whack a woman and would not let anyone else. To this day if I saw a man mistreating a woman I would have something to say.

"I was born into a London boxing family. We were not poor East Enders, I was brought up near Marble Arch and my father was chauffeur to the Labour Prime Minister Ramsey McDonald," said Eric chatting in a Harrogate pub.

"I could never see any side but mine in those days and ran my own team in London. People like Jack *The Hat* McVitie were my close friends — he was a serious hard man who a lot of lies have been written about.

"I used to work with other people occasionally such as Ronnie and Reggie Kray and the Great Train robbers, but I was my own man," he said.

Eric believes that gangsters of yesterday were not nearly so bad as they were painted and had standards criminals of the nineties could not understand.

"Okay I robbed banks and frightened people, but the pellets in my shotgun were carefully emptied of shot and filled with rice before a raid. It was the noise that did the job, I did not want to hurt anyone," he said.

"I have nothing to do with crime any more. I do not regret what happened. I cannot change it, but I will do everything I can to persuade young people of today from going down the same path," he added.

The hardman: Page 7

East End gangster now a charity worker in Yorks

▶ STROLL ON THE STRAY: Former gangster Eric Mason

Krays' jail anniversary

THE notorious Kray twins mark 25 years in jail today and campaigners, including show business figures, are to use the anniversary to revitalise the the fight for the gangsters' release.

Harold Wilson was Prime Minister when identical twins Ronald and Reginald were jailed by Mr Justice Melford Stevenson with a recommendation that they serve a minimum of 30 years.

Carry On actress Barbara Windsor, who has corresponded with the Krays for many years, said: "Even people who hate the Krays feel enough is enough, they are both old men now.

"Ronnie is on medication and has quietened down. He still looks immaculate. Reggie gets up at 4 am and writes and works out. He's hopeful of getting out next year."

Insane

Reggie, 60, once dubbed "England's Al Capone", was jailed for the murder of Jack "The Hat" McVitie and comes up for parole next year. He is held at Blundestone in Suffolk.

Ronnie, convicted of killing George Cornell, is registered criminally insane and unlikely ever to be released from Broadmoor.

Before their downfall, the twins enjoyed a Chicago-style reign of organised crime, controlling East End gangs and West End protection rackets while entertaining politicians, peers and celebrities from sport and showbusiness in their nightclubs.

Ronnie invented the "cigarette punch" – smashing an enemy's jaw with a left hook while he accepted a cigarette. "An open jaw breaks more easily," boasted the man who now uses matches to model gypsy caravans.

● INFAMOUS GANGSTERS – the Kray twins, Ronnie, left, who is in Broadmoor, and Reggie

Reggie claims he became a Christian in jail and has written his life story.

Their "supporters club" organised a march to Downing Street in October in a demand for parole coinciding with their 60th birthday. Barbara Windsor was there with fellow actress Patsy Kensit and singer Roger Daltrey. A petition containing more than 18,000 signatures was handed in.

MALICE

Once upon a crime

JOHN WILLIAMS is sick of the Kray-zee gang

There's a line that jumped out at me in the first episode of the BBC's The Underworld series last week. Bob Hoskins refers to the East End 'with its tradition of street violence and strong sense of community' as if they went hand in hand. As if 'street violence' was just another part of our glorious working-class heritage, like playing football in the road with a tin can — not a rain of boots to the kidney or a razor **slashed** across the face.

The problem with nostalgia is that it has become completely uncritical. It used to be that the past was divided up into Good Things and Bad Things, 1066 And All That-style. Now, in these times of postmodern kitsch, everything in the recent past is absolutely fabulous — Magpie! Seventies **footballers** and their haircuts! Dick Emery! Rick Wakeman! The New Avengers!

Nostalgia may be harmless enough, but when it comes to looking back at our social history, it's positively pernicious. If a programme about superannuated villains has anything to tell us, it should be that there were no good old days — London has always been violent. The Kray Twins were not the GLC, not a couple of benevolent uncles looking after their patch and reluctantly dispensing the occasional mite of street justice. They were not the biggest stars of the swinging world of crime. Crime doesn't have stars. It's not a branch of light entertainment. The Krays were a pair of **murderous** gangsters who made themselves rich and famous through terror and cruelty.

What makes matters worse is the inability of our culture to take old people seriously. Old people can't really be bad, they're de facto lovable old dears. We dress their villainy up in the heritage vocabulary: enforcers and killers become rascals and rogues. They even used amusingly old-fashioned weapons like **coshes** and gelignite — how delightfully quaint. What we refuse to accept is that some funny old East Ender in a dodgy toupee may be just as ruthless a killer as some 16-year-old Angeleno with an Uzi.

The Krays have become a kind of Bloomsbury Set for our times: all those volumes of correspondence from Vita Sackville-West's hairdresser replaced by self-promoting memoirs from diamond **geezers** who once had Ronnie in the back of their motor. Leave it out, my son.

SCANDAL OF KRAY AND LORD

By FIONA MAY

A HOMOSEXUAL scandal involving gangster Ronnie Kray and top Tory peer Lord Boothby threatened to plunge the Government into deep crisis during 1964, according to secret Cabinet documents released yesterday..

The papers – issued under the 30-year rule – reveal that the allegations were even thought to be a Labour Party conspiracy to "wreck" the Government.

The scandal was just a year after the Profumo affair and began after a national newspaper reported the relationship between "Kray and a well-known Tory peer". It referred to Mayfair parties with clergymen and said that blackmail was allegedly involved. Members of the Cabinet quickly learned that the peer was Lord Boothby, former Parliamentary private secretary to Sir Winston Churchill and a household name from countless TV and radio appearances.

GAY: Gangster Kray

The documents from the office of then Prime Minister Sir Alec Douglas-Home show for the first time just how seriously the story was taken.

And a "note for the record" by Sir Alec's private secretary, Sir Timothy Bligh, also linked Lord Boothby with Tom Driberg, a Labour MP known at Westminster for his often flamboyant homosexual lifestyle.

The threat of scandal over Lord Boothby and Kray eased when the politician wrote a public letter of denial.

But some ministers felt there could be substance to the allegations.

And one Downing Street document marked "secret" said that two Tory MPs had told the party's chief whip "that Lord Boothby and Mr Driberg had been importuning males at a dog track and were involved with gangs of thugs."

DENIAL: Lord Boothby

I COULD JUST MURDER ANOTHER McVITIE!

TROUBLE BREWING: Reg, left, and Ron enjoy cuppa at height of their '60s notoriety

KILLER: Reggie Kray

GANG BOSS: Richardson

TORTURER: Fraser

JAILBIRD: Charlie Kray

EXCLUSIVE by GARY JONES

JAILED killer Reggie Kray has made peace with his most hated gangland rivals over tea and biscuits behind bars.

Reggie—serving life for murdering Jack "The Hat" McVitie—requested a prison visit from his old enemies Charlie Richardson and "Mad" Frankie Fraser.

When they walked in for their first meeting in three decades, 60-year-old Reggie hugged them. And he and elder brother Charlie, 67, then sat with them chatting amicably about old times.

The four became tearful as they remembered the "good old days" of the 1960s—when their rival gangs fought a murderous war on London's streets and made fortunes from protection rackets.

Jail chiefs extended their visiting time by half an hour to let them continue the nostalgic chat—and one warder even told them it was "a privilege" to see them together.

Reggie's close pal Dave Courtney was at the get-together in Maidstone jail,

Krays take tea and biscuits with Richardson..and 'mad dog' came too

Kent. He said: "They decided to bury the hatchet.

"They swapped photos of criminal friends and became quite tearful about the past. They admitted a few nasty things they'd done to each other, but laughed about it.

"Frankie kept everyone laughing with his stories. I think they were all surprised how well they got on. They realised they could have been good friends and not enemies.

"Think what would have happened if they'd teamed up 30 years ago instead of fighting. Things might have been very different."

In reality, the Krays and the Richardsons declared an all-out gang war in the early 1960s over control of London gambling dens.

At its height, Reggie's twin Ronnie shot dead Richardson henchman George Cornell in an East End pub. Cornell had called Ronnie "a fat poof."

Reggie later knifed to death small-time crook McVitie at a party.

Both Krays were jailed for life in 1969 for the murders. Charlie got ten years for his involvement in McVitie's killing. Ronnie is still in Broadmoor.

Fraser, now 70, was jailed for ten years in 1967 for torturing enemies of the Richardsons. Charlie Richardson got 25 years for the same offence.

Reggie's pal Dave said: "One prison officer told us it was a privilege to see these criminal heavyweights together."

He added: "They've all promised to keep in touch. They spoke of their hopes for the future—but there's no more talk of going back to their criminal ways. That's in the past."

Malcolm Jones, duty governor at Maidstone, said: "A few years ago, they weren't the best of friends. But with age they've changed."

TWINS LAUNCH PLAN TO BUILD NEW CLUB EMPIRE

JAILED gangland boss Reggie Kray has told the Advertiser about his plans to open a chain of billiard halls.

He has joined forces with twin Ron, elder brother Charlie and a Welsh businessman to launch their first venture in Swansea.

The former East End underworld chiefs promise to give all profits from the combined halls and souvenir shops to charities, especially those that benefit children.

September will see the opening for the Swansea hall which will have 20 tables and a bar.

Reggie writes: "The Krays have built up a strong allegiance with their Welsh supporters since the 1960s when we went to Cardiff to

aid a charity show on behalf of the victims of the Aberfan disaster.

"At the time we went to see the Welsh legend The Mighty Atom, one time flyweight champion of the world Jimmy Wilde who at the time was in an old man's home.

HOMAGE

"But we had tracked him down to pay homage to our fight hero from our schooldays," he added.

Kray merchandise such as T-shirts and videos could be on sale at the billiard hall.

It was way back in 1957 that the Kray Twins opened their first venue - the 14-table Regal Snooker Hall in Eric Street, Mile End.

As Reg writes: "It was the first of our many ventures in the club world."

He hopes the hall in Swansea will be the first of many around Britain.

Reg adds: "It is expected that celebrities such as Eddie Thomas, the ex-fighter along with Howard Winstone ex-featherweight champion of the world will frequent this billiard hall in Swansea."

The Kray Twins were caged a quarter of a century ago after being convicted of the gangland killings of Jack 'The Hat' McVitie and George Cornell.

EXCLUSIVE: Latest photo of Reg taken just last week

Reg's billiard dreams are right on cue

Kraysy caper

☐ REVEALED at last, the Krays' secret plan for gaining an early release. It was pinned on Ivan Lawrence, one of their defence barristers who is MP for Burton but was then a Tory hopeful in Peckham.

"When I went down to say goodbye to Ronald Kray he said, 'Thank you very much, Mr Lawrence, for what you have done for us'," explains the MP.

"We are going to keep our fingers crossed for you in Peckham," continued Ronnie, "so that you can become Home Secretary and let us out early."

However, there were two fatal flaws in the otherwise fiendishly brilliant plan. Lawrence never did become Home Secretary. And he wouldn't have rushed anywhere to get Ronnie out.

Oh God, mother help me!

LAST DYING GASP OF MAD GANGSTER RONNIE KRAY

Ailing . . . Ronnie on a visit last year for tests at hospital where he died

By CHRIS PHARO and PAUL HOOPER

EXCLUSIVE

GANGLAND legend Ronnie Kray died yesterday crying out: "Oh God, Mother, help me!"

The mad former underworld boss, 61, suffered a huge heart attack in a hospital where he had been having tests.

A team of highly-trained medics who happened to be near his bed battled for 15 minutes to save him. But Ronnie — who was serving life in top-security Broadmoor for two killings — had died almost instantly at Wexham Park Hospital in Slough, Berks.

Last night a Broadmoor warder said: "As the heart attack hit him he yelled out, 'Oh God, I'm dying, aren't I? Oh God, Mother, help me.''

Ronnie and twin brother Reggie were devoted to mum Violet, who brought them up in the tough East End they later came to rule.

Reggie, who is in Maidstone Prison in Kent, "wept like a baby"

Continued on Page Two

Death of a failed thug

RONNIE Kray's end was a lot less sudden than it had been for his victims. Not for him a shotgun blast to the head. Instead, a dizzy spell, followed by a heart attack and a peaceful passing away in hospital safe from the threat of vengeful rivals.

With his death, the myth-making will begin in earnest. Not least in the East End where, to this day, the name Kray commands fear and respect in equal measure. In truth, however, getting banged up for the murders of George Cornell and Jack "The Hat" McVitie may well have been the best thing that could have happened to the Kray twins.

For they would have been hopeless inadequates in the modern underworld.

Today, the real "faces" are no longer interested in small fry like £10,000 security van heists or protection rackets operating at the rate of a "bullseye" (£50) a week.

Instead, the big money is in internationally co-ordinated drug rings and large-scale computer fraud. And, as the judge remarked at their trial, the Krays were no rocket scientists.

From the days when they terrorised other children in the playground to the moment they were arrested for murder, they were little more than vicious thugs. Their staple income came from a protection racket whereby anyone who failed to pay the weekly "pension" would either have his premises "torched" or be waylaid in a dark alley and beaten to a pulp.

All attempts to expand on this basic approach ended in failure. The gangsters who operated from the Double R billiard hall failed to make it with West End casino Esmeralda's Barn.

It may have enabled Ronnie and Reggie to impress their mother Violet with snaps of themselves with celebrities like the actress Diana Dors, boxer Joe Louis and Profumo scandal good time girl Christine Keeler, but it went under after four years owing £4,000.

In their business acumen, they lagged far behind their great south London rivals the Richardsons. When Charlie Richardson stood in the dock of the Old Bailey in 1968, he was at the apex of a business empire which ran from South London scrapyards and West End drinking clubs to Welsh slag heaps and South African mines.

He had contacts ranging from the heart of the Conservative Party in Britain to the South African Broederbond, a powerful and secret society of male Afrikaners.

And that was the way the modern underworld was to go.

I'll go to Kray funeral

DUNSTON lifeguard Ray Cann, who has developed a long-standing pen-friendship with jailed East End mobster Reggie Kray, said yesterday that he plans to attend the London funeral of Reggie's brother Ronnie, who died on Friday.

Mr Cann, of Ravensworth Road, said: "I was speaking to Reggie just before Ronnie died but since hearing the news I have kept a respectful silence.

"The funeral will take a lot of arranging. It will be one of the biggest ever seen in London's East End."

Victims protest at tributes to dead gangland boss

Don't cry for killer Kray

RONNIE: Psychopath

VICTIMS of brutal Ronnie Kray were last night shedding no tears for the notorious gangland boss.

They spoke out in protest as underworld figures paid tribute to the mad murderer who died yesterday.

One who suffered from his cruelty revealed how schizophrenic Ronnie attacked him with red-hot pokers.

In an unsigned letter to a local paper, the 64-year-old man recalled: "He said he was going to burn my eyes out until someone behind me shouted out: 'No Ron, not that'.

"Whoever did that saved my life because at that time I thought: 'This is it, he's going to kill me'."

Collapsed

Kray, 61, who collapsed with a heart attack in Broadmoor, died a prisoner as it was intended — without seeing freedom since he was jailed 26 years ago.

His life of infamy ended at 9.07am yesterday in a single room off ward 8A at Wexham Park Hospital, Slough, Berkshire.

Flower-seller Pat Kelly, 38, who works in London's Whitechapel Road, told how Kray and his twin Reggie ruled the East End.

"They were evil men who robbed from the poor. They deserved to be incarcerated.

"I don't think the younger generation will mind too much. But my father was a fan of theirs and he will be pretty upset."

Tory MP Sir Teddy Taylor said the public should not forget the fear and violence inflicted by the twins.

I'M SO GLAD KRAY'S DEAD

A CROOK tortured by Ronnie Kray said last night: "I'm glad he's dead. He was the cruellest man that ever walked."

Lennie Hamilton — blinded with a red-hot poker as Kray laughed in delight — spoke out hours after the 61-year-old gangster died from a massive heart attack.

Chainsmoker Ronnie, who collapsed at Broadmoor top security hospital, died 27 years into a 30-year sentence from which he had no hope of release. And last night as London's East End went into bizarre mourning for a "smashing boy and a good villain" there were growing calls for the psychopathic killer's twin brother, Reggie, to be freed.

Former smalltime hoodlum Hamilton had no regrets.

Inquest on Ronnie Kray held 'in secret'

CONTROVERSY last night surrounded a 'secret' inquest into the death of gangster Ronnie Kray.
East Berkshire coroner Robert Wilson was accused of breaching rules by failing to issue a notice of the three-minute proceedings which he held alone at his home in Waltham St Lawrence.
Mr Wilson, who defended his action last night, recorded a verdict of death by natural causes 24 hours after Kray died from a heart attack in hospital at Slough.
Members of the Coroners' Society claimed it could have been illegal because there was no jury present. The Home Office is investigating.
Kray's twin Reggie is expected to be allowed out of Maidstone prison to attend his funeral.

RONNIE KRAY dies and immediately he's hailed as a latter-day Robin Hood. Strange. I don't remember any stories of Robin burning people with red hot pokers, slicing off bits of them with a samurai sword, or shooting them dead at point blank range.

KRAY'S WHOPPER

Gang boss Reggie Kray has ordered a record-size wreath 18ft long for the grave of twin Ronnie.

Ronnie 'will get stylish funeral'

GANGLAND killer Ronnie Kray will get the stylish funeral he dreamed of, his brother vowed yesterday.

Ronnie — who died of a heart attack on Friday — hoped to go to his grave in a coach drawn by six plumed black horses.

Older brother Charlie warned that East London traffic chaos would rule this out.

But Reggie, 61, phoning from Maidstone jail, told the Daily Mirror: "If you want something badly

LAST WISH: Ron Kray

enough there's always a way to get it. Ron always wanted his coach and horses. I intend to make sure he gets his wish."

Reg also spoke to Charlie, who said later: "I've agreed to meet prison officials, undertakers and a priest to see if there's a way round the problem."

Ronnie is to be buried at Chingford, Essex.

The twins were jailed for life in 1969 after the murders of two underworld figures.

ANGUISH: Charlie Kray outside Maidstone Prison

Krays cry for Ronnie

THE Kray family held a summit in tears at Maidstone Prison yesterday after hearing of gangster Ronnie's death. Elder brother Charlie spent an hour consoling Ronnie's twin Reggie.

Reggie broke down as Charlie arrived at the jail for a specially granted compassionate visit. Afterwards Charlie said: "Reggie is very upset. But he's coping. It's not a nice place to have to cope with it. He's a man and as bad as we feel inside, we have to face up to it."

Reggie's claim

FORMER gangland boss Reggie Kray claims there is "conflicting" evidence about the cause of his twin brother Ronnie's death and believes he may have died after a struggle.

Ronnie Kray, 61, suffered a heart attack and died last Friday after being rushed to hospital from Broadmoor top security hospital.

His brother has since suggested he may have resisted a hospital test involving the insertion of a tube down his throat.

HEAVIES FOR KRAY COFFIN

A TEAM of minders have been ordered by Reg Kray to guard the coffin of his twin Ronnie.

After papers named the funeral parlour where the body of the former East London gangster is lying, it has been plagued by ghoulish callers.

Reg, who has demanded a second post-mortem, fears the corpse may be snatched. He has called on TV actor and celebrity hard-man Dave Courtney to provide a guard.

Kray death saddens villains and police alike

RONNIE KRAY, one half of Britain's best-known criminal partnership, died in hospital yesterday morning at the age of 61, two days after collapsing at Broadmoor hospital where he was serving a life sentence for murder.

Fellow villains and former detectives expressed their regrets at the death of the man who, with his twin brother Reg, became the prototype East End gangster during their brief heyday in the 1960s.

Earlier this week Kray, who was jailed for the murder of fellow gangster George Cornell at the Blind Beggar pub in 1966, was taken to Heatherwood hospital in Ascot where he was treated for anaemia and exhaustion. He had told Reg that he was suffering from a bleeding ulcer, and there were no indications that the illness was life-threatening.

After being returned to Broadmoor, he complained of feeling unwell and was taken to a specialist unit at Wexham Park hospital in Slough, where he died from a heart attack. He had previously suffered heart problems and was a very heavy smoker, smoking more than 100 cigarettes a day.

A former fellow inmate, "Mad Frankie" Fraser, said: "He was pumped full of drugs. He must have had the constitution of a horse." He added: "He was a real gentleman."

A close friend of the Kray family, Eddie Jones, said that the funeral — which will probably take place in Chingford, east London, next week — would "be as big as Kennedy's". Ron had expressed a wish for an old-fashioned funeral, complete with black-plumed horse-drawn hearse.

Reg Kray was told of the death in Maidstone prison where he is serving life for the murder of Jack "The Hat" McVitie. He was comforted in his cell by Freddie "The Mean Machine" Foreman, a former Kray henchman jailed in connection with a Security Express robbery.

The twins' older brother, Charlie, who also served time in connection with the murder of McVitie, said he was "gutted" and "in bits" at the news.

Ron's former wife, Kate Howard, said she had known that Ron was in hospital but had not realised how seriously ill he was. She was very sad to hear of his death.

Leonard "Nipper" Read, the former Scotland Yard detective who tracked the Krays down and brought them to trial for the murders of McVitie and Cornell at the Old Bailey in 1969, said he was also "saddened".

Ron Kray had been certified insane and knew he was unlikely to leave Broadmoor. Reg Kray is hoping to be released after serving the 30 years minimum recommended at his trial.

Reggie says: Farewell Ron

TEARFUL: Reggie   MOURNED: Ronnie

REGGIE Kray arrives at a funeral parlour to say farewell to twin brother Ronnie.

Reggie, who once struck fear into London's East End, looked haggard as he crossed the pavement he and his brothers once ruled to spend a last hour with Ronnie, who died from a heart attack last week.

For an hour before Reggie arrived from Maidstone jail, a squad of plain clothes policmen kept watch outside the undertaker's in Bethnal Green Road.

One said : "Were here because we'd look mugs if someone chose today to spring him." Reggie, dressed all in black and wearing glasses, arrived with an escort of five prison officers. He spent an hour with his twin, wishing him a tender "God bless you Ron" and kissing him on both cheeks.

Earlier in the day the twins' elder brother Charlie spent 15 minutes with Ronnie. But he and Reggie did not meet.

Reggie, who has been in jail since 1969, was driven back to Maidstone past the Blind Beggar pub, where Ronnie shot fellow ganster George Cornell in 1966.

But tearful Reggie just looked the other way.

BODY GUARDS FOR RONNIE

GRIEVING gangster Reggie Kray has posted bodyguards on the corpse of his killer brother Ronnie.

Jailed Reggie is worried that old enemies of his twin might want to spit on his remains ... or worse. Yesterday Ronnie was lying in an open oak coffin at a funeral parlour in his old manor of Bethnal Green, East London.

Solo verdict

MEMBERS of the Coroners' Society claim the inquest into the death of gangland killer Ronnie Kray is not valid because it was conducted in the absence of a jury by a coroner sitting alone in his own home. The "hearing" lasted less than three minutes.

MINDING THE MONARCH: Dave Courtney, front, with fellow carers

133

I'LL DANCE ON EVIL RONNIE KRAY'S GRAVE

By daughter of the villain he shot dead

1967

Doting dad Cornell with baby Rayner

1995

Rayner. . ."I hope Kray rots in hell"

THE daughter of George Cornell vowed yesterday to dance on Ronnie Kray's grave.

Rayner Cornell, 29, who was nine months old when the gang boss shot her dad, spoke out on the eve of Ronnie's funeral.

The mum of two said: "I hope he rots in hell. He was a coward and a thug and all the hero worship of him makes me sick.

"I have been celebrating ever since I heard he died. I would love to kick up my legs up and dance on his tomb."

Ronnie killed childhood pal Cornell in Whitechapel's Blind Beggar pub in 1967 after the rival gangster called him "a fat poof."

Rayner, of Bermondsey, South London, said: "I had just come out of hospital with meningitis.

"Two days before Ronnie killed my father, he sent a big basket of exotic fruit for me.

Laughed

"He knew he would be leaving me without a father. He was evil.

"*I never had a life with my dad. I never knew what it was like to be a daddy's girl.*"

Ronnie was jailed for life for Cornell's murder and was later transferred to Broadmoor.

He died of a heart attack on March 17, aged 61.

Rayner said: "I laughed so much when I

Ronnie Kray . . . heart attack

read how he cried out for his mother. It shows what a coward he was.

"At least my father died like a man.

"According to the autopsy report, his muscles didn't even tense because he knew he was going to die and accepted it."

She added: "Ronnie was a bullying vulture who terrorised the East End, killing people for nothing.

"It's sad that people look up to him."

Geordies to mourn Kray

UP TO 50 former Tyneside friends and associates of Ronnie Kray are planning to attend the funeral of the gangland killer.

The mourners, including relatives and friends of former Newcastle hardman "Mad" Frankie Kelly, were due to meet today to discuss travel arrangements for the service.

The Krays targeted Tyneside in the late 1960s as they sought to expand their empire. The bid failed but the efforts of their Tyneside rivals to resist the move earned them the respect of the notorious East End twins.

Frankie Kelly's nephew, Frankie Donnelly, 38, said: "He was the man who confronted the Krays and got them out of Tyneside. He actually manhandled Ronnie and threw him over a table. After my uncle confronted Ronnie he

● RESPECTED – Ronnie Kray

got their respect."

Mr Donnelly, who lives in Newcastle's West End, said Frankie Kelly later worked for the Krays and struck up a friendship which lasted for many years.

He said the twins were beginning to set up business links in Newcastle when they were arrested and later convicted for two gangland killings.

Mr Donnelly said Ronnie's death had sparked sadness among his former associates on Tyneside.

'Mafia' send-off

RONNIE'S funeral today will be fit for a Mafia godfather. Thousands will line the route through the East End as his coffin is carried to church in a glass coach pulled by six black horses.

Mourners led by Ronnie's twin Reg will travel in 27 limos. Gangsters expected to attend include Freddie Foreman, "Mad" Frankie Fraser, Tony Lambrianou and brothers George and Alan Dixon.

1933 RONNIE KRAY 1995

WHAT A KRAY TO GO
That was some do, Ron Ron

THOUSANDS poured onto the streets of East London yesterday to bid a final farewell to gangland legend Ronnie Kray.

Twin brother Reg, handcuffed throughout to a prison officer and surrounded by burly minders, led the entourage as a horse-drawn funeral carriage took 61-year-old Ron to his grave.

Six black horses pulled the glass sided hearse through Bethnal Green – the heart of the notorious Krays' "manor" which they ruled with a sickening combination of violence and fear. Reg, allowed out of Maidstone Jail for the day, was mobbed by well-wishers as he entered St Matthew's, Bethnal Green, for the funeral service.

In a symbolic gesture, Ron's coffin was carried into the church by former rival gang members. During the service Reggie was supported by his brother Charlie.

The first song played at the service was Frank Sinatra's My Way, a favourite of Ronnie's.

Hundreds packed into the church, hundreds more waited outside and over 7,000 lined the route from there to Chingford Cemetery where Ron took his place near his parents, Violet and Charles.

Reg paid homage to his brother who died 12 days ago from a heart attack: "He did it all his way but above all he was a man."

★ Cartoon – Page 8

FAREWELL: Reggie follows the coffin into the church

TRIBUTE: One of the many wreaths

West goes quietly

MASS murderer Fred West was cremated yesterday at a simple service. There were no hymns at Canley Crematorium, Coventry, where the Rev Robert Simpson, of St Mary's, Newent, Glos, held the service. The body of West, 53, who was found hanged in his prison cell after being accused of 12 murders, was handed to son Stephen and daughter Mae on Monday.

HECTOR BREEZE

"Nice little business you've got here. Pity to see it go up in flames"

Reggie Cry

Ronnie . . . 50,000 paid respects

KRAY TWIN'S ANGUISH AS EAST END BURIES RONNIE

By MIKE SULLIVAN and JOHN TROUP

GANGSTER Reggie Kray cried like a child yesterday after seeing his twin Ronnie buried.

Reggie, 61 — handcuffed to a prison officer — was comforted by elder brother Charlie, 67.

The emotional scene came at an East London cemetery after an extraordinary send-off for Ronnie, who died of a heart attack on March 17.

Around 50,000 people, including dozens of underworld villains, packed the streets to watch a 13-mile funeral procession through the Krays' East London "manor."

A floral tribute from Reggie to his brother read: "To the other half of me."

Overcome . . . Reggie, right, is comforted by brother Charlie yesterday   Picture: JIMMY GRAY

Certain appeal in the Krays

I'M more than a little bored of the high and mighty moral stance taken by some of the Chronicle's rivals over the hoo-ha surrounding Ronnie Kray's funeral.

For the same papers who claimed Ronnie was best buried and forgotten devoted page after page of picture specials on the funeral. I don't question their news sense, I'm as fascinated by the Krays as anyone, but I do question their commitment to their morals. It's time for folk to admit that,

rightly or wrongly, this gangland family has a certain appeal which is based on the black suits, slicked back hair, and dark glasses which could come straight out of a Quentin Tarrantino movie. And as this paper said on Friday, you can guarantee the Kray merchandising machine is well and truly oiled for a resurgence of interest in the wake of Ronnie's death.

So while no-one should mourn his death, let's stop pretending Ronnie and Reg don't hold a certain fascination.

Reggie Kray pauses by the grave of his wife, Frances, after the burial of his brother, Ronnie

Crocodile tears carry Kray away

Tears of the hard men . . .

● GRIEVING Reggie Kray *(right)* is comforted by his brother Charlie as they say their final farewell to brother Ronnie, who was buried yesterday.

★ Full story – Page 2

KRAY'S EAST END

Crowds line the streets to say farewell to Ronnie

MORE than a thousand East Enders saluted the funeral procession of gangland killer Ronnie Kray today.

Ronnie's coffin is carried into the church to the strains of Frank Sinatra's song, My Way

EMPTY MEMORIES: The frame left by the thief

Bravest crook in Britain

HE ROBS RONNIE'S GRAVE

THE bravest crook in Britain was in hiding last night with his loot – a portrait of Ronnie Kray snatched from the gangster's grave.

The ghoulish grave-robber clambered over padlocked gates hours after Wednesday's funeral and stole a colour picture of Ronnie and twin Reggie.

Now the hardmen who guard the Kray legend are looking for the treasured memento.

And Ronnie's ex-wife Kate, 33, said at her home in Headcorn, Kent: "It is an absolutely diabolical thing to do.

"Why can't people just leave things like this alone?"

Gangland killer Ronnie, who died of a heart attack aged 61, is buried at Chingford Mount cemetery in East London.

Tributes

The picture was the centrepiece of a mountain of floral tributes at his grave.

The raider left the gold and white frame bearing the words, "Misunderstood, but simply the best."

Also stolen was a pair of miniature boxing gloves which had been left with the dozens of wreaths.

Nearby graves were destroyed by the crush of onlookers at the funeral.

Yesterday hundreds

NICKED: The picture

filed past Ronnie's grave.

One man travelled 200 miles to see the shrine. Pensioner Bill Reilly said: "They're thieving b****** these days.

"There's no respect for anything.

"I bet it was never like that when the Krays were in charge."

The Kray family are understood to be paying a minder £50 a week to keep watch on the family plot where the twins' parents and Reggie's wife Frances are also buried.

WATCHING OVER RONNIE: Minder Dave is keeping a vigil at the cemetery

Guard for Kray's grave

A BURLY minder is keeping watch over Ronnie Kray – to stop souvenir hunters robbing the gangster's grave.

Security firm boss Dave Courtney was called in after getting a phone call from Ronnie's twin, Reggie, who is in Maidstone jail.

Reggie was furious when he heard that thieves had stolen a portrait of the brothers which was included in a floral tribute from his cousin Rita.

The picture, which had been paraded on the leading limousine at Wednesday's funeral, was ripped from its frame of gold-sprayed flowers.

Wreaths, including one shaped like a boxing glove, have also been taken from Ronnie's grave in Chingford Cemetery, East London.

Shaven-headed Dave, who was wearing a pair of knuckle-dusters said his night vigil would go on for as long as Reggie wanted.

But he is having to do the graveyard shift alone as the rest of the team of minders on his payroll don't like the idea of staying in a cemetery at night alone.

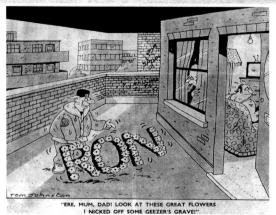

"'ERE, MUM, DAD! LOOK AT THESE GREAT FLOWERS I NICKED OFF SOME GEEZER'S GRAVE!"

Kray foils taxman over secret cash

by Maurice Chittenden

RONNIE KRAY, the East End gangster who died last week, has left behind an unsolved mystery. He and Reggie, his twin, were under investigation by the Inland Revenue over a nice little earner: the fortune their names have generated during their time inside.

The convicted murderer will go to his grave in a gangland funeral at Chingford, Essex, with the secret of what happened to the estimated £1m he made from film deals, book royalties and "Kray-endorsed" merchandise such as T-shirts, postcards and calendars while he was in prison and in Broadmoor hospital.

Friends insist Ronnie gave much of it away to good causes. However, there was no death-bed bequest to Comic Relief and, apart from the occasional gesture to buy a blind boy a computer or auction an autographed book to help a child suffering from muscular dystrophy, no resounding gratitude from charities.

The twins shared £370,000 from a film of their lives, starring Martin and Gary Kemp from Spandau Ballet, and were due to benefit from a sequel. There was more cash from the sale of records featuring taped conversations with the Krays and portfolios of photographs which sold for £250 a time.

However, according to Colin Fry, who wrote the appropriately-titled Doing the Business with the twins' older brother Charlie, Ronnie Kray gave away most of his money and only kept back enough to spend on a world cruise in the unlikely event that he was ever released.

Charlie Kray, who oversaw the cottage industry surrounding the twins, visited his surviving brother Reggie in Maidstone prison, Kent, yesterday. Reggie Kray has been given sedatives to calm him since he learned of his brother's death from a fellow inmate on Friday. "I think half of Reggie died with Ronnie," said the older Kray after a 90-minute visit.

The Kray industry was launched 10 years ago, ostensibly to campaign for the release of the twins. A T-shirt featured a David Bailey photograph of the twins under an EastEnders logo hijacked from the BBC soap opera and the words Steps to Freedom. However, the commercial side of the campaign was such a success that it attracted former gang members, former cellmates and hangers-on all looking for some of the action.

It is likely that the campaign will now concentrate on parole for Reggie Kray, who has served 26 years of a life sentence for murder. Certainly sales will continue. A new disco-style song called It's A Rap, featuring the voices of the twins, is being hawked around record companies.

"Mad" Frankie Fraser, a member of the Richardson gang which vied with the Krays for underworld control in the 1960s, said yesterday: "Ron Kray was always a soft touch and got bundles of begging letters. I think his wealth has been overplayed."

The taxman is not so sure. The Inland Revenue said: "If people have incomes, there is a tax liability. But we can't discuss individual cases. Even Ron and Reg are entitled to privacy in their tax affairs."

The irony was not lost on John Pearson, author of The Profession of Violence, the first authorised biography of the twins: "Ron was into gangster literature and was a fan of Al Capone. He used to have his barber come round to his home each morning to give him a shave just like he had seen Chicago gangsters have it done in the movies.

"Of course, it was the taxman that got Al Capone in the end; that's how they always get gangsters."

THIEF RETURNS RON'S PORTRAIT

THE thief who stole the portrait of Ronnie Kray from his grave has returned it secretly to the East End undertaker who buried him.

Ronnie's brother, Reggie, also in the portrait, is said to be delighted.

☆ THE nauseating spectacle of Ronnie Kray's funeral reminded me of a remark attributed to the great Arthur Mullard.

After hearing someone spout the usual sentimental twaddle about how the Krays only hurt their own, Arfur (allegedly) replied: "Yus. 'uman beings."

Docs have pickled Ron Kray brain

THE brain of gang boss Ronnie Kray was secretly removed from his body on Home Office orders. It is now undergoing medical tests as scientists try to find what made the murdering madman tick. But Ron's horrified widow Kate wants his brain and body reunited. "I've half a mind to sue," she stormed.

Ronnie's ex is so broke

THE ex-wife of gangland villain Ronnie Kray, who died last week, faces bankruptcy.

Kate Kray has had an order made against her by Maidstone, Kent, county court. The one-time strip-o-gram girl wed Kray after visiting him in Broadmoor. They divorced last year.

A Kray-zy legacy

RONNIE Kray's brain is missing. It should be under Jack the Hat.

'If the Krayfish were still around, we wouldn't have all this trouble'

GHOULS SNORTED COKE OFF RONNIE KRAY'S COFFIN

REGGIE: Planning action

COURTNEY: Security boss

SICK jokers snorted lines of cocaine off Ronnie Kray's half-open coffin, his twin brother Reggie has been told.

The ghouls also set up a ouija board next to Ronnie's casket and tried to contact his spirit.

Next, they put a Sony Walkman on the gangland overlord's body and cackled with laughter as one drugged yob said: "Don't he look stupid with the 'eadphones on."

Seething with rage inside Maidstone jail, Reg Kray said last night: "I'm not happy."

He had heard that staff at English's funeral parlour in London's Bethnal Green discovered tell-tale smudges on Ronnie's highly-polished oak coffin.

They also found pieces of paper with letters scribbled on them used

Angry Reg calls family summit over outrage

EXCLUSIVE   By GARY JONES, Chief Crime Reporter

for the ouija session. Former crime king Reggie has now summoned his brother Charlie to Maidstone prison so they can discuss what action to take.

The first person they will want to interview is 36-year-old David Courtney. He was hired to arrange security for the giant funeral which stretched through the East End last month.

Reggie will want him to explain if there was any lapse in the watertight cordon he promised.

Shaven-headed Courtney has a string of convictions—including jail for attacking five Chinese waiters with a meat cleaver. Speaking exclusively to the News of the World, 61-year-old Reggie said: "I've heard some stories . . . and I'm disgusted."

A pal of the ex-gangster added: "He's bloody furious. He can't believe anything like this could have happened.

"There's going to be

repercussions. Make no mistake." Alan Jackson, manager of English's funeral parlour, said: "This is the first I've heard of this. If anything did happen it was without our knowledge."

Ronnie died last month while serving a 30-year sentence in Broadmoor for the murder of George Cornell.

Reggie has been told he must serve his full sen-

tence for killing Jack 'The Hat' McVitie and will not be released before 1998.

Last week he told the News of the World: "When I looked at Ronnie lying there in the Chapel of Rest, I felt somehow comforted. He'd have been overjoyed with the funeral. It was so dignified and respectful."

Anyone who disturbed that dignity may now be a little uneasy.

"It's for that poor geezer who nicked the Kray Brothers photo."

■ **I'M writing to complain about the picture of Ronnie Kray in his coffin last week. How can you justify such a tasteless picture?**
D. MILTON, Devon

SECRET KRAY INQUEST WAS AGAINST LAW

KRAY No.2 GETS PICKLED

NOW both killer Kray twins have had their brains pickled—and mobster Reggie's still alive!

The feared ex-gangland boss got out of his head having a jar or two with pals behind bars—just three weeks after the News of the World revealed how his dead brother Ronnie's grey cells had been preserved for scientific research.

Reggie and three visiting chums made such a noise getting Krayzed on vodka in Maidstone Prison, Kent, that the guards got suspicious. An insider said: "The

lads were so rowdy they were their own worst enemies. Someone was bound to twig what was going on.

"In the end the booze was confiscated and Kray's cronies got booted out."

As punishment Reggie was given a suspended sentence to serve an extra **DAY** in the nick. Not that he will worry—he's doing *life* for murdering Jack "the Hat" McVitie!

Galaxy of stars turn out for Reg's charity party!

Wright little earner to aid sick kid

BY DAVE KEEN

A GALAXY of stars are set to attend an East End charity bash this Saturday organised by Reg Kray.

Top entertainer Shane Ritchie will be the evening's compere and other celebrities at the party will include Arsenal striker Ian Wright.

Former gangland boss Reg Kray, 61, has set up the party in his old East End manor with the help of pal Bradley Alladyce who is caged at Whitemoor Prison, Cambridgeshire.

They aim to raise cash for an eight-year-old boy who suffers from Muscular Dystrophy.

Reg said he wants the young lad, who lives in Nottingham, to "have a better lifestyle."

Stars of hit telly programmes including Eastenders and London's Burning are also expected to attend the event at The Guv'ners in Cleveland Way, Stepney.

Reg's elder brother, Charlie, 67, will host the star-studded party. Other expected guests include top model Debbie Ashbee, Britain's first Page Three model Flanagan, and Minder star Ray Winstone.

Also expected at the party are actor Steve McFadden and Liverpool and Wales striker Ian Rush.

And a number of Page Three girls and Page Seven fellas will be in the crowd of up to 300 party-goers.

East Enders are invited to the £15-a-head bash, but tickets are selling quickly.

On the night, from 8.30pm until late, there will be live entertainment, a raffle, free buffet, and an auction of celebrity items.

These include a pair of gold boxing gloves signed by Reg and Charlie Kray, exclusive drawings by Reg, a firefighter's helmet signed by the cast of London's Burning and Dire Straits CDs signed by Mark Knopfler.

Also up for auction will be a signed book by former boxing champ the Welsh Wizard Howard Winstone, footballs signed by the Arsenal and West Ham team and a holiday for two donated by The Guv'ners Bar.

Twins George and Andrew Wadman, 24, of the Guv'ners, are regular visitors to Reg in Maidstone Prison, Kent.

They hosted the wake after Ron Kray's funeral a fortnight ago.

Of course, the man who set up the evening, Reg Kray, will be unable to attend as he is now in the 27th year of his sentence for a gangland killing. You can turn up on the night, but to book a ticket in advance call The Guv'ners on 0171-702 8656. Dress smart but casual.

Leslie keeps vigil at Ron's graveside

AN old "acquaintance" of the Krays is keeping vigil at Ron's grave at Chingford Mount Cemetery.

Leslie Martin, 52, and his son David, 24, are guarding the grave, with its many wreaths, to deter looters.

Two weeks ago a portrait of the Kray Twins was stolen from the grave. It was later pushed through the letter box of the funeral parlour W English & Son in Bethnal Green Road, Bethnal Green.

Leslie is trying to go to the grave every day to prevent further thefts. He said: "I am doing it out of respect for the Colonel."

He said he will probably carry on the vigil until the end of the month.

Leslie, who now lives in South London, said hundreds of people have been to the grave since the funeral procession that brought parts of the East End to a standstill.

GRIFFIN'S EYE

"He used to be an East End florist until he made a killing on the Kray funeral."

KRAY-DLE SNATCHER

Gangster Reggie's amazing jail bond with a besotted blonde schoolgirl

Reggie . . . 'a true friend'

EXCLUSIVE

By JOHN TROUP

REGGIE Kray gets regular jail visits from a besotted schoolgirl young enough to be his grand-daughter.

A-level student Sophie Williams, 19, hero-worships the 62-year-old gangland killer.

Every month, she makes the 240-mile round trip from her Cotswold village home to Maidstone prison, where Reggie is in the 27th year of a life sentence. They write to each other once a week.

Pretty blonde Sophie – pictured on her way to post a letter to the former East End gang boss – said: "He is the most wonderful man I have ever met. He is a true friend and I try to be one to him.

"It is so cruel to keep him locked away, especially now his twin Ronnie has died."

Sophie, of Milton-under-Wychwood, Oxfordshire, first wrote to Reggie three years ago after reading his autobiography Born Fighter. Her parents know of her visits.

She said: "The train trips cost quite a lot, but Reg is worth it. I think we're good for each other.

"I know he did things that were wrong but he has been punished enough. It would be unthinkable if he died inside like Ronnie."

Reggie was jailed in 1969 for stabbing to death rival gangster Jack "The Hat" McVitie.

Ronnie was also ordered to serve a minimum 30 years for the murders of McVitie and George Cornell. He died after a heart attack in Broadmoor six weeks ago.

A warder at Maidstone told how Sophie sits with East End pals of Reg in the jail visiting room.

Dainty

He said: "It's very strange to see her with all these Cockney wideboys, waiting for Reg to walk in.

"She seems in awe of him. She is very dainty and sits bolt upright, hanging on his every word.

"Reg thinks the world of her and often runs to get her glasses of orange juice or coffee. But when we chat to her, she says very little. She's like a little mouse."

Locals in Sophie's village were stunned to learn of her friendship. One said: "It's not healthy. I'm surprised her parents allow it."

Reggie was unavailable for comment yesterday.

Sophie's picture by NIGEL CAIRNS

Reg Kray pays tribute with 6ft high message to nephew Gary

A kaleidoscope of colour from the many wreaths and oasis from relatives and friends and inset Gary Kray

HE may not have been there in person, but Reg Kray's presence was certainly felt when nephew Gary Kray was laid to rest on Thursday.

The jailed gangland boss, refused day release for the burial by the Home Office, was conspicuous by his absence.

He sent an empty funeral car, reserved two seats at Bethnal Green's St Matthew's Church - for him and his detective - had a taped message played at the service and sent a huge floral tribute as a mark of respect for brother Charlie's son, who died aged 44 after losing his battle against cancer earlier this month.

The 6ft high message, made up of white carnations and red roses, read: "Though not present, I am with you in spirit... God bless, Reg."

The funeral procession left W. English & Son undertakers, in Bethnal Green Road, and travelled a few hundred yards to St Matthew's Church, St Matthew's

BY LEE SERVIS

Row, before leaving for Chingford Mount Cemetery, where Gary was buried close to his nan and grandad, Violet and Charlie, and uncle Ron.

Charlie, the older brother of twins Reg and Ron, said: "The occasion was sad, but it went beautifully.

"The service was fantastic and the funeral directors were magnificent. I would like to thank everyone who attended and sent messages... Gary would have been very proud."

■ Reg Kray has just released a video in tribute to his dead twin Ron.

The film - The Epilogue of Ron Kray - gives a rare insight into Reg's memories of his brother, who died of a heart attack a year ago.

The gangland boss shares his memories of Ron and his recollections of the funeral.

The video is available from major outlets from Friday, price £13.99.

Ex-gangster Freddie Foreman admits the murder of two East End villains

'I killed Ginger Marks'

Freddie Foreman tells all in a new book

EX-GANGSTER Freddie Fore-man has confessed he carried out two underworld killings which have remained unsolved for 30 years.

He has admitted murdering Frank 'Mad Axeman' Mitchell as a favour to the Kray Twins and shooting dead Tommy 'Ginger' Marks in a revenge attack in Bethnal Green.

And he claims to solve the mystery of the final resting places of Mitchell, Marks and Jack 'The Hat' McVitie who was knifed to death by Reg Kray.

He dismisses long-standing rumours that the underworld murder victims were buried in the cement of a flyover or at a remote farm. Instead Foreman says they were weighed down and buried at sea.

He enlisted the help of some fishermen who had been involved in smuggling operations.

Foreman tells how McVitie's body was disposed of: "We had a friend on the coast who wrapped him - McVitie - up in chicken wire attached to weights.

As with Ginger Marks and Frank 'The Mad Axeman' Mitchell, Jack The Hat was buried far out at sea...

"We had been told by American contacts that bodies weighted down in this way would never find their way to the surface but would slowly be disposed of by crabs and other deep-sea dwellers. Many people prefer burial at sea.

"I was protecting the Twins. The rule of thumb was, where there is no

Killed for a favour: Mad Axeman Frank Mitchell

body, there is no evidence and therefore no conviction."

Foreman, who grew up in Sheep-cote Lane in Stepney, was jailed for 10 years for his part in disposing of the body of McVitie.

He writes in his new autobiography: "I got rid of the body for two reasons. One: because it has been put on my doorstep and threatened my own safety and secondly: as a favour to the Krays."

Foreman, 64, in his new autobiography, Respect, shows why he inspired fear in gangland Britain - "don't mess with brown bread Fred or you're dead" was the ominous warning.

He claims the killing of Ginger Marks with a "hail of bullets" in Bethnal Green Road, Bethnal Green, on January 2, 1965, was a revenge attack.

According to Foreman, Marks was

BY DAVE KEEN

an accomplice with George Evans in the shooting of Freddie's brother George at point blank range with a shotgun over an affair he was having with Evans' wife.

In 1965 Evans was acquitted of shooting Freddie Foreman's brother.

And Foreman also tries to justify the killing of Mitchell who had been sprang from jail so that he could campaign for his release from prison!

He writes that the Kray twins "had organised his escape from Dartmoor and came to regret their action almost immediately.

"To unleash him on the public was as irresponsible as taking the muzzle off a crazed rottweiler and letting it loose in a playschool. He was a backward, disturbed child living in a man's body of almost superhuman strength."

Foreman, the self-proclaimed Managing Director of British Crime, writes: "I took part in his killing as a favour to the Twins."

Now Foreman claims he is retired from his criminal career. During the 1980s he was jailed for his part in the £7million Security Express robbery in 1983 after being deported from Spain.

Foreman's actor son Jamie lives in the East End with his actress wife Carol Harrison.

■ Respect, Managing Director of British Crime, Freddie Foreman, with John Lisners, Century, £15.99.

Above: Although the press jumped upon revelations in Freddie's autobiography about how the body of Jack The Hat had been disposed of it was actually Reg himself who first spoke about it in a book several years previously.

REGGIE KRAY LET OUT FOR CANCER TEST

Hospital dash drama

Kray denies claims he is unstable

Gangland killer Reggie Kray today issued a public statement from his Maidstone prison cell to counter a whispering campaign by enemies of the former East End crime boss.

In a statement to a national newspaper Kray said he believes he is the target of a campaign to stop him ever being freed from a life sentence.

In a letter Kray denied claims that he was terminally ill and dismissed a story that a besotted girl visited him.

Kray also rubbished rumours of a gay affair and denounced an allegation that he was due for imminent release.

The 63-year-old gangster, jailed in 1969, also derided recent claims that he paraded on the exercise field dressed in a Red Indian headband.

"This infers that I am unstable and that I am the butt of a joke here at Maidstone jail," Kray complains.

"People from all walks of life have enemies as well as friends, for whatever reason, be it jealousy, envy, scorn, whatever, and I am no different."

Reggie Kray and twin brother Ronnie were once Britain's most feared gangsters. Each was sentenced to at least 30 years in 1969.

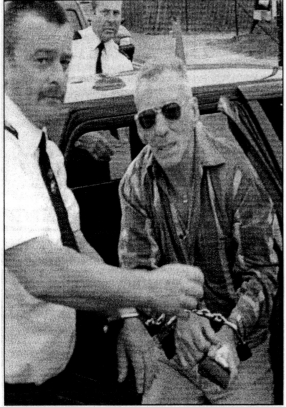

SCARE: Handcuffed to a prison officer, Kray arrives at hospital yesterday

Cancer denied by Kray

Convicted gangster Reggie Kray, who is serving a 30-year sentence in Maidstone Prison, has quashed speculation that he is suffering from stomach cancer by declaring that he is "A1" fit.

A trip to hospital last week was for tests on a "calcium build-up" and showed he was fit and healthy, he said in a statement through a friend.

Kray, whose twin and partner in crime Ronnie died last year, said he had received hundreds of get well cards and messages after being pictured arriving at Maidstone General Hospital.

Kray was jailed for 30 years for the murder of Jack "The Hat" McVitie.

GANGLAND killer Reggie Kray was dramatically rushed to hospital from jail yesterday amid fears that he has cancer.

Kray, 62, was driven the four miles from Maidstone Prison in Kent to Maidstone General Hospital.

Jail officials would not discuss his illness, but there were fears that he has a stomach tumour.

Murder

A prison insider said: "He has not been feeling too well for some time." The Kray twins, jailed at the Old Bailey in 1969, terrorised London's East End in the 1960s.

Reggie was given 30 years for the murder of Jack "The Hat" McVitie.

It was the first time he has been outside the prison since his brother Ronnie's funeral in March last year.

Handcuffed to a prison officer, Kray was driven to hospital in a blue Peugeot 405 estate car.

He chatted to his two burly guards and was helped from the car at the hospital.

Keep-fit fanatic Kray, wearing a maroon and blue striped shirt and jeans, said nothing when asked by a reporter how he felt.

A jail spokesman said he had been taken to hospital for "something that could not be dealt with at the prison."

The spokesman added: "I am unable to say what he is being treated for. However, I understand it possibly involves a scan."

He could not say how long Kray would be in the hospital.

Maidstone Hospital said they could not discuss Kray's condition.

KRAY PAL IS NICKED

STARS' minder Dave Courtney has been arrested at Heathrow airport after customs officers seized £500,000-worth of cocaine.

The 6ft-tall bouncer was one of five men held on Friday after eight kilos of the drug were found in the bags of a passenger from Spain.

Courtney, 38, of Woolwich, a friend of the Kray family, was kept overnight in cells at Twickenham.

He played a mobster in The Krays movie and hires villains for ITV's The Bill.

'Kray' pub gang held

POLICE yesterday smashed a Kray-style gang said to have run a £1million pub protection racket.

Twelve people were held after a dawn swoop – ten in connection with extortion and two over drug dealing.

The gang is said to have muscled in on pubs in the Westminster area.

Friends gather at Ron's graveside

Graveside flypast on the Twins' birthday

PALS of the Kray Twins gathered at Chingford Mount Cemetery last Thursday to pay their respects on Reg Kray's 63rd birthday.

And there was a flypast over the cemetery, where Ron Kray is buried, by two light planes.

One unfurled a banner which read: "Ronald Kray never to be forgotten 1933-1996."

The words in memory of his twin brother were chosen by Reg Kray who is caged at Maidstone Prison.

Pals at the cemetery included former Miss United Kingdom and Miss Great Britain Eileen Sheridan-Price.

Ron Kray was buried at the Kray family plot in the cemetery in April last year.

Also last Thursday a Kray Twins Internet site was launched to provide information on the notorious twins who ruled the East End underworld during the 1950s and 1960s.

Reg was sentenced to life imprisonment in March 1969 for the murder of Jack 'the Hat' McVitie at a flat in Hackney.

His bid for release will not be looked at by his Parole Board until December 1997.

REG: Indian obsession

I'M REG KRAYS-E HORSE!

GANGSTER Reggie Kray has turned his jail cell into a shrine to Red Indians and wants to become a tribal chief.

The former East End crime boss even parades around in a coloured head-dress.

He has such a big collection of bone chest plates, peace pipes, and other Indian memorabilia his cell is full up.

One warder quipped: "Reggie is now known as Krays-e Horse."

Reggie, 63—serving life for his part in the murder of Jack "The Hat" McVitie—entertains other inmates with stories of the Cheyenne River Sioux tribe.

But the crook, whose twin Ronnie died last year, has become the butt of jokes at Maidstone Prison, Kent.

A source said: "They have renamed the jail HM tee-Pee Maidstone.

"And officers threatened to withdraw his phone cards and replace them with a fire and blankets for smoke signals."

KRAY-ZY PRICE

A Christmas card from the Kray twins fetched £77 at a Nottingham sale yesterday — twice as much as a bikini worn by sexy Avengers actress Honor Blackman.

Best man Reg

REG Kray was the best man at a wedding inside Maidstone Prison last Thursday.

He did the honours at the wedding of his pal Bradley Allardyce, 25, to Donna Bates at the chapel within the jail walls.

RONALD KRAY - LEGEND

IN MEMORY OF RON

KRAY WIFE GETS HIS BRAIN BACK

GANGSTER Ronnie Kray's brain has been sent home after his furious widow protested about it being pickled for research.

Doctors removed it without the family's knowledge after murderer Ronnie, 61 — serving 30 years in Broadmoor — died of a heart attack last year. Widow Kate, 39, found out about the research last week.

By CHARLES YATES

She stormed: "After 27 years locked up I thought death had freed him. But I'm outraged there's still part of him imprisoned in a jar."

Ronnie's grey matter, which weighed 2½lb (1.2kg) was taken to Oxford for investigation into criminal behaviour.

Last night an official at Heatherwood Hospital, where Ronnie was pronounced dead, said: "I understand it has been returned."

Ronnie . . . bonce in a bottle

BAN ON REGGIE KRAY'S VIDEO TRIBUTE TO RON

By ALISON BOSHOFF, Showbusiness Reporter

A VIDEO tribute by gang boss Reggie Kray to his dead twin Ron has been banned by W H Smith because it "glorifies" violent crime.

The tape includes footage of Ronnie lying in his coffin after his death at Broadmoor secure hospital a year ago. Reggie, 62, illicitly recorded loving family memories in his cell at Maidstone jail, where he is serving life for murder.

He says: "Ron was not a bad man, he was a good brother.

"He had a terrible temper but he was kind to me and had a wonderful sense of humour." The 55-minute

EXCLUSIVE

tape also shows Ron's massive East End funeral.

W H Smith is refusing to stock it. A spokesman said: "This is about a man who had a more than criminal record."

Reggie . . . illicit tapes

Reg snubs move to cushy jail

EXCLUSIVE by JEFF EDWARDS

GANGSTER Reggie Kray has rejected a move to a cushier jail so he can stay with an armed robber pal.

The feared East End hardman could have paved the way for his eventual release with the transfer.

But Kray, 63, has become close friends with jailed Bradley Allerdyce, 28, at high-security Maidstone prison in Kent.

A member of staff said: "We were astonished but he has made it clear he does not want to be without Bradley." Jail

STAYING: Reg Kray

bosses wanted to move Kray to lower-security Wayland prison in Norfolk — and even offered to transfer Allerdyce there later. But Kray said no.

He will remain a high-security, category B prisoner.

The mobster has hit out at rumours of a gay relationship with Allerdyce, who is serving 12 years.

He said: "I am not gay and nor is he."

Kray got 30 years for murdering fellow villain Jack "The Hat" McVitie.

THE £80M STING

Charlie Kray is held after cops in probe were offered cocaine deal

Held in cops' dramatic swoop . . . pallbearer Charlie Kray at funeral of younger brother Ronnie

Gutted . . brother Reggie   Hardman . . dead Ronnie

THE Kray twins' brother Charlie was arrested after cops posing as drug pushers were offered £80million-worth of cocaine, it was revealed last night.

The undercover police infiltrated a huge smuggling ring during an 11-week operation fraught with danger.

They met a Mr Big who allegedly promised to supply them with five kilos of cocaine every week for the next two years.

Stormed

The sting reached its dramatic climax soon after the cops handed over £62,000 at a hotel in exchange for their first batch.

Two men were arrested. And at the same time officers stormed 70-year-old Kray's home in Crystal Palace, South London.

The former gangster – elder brother of notorious hard-man twins Reggie and Ronnie – was arrested as he watched TV.

Last night he was still being held at Ilford police station, East London. He insists he is innocent

EXCLUSIVE by MIKE SULLIVAN
Crime Reporter

and that the wrong man has been nicked.

The police operation began in May when the undercover officers were offered the cocaine by a man suspected of being a big-time dealer.

They taped their conversation with him using hidden recorders – and pinpointed key suspects for surveillance.

A further series of meetings took place at hotels and car parks. The alleged dealer set up a supply network – and introduced the cops to two Cockney associates.

A test "drop" was arranged for Wednesday night at a quiet hotel in Waltham Abbey, Essex.

The two associates, one in his 40s and the other in his 50s, met the cops over a drink in the foyer at 6.30pm.

Police chiefs claim the officers were given two kilos of top-quality cocaine in exchange for £62,000 in cash.

Parcels were exchanged under a table out of view of guests and visiting drinkers. After the swop, armed police set up a "tail"

which led around the M25 to the Lakeside service station at Thurrock.

Cash and drugs were seized in a swoop as two suspects filled up with petrol.

Another team of officers simultaneously stormed Kray's home.

He was arrested in front of his live-in girlfriend Judy Stanley, 39. The house was searched but no drugs were found.

The sting was carried out by the North-East London Serious Crime Squad as part of the Met's Operation Crackdown on drugs.

Team leader Det Supt Gavin Robertson said conversations between the suspects and the cops had been "corroborated."

Supply

But he added: "It would be inappropriate to name any of the men in custody at this stage."

The three involved have been arrested for conspiracy to supply 522kgs of cocaine with an estimated value of £80million.

Mr Robertson warned drug dealers to take note of the operation. He said: "Unless you have the brains of a rocking horse, pack it in or we'll get you."

Kray was a pallbearer at last year's funeral of brother Ronnie, who died of a heart attack in Broadmoor aged 61.

An underworld source said surviving twin Reggie, 62, who is in Maidstone prison, was "gutted" at Charlie's arrest.

Former Kray henchman Tony Lambrianou was also stunned.

Lambrianou, 53 – who earns a living making "celebrity" appearances with Charlie, added: "Drugs has never been his scene and he doesn't need to get involved. He earns enough from after-dinner speeches."

Kray's neighbours described him as a "perfect gent."

Pensioner Rae Thompson said: "Last week he got out of his car and held up traffic so I could cross the road with my shopping."

'HE'D NEVER PUSH DRUGS'

By KATHRYN LISTER

CHARLIE Kray's lover Judy Stanley last night said he "hated" drugs and would never peddle them.

She added: "Someone has thrown his name into the hat because of who he is. He is no stranger to all this but he's 70 now and doesn't need the hassle."

Blonde Judy, 39, spoke at the shabby semi she shares with Kray in Crystal Palace, South London, after making a vain attempt to see him at Ilford police station. Detectives turned her away, but she managed

to hand over a bag of clean clothes and toiletries. She said: "Charlie is fine and very calm. He has got nothing to worry about."

A friend at the house said: "Charlie and his brothers have always been fiercely anti-drugs.

"Ronnie even hated taking medication for his schizophrenia in prison because of his views."

KRAY-ZY MUSICAL CHAIRS

THE Home Office is to spend £200,000 on prison furniture to keep Reggie Kray and his cronies firmly in their place.

On visiting days up to a dozen of Kray's pals draw up seats around his table—despite a ruling that each prisoner is allowed only three visitors.

Kray, serving life for the murder of Jack 'The Hat' McVitie, bucks the system by bribing other prisoners with phone cards.

Now new chairs are to be bought for the maximum-security jail, in Maidstone, Kent . . . and they will be screwed to the floor.

"This is all because the prison hasn't got the bottle to tell Kray to stop his scam," a source said.

"It's sickening what he gets away with. He was even getting officers to move tables so his mates could be more together."

147

Relaxed . . . Charlie Kray

Kray gives a kiss to his miss

By JOHN TROUP

CHEERFUL Charlie Kray blew a kiss to his girlfriend yesterday as he appeared in court charged with a £78million cocaine plot.

The 70-year-old brother of Kray twins Reggie and Ronnie was relaxed throughout the 30-minute hearing.

Smartly-dressed in a navy suit, he smiled and winked at lover Judy Stanley, 45.

And he blew her the kiss when he was led away after being remanded in custody.

Kray, who lives with Judy in Sanderstead, South London, is accused of plotting to supply drugs with builder Ronald Field, 49, and electrician Robert Gould, 39.

At first JPs in Redbridge, East London, remanded the trio for 28 days. But after learning they had exceeded their powers, they reduced the period to six days.

Charlie Kray in jail heart scare

CHARLIE Kray has suffered a heart attack in jail.

Kray, 70—elder brother of gangster twins Reggie and Ronnie—collapsed during an exercise walk at top-security Belmarsh prison in South London.

Witnesses said he keeled over and his face contorted with agony.

Kray is on remand accused of taking part in an alleged £78 million drug ring.

He has had phone calls and letters from brother Reggie, 61, in Maidstone jail. Ronnie died last year in Broadmoor top-security hospital.

JAIL: Charlie Kray

KRAY IN COURT ON DRUGS RAP

THE elder brother of gangster twins Reggie and Ronnie Kray appeared in court yesterday accused of drug pushing.

Charlie Kray, 70, was charged with conspiring to supply £78 million of cocaine. He is also accused of supplying 4½lbs of cocaine worth £300,000. Two other men charged with him were builder Ronald Field, 49, and electrician Robert Gould, 39, of Wimbledon, south London. Field, of Raynes Park, and Kray, of Sanderstead, Surrey, are also accused of conspiring to supply 1,000 Ecstasy tablets worth £20,000.

They were all remanded in custody by JPs in Redbridge, east London.

Kray stays locked up

CHARLIE Kray was remanded in custody yesterday on £80 million drug charges.

The brother of gangster twins Reggie and Ronnie blew girlfriend Judy Stanley a kiss as he was taken down to the cells at Redbridge Magistrates Court, East London.

Kray, 70, of Sanderstead, Surrey, is charged with conspiring to supply cocaine worth £78 million.

May release plan as Reg is moved

Earlier this year Reg Kray (above) said he didn't want to leave Maidstone Prison because of his friendship with Bradley Allardyce (pictured below)

FORMER East End gangster Reg Kray has move to a lower security prison - and it could signal his release from jail next May.

Both Reg and his supporters are happy with his move from the Category B prison in Maidstone to the more relaxed Category C conditions of Wayland prison in Norfolk.

Earlier this year, Reg, 63, had said he wanted to stay at Maidstone because of his friendship with prison pal Bradley Allardyce.

He also married wife Roberta in a ceremony at the jail in July and she moved into a home nearby.

But supporters believe the move is an necessary step towards release, which Kray would be eligible for in May next year.

BY CHRIS TAYLOR

Kray is coming to the end of a recommended 30 year minimum sentence for the murder of rival gangster Jack The Hat McVitie, which will expire on May 8 1998.

Reg's wife, Roberta Kray, said: "This is one step closer to his eventual release, the first glimpse of light at the end of a very long tunnel."

Kray supporter and the country's first Miss United Kingdom, Eileen Sheridan-Price, said although Kray had been happy at Maidstone and would have to make new friends all over again, the move was something that brought him closer to freedom.

"It's a marvellous step for him," she said.

"It's the impetus he needs to keep him going after all these years."

A spokeswoman for the Home Office said a Category C prison was for those prisoners who could not be trusted in open conditions but did not have the resources or ability to make a determined escape.

Factors such as length of sentence left to serve and the prisoner's record of behaviour influenced the Home Office's decision on downgrading a prisoner, she said.

The Home Office's comments about downgrading criteria fly in the face of a national paper's speculation that Kray moved because he was being investigated for allegedly masterminding a charity fraud from his prison cell at Maidstone.

Freddie Foreman relished murder, ripping out his victims' hearts. So why is he being feted on Britain's celebrity circuit?

Friend of the stars: Freddie Foreman with Barbara Windsor; (left) under arrest in 1989

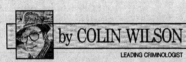

by COLIN WILSON

LEADING CRIMINOLOGIST

FREDDIE FOREMAN is an old-style London gangster who, in January 1969, stood in the dock alongside the Kray brothers.

When his autobiography, Respect — The Managing Director Of British Crime, was published two days ago, he held court at the Cafe Royal, Oscar Wilde's stamping ground, surrounded by minor celebrities such as Barbara Windsor, Scott Harvey, Roy Marsden and Mark Wingett.

The array, admittedly, was not quite as glittering as in the days when the Krays played host to Frank Sinatra, Judy Garland, George Raft — and, of course, Barbara Windsor — but it was pretty impressive all the same.

We cannot turn on a chat show without a former gangster with a smile on his face telling of his shady past and then acknowledging the applause with an upheld hand as if he were an entertainer.

It is a sickening sight to see these men being treated as celebrities. Certainly, these criminals are of interest — after all, I have made my living studying their lives — but you have only to delve in detail into their lives to see why this worship is misplaced.

It was almost 30 years ago that Foreman helped out the Krays by murdering the simple-minded giant, Frank Mitchell, known as the Mad Axeman.

Mitchell had walked out of Dartmoor. The Krays provided him with a hiding place and a mistress while they negotiated his return to prison in exchange for parole. But Mitchell was sick of jail and refused to go back. Reggie Kray called on his pal Foreman, who agreed to relieve him of the embarrassment. On December 23, 1966, Kray henchman Albert Donaghue called at the flat where Mitchell was in hiding and told him he was being taken to a new hide-out. Mitchell climbed in the back of a dark painted van and, as the door slammed, Foreman drew his silenced automatic and another gangster took out a revolver.

Mitchell made a dive for the driver, but he was shot several times and collapsed, groaning. Three more shots were fired into his chest; then, as he raised his head, two final shots were fired into his skull.

When Donaghue gave evidence against Foreman and the three Kray brothers at the Old Bailey, he told how Foreman described hacking up the body — when the heart was ripped open, there were three bullets in it.

'He had a tiny brain,' Foreman told Donaghue, cupping his hands to show how small.

For years after his disappearance, the Mad Axeman was believed to be encased in one of the concrete pillars of the M11. In his autobiography, Foreman reveals this is not true. Mitchell was fed to the fish in the North Sea.

The judge at the Old Bailey ruled that since Donaghue was also involved in Mitchell's escape, his evidence could not be accepted without corroboration. Foreman and the Kray brothers had to be acquitted of the Mad Axeman's murder.

Foreman's autobiography also solves the mystery of what happened to Ginger Marks, a used car dealer who was shot in Stepney in January 1965 and then vanished. Like the Mad Axeman, Ginger was fed to the fish. The law caught up with Foreman in Marbella, Spain, and he was sentenced to seven years in prison for his involvement in the £7 million Security Express raid. He began his autobiography to while away the time in jail.

Like his pal 'Mad Frankie' Fraser, who has just signed a film contract for his autobiography, it looks as if Foreman is going to end up as a rich celebrity regular on late-night TV.

That should please him. Most crooks have a yen to be treated as respectable members of society.

The biographer of the Krays, John Pearson, tells how the twins kept scrapbooks of news reports of their crimes. He says of Ronnie: 'He, who had always longed to be a somebody, discovered his only hope of eminence lay in his power to frighten those around him.'

THAT may be understandable — we all want to be respected and admired. What is altogether stranger is why respectable people should want to be associated with criminals.

It is true that there is no harm in letting bygones be bygones and paying respect to former criminals such as John McVicar and Jimmy Boyle, who have proved their intention of becoming useful members of society. But why this show of affection and respect for someone who is merely confessing to past brutality, including murder?

The late Lord Boothby was a gangster groupie and he almost came to grief in July 1964 when a Sunday newspaper accused him of having a homosexual affair with Ronnie 'the Colonel' Kray.

Boothby outfaced the accusations by writing a letter to The Times, in which he declared 'I am not a homosexual' (raising guffaws throughout London's gay community) and that he had met Ronnie Kray 'on business' only three times. The newspaper backed down, offering an apology to both Lord Boothby and Kray.

The rich find it exciting to sup with tigers — provided, of course, the tigers never growl or show their claws.

It is a dangerous preoccupation for the trouble is that the gangster code demands a criminal should never lose face, and when such men are challenged, smiling good nature gives way to sudden and devastating brutality.

The Krays were particularly prone to unprovoked explosions when they would knock someone to the ground and then kick them unconscious.

The twins had one basic aim: to show they never gave way. Anyone who challenged them — or appeared to do so — had to be flattened. Or, in a few cases, murdered.

The Kray twins, like their old ally Foreman, were not lovable teddy bears pretending to be gangsters or anarchic Robin Hoods who lived by their own quirky code of honour. The reality of their lives was grim, violent and, on the whole, pretty brutal.

Their celebrity friends found it hard to believe ill of them. But then, they never saw them beating somebody to a bloody pulp or slicing open someone's face with a razor. It's an appalling comment on our society that we give such people the time of day.

KRAY-ZEE NAMES

Couple call twin tots Ronnie and Reggie

Steve beats Kray video block

★ Reggie Kray, centre, older brother Charlie on his right, with Steve Wraith in the background at the funeral

A VIDEO that has exclusive footage of the funeral of East End gangster Ronnie Kray is being sold in Gateshead, despite being banned from the shelves of many major stockists.

Steve Wraith, who runs Wardley Post Office, has been a friend of the Kray family for the last seven years and was contacted by Reggie Kray with a view to selling the video.

Funeral

The video, which was released on the first anniversary of Ronnie's death last week, covers the funeral with narration done by Reggie.

Steve agreed to sell the video after major dealers refused to stock it.

By Ian Willis

A WH Smith spokeswoman refused to give a reason why the company weren't selling the tape, only saying: "We are not planning on stocking the production."

Woolworths are also refusing to stock the tape, with a spokeswoman saying: "This video will not be stocked by us as it is not suitable for the Woolworths family image."

Official

"I think some of the big companies are saying that the video is in bad taste, and think it is another example of The Krays trying to make money from crime," said Steve.

Steve, who became interested in The Kray family after doing a school project on the subject, says that there are a lot of people in the Gateshead area who would be interested in buying the video, and doesn't think the video is in bad taste.

"I have done this sort of thing before with things like Krays books and leaflets and people have really been interested in them. This is an official video, which is selling at £13.99 like every other video. It

is certainly not in bad taste, especially with Reggie doing the narration for the footage. If anyone was going to make a film about Ronnie Kray, then Reggie is the right person to do it," added Steve.

Steve was among the mourners at the funeral in March last year, and says that the video gives a perfect showing of the atmosphere at the time.

"This video is a tribute to Ronnie Kray, not a way of Reggie cashing in on his brothers death. The footage follows the funeral cortege from the chapel of rest around the East End streets of London to the cemetery. The atmosphere amongst the people at the funeral comes across on the video," added Steve.

The video, which is called The Epilogue of Ron Kray, lasts for 54 minutes and contains never-seen-before material.

Interest

Steve has asked anyone who is interested in buying a copy of the video to contact him on 0421 350 454.

"The video will be of great interest to anyone intrigued in Ronnie Kray, and there is a chance that the copies can be autographed by Reggie," said Steve.

By ANDREW PARKER

PROUD parents Daryl and Brenda Smith told last night why they have called their twin sons after the Krays.

Burly bouncer Daryl, 31, cuddled month-old tots Ronnie and Reggie and declared: "They are men's names."

And Brenda, 28, claimed the babies were already showing the battling spirit of their East End gangster namesakes.

She said: "They weighed just 3lb 12oz and 4lb 10oz at birth, but they are fighters."

The couple, of Castle Vale, Birmingham, admit many people will brand them barmy for saddling the twins with names of killers.

Admired

But ex-boxer Daryl said he had always admired the Krays, and declared: "We don't give a stuff what anyone thinks.

"When Brenda became pregnant, I dreamed she would have twin boys and that they would be called Ronnie and Reggie."

"As soon as I set eyes on the babies, that was it – job done."

He added: "The Krays were supposed to be a bad lot, but they never attacked old ladies. They only sorted out their own kind."

Reggie Kray, 62, is serving a 30-year sentence imposed in 1969 for the murder of Jack "The Hat" McVitie. Ronnie Kray died in Broadmoor last year.

REGGIE'S A BALLET NICE BLOKE

REGGIE: Gift of paintings

By SIMON DEAN

A BOY dubbed a cissy is on his way to ballet fame, thanks to his fairy godfather–gangland killer Reggie Kray.

The jailed mobster leaped to the rescue when he heard how 11-year-old Daniel James was £4,000 short for his scholarship place at the academy that trained Margot Fonteyn.

"No-one's going to call me names now!" whooped Daniel, revealing how his new tough-guy pal promised to paint three pictures for a fund-raising auction.

"I think Reggie Kray is a very kind man. I've spoken to him on the telephone and he's really nice."

After enduring five years of playground taunts over his dancing, and winning an £8,000 scholarship, Bristol schoolboy Daniel was heartbroken to learn he might lose his promised slot at the £12,000-a-year Legat Academy in East Sussex. And he

was amazed when the notorious Kray twin rang from Maidstone Jail, Kent, in response to an appeal.

"Not many boys do ballet so the other kids have given me a hard time," admitted Daniel. "Now with Mr Kray's help I'm determined to make it to the top one day."

150

BRAVE BARMAID'S EVIDENCE HELPED JAIL EVIL KRAY TWIN

IT was 8.15 on a March evening. Things were quiet in the East End pub where a Walker Brothers record was playing on the jukebox.

Then Ronnie Kray walked in. Without speaking, he made straight for the bar where George Cornell was drinking with two friends.

He fired three shots at point-blank range and Cornell fell from his barstool onto the floor.

Another brutal gangland killing. Another chapter in the bloody feud between the Krays and the Richardsons, rivals in the capital's murky underworld.

Police seemed helpless to stop the escalating violence. Fear and misguided loyalty put the gang leaders seemingly out of their reach.

But this time it was different. This time, someone was prepared to speak out in a remarkably brave effort to break the vicious circle of violence.

Grip of terror

One young woman had seen it all. The barmaid that evening in the now-infamous Blind Beggar pub was chatting to Cornell when Kray walked in.

She watched in horror as he was gunned down. She cradled his head as he lay dying.

Such was the Krays' grip of terror that, for almost three years, no-one spoke out against them.

Except for that barmaid. Risking her life to tell the truth, her evidence put Ronnie behind bars for life.

Now, after life in hiding, she's written book telling story of fateful night Ronnie Kray walked into Blind Beggar pub

WEEKLY NEWS EXCLUSIVE

Today, she has a new identity, a new name, a new home. She has been forced to move time and again, from one "safe house" to another.

Standing in an Old Bailey witness box ensured she would forever be looking over her shoulder.

Only a few of her closest friends stuck by her. Even her family shunned her for "grassing on one of her own".

For 30 years she has not spoken about the chilling events of March 9, 1966, or the nightmares that followed. But she has at last decided to tell her fascinating story.

In her book, *The Barmaid's Tale*, she tells in her own words how one moment on a quiet night at the pub where she worked changed her life forever.

It is written using the pseudonym "Mrs X" — the name she asked us to use in an exclusive Weekly News interview.

She feels no safer now than she did then. Despite Ronnie Kray's death last year, she still believes she would be killed if her identity is revealed.

"I have no doubt that something would happen to me if I was discovered," she said, drawing deeply on a cigarette.

"You have to have lived through those times to know what influence Ronnie and Reggie had. They only had to snap their fingers to get something done."

But now that Ronnie is dead, surely the threat is gone?

"Only to a degree," she said. "I felt a mixture of emotions when I heard on my radio that Ronnie had died.

"Of course there was relief. But there was disbelief too. I know it sounds ridiculous, but I didn't believe Ronnie could die.

"I wasn't alone. Ask anyone who knew them. Everyone thought they were immortal."

Ronnie's twin, Reggie, is still serving time for the 1967 murder of Jack "The Hat" McVitie. He was tried alongside his brother in 1969.

Funeral

"They still have a lot of influence," said Mrs X. "They have become legendary figures. Just look at the turn-out for Ronnie's funeral.

"Anyone who thinks they don't have friends today who would settle old scores is kidding themselves."

So why did she put herself in that position? Why risk her life — and the lives of her three young children — in order to testify?

"Strange as it sounds, I did it for my kids," she said. "They were only

tots at the time. It was time someone made a stand.

"I looked around and saw a lawless world where someone could walk into a quiet pub and shoot a man dead, then calmly walk away.

"I couldn't stand by and let that happen. If I had kept quiet, I would have been helping to make this a more dangerous world for my children to grow up in.

"I also had to speak up to clear my own

conscience," she said. "I had to be able to live with myself.

"I am still haunted by what I saw that night. I can still see everything crystal clear. Things like that, you can never forget.

"When you see something that is so horrific right in front of your eyes, when you see a human being lying on the floor, shot in cold blood, you have to speak out.

Whisper

"How could you carry on if you didn't?" she asked, her voice now hardly more than a whisper.

During the trial, and for some time afterwards, Mrs X was given a police guard. Officers lived with her, providing round-the-clock protection.

Those officers became friends. Today, she still keeps in touch and one, whom she refers to only as Helen, has become one of her closest confidantes.

"We are very close," said Mrs X. "One of the few bonuses of this whole business is that I came out of it with some good friends.

"I still see Nipper," — Leonard "Nipper" Read, the Scotland Yard detective given the task of rounding up the

Krays. "We have a meal every now and again.

"In fact, it was his suggestion to write the book.

"At first I was unsure. I didn't want to drag up all those memories again.

"Then I talked to a few people and thought, 'why not?' All the books written so far have been from the criminal side. I could at least set the record straight as to what really happened."

Despite moving out of the East End, Mrs X spent the years immediately after the Kray trial concealing her appearance with a succession of wigs.

Whether she resorted to plastic surgery or other ways to change her looks, she won't say.

Now she feels that time is her best disguise.

"I'm getting to be an old woman now," she said. "No-one would know me from my time at the Blind Beggar.

"Despite everything, I would do it all again. I would take to the witness box again given those circumstances.

"I have just one regret — that I was ever there in the Blind Beggar that night.

"I would have given anything not to see what I saw. But I did, and the rest is history."

The Barmaid's Tale is published by Little, Brown, priced £16.99.

The Kray Twins with brother Charlie.

Reg Kray in charity event bust-up

By PETE LEYDON

FORMER gangland boss Reggie Kray has pulled out of a charity bash for Tyneside burns victim Terry Moran – after a bust-up with organisers.

Reg's brother Charlie, who was due to host tomorrow night's fundraising event in Gateshead with a host of other stars, will not now attend.

The party is being staged for 16-year-old Terry, of Felling Dene Gardens, Gateshead, who was too ill to attend the original one in July for more than a few minutes.

Organiser Steve Wraith wanted Terry, who celebrates his birthday in two days, as the guest of honour at the Elysium Lane Club event in Dunston tomorrow.

But it led to a row between Steve and Reg Kray – currently serving life in Maidstone jail for the murder of Jack McVitie – who wanted some of the money raised to go to charities in the South.

Argument

Steve, a friend of the Krays for seven years, said: "This is not a Krays supporters party. It's a charity night for Terry Moran.

"There's an argument or two between me and Reg. It's down to artistic and professional differences.

"As far as I'm concerned the party is being held in the North East and the money should go to the North East area."

Terry, who spent eight months in hospital with horrific burns after fuel exploded in his hands at a bonfire last year, will get to meet a host of celebrities at the £10-a-head bash.

They will include Newcastle United footballers Lee Clark and Steve Watson, and stars from hit TV show *Byker Grove*.

Fists of fury — the twins in their younger days.

151

REGGIE WANTS A STAG NIGHT OUT WITH LAGS

JAILBIRD Reggie Kray shocked prison bosses by demanding a last night of freedom—a boozy stag party.

But the gangland killer got a shock in return—he was told to sling his hook.

A prison officer quipped: "We're bracing ourselves for Kray to ask for a two-week honeymoon in Marbella!"

Kray-zy Reggie, 63, who is serving life at Maidstone Prison, Kent, for his part in the murder of Jack "The Hat" McVitie, even asked for his best man—convicted armed robber Bradley Allardyce—to be transferred from another wing of the jail so he could attend the bash tonight.

Two months ago we exclusively revealed that the ageing gangster was to marry sexy 38-year-old blonde Roberta Jones tomorrow at the jail's chapel.

Roberta moved from East London to a house 100 yards from the prison to be near her sweetheart.

A prison source said: "Kray lives in a world of his own and has no sense of reality.

"He expected his re-

KRAY: 'Obsessed'

ROBERTA: Moved

By IAN EDMONDSON

quests to get the go-ahead. Since he decided he was getting married he has become self-obsessed.

"For weeks he has been plotting and planning every last detail.

"He has even organised the flowers, the cake and the full guest list from his prison cell."

Wedding cells for Kray twin

JAILED gangland leader Reggie Kray tied the knot with Roberta Jones, above, yesterday. Kray twin Reggie, 63, and Roberta, 38, got hitched in Maidstone Prison, Kent. But there'll be no nookie until he's released. He's up for parole next year.

HITCHED: Reggie

KRAY IT WITH FLOWERS

By DAVID DILLON

BLUR star Damon Albarn has a new fan – gangland killer Reggie Kray.

The jailed mobster sent the Britpop heart-throb a huge bunch of flowers after listening to the band's music with his cell mate Bradley Allardyce at Maidstone Prison.

Kray, 62, was so touched by Damon's hit song Charmless Man, which mentions Reggie's dead twin Ronnie, that he sent a bouquet to the singer's London record company, Parlophone. Last night Damon said he was "delighted" with the gift and had sent a note of thanks. He added: "It was really nice of him to let us know how much he likes the album."

Kray said in a telephone call from jail: "I'm a big fan of Blur. I was very impressed with the songs and liked the fact they'd mentioned Ronnie. They didn't have a go at him and I respect them for that."

● DRUG CHARGE – Charlie Kray

ACCUSED: Kray

Kray: I told pop hero to punch rival

CHARLIE Kray told a jury yesterday how he once asked Spandau Ballet pop star Martin Kemp to thump a man on a film set.

The older brother of ex-gangsters Ronnie and Reggie said Peter Gillet had crossed Ronnie in the 1960s.

Asked at Woolwich Crown Court if Kemp – Reggie in the Kray movie – hit Gillet during filming, Kray said: "I think he did."

Kray, 70, of Sanderstead, south London, denies masterminding a £39million cocaine plot.

The case continues.

NEW BOMBSHELL FOR PM (OR IS IT BLAIR?)

VOTE KRAYBOUR

REGGIE: I AM BACKING TONY

FORMER gangster Reggie Kray is urging friends to back Labour.

He has told staff and fellow inmates at the jail where he is serving life for murder that if prisoners were allowed to vote "I would vote for Tony Blair."

Kray, 64, was once an admirer of Margaret Thatcher. He now favours a more caring society. In a statement released exclusively to The Mirror he says: "Love thy neighbour, vote Labour.

By JEFF EDWARDS
Chief Crime Correspondent

"The Tories advocate a tougher prison regime. One should remember it is the streets that need to be safe for the citizens. We in prison are already locked away...

Harmony

"Do not let the smokescreen of hard line prison reform cloak more serious issues.

"The theme should be that coloured, white and Jew live in harmony regardless of what we think of each other because at the end of the day we all have to live together.

"My supporters all over the country, and across the world, agree with me in this philosophy that the people stand united and show compassion and understanding. God bless. Reg."

Kray and his late twin Ronnie were kings of London's underworld in the 1960's.

One close friend said: "Reg has often said that if he had not made the mistake of getting involved in crime he'd have liked to have gone into politics.

"He had many of the qualities that make a good MP.

"He could be very persuasive."

Kray is in Kent's Maidstone Jail. The judge who sentenced him in 1969 recommended he serve at least 30 years.

Undercover cop's lived it up – claim

A POLICEMAN trying to snare alleged drug dealer Charlie Kray, 70, lived it up with him at a Tyneside hotel, a court heard.

Jonathan Goldberg, QC, defending the brother of the notorious twins Ronnie and Reggie on two drugs charges accused police operating undercover of living a life of Riley while on duty.

Kray, of Sanderstead, south London, denies offering to supply cocaine and another charge of supplying two kilogrammes of the drug.

The prosecution alleges that he was involved in a deal to supply £39 million of cocaine, but was caught while dealing with undercover Scotland Yard officers.

A jury at Woolwich Crown Court heard Mr Goldberg accused an officer of drinking rare malt whisky out of half-pint glasses during one meeting with Kray at an hotel outside Newcastle.

The officer admitted he drank quite heavily that night, but denied Mr Goldberg's claim. He told the court: "I was drinking it in the tall glasses that it was served in."

Charlie drug cops'drinks with Posh Spice

UNDERCOVER cops had drinks with Posh Spice Victoria Adams while they waited for Charlie Kray to hand over drugs, a court heard.

The policeman met the chart-topping singer at a hotel in Essex while they were investigating 70-year-old Kray, Woolwich Crown Court was told.

But it was claimed dealers failed to arrive for the delivery and the cops went to the bar where they met Posh Spice.

Kray had earlier offered a ton of cannabis before promising to supply cocaine worth £39 million to the undercover police when they met in a Birmingham club, the jury heard.

Kray - elder brother of Ronnie and Reggie - bragged he knew people could supply the Class B drug.

Kray allegedly told an undercover cop that he could put his "name on it" if he wanted the drug, Woolwich Crown Court was told.

Kray made the offer as he quaffed champagne at a Birmingham nightclub with a cop, who was posing as a rich businessman, the court heard.

The undercover policeman, who is shielded from the public behind screens, said he went to "the dam" (Amsterdam) on regular business.

The cop - known as Jack - said: "I told him that until December of last year I had been visiting the dam regularly, but the man I had been trading with had been topped and that had left me a bit dry.

"He said he had people who sat on a ton and he could put my name on it if I wanted it. I said that's a lot of puff."

The conversation was not taped because they were at a nightclub and the cop's cover might have been blown, the jury was told.

They agreed that it was too dangerous to continue the conversation and Kray suggested discussing it further the next day. The pair then shook hands and left, both going back to a hotel for more drinks, the jury heard.

Kray was said to have first met the detective at a party held for a pal. But they then went on to The Elbow Room nightclub, where the cop splashed out on champagne

Posh Spice Victoria Adams drank with undercover cops investigating Charlie Kray

Kray pals welcome Reg's jail wedding to Roberta

Kate Kray: "I wish Reg and Roberta all the luck and happiness in the world"

Flanagan: "I am happy for Reg to be happy for the rest of his life"

FAMILY and friends of Reg Kray this week wished him all the best as he prepares to marry sweetheart Roberta Jones next month.

The jailed former gangland boss has applied to Maidstone Prison bosses for permission to wed the 38-year-old, who has been a "truly loyal friend" during the past year.

It is believed Reg, 63, and Roberta will tie the knot at the prison chapel on June 4, with jail pal and armed robber Bradley Allardyce being the best man.

Roberta, a former research company worker, first met Reg during a jail visit just over a year ago.

She has since moved from Hackney to Maidstone - just a short distance from the jail.

This week she refused to comment, other than to confirm the big day was just around the corner, and added: "I'm sure our friends may have something to say about the wedding."

Kate Kray, who married Ron, said: "I wish Reg and Roberta all the luck and happiness in the world. I can't say I am that surprised by the news. Reg is a good-looking man whose heart is in the right place.

"Roberta has obviously made quite an impression on Reg. I wish the pair of them all the best."

Flanagan, a close pal of Reg - and Britain's first Page Three girl - said: "I was a little shocked when I first heard, because he has never really mentioned marriage since

BY LEE SERVIS

the death of his first wife Frances.

"But then Roberta has been a truly loyal friend to him and loyalty is one of the most important things in the world to Reg.

"He has had a hell of a lot of offers from girls over the years. But many of these would then try and sell his 'love letters' to the newspapers and that cuts no ice with Reg.

"He obviously has a deep affection for Roberta - she is a kind and loyal lady - and I am happy for him to be happy for the rest of his life."

Actress Helen Keating, a long-time friend of the Krays, said: "I'm over the moon for Reg and Roberta. If anyone deserved some happi-

ness it's Reg - the man has had a lot thrown at him over the years. I wish them all the very best for their future together."

Reg was jailed for life in 1969 for the murder of Jack 'The Hat' McVitie, while Ron was given the same sentence for killing gangster George Cornell.

Ron - who married twice while inside - died in Broadmoor two years ago.

Reg Kray is marrying in jail

Reggie's £2,500 knees-up

GANGLAND killer Reggie Kray has spent £2,500 on two EastEnders-style bashes for pensioners and needy children.

Jellied eels and pie and mash were delivered specially to the Phoenix pub at Gedling, Nottingham.

The parties were arranged for 63-year-old Reggie by his pen-pal Barbara Hall who lives at nearby Carlton.

Reggie, jailed in 1968 said from Maidstone jail Kent: "I'm bored and love organising treats—especially for children."

DEAL DRUGS? KRAY COULD NOT EVEN DEAL CARDS

He's a never was, jury told

CHARLIE KRAY was a living myth who "could not deal cards let alone drugs", a court heard yesterday.

Nightclub security boss Dave Courtney, whose life story was used in an episode of The Bill, told the jury: "I would say he is a 70-year-old has-been except he is not even a has-been. He has never done anything."

Kray, older brother of gang-

land twins Reggie and Ronnie, is alleged to have masterminded a £39million cocaine smuggling plot.

But Mr Courtney said: "Charlie has got holes in his shoes and he wears a £10 watch."

The security boss recalled spending £10,000 organising Ronnie Kray's funeral two years ago.

He said: "I liaised with the chief of police Sir Paul Condom."

To laughter, the defence counsel pointed out: "I think it is Condon." Mr Courtney: "Oh yeah?" Author Robin McGibbon,

who ghost-wrote Kray's biography, told Woolwich Crown Court in south London that Charlie was a dreamer who tried one hare-brained scheme after another.

He once told top photographer David Bailey "I am into oil."

Mr McGibbon said: "David was just gobsmacked."

Kray, from Sanderstead, south London, denies two drug charges. The trial continues.

TALL TALES: Charlie Kray

STAY AWAY PATSY YOU'RE BAD FOR REGGIE'S IMAGE!

Kray twin fears the Oasis link

By CLAUDIA CONNELL

SWEET little Patsy Kensit had better watch her step – for murdering crime boss Reggie Kray reckons SHE is giving HIM a bad name!

Amazingly the notorious gangster's henchmen have warned the blonde actress not to visit her old pal in prison. They fear her engagement to Oasis brat Liam Gallagher will taint the East End racketeer's jealously guarded butter-wouldn't-melt image. . .

Kray's former sidekick Joe Falcon is heading a campaign to have his mate freed from Kent's Maidstone jail after 30 years behind bars." The fact that Reggie's been inside for that long is criminal in itself," he declared.

"Even child abusers are going in and out in no time these days.

"We can't afford to slip up now and further delay Reggie's release, especially when we're all convinced that it's just around the corner.

"We need support and there's concern that Patsy will bring us bad publicity that we really don't want.

"After all, she's had a few problems with that lad she's living with, especially that drugs bust of his what made the papers.

Chilling

"Reggie mustn't be associated with anything like that."

While tut-tutting about 24-year-old rocker Liam's shame which ended in a police caution for carrying cocaine during a night on the town, Joe forgot to mention any of Reggie's run-ins with the law when he and twin brother Ronnie ruled London's underworld with chilling violence.

Their reign of extortion and terror ended in a sensational Old Bailey trial and life sentences for murder.

When the brothers went down, longtime friends the Kensit family, headed by Patsy's pickpocket dad Jimmy the Dip, stayed loyal.

Petty crook Jimmy had earned the twins' respect by running errands for their evil crime syndicate. He even risked his neck by giving evidence at the trial of their rivals from south of the Thames, the much-feared Richardsons.

And Jimmy cemented his bond with the villains by making 62-year-old Reggie godfather to Patsy's older brother Jamie.

Even after her dad's death 10 years ago screen star Patsy, 28, who found fame in the hit movie Absolute Beginners, was determined to remain close to her roots.

She regularly visited Reg- and Ron until he died in 1995 - and joined the movement dedicated to fighting for their release.

Last night it looked unlikely that Patsy would ever see her old friend again unless that battle proves successful.

Joe Falcon revealed: "I don't know what Reggie thinks of Liam Gallagher but he's still very fond of Patsy and follows her career from inside.

"Sure she's been a visitor in the past but now she's been asked to steer clear.

"I think she understands why. She's a good girl."

Reg set to hand out £100,000 lottery win to East End

Reg Kray: Hand out

BY MARK OVERINGTON

EAST End gangland killer Reg Kray is giving away a £100,000 donation to worthy causes in the East End..

Millionaire Karl Crompton - who landed an £11million lottery jackpot last May - gave Reg the cash as a "token of respect" soon after his win.

Friends claim former crime-boss Reg has since been anonymously donating the money to old folk and kids homes in his old East End manor.

And Reg has ensured the story of his secret donations is proving to be a nice little earner as well.

BOMBARDMENT

His new manager Capital Radio DJ Caesar the Geezer said of the astonishing lottery-cash story that hit the headlines last weekend: "I sold that story for Reg."

And he revealed Reg planned a media bombardment that would earn thousands for the ex-gangland boss.

"I've got a whole serialisation to sell about Reg's life in prison," Caesar claimed.

And he said: "There are pictures of Reg in the gym, showing how he looks.

"It will go to the highest bidder and all the money goes to his old manor."

Caesar claims he has already turned down offers of £50,000 for exclusive rights to the new pictures. The last time the gangland killer was photographed was at twin Ron's Bethnal Green funeral service in 1995.

Reg is eligible for parole in May, 1998, when he will have served a minimum 30-year sentence for the murder of Jack 'The Hat' McVitie.

And Caesar claimed: "There are very good odds of Reg Kray being released. Reg Kray will be released. I know so."

I STAND BY CHARLIE KRAY

THE GATESHEAD
POST
EXCLUSIVE
BY ROGER
WOODCOCK

★ SIDE BY SIDE – Steve Wraith, left, with Charlie Kray at the Gateshead charity night two years ago

Court told of 'good deeds' at Gateshead charity night

THE man who invited Charlie Kray to a Gateshead charity night is standing by the gangster as he starts a 12-year prison sentence.

Steve Wraith, from Wardley, was called as a character witness in the trial of Charlie Kray, 70, who was convicted of masterminding a £39 million drugs ring.

Steve, who mentioned the Gateshead Post's coverage of the charity night in his evidence, said:

★ TRIAL DOUBTS –
Tony Lambrianou

"Everybody who knows Charlie Kray is devastated by Monday's sentence at Woolwich Crown Court.

Kray came to the Elysium Club in Bensham on July 8, 1995, as the main guest at a charity event Steve helped to organise in aid of teenage firework accident victim Terry Moran, from Felling.

"The Gateshead Post's coverage of the event came up at Woolwich Crown Court when I was giving my evidence in my personal attempt to convince the jury that Charlie Kray, despite his past, is now a very different person to the Charlie Kray of legend," said Steve.

A subpostmaster at Wardley, Steve got to know Charlie Kray after establishing a friendship with his younger brother Reggie — the surviving half of the notorious East End Kray twins — through a pen-pal relationship.

Steve said: "I had no hesitation in going to speak up for the Charlie Kray. I know and I believe that

■ Turn to Page 2

CHARLIE KRAY: JUST A NAIVE SKINT OLD FOOL

Drug boast 'a lie'

THE Kray twins' brother Charlie is "an old, skint, naive fool" who was duped by cops into pretending he was a drug baron, a court heard yesterday.

Kray, 70, told undercover detectives posing as drug dealers that he could supply them with cocaine worth £39million.

But yesterday his lawyer Jonathan Goldberg insisted it was a pack of lies, adding: "This old fool who is now in the dock thought he could con them for money.

"He told them what they wanted to hear – he'd have promised them Scud missiles and gold bullion if he'd thought it helped." Mr Goldberg painted a picture of Kray as a charming old rogue who had survived on "bull" for decades by exaggerating his criminal exploits.

But the lawyer insisted Kray was **NOT** like evil younger brothers Ronnie and Reggie, gangland bosses who terrorised 1960s London.

Mr Goldberg said: "He is a pathetic old has-been, an utterly washed-up figure made to appear something he's not.

"He is sociable, loveable, anti-crime, anti-drugs, anti-violence and a man with a heart of gold.

"He is naive and gullible. He doesn't recognise where his charm ends and reality begins." Mr Goldberg told Woolwich Crown Court that Kray had just two previous convictions.

In 1951 he was fined £5 for theft. In 1969 he was jailed for ten years for being an accessory to his brothers' murder of gangster Jack "The Hat" McVitie.

Bask

Kray was trapped by the undercover cops after they "showered him with champagne," it was claimed.

Mr Goldberg accused them of acting with "utter deviousness" because they wanted to bask in the glory of arresting one of the Krays.

Prosecutors say Kray would have netted £8million profit from the drug deal.

Kray, of Sanderstead, South London, told the court his infamous brothers were "kind-hearted" men.

He said of Ronnie, who died of cancer in Broadmoor in 1995: "He would help anybody – but he was not responsible when he got into one of his moods."

Of Reggie, who is serving life for murder, he admitted: "He had a few fights and things like that."

Kray said the twins treated people "with great respect," adding: "They always helped as best they could."

Kray denies offering to supply cocaine and providing two kilograms of the drug. The case continues.

Charlie Kray . . . 'not a crook'

'I'm not out to make money' says Reggie

FORMER East End crime boss Reg Kray is to act as his own PR man to scotch rumours that he is to profit from press stories.

Reg is getting a grip after damaging rumours spread that a high-profile radio DJ planned to help him raise funds for good causes by selling stories to the press.

But this week Reg slammed the claims as "out of order". And he told the Advertiser: "I prefer to put things out myself because that way you get it straight from the horse's mouth."

Capital Radio DJ Caesar the Geezer has been doing good works for Reg and speaking as his PR man ever since meet-

BY MARK OVERINGTON

ing him in prison earlier this year.

This week Reg said Caesar had good intentions. But he insisted: "He is not my PR man or manager. I can do both those jobs and I've been doing them for a number of years."

Calling from Maidstone Prison, Reg spoke to the Advertiser about his hopes for the present and future.

Reg shrugged off controversy surrounding his involvement with a Nottinghamshire football club.

The former gangland killer and his prisoner pal Bradley

Allardyce hit the headlines this week after Ashfield'95 FC appointed them president and vice-president following a £2,000 joint donation.

Nottinghamshire Football Association is demanding an explanation and team manager David Howard has been accused of accepting "bloodmoney".

But Reg is staying cool over the heated episode. He told us: "I don't let it get to me. Some people like me and some people don't."

And the former gangland boss - jailed for a minimum of 30 years in 1969 for the murder of Jack 'The Hat' McVitie and up for parole later this year - reflected: "It's not necessarily the case that I'll get parole.

"I don't hope one way or the other. I'll just let things take their natural course."

But Reg revealed he still misses his old manor. He said: "I miss Pellici's cafe in Bethnal Green Road. I've been going there since I was a kid. And Vallance Road of course. Give all my supporters a message that I'm well and very fit."

Meanwhile Ashfield Football Club manager David Howard said: "All the lads are over the moon. As far as they are concerned they couldn't have a better backer than Reg Kray.

"They object because of who he is. Why shouldn't we take his money when all these do-gooders end up giving us nothing."

MATCH OF THE KRAY

Reg honoured by soccer club

JAILED gangland killer Reggie Kray has given £1,000 to a football club – and been made its president in return.

Kray, 63, made the donation to an amateur team in Nottinghamshire.

Speaking from Maidstone Prison in Kent yesterday, he said: "I am very pleased the team has honoured me in this way.

"I have always had a soft spot for Nottinghamshire since I spent a few years in Nottingham Prison."

But soccer bosses are demanding details from officials of Ashfield 95 FC at Kirkby-in-Ashfield.

Ruled

Mick Kilbee, assistant secretary to the Football Association, said: "We have written to the club asking them to explain the situation in writing."

Reggie and his twin Ronnie ruled the East London underworld in the 1960s and were

LIFER: Former gang boss Reg Kray

By STEVE ATKINSON

jailed for life in 1969. Ron died of a heart attack nearly two years ago.

Reggie, serving 30 years for the murder of Jack "The Hat" McVitie, responded to an appeal by the Ashfield club for money to improve their facilities.

In January, Kray sent £2,000 worth of

food, including jellied eels and pie and mash, for a pensioners' New Year knees-up in a Nottingham pub.

He said yesterday: "The people of Nottingham are really friendly – it's my second favourite city after London."

The twins were paid £255,000 by the makers of the film The Krays.

Reg has reportedly given a fortune to good causes.

MYSTERY THREATS FOR KRAY PLAY CAST

ACTORS playing the Kray twins in a stage play have been the targeted by anonymous threatening letters..

The letters were sent to the two actors playing the gangsters at the Queen's Theatre in Hornchurch which is staging the production of Inside The Firm based on the book penned by Kray insider, Tony Lambrianou.

Bow-based director, Marina Caldarone, said: "We've had a few, two were serious and one might have been a hoax. They are quite threatening, all they want is that we don't rubbish them on stage."

The letters penned to actors Jimmy Puddephat and Mark Leadbetter warned them 'not to represent the twins in any way other than the good people they were' or else.

Marina said: "We're just representing a situation as it was - we're not commenting on it, it's really a play about homeless people in the nineties."

Scriptwriter Jon Ivay has interwoven two homeless characters into the play who get involved in a life of crime to draw parallels with 60s gangsters.

Since the play opened last week the letters have so far stopped and Marina hopes the anonymous writers had been to see the play and were satisfied.

'They even used the death of the son as a tool to get to the father, that's how charming this operation was. The police should be ashamed of themselves'

Jonathon Goldberg, Kray's counsel

The judge (left) listens to Jonathon Goldberg QC (second left) defending Charlie Kray (right) against charges of supplying cocaine   DRAWING: SIAN FRANCES

Patsy fury at 'Kray pals' slur

ANGRY Patsy Kensit has denied a report that she visited the Kray brothers in jail and campaigned for Reggie's release.

A Sunday newspaper claimed that Patsy, 28, had been told not to call on the convicted murderer because of her relationship with Liam Gallagher.

It said Reg's henchmen feared her engagement to Oasis star Liam, 24, would taint the Kray image!

Visit

But yesterday Patsy's spokesman said: "She has never visited Reggie or Ronnie Kray or indeed ever met either of them.

"She has no intention of trying to or asking to visit or contact Reggie.

"And Patsy has **NOT** joined the movement fighting for Reggie's release.

"She is appalled that her name has been used in this untrue story."

MY HOTLINE TO REGGIE KRAY

By JULIE STEWART

GRIEVING Allison Harvey today told how she turned to gangster Reggie Kray for comfort after her mum's death.

In a fit of depression, the 28-year-old housewife went to a phone box in Jarrow and rang the notorious killer, who is serving a life sentence.

Allison told warders at Maidstone Prison she had long admired the Krays and begged them to ask him to call her back.

And she was amazed when Reggie rang her back - and talked her out of her depression.

Allison said she felt she had no-one after her mum died.

Reggie, 63, had lost his mum and brother Ronnie while he was in prison. Allison thought he might understand how she was feeling.

Allison, of Saxon Way, said: "We chatted for 10 minutes, I never expected him to phone me back. I felt so privileged. It made me feel like someone special.

"I thought I'd only give him half a hour and then go home because it was really cold waiting in the phone box. When he rang me, I couldn't believe it.

"I wanted to send him a present and I decided to ask him what he wanted.

"He said he would want a shirt and he described what sort suited him. Then I told him about my mum and he was so sympathetic.

"I'd always been a fan of the Krays - but I don't know what made me phone him. It was all on the spur of the moment."

Now she and the ageing gangster have struck up a friendship and keep in touch by letter.

"He's a kind man - a gentleman. I felt like he was the only one who cared about me - he's saved my life."

■ Reggie and his brother Ronnie, who died in 1995, were sentenced in 1969 to not less than 30 years for two killings.

6 THIS statement is in protest at allegations that have been printed and directed at me over a recent period of time.

Allegations that I refute not only for truth's sake, but to protect friends inside the jail and out from any adverse effect that may stem from gossip and incorrect Press reports.

It has been said that I am seriously ill with a tumour, that I had a besotted young girl visit me over a period of time, that I am gay, that I am due for imminent release and the most recent allegation — that I parade around the exercise field wearing a Red Indian head band and that Indian trophies have been removed from my cell.

This infers that I am unstable and that I am the butt of a joke here at Maidstone jail.

It could also imply that I am not happy in my present environment.

I choose to delve into the latter allegation first instead of in order of sequence, such as those that said I was due for C-category prison soon and others that

From Reg Kray, HMP Maidstone

claimed that I had property and businesses all over England — implying they had come from ill-gotten gains.

I have no property or investments in England or anywhere else in the world; I've not even got a tent.

I delve into the latter because I do not think the former are worthy of any consideration.

False

The latter speaks for the former in that there is no credibility or substance to the allegations.

In fact my solicitors are in possession of a letter that came from the governor of this jail, Mr Jones, in which Mr Jones states categorically that there is no truth whatsoever.

I should also mention that I am very happy in this environment in Maidstone Jail. In fact, I consider it the best jail I have ever been in and, although it is a matter of

in the Red Indian story. It is completely false.

As for the claims about my illness, I have a medical certificate, which is held outside the prison and can be produced, showing the results of blood tests and proving that I am fit and well.

People from all walks of life have enemies as well as friends, for whatever reason, be it jealousy, envy, scorn, whatever, and I am no different.

We all have to bear the cross of human nature.

Some of my friends outside have had anonymous phone calls about me, over a period of time, which are in the vein of gossip on all aspects of life that I am supposed to be leading inside this jail.

Proud

Those who would spread malicious gossip can only strengthen our resolve to stand as one pillar, one family, from within the walls and beyond the walls.

Last but not least I know that my supporters will be loyal as sure as night follows day, so if there are

personal opinion, I've been in a few.

The inmates here are also the very best.

I've got friends all across the country and some across the world and I know these will stay loyal.

I know without a shadow of doubt that friends who keep company with me in prison at association time are also loyal and we consider ourselves family, the same as my friends outside do and I do.

any more allegations in the future I will not trouble to make further public statements.

There is no news of imminent release or any future release, but should there be so I will be proud and honoured to join my friends on the outside.

I have spent almost 28 years in prison.

I have got no intention of spending the rest of whatever life I may have left inside the walls of courts, debating court cases or denying allegations, so let the tide flow, whichever way I am depicted to be.

My philosophy is that I live for the moment, so I've got no intention of worrying about the future or about any future allegations.

I wish to thank all my loyal friends and supporters in full — this is paramount in my thoughts at the moment. The main theme in this statement is that I count my blessings. **9**

I thank everyone again who has stood by me. God bless,

Yours, Reggie

I'M NOT REGGIE GAY

And I haven't had a besotted young girl visit me.. and I don't parade on the exercise field dressed in a Red Indian headband

Santa Reggie

GANGLAND killer Reggie Kray turned into Santa Claus to give 90 pensioners and needy kids an EastEnders-style Christmas bash.

Britain's most legendary villain forked out £2,500 for lashings of pie, mash and jellied eels to be driven from London to a Nottingham pub. And yesterday, from his cell in Maidstone prison, Kent, delighted Reggie, 63, said: "It's the best dosh I've ever spent.

"I love kids and pensioners, so doing something like this gave me great satisfaction."

Poor

The party was organised by Reggie's pen pal, Barbara Hall, after he asked her "to do something for old folk and poor children at Christmas".

Barbara hired the Phoenix pub in Gedling, for the East End bash.

Last night at her home in Carlton, Nottingham,

■ FRANK CURRAN

Barbara said: "It was Reg's idea and a lovely gesture. It went down a treat with the old folk and kiddies."

The mother-of-two met Reggie after reading his book, Born Fighters.

Barbara added: "Reggie has a kind heart and I believe he is a changed person. This shows he is worthy of his freedom."

Reggie and late brother Ron, were jailed for the murder of Jack the Hat McVitie in 1963.

GENEROUS: Reg

Kray tribute for brother

EAST End gangster Reggie Kray has recorded a message to be played at a memorial service today to mark the second anniversary of the death of his twin brother Ronnie.

Reggie, 63, who has spent 29 years behind bars for murder, said he had not asked to be let out of Maidstone Prison for the service. Friends were gathering at a cemetery in east London, where Ronnie Kray is buried.

PROPER CHARLIE

Guilty Kray fears he'll die in a cell

■ PETER BOND

OLD-age pensioner Charlie Kray was behind bars last night, fearing he will NEVER get out alive.

The 71-year-old brother of gangland killers Ronnie and Reggie was convicted of masterminding a £39 million cocaine plot and will be sentenced on Monday.

But friends warned that Charlie had grown "soft" in the twilight of his life and wouldn't be able to serve a long sentence.

They fear the only way he'll leave prison is in a box.

Prosecution lawyers said Kray thought he was going to make £8 million from two drug dealers — but unknown to him they were undercover cops.

The former professional boxer was convicted of offering to supply five kilograms of cocaine every fortnight for two years to the officers. He was also found guilty of supplying a two-kilogram consignment.

Silver-haired Kray gave a resigned shrug as the jury delivered their verdict at Woolwich Crown Court, London.

Looking his age and wearing the same blue suit he'd worn throughout the five-week trial, he turned to the public gallery and gave a woeful smile to his sobbing common-law wife Judy Stanley, 42.

Tears

There were also tears from his friend, Page Three pioneering model Flanagan who was comforted by pals when she broke down outside the court.

Judge Michael Carroll told Kray and his partners in crime — electrician Ronald Field, 49, and builder Robert Gould, 39 — that he would sentence them on Monday.

They were warned to brace themselves for tough jail terms.

The jury heard how the trio were trapped by cops posing as "heavies" interested in buying drugs. During a series of secretly-taped phone calls and meetings, Kray spoke of having access to Ecstasy and a ton of cannabis.

But it was cocaine he finally offered to supply — 92 per cent pure and at the rate of five kilograms a fortnight for two

TEARS: Former Page Three girl Flanagan is comforted by friends outside the court yesterday

OLD FIRM: Charlie, centre, with brothers Ronnie and Reggie

years. After lengthy negotiations, Field and Gould turned up at the Swallow Hotel, in Waltham Abbey, Essex — popular with Posh Spice Victoria Adams — and handed the undercover officers a Jiffy bag containing two kilos of coke, worth £63,000.

They were arrested and Kray was detained a short while later at his home in Sanderstead, south London. John Kelsey-Fry, prosecuting, said Kray was careful not to be around when the

drugs were actually delivered. But he pulled both ends of the deal together and acted as a "conduit."

The jury was asked to decide if the old codger in the dock was the mastermind behind a plot to flood Britain's streets with cocaine.

Or if he was nothing more than a sad old man, with a £10 watch and holes in his shoes, who traded tall tales of East End thuggery for a couple of pints,

because he was too skint to afford a packet of fags or a trip to the barber.

Mr Kelsey-Fry told them: "Don't be fooled by his affable, slightly down-at-heel character."

Jonathan Goldberg QC, defending Kray, argued in vain that his client was the victim of carefully-crafted police hype.

Mad Frankie Fraser, a former gangland enforcer, told the court Kray was a "big softie" who "wouldn't know how to pinch a penny".

Looking at the judge, he said: "He is as innocent as you are, sir."

But it was the shock revelation about Charlie's brother Ronnie that provided the trial's most bizarre twist.

The court heard Ronnie was buried without his brain. It was removed by a Home Office pathologist for experiments.

Frankie Very Much: Gone Too Far Page 3

JAILED CHARLIE IS STIR KRAYZY

PETER BOND

YOUNG jail hoodlums were waiting last night to "boot hell" out of ageing hard man Charlie Kray.

The white-haired gangster was jailed yesterday for 12 years — but his lawyer and pals fear he will **NEVER** survive the sentence.

His brief Jonathan Goldberg QC warned that young thugs, desperate to boost their tough-guy image, would be anxious to have a go at him.

He asked Judge Michael Carroll to extend "the hand of mercy" to the infamous villain turned drugs pedlar, but his pleas were rejected. Mr Goldberg said: "Every young hoodlum will want to take a pot shot at the famous Charlie Kray."

The judge described 70-year-old Kray as a "hypocrite and liar".

Tough

As he despatched the ex-boxer to 12 years inside, a dozen women in the public gallery yelled and screamed in disbelief.

Former Page 3 model Maureen Flanagan, a lifelong friend, said: "It's too much, far too much. He's a tough old bird, but he can't take this. It could kill him."

The brother of gangland killers Reggie and Ronnie was convicted of master-minding a £39 million cocaine plot.

He didn't know the two drug dealers he talked to were cops.

The pensioner denied offering to supply them with five kilos of cocaine every fortnight for two years.

Last week the jury rejected his cries of innocence.

Kray, of Sanderstead, Surrey, looking his age,

KRAY: "He can't take it"

made an impassioned plea from the dock.

He begged the judge at Woolwich, London, to believe he was only guilty of a stupid money-raising scam.

"I swear on my son's grave I have never handled drugs."

Kray's cohorts, electrician Ronald Field, 49, of Raynes Park, south London, got nine years and builder Robert Gould, 39, of Wimbledon, got five years.

The Star Says: Page 2

Kray jailed for 12 years in drug plot

CHARLIE KRAY was yesterday jailed for 12 years for master-minding a £39million cocaine plot. The elder brother of the Kray twins was told by Judge Michael Carroll at Woolwich Crown Court, South East London: 'Throughout this case you have professed your abhorrence against drugs, but the jury's verdict has shown your protestations to be hypocrisy.' Kray, 70, (pictured) was convicted of offering to supply five kilograms of high-purity cocaine every fortnight for two years and of actually supplying two kilograms of the drug, dropped off by his partners-in-crime, Ronald Field and Robert Gould.

The Krays I knew — Page NINE

KRAY OWES £5,000 ON SON'S PLOT

By SEAN O'BRIEN

CHARLIE Kray swore on his son's grave that he was not a drug dealer—but he hasn't even paid for it.

Kray, jailed for 12 years for supplying £3 million worth of cocaine, owes £4,800 to a firm of East End funeral directors.

They were unimpressed by his impromptu oath at his trial in south-east London last month. Kray's son, Gary, 44, died of lung cancer a year ago.

An undertaker, who asked not to be named, said yesterday: "There is still a substantial balance outstanding, and it doesn't look like it's going to be paid now he's in prison."

The only person to make any attempt to meet the bill was brother Reg Kray's new wife Roberta, whom he married last week at Maidstone Prison.

The undertaker added: "She has paid £1,000 towards the bill." The funeral directors have been sending final demands for months.

'I said, bring a CAKE with a file in it'

Tears over removal of Ron's brain

CHARLIE Kray told how his gangland brother Ron's brain was removed for "experiments" before his funeral without his family's knowledge.

Kray said: "Everyone was ringing up the Home Office about it and everyone was very upset."

"We eventually got the brain back in a casket and it was reburied."

A complaint had been made to the Home Office.

Asked if any action was taken by Home Office Mr Kray replied: "No."

Fighting back tears Charlie said: "We didn't know at the time, we thought we were burying the whole body."

GIFT TO ACTOR IN 'THE BILL'

ACTOR Bill Murray, who plays Det Sgt Don Beech in The Bill, said Charlie Kray gave him his first step on the acting ladder.

Mr Murray said Charlie gave him £400 for drama school fees.

Murray used to spar with Charlie at the Double R club.

"I went to drama school to train as an actor at 22 to 23.

He added: "I mentioned it to Charlie and the next thing I knew he told me he had paid for my first year at drama school. When he repaid the loan: "Charlie said 'keep it.'

"Charlie was a generous man. He was regarded as a gentleman. He was entirely different from the other two."

He said: "I gave him £200 18 months ago. I heard that he was really broke."

Why George Cornell was shot by Ron

WHEN Frankie Fraser was cross-examined by prosecutor John Kelsey-Fry, he told the tale of how Ronnie Kray murdered George Cornell, in the Blind Beggar pub in Whitechapel Road in 1966.

He exploded years of popular gangland myth by saying that Cornell had not in fact sparked the row by branding Ronnie "a fat poof".

Fraser said: "He must have spoken to Ron not as well as he should have done. That is what hurt. When he saw his opportunity he took it."

He said of the Blind Beggar: "It is a nice pub. I recommend it to you to go for a drink in there."

REG KRAY PUNISHED FOR HIS RADIO RAGE

By ADRIAN SHAW

EXCLUSIVE

KILLER Reg Kray was in solitary confinement yesterday after a radio outburst against his brother Charlie's 12-year jail term.

The 63-year-old ex-gangster phoned commercial Talk Radio in a rage after Charlie's sentence for masterminding a £39million plot to flood Britain's streets with cocaine.

He claimed Charlie, 70, did not have "the criminal intellect" to commit such and offence and had been framed.

"I'm the main target," he stormed. "Charlie is just a pawn in the game."

Reg, who terrorised London's East End in the 1960s, is in Maidstone Prison, Kent.

A source said: "Reggie has said his bit on TV and radio before and had been warned.

The governor blew his top and Reggie got seven days' solitary."

Kray, whose twin Ron died two years ago, was jailed for a minimum of 30 years for a gangland murder.

Charlie was sentenced in London on Monday.

SOLITARY: Reg Kray

KRAY BEGS VICTIM'S SON FOR CASH HELP

By IAN EDMONDSON

GANGLAND killer Reggie Kray has stunned pals by begging the son of one of the twins' victims to help him.

His brother Ronnie—who died in Broadmoor in 1995—gunned down enforcer George Cornell in East London's Blind Beggar pub in the 1960s.

But Reggie, 63, wanted Cornell's car dealer son Jack to appear at a fundraising bash for him in Hackney last Saturday.

Not surprisingly, Jack told him: "No way." And he remarked to a friend: "He must be desperate if he wants me to go!" Kray and his blonde wife, Roberta, are anxious to scrape together as much money as possible before his release from jail.

The couple—wed at Maidstone prison, Kent, in July—are convinced he is about to be freed.

Though not eligible for parole until 1999, he was recently moved to low-security Wayland prison, Norfolk. And sources say Reggie is furious pals shunned his 'benefit'. In contrast, underworld figures, including Mad Frankie Fraser and Freddie Foreman, flocked to a lavish fund-raiser the next night at a Kent golf club for his surviving brother, Charlie, 70.

He was jailed in June for 12 years for drug smuggling. Money raised by the £100 a head do will finance an appeal.

Organiser and former Kray gang member Tony Lambrianou said: "Many people believe Charlie's innocent. Reggie must realise he's not the only person in the world."

Kray in fight for release

REGGIE Kray's lawyer attacked Home Secretary Jack Straw today for refusing to consider releasing the former gangland boss from prison.

Trevor Linn made his criticism on the day Kray, 64, completed his 30th year in custody – the minimum sentence recommended by a judge – and hinted that the convicted murderer may take legal action in a bid to win freedom.

He accused Mr Straw of "avoiding" making a decision even though Kray had already served one of the longest sentences in legal history and had been assessed be experts as being of "negligible risk to the community".

Mr Linn revealed the Parole Board, which decided Kray should remain in a closed prison, could not consider release unless asked by Mr Straw.

Reg draws in Krayon

GANGLAND killer Reggie Kray is trying a new career—as an artist.

Reggie, 64, has taken up drawing at Wayland Prison, Norfolk, to raise money for Angels With Dirty Faces — a Down's Syndrome kids' charity.

He plans to auction a crayon sketch of a cowboy. But Evening Standard art critic Brian Sewell called it the work of a "mental defective."

A serving of porridge hautes

PS AN unlikely friendship has formed between old lag Reggie Kray and the former newspaper magnate Lord Hartwell's youngest daughter, the eccentric writer Eleanor Berry, whose thriller, The Most Singular Adventures Of Eddy Vernon, is published next month.

Reggie, a resident of Wayland Prison in Thetford, Norfolk, wrote to Eleanor after reading one of her books. It was apparently her comely picture on the dust jacket rather than the subject matter that caught his attention. 'Reggie subsequently sent me two solid silver keyrings bearing his initials as a gesture of affection,' says Eleanor, 48. 'But our friendship soon ran into trouble on account of his indecipherable handwriting. 'I had to go to the East End and hunt out old taxi drivers who had known Reggie and who could translate it. But after a while, it became too much of a bore.'

Murderer Kray set to be released

GANGLAND killer Reggie Kray is fit to be released from prison say psychiatrists who have interviewed him, it was reported today.

They say Kray, now 64, has expressed remorse for his crimes and reads poetry, dislikes bad language and writes to soldiers in the Gulf and Bosnia.

The interviews were carried out for a confidential parole board report, a copy of which has been passed to a national newspaper.

It says the report includes a medical assessment which suggests Kray "has shown no serious instance of violence over the past few years", while a probation officer is quoted as saying the "likelihood of further offences on release is probably minimal".

Kray was arrested for the murder in 1968 of Jack "The Hat" McVitie. He was stabbed to death in a flat in north London, because he had threatened Kray's twin brother,

Ronnie, who, in a feud with a rival gang, had shot George Cornell dead in the saloon bar of the Blind Beggar pub in east London.

The twins were convicted of the respective murders at the Old Bailey in 1969 and sentenced to life, with a recommendation they serve not less than 30 years. It is said the parole report concludes there is no reason why Kray should not be released after completing his 30-year tariff on May 9.

Kray's parole denied 'because of his drinking'

By Richard Ford, Home Correspondent

REGGIE KRAY, the gangland killer, was refused parole last month because he drinks alcohol in jail and remains a devious and manipulative personality, according to the Parole Board.

The board also expressed concern that the former East End gangster had failed to complete programmes helping him to understand his criminal behaviour or to undertake a full psychological assessment.

A letter from the Lifer Review Unit of the Prison Service informed Kray, 64, that the Parole Board had refused to release him on life licence or even transfer him to an open prison because the "risk is too high for release or a move to open conditions at this stage". The letter told Kray, who had hoped to settle with his new wife in East Anglia, that the next formal review of his case would be in March 2000.

The Parole Board reviewed Kray's case because this week he completed the minimum 30-year term imposed on him for "retribution and deterrence" when he was jailed for life at the Old Bailey in 1969.

The tariff ends this week because Kray was arrested in 1968. He was transferred last August from Maidstone prison to Wayland jail, Norfolk.

Kray's solicitor today challenges the reasons given by the board and in a letter in The Times says that they are "factually incorrect". Trevor Linn writes that Kray has no disciplinary findings recorded against him in respect of alcohol, is willing to complete any course required of him and has been assessed by two psychiatrists and two psychologists for the Parole Review.

Confidential reports prepared for the parole hearing indicated that Kray had changed from the confrontational inmate of 30 years ago to one who liked reading and poetry, and disliked watching television. A psychiatrist who examined Kray said that he could be deemed entirely capable of independent living.

Another medical report suggested that Kray showed no serious instance of violence over the past few years, although it said that there were "strong intimidating eye contact [that] conveyed feelings of suppressed aggression or defensiveness with a paranoid and contemptuous flavour".

Kray and his twin brother, Ronnie, were convicted in 1969 for the murder of Jack "the Hat" McVitie and George Cornell. Ronnie Kray died of a heart attack in 1995 while in Broadmoor top security hospital and was given a traditional East End funeral.

Even if the Parole Board had recommended that Kray be released, the final decision would rest with Jack Straw, the Home Secretary.

Kray: has now served 30 years for murder

Diary, page 22
Letters, page 23

Sky-high attempt to free Reggie

GANGLAND killer Reggie Kray watched proudly as the campaign to secure his freedom took to the skies yesterday.

Wife Roberta arranged for a light aircraft to fly around his jail, pulling a 100ft banner with 5ft high red letters reading: "Reg Kray Political Prisoner 1968-1998."

Prison officials were powerless to stop the stunt which marked the 30th anniversary of Kray's arrest.

Kray, 64, and other inmates on their exercise session saw the single-engined craft spend 20 minutes circling Wayland Prison, Norfolk.

Roberta, 39, said: "He was very pleased.

"He knows the decision to keep him inside is a political one. It is inhumane that he is still locked up.

"All he wants to do is live quietly in East Anglia for the rest of his life."

Kray, jailed for life for murder has just had his request for parole turned down and must wait two years before he can apply again.

Pilot Jim Stevens, 49, agreed to do the flight at a cut price rate for Roberta because he supports her campaign.

He said: "I could see prisoners looking up and pointing but I couldn't tell which was Reg."

Kray appeal is rejected

APPEAL REJECTED –
Charlie Kray

DRUG dealer Charlie Kray has lost the first round of his appeal against a 12-year jail term for masterminding a £39 million cocaine deal.

Kray, 71, elder brother of gangster twins Ronnie and Reggie, was jailed last year after offering to supply undercover police officers with cocaine.

One of the deals was set up in Linden Hall Hotel, Longhorsley, Northumberland, and £500,000 worth of cocaine was destined for the streets of Tyneside.

Kray shook hands on a deal with an undercover officer who he agreed to supply five kilos of 92 per cent pure cocaine once a fortnight for two years.

By DAVID TROUT

The officer posed as a businessman with a criminal background.

The Court of Appeal yesterday rejected a written application from Kray's legal team for leave to appeal against the conviction.

Solicitor Ralph Haeems said: "We are disappointed but will now prepare a legal submission to be heard before three judges."

The legal team has 14 days to submit a second application on behalf of Kray, who is in Long Lartin jail, Leicestershire.

Kray's girlfriend Judy Stanley said the fight would go on.

REG CHOSE WRONG CRIME

REGGIE Kray's application for parole has been turned down again, even though he has already served nearly 30 years inside and no one seriously believes he poses any threat to society.

Even his most vociferous supporters make no attempt to condone his crimes and they acknowledge that he used to be a very violent man.

But he has long since served his time. If instead of killing another gangster, he had raped and murdered a child he would not only have been out by now but would also have his own luxury hideaway with a wide-screen television and hot and cold running room service, courtesy of the police and the British taxpayer.

STAR SAYS I'LL DO IT MY KRAY

FORMER Bros heart-throb Matt Goss has paid a secret visit to jailed gang boss Reggie Kray–to help him write a song.

The unlikely duo teamed up to set to music a poem written by Reggie, 64, about his dead twin brother Ronnie.

It will be featured on an album highlighting Reggie's campaign for release. He invited Matt, 29, to visit him at Wayland Prison, Norfolk, to launch the project.

Manager Rob Ferguson told the News of the World: "Reggie was particularly keen for Matt to work on this song because he is a twin himself and will understand the special bond between the brothers.

"They hit it off

By VANESSA LARGE

straight away and swapped stories about growing up."

Rob added: "It seems very unjust that an old man like Reggie is still held after 30 years."

Jail sentence stands on Charlie Kray

THE 12-year sentence given to Charlie Kray for his part in a £39million cocaine deal was upheld yesterday by the Court of Appeal. Kray, 72, (pictured) of Sanderstead, South-East London, older brother of Ronnie and Reggie, sat impassively as his plea to have his sentence reduced was thrown out. His appeal against conviction, on the grounds that he had been set up, was dismissed at an earlier hearing.

DON'T MESS WITH THE NEW PREMIERSHIP ENFORCERS

FIND OUT WHO ON PAGE 52

REGGIE KRAY:
I'M FIT TO BE FREE

Reggie Kray proudly displays his lean, muscular body at 65 — and claims he is fit to be freed from jail. The ex-boxer has been inside for 30 years for a gangland murder. He works out daily to stay in shape for his release

SONY KRAYSTATION

EXCLUSIVE by JOHN TROUP

Mod cons . . PlayStation

Video games for Reggie jail

Game fun . . Reg Kray

PAMPERED cons at a jail housing killer Reggie Kray have been given Sony PlayStations to encourage them to behave themselves.

Thirteen of the video game consoles have been placed in recreation rooms for prisoners to use.

But the move has appalled warders, who say it is the latest example of criminals getting kid glove treatment.

The £79 PlayStations were delivered to Wayland Jail near Attleborough in Norfolk on Tuesday. Last night one warder said: "Prison life is getting cushier all the time for these blokes. They have access to televisions and videos and now get given games for which kids spend months saving up their pocket money. It's ludicrous.

"It makes you wonder just what they will end up being deprived of in here. They should be experiencing a life bereft of luxuries. Instead they spend their association time sitting around playing football games and flight simulators." The Home Office defended the decision to buy the PlayStations, which were paid for out of proceeds from the prison shop and cost taxpayers nothing.

A prisons spokesman said: "They are not for the use of individual prisoners in their cells and inmates will be restricted to an hour on the machines at a time.

"Three PlayStations have been placed on each of the four wings of the jail. Each wing accommodates 120 men.

"Another has been placed in the recreation room used by inmates who are attempting to stay clean from drugs.

"The consoles will be used to encourage good behaviour and will be forfeited if prisoners fail to maintain standards.

"The games they play will be purchased by prison staff. No games featuring excessive violence or criminal themes will be purchased and inmates will not be able to play games brought in for them by visitors."

news

FUN LOVIN' CRIMINALS have made a new friend – the original fun lovin' criminal! Huey and co are launching a musical project with jailed Sixties gangster Reggie Kray.

Kray twin Reggie – who rose to notoriety with his late brother Ronnie – has been writing song lyrics while he serves his sentence.

And Fun Lovin' Criminals intend to set the words to music for release on an album next year.

Although all of the band, and possibly some special guests, will be involved, it's not thought at the moment that the release will be under the banner of Fun Lovin' Criminals.

Huey has been to visit Reggie at HMP Wayland in Griston, near Thetford, Norfolk, and he said afterwards: "Reggie is a man without a voice, and I'm going to give him the voice that he needs."

Reggie Kray: the East End's answer to John Gotti

Huey (centre) and co: having fun on the outside

FUN LOVIN' CRIMINALS: 'FREE REGGIE KRAY!'

The Kray twins, in their day, were renowned as much for their glitzy showbiz parties, their enthusiastic clubbing and their pub piss-ups as they were for the iron fist with which they ruled London's East End.

But the good times came to an end in 1968, when the twins were arrested and later sentenced to a recommended minimum of 30 years in prison for the murders of Jack "The Hat" McVitie and George Cornell.

Ronnie Kray has since died in captivity, and Reggie has clocked up 31 years with no prospect of release.

Huey has added his voice to the "Free Reggie" campaign and wears the official T-shirt.

He flew into Britain three days early for the band's Reading Festival appearance to make the jail visit with FLC manager Jonathan Block.

Reggie Kray told The Maker: "Huey and I have become firm friends. We're keeping in contact. I would walk to the ends of the earth to do anything for him.

"I spoke to him five minutes before he went onstage at Reading Festival. He told the audience what he was doing for me. He dedicated the John Gotti song, 'King Of New York', to me and changed the chorus to 'Hey, hey, free Reg Kray', and got the crowd singing it."

Talking of the musical project, Reggie said: "We've put things together very quickly. We've got great expectations for the future. We did a lot of it by phone, with a great deal of help from my wife Roberta."

Roberta adds: "Someone told us that Huey was sympathetic to Reg and so we got in touch with EMI and I sent half a dozen sets of lyrics. They were given to the band at Glastonbury, and it went from there. I believe they've already put music to one song, and I've got to send them out a lot of new lyrics. They're going to decide which ones to use.

"Huey is very sympathetic. He's completely behind Reg."

Fun Lovin' Criminals and Reggie hope to launch the project to tie in with his next parole appeal, around March next year.

Jonathan Block told us: "I can confirm that myself and Huey met with Reg and we're in discussions with him to collaborate on a musical project. He's a really, really nice, kind man, and should not be in jail."

THE SUN SAYS
Free Reggie

IN the Sixties, Reggie Kray was a murdering gang boss.

His reign of terror in London's East End deservedly got him a 30-year jail sentence.

But today that 30 years is up. He has done his time.

He may keep himself fit in prison, but he is now an old age pensioner.

No one can seriously believe he is a danger to anyone.

So why on earth is Reggie Kray still inside?

IRA bombers who killed dozens of innocent people have been freed.

Criminal

Child killers can be out after less than 10 years.

Kray is not like Myra Hindley. The man Kray killed was another criminal.

That doesn't excuse the crime— but it does put it into context.

Sun readers have voted overwhelmingly to back Kray's bid for freedom.

Keeping him locked up is not justice - it is vengeance.

My bloody memories, by Reggie

EXCLUSIVE BY **IAN EDMONDSON**

JAILED mobster Reggie Kray is to boast about his murderous past—in a magazine column.

He will write each month in a glossy called Front.

Kray, 64, who has so far served 30 years for knifing Jack 'The Hat' McVitie, is campaigning to be released.

He told cronies he want, to "raise his public profil-

His first column recall the notorious shooting club owner Jimmy Cooney villain Jimmy Nash.

Kray writes: "Jimmy had a short bull ne crew cut and a lik Nazi memorabilia ar on torture."

Kray fan jailed for 49p robbery

A FAN of the Kray twins was jailed yesterday for setting up a protection racket in a skateboard park which earned him just 49p. Cardiff Crown Court was told Jason Clowes, 20, approached a 16-year-old, saying: 'We are the Krays, you have to pay taxes.' He had a knife with a serrated edge and the boy handed over 49p. Clowes admitted robbery and was sent to a young offenders' institution for a year.

Kray sees brother in hospital

GANGSTER Reggie Kray has paid a visit to his brother in hospital as concern mounted over Charlie Kray's condition.

The 73-year-old elder brother of the Kray twins is in St Mary's Hospital, Isle of Wight, after collapsing at Parkhurst Prison last month.

He is serving 12 years for his part in a drugs plot.

Reggie's visit yesterday appeared to be a break from routine, prompting speculation that his brother's condition was grave.

Reggie, 66, whose twin Ronnie died five years ago, was moved last month from Wayland Prison, Norfolk, to Parkhurst to be near Charlie.

PATSY: 'A real natural'

PATSY'S KRAYS

BY SANDRO MONETTI
TV CORRESPONDENT

FORMER EastEnders star Patsy Palmer is to host a documentary on The Krays.

She quizzes admirers and neighbours of the mobsters in her new TV series, Patsy Palmer's Real East End.

Patsy said: "The East End is THE place to be. The bad image of the Krays and the explosion of bars and clubs has made the area dangerously trendy."

The shows go out on BBC Choice from May 25. A TV insider said: "We think she's a real natural."

Patsy, 28 — who played Bianca in EastEnders — returns to acting tonight as a troubled backpacker in Sky One's Do or Die at 9pm.

Get Krayzed on Chateau Reggie

Gangster sells wine that will blow your head off

BEST SERVED BEHIND BARS

Beaujailais

1999 VINTAGE

DRY REG WINE

WITH PLENTY OF BODY

PRISON VAN ORDINAIRE: Kray hopes to make a killing

JAILED gangland killer Reggie Kray is swapping prison screws for corkscrews — and launching his own brand of wine.

The mobster has seen more exercise yards than vineyards for the past 30 years inside.

But he hopes his new range of jailhouse red and white will raise cash to fund his campaign for freedom. A prison insider told us: "Reggie's spilled plenty of claret in his time—now he's decided to flog it.

"At least this makes a change from his usual whine, 'Why am I still behind bars?'"

Kray, serving life for the murder of Jack 'The Hat' McVitie, hopes the specially imported French plonk will be a vintage to die for.

His joint venture with a drinks distribution company is being masterminded by 39-year-old wife Roberta.

Bang

The wine, featuring a picture of the 66-year-old villain holding up a glass of the brew, is to be released for sale in pubs, clubs and off-licences later this month at £80 for a case of 12.

Plans are under way to produce up to 1,000 cases, using the Free Reggie internet site to advertise the booze.

One of Kray's guards at Wayland prison, Suffolk, told us: "Reggie's very excited about going into the wine trade and has told everybody they've planned the launch to cash in on millennium celebrations.

"With his record I reckon it'll make any party go with a bang. Loathe him or love him, he's always had plenty of bottle."

And if there's any leftovers the brut version can always be relied on for a killer punch...

The Noughties & Beyond

"I won't let them carry me out of here in a box."
Reg Kray

"I lost my appeal but I have many people helping me so the truth will come out in the end, I hope its not too long."
Charlie Kray

"Reg was no angel but he was not the devil either.
He had reason, intelligence and warmth - and he never lost his capacity for love"
Roberta Kray

KRAY-ZY GANG

Lover feared the Kray Twins after village sex romps

By LEE HANNON

THE man who tried to steal Mike Reid's wife Shirley was terrified that the infamous Kray Twins would come after him after news leaked out about their passionate affair.

And Reg Turner, now in his late 40s, is still reluctant to talk about what happened. He said: "It's all water under the bridge now.

"I don't want to talk about it. I used to get into all sorts of scrapes and fights back then, but I keep myself to myself now."

At the time of the affair, Reg and brother Kenny were the Mitchell brothers of the tiny Nottinghamshire village of Sutton.

They were notorious for their womanising and drinking in the local pub, The Gate.

When we tracked him down, Reg admitted: "I am the Reg Turner you are looking for."

ROMANCE: Reg Turner

Amnesia

But he claimed not to remember anything about his romance with Shirley.

"I can't remember what I did last week, never mind then," said Reg, who now lives in the nearby town of Retford.

"I have got a sort of amnesia. I can not remember anything about it, but no harm was meant."

Brother Kenny, though, said: "Reg was worried the Krays would become involved and has kept his mouth shut since.

"I know one twin is dead and the other is in prison, but back then Reg believed this and it worried him. He just doesn't want to talk about it."

Kenny still lives in the village just a stone's throw from the Gate Inn where Mike "knocked Reg's lights out".

But he added: "It is all over now and we don't want to discuss it."

A fright at the theatre

■ by CHRIS WHITE

A BUNCH of celebrity East End gangsters menaced a theatre audience watching a play – about the notorious Kray Twins.

Many were scared to go back to their seats when Roy "Pretty Boy" Shaw, Charlie Richardson and other heavies got stroppy in the stalls.

The mob, including Page Three model Sam Fox and her mum, set off fire alarms, ejected people from their row, interfered with set props and heckled the actors.

Manners gave way to mayhem at genteel Wimbledon Studio Theatre, south London, at a preview of Jump To Cow Heaven.

The atmosphere soured when tough guy Roy Shaw – dubbed the hardest man in Britain in the 60s – and his mates turned up to the play 15 minutes late.

The firm were accompanied by minders, while Sam Fox was with her mum, who was dating one of the cast.

WELL 'ARD: Richardson

INSPIRATION: Twins Ron, left, and Reg Kray

Terror

Actors who were portraying the notorious Krays and fellow gangster Frank Mitchell did their best against the odds.

But when the one-time villains discovered that they could not sit together, they sorted matters in their own trusty, time-honoured way.

A scary bloke "had a word" with manager Jonathan Kennedy, telling him straight: "Rectify the situation ... before we do."

Mr Kennedy said: "I wasn't going to argue. And neither were the audience."

The second act was forced to start late as terrified members of the audience had to be coaxed out of hiding in the bar, and sent trembling back to their seats.

But the off-set palaver carried on when some of the mob ignored no-smoking signs, which immediately set off fire alarms.

Firefighters were called and the actors bravely continued despite the bells.

Meanwhile, one of the firm decided a coat stand prop was perfect to hang up his jacket, and another casually helped himself to fake whisky from the set.

One watcher said: "There was an air of menace in the bar after the show."

And tough cookie Roy Shaw's verdict?

"The play was 100 per cent accurate," he said. "But it could've done with a bit more violence."

Ronnie Kray was my baby-sitter

Ask Jamie Foreman about playing an underworld boss in Gangster No 1 and the talk inevitably turns to his notorious father Freddie. **PETE CLARK** tries the diplomatic approach

I 'VE been coming here since I was 10," says Jamie Foreman, taking a ruminative puff on his Camel filter. "My dad used to bring me. We came here for lunch last week and left at one in the morning. Good lunch, that. And, you know, the service is always good." The service at Sheekey's is, indeed, good. Our waiter is so attentive that I feel that at any moment he might take up permanent residence in my lap. Jamie's usual, a sprightly Puligny Montrachet '97, is rushed to the table every time one of us looks at our glass. They know Jamie. He is a valued customer. Janet Street Porter is at a table across the way giving it a bit of rabbit, although she is eclipsed by the Richard E Grant lookalike at the table next door who is wowing his rapt audience with tales of the parts he should have got. Despite all their efforts, our table is the cynosure.

Jamie Foreman is an actor of the most plausible kind. In his latest film, Gangster No 1, he plays a gangland boss called Lenny Taylor, who manages to remain threatening throughout a protracted and untimely end. As Lenny, Jamie has the distinct look of a Kray. As Jamie, Jamie has a similar sort of feel of meritocratic menace. I ask him about the Kray thing. "That was deliberate, yeah. I went for Ronnie — smile on your face, stab you in the back. Ron was the look." Knowing that Jamie's dad is Freddie Foreman, charismatic Sixties enforcer, I feel it might be possible that young Jamie was basing his performance on a character he had personal knowledge of. "I was about 10 in 1968," he reflects. "Ronnie used to look after me when I was a kid. My dad used to say to him, 'Mind Jamie for a bit, I've got to go see someone'." For

"I've one of the best names in London behind me": Jamie Foreman has maintained a strong relationship with his father Freddie, left

The super high-Kray

NOTORIOUS gangland killer Reggie Kray has launched his own website.

The move is part of a campaign to win his release from jail after 31 years behind bars.

His solicitor Trevor Linn said: "I'm beginning to wonder in just which millennium they intend to release Reg."

The website address is at http://www.thekrays.co.uk

Kray movie got it wrong

I never knew Violet Kray. The nearest connection I have with the Krays is that one of the actresses in the film (Barbara Ferns) went to school with my mother.

However I can well believe Lawrie O'Leary's statement that she was nothing like the character played in the film.

I'm no expert on the Krays, but noticed several inaccuracies in the film.

For instance, I doubt if their grandfather really spoke in a Northern accent; I believe the Kray twins fought each other in proper contest rather then a booth fight and as kids rather than adults.

Their Aunt Rose died years before Reggie Kray got married, not during his honeymoon; Frances Kray was a redhead (I found that change inexplicable); and the murders of Cornell and McVitie did not happen in the way they were depicted. Ironically the truth was more "filmable".

If the film could make errors like that I can well believe that it would depict Mrs Kray (who I believe to have been a very nice lady) inaccurately. Would the producers care to explain themselves?

My feelings are, I admit, partly due to the fact that the way the Kray brothers talk about their mother is the way a friend of mine talks about his.

My friends mother sound like the nicest person I've ever heard of Need I say more? May I suggest a TV serial on the Krays, simply showing the truth.

And yes I do believe that Reggie Kray should be released, as should Ronnie if he's able to cope with life on the outside.

They were not after all, child-killers, cop-killers, terrorists or traitors.

Mark Tate, Forbing Road, Highgate.

Issue of the Week
Should Reggie Kray be freed from prison?

WHEN the Kray twins were sentenced to life imprisonment for murder it was with the recommendation that they should serve no less than 30 years.

Certified criminally insane after murdering George Cornell, Ronnie Kray died of a heart attack on March 17 1995 at Broadmoor maximum security psychiatric hospital.

His brother Reggie is still jailed in Wayland Prison, Norfolk, with better surroundings than Parkhurst Prison on the Isle of Wight. He spent 20 years there as a Category 'A' prisoner, largely in isolation and under constant surveillance, after the murder of Jack 'The Hat' McVitie.

Their older brother Charlie was jailed for 12 years in 1997, aged 70, for dealing in cocaine.

But Reggie's next parole review in March will consider his eligibility for transfer to an open prison. The question on the Home Secretary's mind is should he be released now he's served his sentence? Or should he be kept behind bars and used as a warning to others?

Tamara Sternberg asked what you thought.

Reformed?: Reggie Kray

PETER KAUNE
No. 1 Scaffolding

HE'S served his time. There are people out there who have done a lot worse but done less time. He's paid his debt to society.

YES

MARK STIMPSON
Millcroft Scaffolding

HE committed his crime over 30 years ago, and he was killing another convict. Today, rapists and paedophiles get half the sentences.

YES

GEORGE JOHNSON
ABB Stuart

THERE are so many people who commit worse crimes but get much shorter sentences. I don't agree with what he did, but people do worse.

YES

ELIZABETH VAUGHAN
O'Rourke's

HE'S an old man. If he's going to do any more damage, he could do it from inside jail just as well as from on the outside, so they should let him go.

YES

ELAINE BROWN-CRAWFORD
Barclays Capital

FOR someone who's killed so many people, he should get life meaning actual life. It's not fair to other lifers who have to serve their full sentence.

NO

STEVEN PROCTER
ArtLite International

HE'S a victim of his own fame. Plenty of people have committed worse crimes. But politicians are afraid of the backlash if they let him out.

YES

KRAY BROTHER IS 'CLOSE TO DEATH'

Villain Reggie rushed from cell to bedside of sick Charlie

Kray's agony

FEARS: Reggie visits brother Charlie yesterday

FORMER gangster Reggie Kray was last night at the hospital bedside of his "desperately ill" elder brother.

Warders took the East End hardman from his cell 30 minutes after lock-up for the mercy dash.

Reggie, 66, was said to be distraught after his brother Charlie's condition suddenly worsened.

Reggie was allowed out on compassionate grounds from C Wing of Parkhurst Jail on the Isle of Wight to travel to nearby St Mary's Hospital.

A source said: "Charlie is in a very bad way now. We all feared the worst when we heard.

Serious

"He is hanging by a thread. Reggie is with him at the hospital and is very worried. Doctors have told him it doesn't look too good."

Sick Charlie, 73 – serving 12 years for cocaine smuggling – has been suffering from serious heart problems.

Pals have already voiced their concern that he could die behind bars. This is already his third spell in hospital this year.

Reggie, who was jailed for life in 1969 for the murder of gangster Jack "The Hat" McVitie, was recently moved temporarily to Parkhurst from his jail in Norfolk.

He has seen sick Charlie at least twice since the switch – including a 45-minute get together in a hospital side ward.

It was the first time they had seen each other since the funeral of Reggie's twin brother Ronnie, in 1995.

Charlie, left, and Reggie at Ronnie's funeral and, below, the three brothers in the 60s

EXCLUSIVE by ANTHONY WALTON

Charlie was convicted of masterminding a plan to supply cocaine worth £39 million in 1997.

A boxer, it was he who taught Reggie and Ronnie the fighting skills that helped them set up their East End crime empire. Yet he hated violence himself.

"Nipper" Read, the detective who broke the Krays, said: "When they were in trouble the twins always turned to Charlie."

HAGGARD Reggie Kray leaves the hospital bedside of his older brother Charlie yesterday, knowing it could be for the final time.

The gangland killer spent 70 minutes yesterday with 73-year-old Charlie, whose condition was said to be "extremely poorly".

Lifer Reggie, 66, was taken by van from the Isle of Wight's Parkhurst Prison to the nearby St Mary's Hospital in Newport on Monday evening – when it was feared his brother might not make it through the night.

Yesterday he looked increasingly drawn and distressed as he was led in and out of the hospital handcuffed to a prison officer.

Reggie was transferred 18 days ago from Wayland jail in Norfolk to Parkhurst, where Charlie was doing 12 years for his part in a £39million cocaine smuggling plot.

He has made regular visits under escort to his brother since then.

Kray's hospital vigil

REGGIE Kray strides from hospital flanked by jail guards after visiting stricken brother Charlie yesterday.

The gangster, 66, wore jeans, an open-necked shirt and medallion on one of the few times he has been outside prison walls since being locked up 31 years ago for murder.

Charlie, 73, had collapsed with chest pains at Parkhurst jail, Isle of Wight. Reggie has been transferred there — where he served 18 years — to visit daily. Afterwards he will go back to Wayland Prison, Norfolk.

Wife Roberta, 41, said: "He desperately wanted to be with Charlie."

Charlie was jailed for 12 years in 1997 for a £36million cocaine plot.

CLOSE FAMILY – Charlie Kray with a copy of his autobiography of life with his twin brothers

Charlie's gone, so let the myth die with him

NEWSFLASH: A kindly, elderly gentleman passed away this week after a protracted heart condition. Charlie "gentleman" Kray was loved and respected by all he knew, was kind to his dear old muvver and liked playing with kittens. His masterminding of a £39 million cocaine plot and his invaluable help in disposing of Jack "The Hat" McVitie's body were unfortunate incidents which in no way detracted from his general human decency and charitable approach to life.

State funeral, with requisite weeping EastEnders' stars and preposterous Sixties has-beens wearing dark glasses whatever the weather, will take place as soon as Barbara Windsor can clear her filming schedule. Flowers welcome, particularly if over-elaborate and fashioned into the words "Bruvver" or "Respect". Donations, please, to the Charlie Kray Twilight Home for Honourable Violence (we knew where we stood).

Don't blame Charlie

HAVING known Charlie Kray for most of my life, via my friendship with his son, Gary, I find John McVicar's comments (Mail) sad.

But I recall the film in which McVicar was portrayed by The Who lead singer Roger Daltry, adding glamour to a story which seemed to show McVicar suffering more for his problems 'inside' than for his actions as a criminal on the loose.

McVicar's parting shot about Charlie's dress sense was confusing. When I saw McVicar on a chat show some months ago, he looked like someone caught in a juvenile/skinhead time-warp.

Perhaps, like Charlie, his time spent in prison makes him inadvertently try to buy back the years of a mis-spent youth.

For most of the years I knew him, Charlie was a Kray in name only. He loved his brothers unreservedly — not because of their notoriety or glamour.

They were his brothers and he loved them as he did his poor son, Gary.

Charlie had different ideals, a different lifestyle, but he came from the same human race as you or me.

BARRY A. MAHONEY,
Thorpe Bay, Essex.

Kray brother dies

FAMILY and friends of Charlie Kray, elder brother of gangster twins Ronnie and Reggie, were mourning today after his death at the age of 73.

Kray, who had a heart condition, died last night in St Mary's Hospital, Isle of Wight, near Parkhurst Prison, where he was serving a 12-year sentence for his part in a drugs plot.

His girlfriend, Diane Buffini, and two other friends were at his bedside when he died at 8.50pm, a hospital spokesman said.

Reggie, 66, went to see his dying brother on Monday evening and again yesterday afternoon but was not with him when he died.

Reggie was moved from Wayland Prison, Norfolk, to Parkhurst Prison to be near Charlie.

Tyson: I won't be visiting Reggie Kray, even though he wrote to me when I was in jail

MIKE TYSON last night announced he would cut his links with jailed East End gangster Reggie Kray to avoid tarnishing his image any further.

It had been claimed Tyson would visit Kray in prison after he fights Julius Francis in Manchester on January 29.

But Tyson said: "I would not glamourise him." And he insisted he never returned letters sent to him by Kray while serving his own sentence.

Fight promoter Frank Warren has lined up a series of hospital visits aimed at showing a softer side to Tyson.

The former world heavyweight champion did admit, though, that messages from Kray were a source of comfort while he was behind bars.

Tyson said: "When you are in prison, you will talk to anybody. Prison is the closest thing to death. I appreciated him writing me. I respect him for that.

GOODBYE BROTHER

Cheers as crowds get a glimpse of Reggie

REGGIE Kray was greeted by cheering crowds as he arrived in Bethnal Green for his brother Charlie's funeral yesterday.

East Enders lined St Matthew's Row to catch a glimpse of the last remaining Kray brother as he was escorted into the hour-long service at St Matthew's Church handcuffed to a woman police officer.

Fellow former hard man 'Mad' Frankie Fraser led "three cheers for Reggie" as the convicted gangster left the church on the way to Chingford Mount Cemetery for the burial.

Reg Kray waves to the cheering crowds as he enters St Matthew's Church for the funeral. Left: Brother Charlie Kray's coffin is carried into the church for the hour-long service

Reggie Kray says a last farewell . . .

GANGSTER Reggie Kray got a brief taste of freedom yesterday to go to his brother Charlie's funeral.

Reggie, 66, had been let out of Wayland jail, Norfolk, where he is serving life for murder but was handcuffed to a female prison officer throughout the 50-minute service in London's Bethnal Green.

Charlie, 73, died in Parkhurst prison, Isle of Wight, while serving 12 years for a cocaine smuggling plot.

BYE BRUV

Gangster's day out

Returning to the East End for the funeral of his brother, Reggie Kray is treated like a hero

By **Bill Mouland**

HIS crimes are heinous, his name synonymous with terror.

But yesterday the pavements were lined three deep to mark the return of Reggie Kray to the streets he and his twin once ruled with fear.

The crowds were there not to boo or heckle this convicted murderer but to cheer him as if he were a conquering hero, not the sadistic gangster that he really is.

He was released from prison to attend the funeral of his 73-year-old brother Charlie. But nobody pretended that the star attraction was anything other than Reggie, 66.

'We love you Reggie,' they cried beneath banners hailing this infamous son of the East End. Even the parish priest who conducted the service declined to condemn the ungodly activities of the Krays.

Reggie's old gangland mate 'Mad' Frankie Fraser was there too. Twice 'Mad' Frankie called to the heavens for 'three cheers for Reggie'. Both times he was raucously answered.

And Reggie acknowledged their cheers, raising his hands to wave. But it was an awkward wave, the steel cuffs around his wrists restricting his movement. Indeed, he spent the entire day handcuffed to a woman prison officer

They weren't happy about that, his supporters. Many thought that his hands should have been free, as a gesture of mercy. Not that Reggie was big on mercy for anyone else when he was at large.

'People do love him,' insisted 63-year-old Rose Chatfield, who has visited him in prison where he is serving life for the murder of Jack 'The Hat' McVitie. 'He has done his time and should come out.'

Unlike the arrangements he had orchestrated for his twin Ronnie's funeral five years ago, Reggie hadn't laid on the the six plumed black horses and glass hearse for Charlie.

Where Ronnie got 26 Daimlers, Charlie got just 12. For that matter, while Ronnie and Reggie got life imprisonment for callous murder, Charlie, who died in prison on April 4, had been given 12 years for a bungled drugs deal.

As the older brother of Britain's most notorious twins, he was still guaranteed a send-off with all the gaudy trimmings.

Thousands stood three deep on the pavement in the busy bits of the 12-mile route from church in Bethnal Green to family plot in Chingford via Walthamstow. Reggie was riding along, just behind the hearse, in an electric blue V-registered Mercedes convict carrier.

He had emerged from the scrum of people outside W. English and Son, Funeral Director, a wizened little man now with grey hair and a shaky demeanour. To ragged cheers, the cortege then made its way slowly along to St Matthew's Church. Inside, Father Ken Rimini said: 'It's not for me to judge Charles. He is before a greater authority than I ever had in life.'

Reggie had not trusted his grating voice to carry far in the church so he had recorded his own message, to be relayed over loudspeakers. In fact, the congregation was told, it was the poem he wanted for his own funeral, written by a real hero Stephen Cummins, a soldier who was later killed in Ulster. 'Do not stand at my grave and weep,' it began.

Crowds lined St Matthew's Row when the coffin was brought out of church past a ragtaggle 'guard of honour' made up of men with shaven heads and leather jackets. People hung banners on the route. A wreath in the shape of a boxing ring was from Reggie.

At the cemetery, as he stood at Charlie's graveside, Reggie was allowed to put his arm round his wife Roberta for the final prayers, but it was the prison officer who had to hand him the red roses which he threw on the coffin.

Afterwards, the shaved heads, the grey heads and the bottle blondes engulfed him and it seemed he might be shedding a tear. The old gangland types said hello – Mad Frankie, Charlie Richardson, Tony Lambrianou.

And while the crowds may have cheered yesterday, how many thought that the next time Reggie sees Chingford Mount Cemetery he will be being buried in it himself? Who will be cheering then?

REGGIE KRAY – 31 YEARS ON!

Kray legend may be behind the reluctance to free Reg

THE campaign to free former gangland killer Reg Kray will receive another boost with a special documentary screened tonight (Thursday) on Channel Four.

It is now almost 31 years since Kray twins were sent to prison for a minimum of 30 years and the Cutting Edge Special examines the case for freeing Reg.

When Ronnie died in 1995, tens of thousands of East Enders lined the streets to pay their respects and the documentary looks at how the prevailing Kray legend may be behind the authorities' reluctance to free Reg.

His wife Roberta, friends and former victims of the Krays are interviewed about difference between the Reg Kray of 30 years ago and the man as he is today.

Although Roberta hasn't seen the finished product, she told the Advertiser she and Reg were encouraged that it would be constructive for the campaign.

"We're hoping the documentary will show that justice is for the majority and not that there's is not one rule for Reg Kray and one rule for everybody else."

Reg is due for another

BY CHRIS TAYLOR

parole review next month and Roberta, who married him in 1997, is hopeful the authorities will see that Reg has served his time.

Another person interviewed, childhood friend of the Krays, Johnny Squibb, tells the documentary team that although both twins were gang leaders, they were by no means similar in their personalities.

"If Reggie sent for you....you'd go round and see him....if Ronnie sent for you, you'd take six pairs of pants with you." he claims.

Former Krays' victim, Lennie Hamilton, paints an even less flattering picture of Ronnie for the programme makers.

"I have nightmares today over what Ronnie Kray did to me and I'm bloody glad he's dead and f*** him," the documentary hears.

■ Cutting Edge Special: Reggie Kray will be shown on Channel Four, on Thursday, February 17, at 9pm.

A young Reggie in the Kray heyday, Reggie when released to attend Ronnie's funeral and above a delighted Roberta on her wedding day

NEW KRAY MURDER QUIZ

SHOT: Mad Frankie

BOSS: Twin Reggie

HITMAN: Foreman

CRIME king Reggie Kray is set to be quizzed again in jail over a 35-year-old underworld murder.

Files have been re-opened into the shooting of Frank "Mad Axeman" Mitchell after Kray henchman Freddie Foreman made a dramatic confession on TV.

Foreman, a close friend of Eastender Reggie and his now-dead twin Ronnie, came clean in a two-part Carlton documentary about the brothers.

In front of millions of viewers Foreman admitted he had pumped Mitchell full of bullets at Christmas 1966.

The axeman was on the run from Dartmoor and the Krays gave him a hiding place while they tried to negotiate parole if he gave himself up.

But when Mitchell backed out of the deal, hitman Foreman was called in to get rid of him. Detectives from Scotland Yard's elite Organised Crime Group have studied recordings of the ITV documentary and will interview Foreman as well as Kray.

The pair cannot be charged with the murder because they

already stood trial for it in the 1960s and were cleared when the evidence of a vital witness was ruled inadmissable.

But following his TV revelations Foreman could face charges of perverting justice over the evidence he gave at his trial. Police believe Reggie Kray could face conspiracy charges.

Reggie is currently serving life for killing George Cornell and Jack "The Hat" McVitie.

177

Kray crony held after TV murder confession

Frank Mitchell: 'Mad axeman'

Freddie Foreman: He claimed he carried out killings on Krays' orders

ONE of Britain's most notorious criminals was yesterday arrested after he admitted on television that he carried out at least two murders on the orders of the Krays.

Freddie Foreman was acquitted of the murders but detectives launched a new investigation after he made his confession to millions of viewers.

Under the 'double jeopardy' rule, he cannot be tried again for the murders but he could face prosecution for perjury and perverting the course of justice.

Earlier this year, Foreman, 68, admitted in two TV documentaries that he intimidated witnesses who had seen Ronnie Kray shoot dead George Cornell in the Blind Beggar pub in Whitechapel, East London in 1966.

He confessed that a few months later he helped the Krays by murdering Frank Mitchell, known as the Mad Axeman, and feeding his body to fish in the North Sea.

Mitchell had escaped from Dartmoor Prison and the Krays provided him with a hiding place while they negotiated his return

By Peter Rose
Chief Crime Correspondent

to prison in exchange for parole.' Sick of jail, Mitchell refused to go back so Reggie Kray called in Foreman.

During the subsequent Old Bailey trial, another gangland figure, Albert Donaghue, gave evidence against Foreman, the Kray twins and their brother Charlie. He described how Foreman had hacked up the body.

But the judge ruled that because Donaghue was also involved in Mitchell's escape from prison, his evidence could not be accepted without corroboration. Foreman and the Krays were acquitted.

Foreman's television confession could also result in Reggie Kray being charged again. Scot-

land Yard detectives arrested Foreman yesterday and questioned him after studying tapes of the two documentaries. He was later bailed until July for further questioning. They have not yet questioned Reggie Kray.

On the programmes, Foreman also solved the mystery of what happened to Tommy 'Ginger' Marks, a used car dealer whose body vanished after he was shot in Stepney, East London, in 1965. He was also fed to the fish.

Ten years later at the Old Bailey, Foreman and three other men were cleared of Marks's murder on the judge's directions.

In 1969, the Kray twins were sentenced to life for the murders of George Cornell and Jack 'the Hat' McVitie. Foreman was jailed for ten years as an accessory.

Last night, asked about Fore-

man's arrest, a police spokesman would only say: 'We can confirm a 68-year-old man attended a Central London police station and was arrested in connection with allegations of perjury and perverting the course of justice'.

The programmes, produced by Carlton Television, have fuelled the debate over whether suspected criminals who are acquitted of serious

crimes such as murder can be recharged and tried again.

Police chiefs last year stepped up their campaign for the law to be changed to allow this.

The Home Office is reviewing the 'double jeopardy' rule and Home Secretary Jack Straw is considering changing the law.

p.rose@dailymail.co.uk

EXCLUSIVE by MIKE SULLIVAN, Crime Reporter

REGGIE KRAY FIGHTS BIG C

GANGSTER Reggie Kray is fighting cancer of the stomach, The Sun can reveal.

The former crime lord underwent surgery yesterday and was said to be "in a bad way".

Reggie, 66, was moved from Wayland jail in Norfolk on Tuesday after complaining of an obstruction in his stomach.

He was taken to Addenbrooke's Hospital in Cambridge, where a tumour was diagnosed.

Doctors transferred him to Norfolk and Norwich Hospital for an exploratory op.

A hospital source said: "Reggie's condition is not good. He's in a bad way but is putting a brave

face on it." The gangland killer has vowed to lick the Big C — and is determined not to die in jail like his brothers.

Guard

Reggie has served 32 years of a life sentence for murdering rival Jack "The Hat" McVitie.

He ruled East London's underworld in the 1960s with twin Ronnie, who died of a heart attack at

Broadmoor in 1995. Brother Charlie, 73, also died from a heart attack at Parkhurst last April while serving 12 years for drug offences.

Reggie's wife Roberta, 40, was last night at his hospital bedside, where a prison guard is also posted.

A pal said: "It's the biggest fight of Reggie's life and he has had a few.

"But he's determined to survive and finish his sentence so he can be free."

Kray . . . stomach cancer op

Jailed gangster may have been key player in West End shooting, Yard reveals

Charlie Kray 'link to tycoon's murder'

By Chester Stern

CRIME CORRESPONDENT

EAST END gangster Charlie Kray may have had links with the 1993 contract killing of millionaire Donald Urquhart, Scotland Yard has revealed.

Detectives believe they are closing in on the syndicate behind the assassination of the property tycoon, who was shot in a London street in front of his Thai girlfriend.

Fresh evidence points to the older brother of Kray twins Ronnie and Reggie as a key player in the shooting. He died last April after collapsing in Parkhurst Prison on the Isle of Wight.

Yesterday police arrested two men in London and the Home Counties for questioning about the murder. Both have been released on bail.

Last night, a senior Yard source said: 'We have a clear insight into the South London nightclub scene and have established Charlie Kray's role as an adviser after the murder.

'He was a close associate of those identified as being responsible and was a vital conduit between criminals in Central London and South London.' Detectives, who launched a new inquiry into the killing a year ago under a programme set up to review unsolved murders, may go to America next month to interview 'important new witnesses'.

When Urquhart was killed there were claims that his death was linked to international gun-running and drug smuggling, but police found a secret will which left his wealth to his lawyer and business associate Jonathan Levene.

Mr Levene, who went on the run shortly after the killing, remains the prime suspect. Last year The Mail on Sunday tracked him to his Swiss hideaway.

The hitman, Graeme West, and his accomplice, Geoffrey Heath, were jailed for the murder seven years ago but the person who paid for the killing has never been caught.

'We have interviewed important new witnesses, including a contract killer in prison,' said the Scotland Yard source.

Officers now believe the motive for the murder was rivalry between Urquhart and his business partners.

The shooting happened on Saturday, January 2, 1993, shortly after Urquhart had left a pub in Marylebone High Street. West, wearing a motorcycle helmet, strolled up to the tycoon and fired a .32 revolver three times into the side of his head and neck before making his escape on a motorbike.

AILING REGGIE KRAY HAS OP FOR CANCER

Wife at gangster's bedside

By GARY JONES

GANGSTER Reggie Kray has been diagnosed with cancer after undergoing emergency surgery.

Frail Kray, 67, was said to be stable and comfortable. Last night his wife Roberta, who is campaigning for his freedom, was at his bedside. She is expected to make a statement today.

A prison source said: "Reggie has had exploratory surgery, which has found cancer in his body. No-one is sure at the moment just how bad

DRAMA: Hospital treating Kray, left

CANCER-HIT KRAY WILL FIGHT FOR HIS FREEDOM

'My Reg has suffered enough'

By GARY JONES

THE wife of notorious gangster Reggie Kray yesterday called for him to be freed from jail after confirming he has cancer.

Last week The Mirror revealed that the 67-year-old killer was being treated in hospital for the disease.

Roberta Kray, 41, confirmed surgeons had removed a malignant tumour from Kray's small intestine in a four-hour operation.

She said: "The obstruction is a secondary growth, and we are awaiting further scans to determine the source." His solicitor would now apply for compassionate parole, she added.

"What is the purpose of keeping him in any longer? I feel after 32 years in prison he has suffered enough.

"In the light of this, and of the severity of his illness, we are hoping he will be granted his long-awaited freedom."

Kray is serving a life sentence for the murder of Jack "The Hat" McVitie in London in 1969.

Old friends from those days are also calling for the Home Secretary to make Reggie a free man.

Les Martin, who has known Reggie since the 60s, said: "Jack Straw should sign on the dotted line and order his release. Reggie has done his time and suffered enough."

The Prison Service said compassionate parole was only given in "exceptional circumstances".

A spokesman said: "It is very rare to release them under this section and it will only happen when it will not put the safety of the public at risk."

A scheduled parole review has been postponed because of his illness.

Kray went from Wayland Prison, Norfolk to Norwich hospital for the operation on August 3.

A spokesman said: "He continues to improve"

SURGERY: Reggie

APPEAL: Roberta Kray talks yesterday

SET DYING KRAY FREE BEG PALS

GANGLAND killer Reggie Kray could be freed from jail after tests revealed he has several cancer tumours.

The 67-year-old's worst fears were confirmed yesterday after surgeons removed a malignant secondary tumour from his small intestine.

Kray, who has been in jail 31 years, will now be able to add compassionate grounds to his forthcoming application for parole – and the strongest cases are terminal illnesses.

Friends were concerned about his dramatic weight loss at the funeral of his brother Charlie in April. He has been reduced to drinking liquids and doctors put him on painkillers.

One pal said last night: "I think it's about time they let Reggie out."

Now the Home Secretary is likely to look favourably on Kray's next bid for release from Wayland Prison, Norfolk, on compassionate grounds.

Kray had been due before a parole board to decide his future next Friday, but he

ILL: Reg has had tumour removed

■ by ROSS KANIUK

asked for an adjournment after serious health problems emerged.

Before going into hospital, he would have argued that he should be released because he had behaved in prison, served his time, and he was no danger to the public. But now he will apply on compassionate grounds to his governor, who can forward the application to the Parole Board. The Home Secretary will make the final decision.

The notorious gangster is serving a life sentence for the murder of another gangland character, Jack "The Hat" McVitie in London in 1969.

180

Straw frees Kray after 31 years – but he's too sick to go home

BY LOUISE JURY

JACK STRAW, the Home Secretary, yesterday ruled Reggie Kray can be freed from jail on compassionate grounds, but the dying gangster was too ill to go home last night. His solicitor, Trevor Linn, said Kray could be released from hospital in the next few days so he could die a free man under the care of his wife Roberta.

Kray, the notorious East End criminal, has been undergoing treatment for terminal cancer of the bladder in hospital near the jail where he was serving life for murder. After it became clear he had just weeks to live, his lawyer had asked the Home Secretary to allow Kray to spend his last days at home with Roberta.

Kray has to stay

By JOHN TROUP

DYING gangland killer Reggie Kray will not leave hospital this week, doctors said last night.

Kray, 66, was released from jail on compassionate grounds by Home Secretary Jack Straw on Saturday.

A hospital spokesman said: "He is stable and had a comfortable night but he will be here for the foreseeable future.

"His wife has confirmed he will definitely not leave this week."

Conscious

Wife Roberta, 41, said: "His freedom is something he's waited so long for but he's seriously ill.

"We're hoping he will be able to get out for a few days. He is conscious and able to speak."

Kray, who has bladder cancer, went to the Norfolk and Norwich Hospital three weeks ago from Wayland Prison.

Kray's solicitor Trevor Linn said: "I hope he'll get out soon — he's as tough as old boots."

Reggie Kray set free to die

REGGIE KRAY was freed from custody by the home secretary yesterday, but remained in his hospital bed, too sick to be moved, *writes Nicholas Rufford.*

The last surviving member of the family gang that terrorised London's East End in the 1960s was terminally ill with bladder cancer and tumours in his intestine.

Doctors at the Norfolk and Norwich hospital said he would not be fit enough to leave for several days, if at all. He is too weak to walk and has to be helped by staff.

Trevor Linn, his solicitor, said Kray was overjoyed at Jack Straw's decision to free him from custody. Kray has spent the past 32 years in jail.

Straw took the decision to

Profile, page 15

release Kray, 67, after being told by a hospital consultant that he may have only days to live.

Kray was serving a life sentence in Wayland prison, Norfolk, for the fatal stabbing of Jack "The Hat" McVitie.

Ronnie Kray, Reggie's twin, died five years ago in Broadmoor, where he was serving a life sentence for murder.

THANK YOU SUNDAY **PEOPLE** **FOR MY FREEDOM**

Dying Reggie's message after YOU win fight to let him spend his last days with dignity

The shocking picture that made Jack Straw act

KRAY-ZY

They keep Reggie Kray in jail until he's just days from death.. but release child sex offenders to strike again and again

REGGIE KRAY: Free after 32 years' jail

BY JON CARTER

DYING gangster Reggie Kray was officially released yesterday—after seeing some of Britain's most evil monsters freed long before him.

Last night Kray's supporters celebrated his freedom—and slammed the system which kept him in jail for 32 years while showing extraordinary leniency to predatory paedophiles and terrorists.

Kray's wife Roberta, 41, said: "Reggie has been in jail almost as long as the Moors Murderers, and probably twice what the monster who murdered Sarah Payne will get."

Cancer-ridden Kray, 66—jailed in 1969 for killing a fellow gangster—expects to die within days.

His solicitor Trevor Linn had pleaded with Home Secretary Jack Straw to grant compassionate parole.

He said: "It is a complete outrage that it's taken this man's terminal illness to make the Home Secretary release him. This is long, long overdue."

Amazingly he said Kray was in "good spirits and cracking jokes."

Kray supporter Maureen Flanagan said: "Reggie has sat there in his cell watching paedophiles and terrorists released without having to serve their full sentences."

Full Story: Pages 2 and 3

LAST FIGHT OF THE LAST KRAY

By AIDAN McGURRAN

THIS is the first picture of dying Reggie Kray as a free man.

The cancer-ravaged mobster — last of the brothers who ruled the East End — is seen in hospital yesterday after being released from nearly 32 years' jail.

Kray, 66, took his first steps in weeks. He was also visited by old mate "Mad" Frankie Fraser, who said: "He was in good spirits and good humour."

SEE PAGES 4 & 5

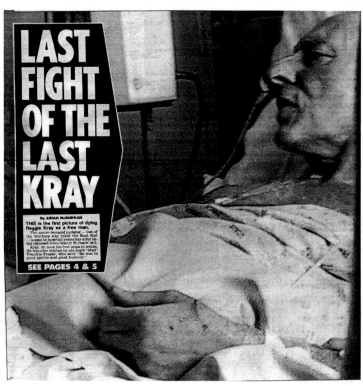

THE SUN SAYS
Kray saga

REGGIE Kray is a free man again after 32 years in jail.

But chances are he will not live to enjoy that freedom for long.

There is no doubt his funeral, when it comes, will be a huge spectacle.

Stars and famous criminals will join the mourners, ordinary Londoners will line the streets and drinkers in East End pubs will raise a glass to "good old Reggie".

It will be bigger than the state funerals for genuine national heroes such as Field Marshal Montgomery.

That glamorisation of the Krays is precisely why they were kept in prison for so long.

How could any parent try to teach a child right from wrong if for the past 15 years or so the Kray twins had been arriving in stretch limos at royal film premieres, taking part in TV panel games or hosting Who Wants To Be A Millionaire?

Certainly the Krays' 30-year sentence was out of proportion to their crimes.

Their victims would say the "gangland justice" handed out by the Krays was out of proportion too. One market trader who argued with the twins' mother was stabbed with a bayonet and left a mental wreck.

George Cornell called Ronnie a "fat poof" and was shot dead.

Yet many eloquent voices still speak up for the Krays.

However, no one can object to dying Reggie being released now.

Thankfully the final curtain will soon come down on the Kray twins saga.

BBC in row over cash for Kray film

THE BBC was last night embroiled in a row over a £280,000 fee paid for Reggie Kray's deathbed interview.

Insiders suggested that the programme would leave the corporation open to charges of glamorising violence.

And victim support groups were outraged at the amount of money paid for footage of the gangster who, with his twin brother Ronnie, once terrorised London's East End.

The hour-long documentary, Reggie Kray – The Final Word, will be screened next Thursday.

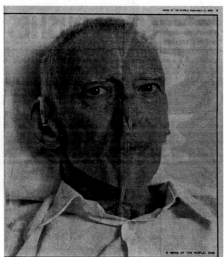

DEADLY BORING: Reggie Kray

Final word on Reggie: A dead loss

FASCINATING documentary the other night about some terrifying siblings who brought panic and fear to everyone who saw them and still give people nightmares even now.

And once I'd finished watching **The Sound Of Music Children** (ITV, Wednesday) I moved on to **Reggie Kray: The Final Word** (BBC1, Thursday) in which the Beeb attempted to show that a life of crime shouldn't be celebrated.

They did this by talking to the victims of the Kray twins and "the people who really knew them".

So anyone who thinks that fleshing out a sensationalist but actually quite boring deathbed interview with Reggie with loads of guff we've heard before was just a shameless attempt by BBC1 to give ITV a kicking in the ratings must be mistaken.

DYING KRAY SHOCK: I KILLED ANOTHER

GANGSTER Reggie Kray owned up to another killing in a deathbed confession, it will be revealed this week.

Kray did not name the victim but he is believed to be Edward "Mad Teddy" Smith, an occasional minder for the Kray twins who vanished during their 60s reign of terror in London's East End.

His body has never been found and no one has told of his fate.

But Kray, serving life for the murder of Jack "The Hat" McVitie, admitted more blood on his hands before his cancer death last

CONFESSION: Kray

EXCLUSIVE
By JAMES MURRAY

year. In a BBC TV interview to be shown on Thursday he was asked whether there had been other killings which influenced the decision not to parole him. He paused before replying: "One. One."

Scotland Yard's Leonard "Nipper" Read, who smashed the Krays' empire, said: "I should imagine that would be Teddy Smith."

Dying Reg climbs out of his bed and walks

KRAY FREEDOM
Exclusive FIRST picture of Reg outside

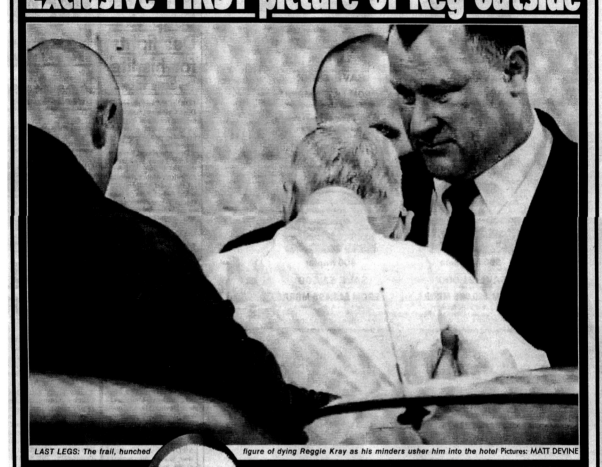

LAST LEGS: The frail, hunched figure of dying Reggie Kray as his minders usher him into the hotel Pictures: MATT DEVINE

By DAVID BROWN and LUCY PANTON

DYING Reggie Kray is a pitiful sight as he takes his first steps to freedom helped by a group of burly minders.

The hardened heavies were visibly moved as the gang leader who once strutted cockily through London's East End was hunched and frail as he arrived at a Beefeater hotel.

One onlooker said: I was shocked at how ill he looked. I'm used to seeing pictures of him in his younger days.

"But Reggie is a shadow of his former self. His eyes were sunken and his skin pale and yellowing."

His minders will be at his side again today when the cancer-stricken killer finally buries the hatchet with his Sixties mobster rivals – in the hotel carvery.

Old South London adversary Charlie Richardson, 66, and his brutal enforcer "Mad" Frankie

DYING: Killer Kray

Fraser, 77, will be among the guests as Kray hosts Sunday lunch at the Town House in Norwich, Norfolk.

An insider said: "Reggie has been dreaming about this reunion for ages.

Cigars

"The Krays and the Richardsons were at each others' throats 40 years ago. It was war, but all that is forgotten now. Reggie's quite a sentimental sort and will be chuffed to bits at the turnout for the roast lunch.

GETAWAY: The Krays' honeymoon hotel suite is ringed

"He won't be able to eat that much but I'm sure he'll enjoy reliving old times. He'll say his goodbyes. It will be quite emotional."

Kray, 66, jailed for life in 1969 for the murder of Jack "The Hat" McVitie, was freed on compassionate grounds by Home Secretary Jack Straw five weeks ago after a Sunday People campaign.

But he didn't return to the outside world until Friday, when he was whisked out of Norfolk and Norwich Hospital.

He was greeted by his entourage of dark-suited heavies at the hotel. Security guards then carried him up the stairs in a wheelchair to the £50-a-night honeymoon suite – where wife Roberta, 41, was waiting.

Kray, who has seen his twin Ron and older brother Charlie both die in jail, wasted no time.

A hotel source said: "He is living like a lord. He wants to make the most of all the time he has left.H e's relaxing in the room, chatting to Roberta and taking calls from friends. He is

dressed in a silk Versace robe and indulging in Bollinger champagne and Henry Winterman cigars.

"He has a magnum of champagne by the bed and is enjoying all the things he has not been allowed for 30 years.

"But although he can walk he is still frail from all the time spent in a hospital bed."

Kray knows his days are numbered. He specifically requested a room with a tranquil river view as he lives with Roberta for the first time since their Maidstone prison wedding three years ago.

And shortly after his arrival, minders brought in his deathbed. The pink double mattress was replaced by a clinical blue version.

Other guests in the 16-room hotel complained that their peace has been shattered.

One said yesterday: "The place is crawling with big blokes dressed in black."

● **People HOTlinks**

d.brown@people.co.uk
For more info on the Krays:
www.the krays.co.uk

REGGIE KRAY RUINED OUR WEDDING NIGHT

Couple lose honeymoon suite

By STEVE ATKINSON

A COUPLE protested yesterday that their wedding night was ruined because they had to give up their honeymoon suite for dying Reggie Kray.

Kevin and Michelle Baker were booked into the £52-a-night room with four-poster bed and river views after their wedding and reception last Saturday.

But they were told it was needed for a "sick person". The newlyweds reluctantly accepted an ordinary room at the hotel costing £37.50 a night with free champagne and breakfast as compensation.

They only realised that 66-year-old Kray had moved into the honeymoon suite with his wife Roberta, 41, when they watched the TV news the following evening.

Kray, who has inoperable bladder cancer, went to the Town House Hotel near Norwich after his release from hospital.

Kevin, 38, from Norwich, said: "The room we got was small, badly decorated and had creaky floorboards. It took the shine right off our day."

Michelle, 32, added: "We were looking forward to a room with a nice river view. All we got was a view of a flat roof and a

NEWLYWEDS: The Bakers yesterday — and the four-poster bec

DYING: Kray

kitchen window. The hotel ended up waiving the charge for the room and gave us free champagne, breakfast and flowers — but it did not compensate for the disappointment."

Ex-gangster Kray, jailed for life in 1969 for murder, has spent the past week enjoying red wine and a tot or two of whisky — and has even talked of doing some fishing.

His solicitor Mark Goldstein commented: "It's really a matter for the hotel. Neither Mr or Mrs Kray would want anyone moved because of them — certainly not a honeymoon couple."

Hotel manager Gordon Graham-Hall, 42, said: "The intention was to move Mr Kray from the suite but he was too ill.

"We have now offered this couple a free stay in the honeymoon suite at a later date."

Held up by Cray twins

A ROBBER armed with two live lobsters forced a shop assistant to hand over the takings.

Carol Bywater, 23, emptied the till when the robber threatened her with the crayfish-like claws. Cops in New York believe the weapons have now been eaten.

Kray letters

Letters by the gangster Ronnie Kray covering his decline into madness are to be auctioned. The 23 letters are on 40 pages of his personal headed notepaper. Kray, who died in Broadmoor in 1995, once wrote 14 letters in a day. The sale is at Mullock Madeley, Shropshire, on July 31.

BIG C KILLS KRAY

VILLAIN: Reggie Kray

Reggie loses cancer fight

GANGSTER Reggie Kray died in his sleep yesterday after a battle against bladder cancer without fulfilling his dying wish — a countryside stroll with his wife.

Kray, 66, died in the honeymoon suite at the Beefeater Town House Hotel in Thorpe St Andrew, near Norwich.

His wife Roberta, 41, who had maintained a bedside vigil since his release from prison on compassionate grounds in August, and gangland pals Freddie Foreman and Jerry Powell were at his side.

Kray's lawyer Mark Goldstein said: "The last couple of weeks have been spent in the hotel.

"He has been very sickly most of the time and has been listening to music.

"The hotel was chosen because it was near a river. It was hoped that he and Mrs Kray could go for a walk, but because of the illness that never transpired."

Heroes

Kray was released after serving more than 30 years for stabbing to death fellow gangster Jack "The Hat" McVitie at a flat in Stoke Newington, north London.

McVitie had allegedly issued threats to his homosexual twin Ronnie.

The Krays are still thought of as heroes in their home district of Bethnal Green in east London, where they ran a string of protection rackets controlled through Mafia-style gangs.

The pair were sentenced to life at the Old Bailey in 1969 with a recommendation that they serve not less than 30 years.

Reggie was officially freed on August 26 by Home Secretary Jack Straw because of his deteriorating health.

He had been moved to the Norfolk and Nor-

wich Hospital from Wayland Prison near Watton, Norfolk, 10 days earlier.

Actress Barbara Windsor said: "It's a great loss. People knocked me for talking about him, but you can only speak as you find."

She described him as "charming and polite" after she met him through the showbusiness scene.

The Kray twins' life of crime began at 12 years old when they were put on probation for firing an air rifle from a train.

At the age of 16 they bought their first revolver and hid it under their bedroom floor.

Ronnie was given a three-year jail sentence in 1958 for a pub attack, and certified insane.

Before they were arrested for the last time in 1968, the twins, known as The Firm, sprang Frank "Mad Axeman" Mitchell from Dartmoor Prison. He

MOURNING: Wife Roberta (above) and actress Barbara Windsor

was hidden in a council house with a prostitute for company.

But he fell foul of the Krays and was killed.

One of the Kray gang cut up Mitchell's body and put it through a meat mixer.

Later Reggie threatened gangster Charlie Mitchell with a gun and said: "We've done one Mitchell already, it's easy."

The twins sometimes soaked enemies in petrol and flicked lighted matches at them.

Cronies

Years later, in a feud with a rival gang, Ronnie shot George Cornell dead in the Blind Beggar pub in east London.

The same night Reggie killed McVitie. He was supposed to be shot but the gun didn't work so Reggie stabbed him while cronies looked on.

They were convicted of the murders at the Old Bailey in 1969.

Ronnie died in prison five years ago. Their elder brother Charlie died in April this year, aged 73.

TIME TO LET GO REGGIE

Reggie... died in hotel bed

Gangster Freddie tells of Kray's last moments

By MIKE SULLIVAN, Crime Editor

EXCLUSIVE

GANGSTER Freddie Foreman told last night how he urged pal Reggie Kray to "let go" moments before the infamous villain died.

Cancer-stricken Reggie's life finally ebbed away as he clasped the hand of wife Roberta who was at his bedside.

Freddie said: "He was breathing very badly and the space between his breaths was getting longer. But he was still fighting it.

"I put my hand on his head and said, 'Let go, let go, Reg. Just let go, old son'. A couple of breaths later he was gone."

Reggie, 66, died yesterday at The Town House Hotel, Norwich, only 36 days after Home Secretary Jack Straw ordered his release from jail on compassionate grounds. He

Continued on Page 13

I NEVER met Reggie Kray but I am annoyed with Sun readers who slagged him off. He did his time but was kept inside longer than needed.

My young son was kicked to death and the person who killed him got three years but only did 14 months. Things were different in the Krays' days.

Mrs D ANGUS
Basildon, Essex

OUR brother Frank Mitchell was one of the Krays' victims. Our family would like to thank Sun reader David Clarke for recognising that we are left to cope without our brother. The Krays were no heroes, just murderers.

LINDA and MAY MITCHELL
Bow, East London

A gangland era has ended with Reggie's death

REGGIE Kray died in his sleep yesterday – the last of the big time East End gangsters.

He was as infamous and murderous as the twin, Ronnie, he follows to the grave.

And, after the death of their older gangland brother Charlie earlier this year, the legend of the Krays has finally been laid to rest.

TIME TO GO, PAL

Continued from Page One

was suffering incurable cancer of the bladder.

Reggie was the last of the notorious Kray clan which — led by him and his twin crazed Ronnie — ruled London's East End during the 1960s.

He served 32 years of a life term for murdering crook Jack "The Hat" McVitie in 1967.

Freddie, 67, who was locked up for ten years for being an accessory to the killing, went to see Reggie yesterday with fellow mobsters Joey Pyle, 63, Johnny Nash, 66, and Wilf Pine.

He said: "It felt like he had been hanging in there to see us.

"We had a chat for a couple of hours and Reg was talking about the old days, his family and Norfolk, which he loved.

"He was very ill but the last thing he said to us was he wanted us to be his pallbearers." Roberta, 41, sobbed as her

Mike Reid . . . grief for Reggie

husband lay dying in a huge four-poster in the hotel's honeymoon suite.

Freddie, who claimed on TV this year he carried out two murders for Reggie and Ronnie, added: "After he died we went down to the bar and toasted him."

Reggie weighed only 5st at the end and he had not eaten in days.

Twin Ronnie died, aged 61, after a heart attack in Broadmoor in 1995. Their older brother Charlie, 73, died in April this year while serving a 12-year sentence for conspiring to smuggle cocaine.

Reggie's arch rival in the Sixties, South London crime boss Charlie Richardson, had been due to see him last Tuesday and make peace.

But the visit was called off because Reggie was deteriorating.

Former Kray henchman Tony Lambrianou, 58, said last night: "It's the end of a dynasty. The Krays are now the stuff of legend."

EastEnders actress Barbara Windsor, an ex-girlfriend of Reggie, said: "I was hoping he would have more time out of prison with Roberta."

And Mike Reid, who stars with her in the soap, said: "Reggie and Ronnie were pussycats compared to some of the villains nowadays who only serve a few years."

...THEN THERE WERE NONE

Four poster finale for the last Kray

BY PAUL MARINKO

The four poster in the hotel honeymoon suite where Reg Kray died on Sunday. Right: Reg and wife Roberta spent their last days together in the Norfolk hotel room

REGGIE Kray was surrounded by former associates from his criminal past when he breathed his last in the four-poster bed of a Norwich hotel's honeymoon suite on Sunday.

The 66-year-old former gangland boss who, with twin brother Ronnie, ruled the East End through violence and intimidation during the sixties, died weeks after being diagnosed with terminal bowel and bladder cancer.

Weighing just five stone at the end Reggie had managed to leave his hospital bed in the city's centre and travel the short distance to The Town House hotel two weeks earlier.

There he and wife Roberta, 41, had booked into the £52-a-night honeymoon suite but hopes the move may help him live a little longer and allow him to entertain the many friends who wanted to visit and pay their last respects faded quickly.

Reggie's condition only went down hill but four former associates, Freddie Foreman, Joey Pyle, Johnny Nash and Wilf Pine had made the trip up to see him on his last day.

The group chatted for a couple of hours before Reg, who served 32 years in prison for the murder of Jack 'The Hat' McVitie in 1967, eventually died at 2pm.

Foreman, who served 10 years in prison for being an accessory to the crime, said: "It was just like Reg was waiting for us to get there so we could pay our last respects to him."

A sobbing Roberta held her husband's hand as Joey Pyle held the other while they watched him slip away.

Forman said: "When your number's up the old grim reaper ain't going to pass you by, whether you're going upstairs or down."

Reggie had only been freed by Home Secretary Jack Straw six weeks ago on compassionate grounds, when the extent of his cancer became clear.

He will now be buried at Chingford Mount Cemetery, alongside other members of his family, including twin Ronnie and older brother Charlie.

Solicitor announces Kray funeral date

FUNERAL The funeral of Reggie Kray will take place next week, his solicitor said yesterday.

The former East End gangster, who died of bladder cancer on Sunday aged 66, will be buried next Wednesday. His funeral cortege will leave from W English and Son undertakers in Bethnal Green, East London.   (PA)

REGGIE KRAY   1933 - 2000

THE END OF AN OGRE

CONFLICTING reports over Reggie Kray's final few hours. However, despatches from outside his Norwich hotel suggest the gangland chief had a deathbed audience with four leading underworld figures.

No sign of them here. But dear old Reggie must have gone to meet his maker with a smile on his face after receiving a surprise visit from the directors of Man At C&A.

Reggie, God rest his soul, must have marvelled at how little men's fashions had changed since he was jailed in 1969.

Chivalrous Krays

AS AN East Ender, I'm not seduced by the myth of the Kray twins, but folk who knew them said they were 'only a threat to their own' and my husband always found them to be gentlemen.

I met them three or four times. The first was in 1955, when I was 15, acting 18. There was a cafe in Hackney where we used to spend a lot of time and I recall saying one night to my friend: 'I wish something exciting would happen.'

Along came a car and someone said: 'That's the twins; I wonder what they're doing here.' My friend and I waved and shouted: 'Give us a lift!' The car stopped and we got in. 'Are you the Krays?' we asked and the answer was yes. One of them asked our ages and I said: '18'

They drove us to High Beach, a beauty spot in the middle of Epping Forest. I thought: 'My dad will kill me.' Then one of the twins asked again: 'How old are you?' and my voice was shakey as I replied: '14 and 15.' They asked where we lived and drove us home to Dalston.

They said they would be back the next night to make sure we weren't hanging around at the cafe or they would tell our parents and tan our backsides. We got a right earful and I was grounded for a week by my dad.

Friends told us the twins came back to the cafe all that week to check we weren't there. The East End was a safe place. Had we made a similar encounter at the cafe today I'm sure we would have been raped.
Mrs P. SLATER, Rayleigh, Essex.
week to check we weren't there.

The East End was a safe place. Had we made a similar encounter at the cafe today I'm sure we would have been raped.
Mrs P. SLATER, Rayleigh, Essex.

Reggie's taunt from the grave

GANGLAND killer Reggie Kray will have have one last jibe at the Government from the grave.

His widow Roberta, 41, has ordered a bouquet bearing the words "Free at last" to sit on Kray's coffin at his funeral on Wednesday. Thousands are expected to line East London streets for the procession.

The floral tribute is an attack on Home Secretary Jack Straw, who refused to release Kray until five weeks before he died.

Tony Lambrianou, his former assistant, said: "I think Roberta is sending a message to the powers that be that Reggie was kept inside for too long."

Kray, 66, died of cancer last week after serving 32 years for the killing of Jack "The Hat" McVitie.

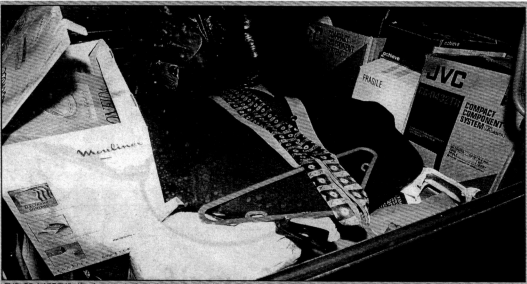

END OF A LEGEND: Kray's suit and other belongings are loaded into a cab yesterday at the Norwich hotel where he died   Picture: ARNOLD SLATER

Bundled into the back of a cab.. Reggie's gear returns to his manor

By LORRAINE FISHER

REGGIE KRAY returned yesterday to the manor he once ruled by fear.

And the ex-gangster's personal belongings were bundled into the back of a black cab after being removed from the hotel where he ended his days.

The body of 66-year-old Kray — who died from bladder cancer — was taken to Bethnal Green in East London where Reggie and his twin Ronnie were born.

His old black suit and silk blue-patterned tie were loaded into the taxi along with a kettle and ghetto blaster, boxes and carrier bags. Many of the packages were marked with the words "Kray" and "Parkhurst".

Also removed from the hotel in Norwich where Kray spent the last 10 days of his life was his special mattress.

Reggie will be buried at the family plot in Chingford cemetery after a funeral procession from Bethnal Green at the heart of the area he terrorised in the 1960s but where many now regard him as a folk hero.

The funeral will follow the same route and be similar in style to the East End send-offs for Ronnie and the twins' older brother Charlie.

Thousands of mourners lined the streets.

Relatives and friends of Reggie have asked that all donations should go to Macmillan nurses, who care for cancer patients.

Kray spent 32 years behind bars for the murder of fellow gangster Jack "The Hat" McVitie.

Yesterday his widow Roberta, 41, left the Town House Hotel where she had kept vigil beside her dying husband.

A former cellmate of Kray said: "She's absolutely devastated at the moment and doesn't want to say anything."

Funeral arrangements have not yet been finalised.

Kray chose the £40-a-night honeymoon suite, with four-poster bed, for its river views.

Staff at the 18-room Town House Hotel are worried that it could now become notorious as the place where Reggie Kray died. One worker said: "I'm sure there is going to be a lot of macabre interest in the room."

Hotel manager Gordon Graham-Hall, 42, said: "It's possible it will attract some ghouls, only time will tell."

lfisher@mirror.co.uk

GOING HOME: Reggie's body was taken to the East End yesterday

£1m REG CHEATS TAXMAN IN DEATH

■ *by TONY BONNICI*

REGGIE Kray salted away a fortune from dozens of deals made behind bars.

The former gangland boss, who died from cancer on Sunday, could have built up a **£1MILLION** pile.

But the crafty con's biographer reckons he hid most of his money in secret accounts – to make sure the taxman doesn't see a penny – in a beyond-the-grave revenge for being kept in jail past his 30-year recommended sentence.

The revelations about the East End hardman's finances were made yesterday by Colin Fry. The author of Doing The Business said that unlike his twin Ronnie, who gave thousands away to charity, Reggie became a tightwad while inside.

Fry said: "As time went on Reg didn't like spending his money even though he was raking it in.

"He made £500,000 just on his new book A Way of Life.

"And there was so much more coming in because he didn't mind what was done in the Kray name as long as the money was right.

TIGHTWAD: Reggie Kray

Expenses

"But Reg wasn't stupid. He put all his money into offshore accounts through his many contacts."

Fry added: "He wouldn't like the Government getting their hands on his dosh after they locked him away for so long.

"So it wouldn't surprise me if, on paper at least, Reggie only has enough money to cover his funeral expenses and little else."

During his 32 years in prison Reggie, 66, built up a huge empire.

As well as several books, the twins got £370,000 for a film on their lives starring Martin and Gary Kemp.

More cash rolled in from the sale of autographs, photos and T-shirts.

And yesterday it was revealed Reggie could still attract cash – because staff at the £40-a-night Norwich hotel where he spent his last days believe the four-poster bed in which he

WIDOW: Roberta Kray

died could be a booking target for ghoulish fans.

Meanwhile, his widow Roberta, 41, said Kray would be reunited in death with his brothers Ronnie and Charlie at Chingford cemetery, east London.

No funeral date has yet been arranged but the procession will definitely begin in their Bethnal Green birthplace.

☐ TUESDAY. And a phone call from underworld legend Joe Pyle in an agitated mood over last week's Reggie Kray gag.

Fair to say Joe, Johnny Nash and Freddie Foreman — pictured below — were none too thrilled by my suggestion Reggie had received a death bed visit from the directors of Man At C&A.

In purely comedy terms, I still think it's a valid gag. But as Joe points out, quite passionately, visit-

VISIT . . . Freddie, Johnny and Joe

ing his Reggieness dressed like members of Hawkwind would have been disrespectful.

And sometimes it's best to keep these jokes to yourself and shut the **** up.

Sorry fellas.

And, without wishing to give the appearance I've been leant on here, I would like to add, the Krays only hurt their own.

Furthermore, it was a lot safer in them days and you could leave your front door open, etc etc.

Soccer Kray-zy

AN amateur soccer club in Kirkby-in-Ashfield, Notts, is naming a stand after dead gangster Reggie Kray, who gave them £1,000 in 1995.

REGGIE Kray's widow has snubbed his gangland pals — by refusing to let them carry the killer's coffin.

REG'S WIDOW SNUBS MOBSTERS AT FUNERAL

Grieving Roberta Kray, 41, has instead asked two figures from the **POP** world to be pallbearers at Wednesday's funeral.

Former East 17 heart-throb Tony Mortimer and The Who's manager Bill Curbishly will perform the honour along with Reggie's lawyer and an ex-lag he met just six years ago.

Last night furious underworld henchman Freddie Foreman — who claims Kray asked him on his deathbed to carry the coffin — vowed to **BOYCOTT** the funeral in London's East End.

He stormed: "It's out of order. Reggie's dying wishes are not being complied with.

"There has been a lot of wrangling over who is carrying the coffin and sitting in the church.

Enemies

"Friends of Reg for the last 40 years are being ignored or cast aside while new acquaintances, complete strangers and even his old enemies like Frankie Fraser are getting front row seats."

Roberta wants to stop Kray's funeral in London's East End being turned into a gangland spectacle — like the send-offs for his twin Ronnie and their brother Charlie.

But one former villain fumed: "Roberta has completely squeezed out the gangsters. She has put a few noses out of joint. The Krays always loved showbiz and regarded themselves as celebrities.

"But it's a bit rich that a young pop star who only knew Reg for a couple of years is being made a pallbearer."

Fuming Foreman carried the coffins of both Ronnie Kray and older brother Charlie.

Lyrics

He and fellow hardmen Johnny Nash and Joey Pyle visited Kray in his hotel room hours before he lost his cancer battle on Sunday.

Foreman told The Sun: "The last thing Reg said was 'Nobody but you is to carry the coffin.'"

But schoolteacher's daughter Roberta — who wed Kray in Maidstone prison in 1997 — insisted: "For the last few hours of his life Reg was barely conscious.

"Sadly he was unaware of any visitors at this time."

She claimed Kray had earlier named the men he wanted to bear his coffin into church.

East 17 frontman Mortimer met the legendary crime boss in jail two years ago after Kray said he liked the pop star's music.

They struck up a friendship and Kray even wrote lyrics for Mortimer's new band Sub Zero. Cock-

Showbiz pals will carry his coffin in church

Final journey . . . the coffin of Reggie's twin Ronnie is carried by pallbearers including gangster Freddie Foreman — bringing up the rear on the far left — and the pair's older brother Charlie Kray, right, in 1995

Grief. . Roberta Kray with Reggie at brother Charlie's funeral in April

Charlton Athletic soccer boss Alan — had long campaigned with Kray's lawyer Mark Goldstein for the killer to be freed.

The final pallbearer — former lag Bradley Allardyce — was best man at Kray's wedding. Roberta said her husband — who died aged 66 after serving 32 years for murder — regarded all four as his "special" friends.

But one chum who knew Kray in the 1960s — when he and Ronnie ruled the East End — said: "Some of us believe Reg will be turning in his grave over it."

Pop star . . Tony Mortimer

Best man . . Brad Allardyce

Rock manager . . Curbishly

Lawyer . . Mark Goldstein

FREE AT LAST

'Old guard' missing as thousands bid a final farewell to the last of the Krays

Pall-bearers carry Reg Kray's flower-bedecked coffin into the church. Right: Reg Kray in April

REGGIE Kray's funeral brought the East End to a standstill yesterday but feuding between friends and family led many famous faces to stay away.

The former gangster's wife Roberta had sidelined his old gangster friends by refusing to let them be pallbear-

BY PAUL MARINKO

ers.

She stamped her authority on proceedings by largely excluded villains from Reggie's past.

As the service began at St Matthew's Church, St Matthew's Row in Bethnal Green with the hymn 'Morning Has Broken' it was clear the snubbed pallbearers and their old associates from the East End's 60s underworld were staying away.

Minders stand in front of a crowd at Chingford Cemetery during the burial of convicted killer Reggie Kray, who died of cancer last month.

Crowds watch murderer buried

Thousands line the streets

SPECIAL REPORT BY LAURA HOLLAND

East Enders turn out to remember Reggie

THEY came from all over Britain yesterday to see the funeral of the last member of the infamous Kray family to die.

Many came to say goodbye to Reggie Kray, some just to watch, and a few came to make sure this really was the end of them.

Reggie, the last of the Kray clan, who violently ruled the East End in the sixties, was finally laid to rest yesterday after dying of terminal bowel and bladder cancer.

Crowds lining the pavement were held back by security guards as they waited for the coffin to appear outside funeral directors, W. English and Son.

One woman caught in the battle shouted in frustration: "Let me say goodbye to my Reggie!"

At 11.15am, the coffin was brought out and taken in a glass-sided hearse pulled by six plumbed black horses, down Bethnal Green Road.

From there the cortege including 17 cars laden with flowers turned into Vallance Road, where Reggie was brought up with twin Ronnie and older brother Charlie.

THREATENING

As the horses turned into Cheshire Street, the sun managed to shine through the threatening rain clouds onto the many people waiting to follow them to the church gates in St. Matthews Row.

From there the mourners grew silent and a few shed tears as the coffin was carried inside St. Matthew's Church by six pall-bearers.

They included Mark Goldstein, Reggie's lawyer and Bradley Allardyce, who was best man at Reggie's second wedding to Roberta.

A police officer from Bethnal Green Police estimated there were several thousand well-wishers lining the route from the funeral directors to St. Matthew's Church.

Danny Faulkner of Shipton Street, Bethnal Green said: "He was an inspiration.

RELEASED

"It goes to show that you can make something of yourself in an area like this.

"It feels like the area has died."
Emma Backman of Brady Street, Bethnal Green, said: "It's really sad. I'd say it was a safer place here when they was around"

Matthew Dalton, who travelled all the way to the East End from Littlehampton in Sussex said: "From an outsiders point of view they certainly made the streets a lot safer.

"They should have been released years ago. Both of them."

But Derek Handley, originally of Hedlam Street, Bethnal Green said: "I think it's a good job we're celebrating him going. Thank God the last one's gone."

Mourners included Toby von Judge (right)

Media frenzy as 'Mad' Frankie Fraser arrives. He was the only 60s crime figure to make an appearance

Crowds line the railings outside the church

■ Former Page 3 model Flanagan waiting outside the church for the funeral cortege

FITTING EXIT FOR A KILLER

Dry eyes and sunglasses for security staff outside St Matthew's Church in Bethnal Green where the funeral of gangland murderer Reggie Kray was held today   Picture: KEN TOWNER

194

REG KRAY
Born 1933
Died 2000

■ FROM PAGE 1

Bernie Lee, an old friend of Reg - who died of terminal bowel and bladder cancer last week - said two of the snubbed pallbearers, Freddie Foreman and Joey Pyle, would definitely be staying away.

He said: "It's caused a lot of bad blood."

Freddie Foreman is said to be furious at Roberta's decision to allow new friends that Reggie, 66, made recently while in prison, carry the coffin.

Foreman, who was sent to prison for his part in disposing of Jack 'The Hat' McVitie's body - the murder for which Reggie served 32 years in jail - was joined by Joe Pyle, another old gangland friend of the Krays who was also snubbed as a pallbearer.

BOOK

Tony Lambrianou, who was in the Stoke Newington flat in 1967 when Reg knifed McVitie to death and subsequently served 10 years for his part in the crime, also stayed away allegedly in support of Foreman, who he is reported to be writing a book with.

In the place of these old faces Roberta chose Reggie's lawyer Mark Goldstein, former member of pop group E17 Tony Mortimer and Reggie's prison friend Bradley Allardyce to be pallbearers.

Although former Page Three girl Flanagan was in the thick of it seating guests, who included former gangland enforcer 'Mad' Frankie Fraser, great train robber Bruce Reynolds bare knuckle fighter Roy Shaw and boxer Nosher Powell, figures from the 60s underworld played very little part in proceedings.

The main address was made by Dr Ken Stallard, the Christian minister who married Roberta and Reg three years ago in Maidstone Prison.

Free at last: The horsedrawn hearse with black-plumed horses also carried Ron Kray to his final resting place

He told the gathered guests and the crowds outside, who listened to the service on loudspeakers held back by the 400 private security guards from Reading, that he had first met Reggie's twin Ronnie in 1983 on a visit to Broadmoor.

Reggie, Dr Stallard said, had asked to see him because he had made such an impression on "our Ron".

Since then he had been the twins' 'spiritual guide' until they had both died.

He said Ron and Reg were both "honest and up-front", adding that Reg had turned to Christianity in his later years but made Dr Stallard promise not to say anything until he died.

Before reading a poem written for the occasion Dr Stallard said: "It was very sad that Reg was away for so long, we all thought it was a grave injustice."

The poem ended with the line 'toast my freedom with a beer'.

Finally he quoted Sir Winston Churchill: "My friends, my friends, I say to you now, never, never, never give in."

Reggie's lawyer Mark Goldstein also addressed the service saying: "Reg was an icon of the 21st century.

"It is sad he never really truly tasted freedom."

GOD BLESS

He finished with one of Reggie's favourite phrases, God bless.

The congregation, which also included actors Billy Murray, DS Don Beach in The Bill, and Helen Keating of London's Burning fame, then sang the hymn 'Fight the Good Fight'.

Finally there were two more prayers and the closing hymn, also sung at Reggie's older brother Charlie's funeral in April, 'Abide With Me'.

As people filed out of the church into the bitter October wind, one of Reggie's favourite songs 'My Way' by Frank Sinatra was played.

His coffin was carried to the hearse which took Reggie, at the head of a procession of 35 cars, down Bethnal Green Road, Roman Road and Grove Road past the thousands of East Enders, who had turned up for the funeral, and out of the East End for the last time.

He was buried at Chingford Mount Cemetery alongside his twin Ronnie at the family plot where a headstone is planned reading 'Here lie the Kray twins'.

Widow Roberta Kray

Actress Helen Keating

The Bill actor Billy Murray

Ex-fighter Roy Shaw

'Bad blood' as Reggie Kray goes to grave

❛ None of the Kray brothers were lovable rogues, they were vicious, committed career criminals with both Ronald and Reggie committing the ultimate crime of murder ❜

"An East End event": crowds gather to see off Reggie Kray, right, the last of the Kray brothers who terrorised the East End in the Sixties

East End send-off blurs myth and fact

HERE LIE
THE KRAY TWINS

"What you lookin' at?"

REGGIE Kray has dedicated the first track of a music CD completed days before his death to the memory of murdered black teenager, Stephen Lawrence.

It is seen as a direct attack on the racist thugs who were believed to have killed Stephen in April, 1993.

The Haggerston-born hood was furious when the gang announced they were the next Kray firm, said Rob Ferguson, of the Kray Kampaign.

"They put themselves forward as the next Krays and that really infuriated Reg," he said. "He was never racially motivated."

The five-track CD called *Freedom of Thought* contains two tracks penned by the former gangland boss. Other tracks include Reg's recital of an American Indian prayer.

One tune is dedicated to his twin, Ronnie, and another to his second wife, Roberta.

Reggie had numerous visits from pop stars while in jail –

including one from the hit New York-based band, The Fun Lovin' Criminals – to discuss possible collaborations.

"Reggie had a list as long as his arm and on the strength of that we took several pop stars to visit him," said Mr Ferguson.

"Some of them just wanted the association because none of them came through."

Instead, the CD was recorded using a session musician. It includes a special message from Reggie, which Mr Ferguson said "sounds like a goodbye".

"No one has ever heard Reg in this light before," he added.

Further information is available from the Kray Kampaign on www.thekrays.co.uk.

Rebuke for Lawrence gang on farewell CD

● *Reggie Kray's CD.*

THEY tried to turn the clock back 40 years to bury Reggie Kray yesterday.

Grandfathers in ill-fitting funeral suits, hard men wearing gangster black – all of them talking a great deal about loyalty and 'respect'. Especially respect.

For a few hours on a bleak and cloudy afternoon, they said it was as if Reg and his late twin brother Ron had returned to rule their East End manor, just like they used to in the 1960s.

Reality was different. It was more as if thousands of people had turned away from glamorising the life of a sadistic murderer, or that they simply didn't see a reason to keep the Kray legend alive in the 21st century.

Only about 3,000 of the predicted 100,000 lined the streets for what was billed almost as a state funeral. The much-vaunted galaxy of stars eventually managed barely a sprinkling of glitter between them.

Perhaps it was the plea from the 66-year-old gangster's widow Roberta, 41, that persuaded them to keep it comparatively low key – although it was still extraordinary to witness such mock grandeur afforded to a ruthless murderer.

Many onlookers spouted the usual nonsense about the brothers' big-hearted gestures, how they only ever hurt their own, and how the streets of London were far safer because of the Kray regime than they ever were now.

Then in a church service that enlisted Shakespeare, Churchill and Sinatra to send Kray to his grave, he was eulogised as 'an icon of the 20th century'.

There are usually two sides to every life story. Certainly, the one presented to the 300-strong congregation at St Matthew's church in Bethnal Green tried to focus on what was described as 'the real Reggie Kray'.

This was the quiet Christian who came to seek spiritual forgiveness in prison before his release from a life sentence to die from cancer.

Kray, as the floral tributes said, was now 'free at last'. The quotes from Shakespeare ('All the world's a stage...') and Churchill ('Never, never, never give in...') sat less happily in the speech than Sinatra's 'My Way', which – naturally – was Kray's choice for his send-off.

'George Cornell' joins the funeral

ONE surprise guest at the funeral was George Cornell, one of the twins' victims.

Not the real George Cornell, who Reggie's twin brother Ron shot dead in The Blind Beggar, but Steven Berkoff, the Narrow Street-based actor who played the crook in the 1989 film of the twins' life of crime The Krays.

Wearing a brown scarf and black baseball cap the actor, pictured above, mingled with invited guests outside W. English and Son funeral directors as they waited for the coffin to appear containing the last of the infamous Kray brothers to die.

He made his way down to St Matthew's Church for the service from which he emerged chatting to Nick Reynolds, the sculptor son of one of the Great Train Robbers Bruce Reynolds.

OH GAWD! REG WAS A CLOSET CHRISTIAN

...but he didn't want gangster pals to find out

TEARS OF FAREWELL: Old folk weep at St Matthew's Church

REGGIE KRAY'S secret life as a Christian was revealed after he returned to his East End stamping ground yesterday – in a coffin pulled by six black horses.

The 66-year-old villain had turned to God in jail, but he didn't want anyone to find out until after he died from cancer.

Evangelist Ken Stallard, who officiated at Reggie's wedding to Roberta, 41, told mourners how the gangland boss had repented his sins on his deathbed in the honeymoon suite of a Norfolk hotel.

Terror

"I asked Reg if he wanted to repent and Reg said 'Of course, of course'," said Mr Stallard.

Reggie told Mr Stallard: 'I want to be like you Ken, I want to be a Christian. But don't tell anybody until I'm gone. I don't want anyone to think I became a Christian to get parole'."

I N THE wake of the death of the last of the Krays, "Mad" Frankie Fraser, our remaining celebrity hoodlum, has been telling anyone who will listen that London's East End was a safer place when Ronnie and Reggie (left and right above with mother Violet) reigned because, in their day, you could leave your front door open safe in the knowledge that nothing inside would get nicked.

He's absolutely right. I lived on the Krays' manor from birth to young adulthood and I am here to tell you that, in the Fifties and Sixties, and entirely thanks to the wonderful security provided by the local thugs, not a single one of our neighbours in Hackney ever got their video stolen.

We never worried about leaving our stereos unguarded or whether our home computers were nailed to the desk. While the Krays ruled, we didn't give a second thought about our DVD equipment, our in-car CD players or our digital cameras and if anyone on our estate ever thought to lock up their credit cards I never knew about it.

Reality check, Frankie: the reason nothing ever got stolen in the East End was because, in those days, nobody had anything to steal. Except the Krays and their chums — and not even Frankie was mad enough to steal from them.

KRAY SECRETS TO BE REVEALED

Reg Kray: Dead at 66

NEW revelations about Reg Kray's past are about to surface in a new book by one of the twins' victims.

Lenny Hamilton, an East End thief who was savagely burnt in the eye with a red hot poker by Ron Kray in 1962, is launching his own account of the notorious twins in his new book Branded.

The book was due to come out this week but has been delayed since Reg's death at the weekend so Lenny can put in a chapter about how the twins allegedly mistreated his first wife Frances Shea.

Lawyers for his publishers Pegasus made him drop the chapter originally fearing Reggie, 66, may sue.

But now the former gangland boss has died Lenny is free to put the revelations into the book, which is now likely to come out at the end of the month.

Lenny is staying tight-lipped

BY PAUL MARINKO

about the new information but admitted it was about how the Kray firm mistreated Frances and he has no kind words for his old foes.

"They weren't Robin Hoods they were robbin' bastards," he said.

"She was a lovely girl, he only married her to have a nice girl on his arm. It was terrible what they did to her."

OVERDOSE

Reg married Frances, 11 years his junior, in 1965 but it turned out to be disaster and she was back living with her parents in Ormsby Street, Bethnal Green, eight weeks later.

But within two years, which saw a number of failed attempts by Reg to get her back, she was dead.

She is believed to have committed

Victim of the Krays Lenny Hamilton has written a book about the Kray empire

■ TURN TO PAGES 6.7.9

199

Killer for the Kray gang escapes again

By Wayne Francis

Freddie Foreman: Once feared

A GANGLAND hit man has escaped prosecution after admitting on television that he carried out at least two murders on the orders of the Kray brothers.

Freddie Foreman was arrested by Scotland Yard detectives following his confession to millions of viewers.

He had already been acquitted of the murders and could not be tried again for the killings under the 'double jeopardy' rule.

But he could have been charged with perjury and perverting the course of justice.

The Crown Prosecution Service, however, has now told 68-year-old Foreman that he will not face trial.

A Scotland Yard spokesman said: 'The CPS decided not to proceed as there was insufficient evidence.'

Foreman and his common-law wife Janice celebrated the news at home in North-West London with their family, including son Jamie, 42, who starred in the film Gangster No 1, playing a gangland boss.

Jamie has recently been dating actress Patsy Kensit, following her split from pop star Liam Gallagher.

According to a friend, Foreman received a letter from the CPS just before Christmas, which was 'the best present he could have had. Freddie is in good shape for his age but another trial and stretch inside would have finished him.'

Foreman, once one of the most feared men in London, has spent more than 16 years in jail for crimes including handling proceeds of the £7million Security Express robbery in 1983 and disposing of the body of Jack 'The Hat' McVitie, who was murdered by the Kray twins.

Earlier this year, he admitted in two TV documentaries that he intimidated witnesses who had seen Ronnie Kray shoot dead George Cornell in the Blind Beggar pub in Whitechapel, East London, in 1966.

He also confessed that a few months later he helped the Krays by murdering Frank Mitchell, known as the Mad Axeman, and feeding his body to fish in the North Sea.

'I'd be a happier man if I hadn't done it,' he added.

He said the Krays had asked him to get rid of Mitchell, who had escaped from Dartmoor.

The Krays had given Mitchell a hiding place and a mistress while they negotiated his return to prison in exchange for parole.

But Mitchell refused to go back. Foreman described the decision to kill Mitchell as similar to one that 'a veterinary surgeon has to make when confronted with a mad dog'.

On the TV programmes, Foreman also solved the mystery of what had happened to Tommy 'Ginger' Marks, a used car dealer whose body vanished after he was shot in Stepney, East London, in 1965. He was also fed to the fish.

Foreman was acquitted of the two murders in separate trials at the Old Bailey.

He first made his confessions in his autobiography, Respect, and then repeated them on television.

He was arrested and questioned by officers of Scotland Yard's elite Organised Crime Group and released on police bail to await a decision.

The confessions fuelled the debate over whether people who are acquitted of serious crimes such as murder should be recharged following fresh evidence and tried again.

The Home Office is reviewing the 'double jeopardy' rule and Home Secretary Jack Straw is considering changing the law.

THE CRAYS

THE Krays once brought terror to the underworld – but now their namesakes are having the same effect in the underwater world.

Experts have discovered a new super-strain of crayfish which can reproduce without mating – meaning they could wipe out rival species in scenes reminiscent of Star Wars: Attack Of The Clones.

They are also worried that the 3in crustacean – named marmorkrebs – is closely related to a notorious North American species.

'Nice waterway – be a shame if anyfink was to 'appen to it!'

BANNED! THE KRAYS' SECRET ROYAL DOSSIER

EXCLUSIVE by NIGEL NELSON

A SECRET dossier on Princess Margaret by gangster Ronnie Kray is to be locked away for 50 YEARS.

The astonishing move was ordered by the Lord Chancellor's department after officials read its explosive contents.

In his memoir, Ronnie named royals and top politicians he and twin Reggie rubbed shoulders with when they terrorised London in the 1960s. And last night it emerged that Margaret, now 70, visited a Kray GAMBLING CLUB at least twice.

VISITS: Princess Margaret and killer Kray twins Ronnie and Reggie

A gangland insider said: "The boys were chuffed when she turned up."

Home Office minister Charles Clarke revealed that nine police files on the Krays – both now dead – have been handed over to the Public Record Office.

But eight will remain shut for 50 years and the ninth cannot be made public for 30 years.

Among police reports and witness statements is the memoir penned by Ronnie. He wrote it while serving 30 years for shooting dead rival gangster George Cornell in East End pub The Blind Beggar.

Historic

The Government admitted to Labour MP Harry Cohen that it had ordered the documents kept under lock and key after a constituent asked to see them.

Mr Cohen, MP for Leyton and Wanstead, said: "These files should be made public.

"They contribute to East End history. It's unreasonable they are being covered up because there cannot be any implications for national security.

"What secrets could Ronnie Kray have known to treat these files like Cabinet papers? This dossier is historic and should not be kept hidden."

The Public Record Office said the files were being kept under wraps to protect police informants and avoid upsetting families of Kray victims.

"They contain information which would cause substantial distress or endangerment," a spokeswoman said.

REGGIE KRAY CONFESSES FROM GRAVE: I AM GAY

Letter to PEOPLE man reveals gangster's darkest secret

OWNING UP: Letter that Reggie (right) wrote in jail revealing his lust for young men

GANGSTER Reggie Kray has made an amazing confession from beyond the grave – his hardman image concealed that he was GAY.

Reggie poured out his darkest secret in a letter written as he faced blackmail over his homosexuality.

He handed me the astonishing two-page admission in a prison visiting room and asked for it to be published after his death.

The once-feared East End crime boss wrote: "I wish for the public to know that I am bisexual."

Today the Sunday People can exclusively reveal how Reggie, who died last Sunday aged 66:

● **KEPT** a string of handsome young lovers while behind bars,

● **PESTERED** new prisoners he fancied – earning him warnings from jail chiefs;

● **SHOWERED** his gay lovers with gifts of expensive jewellery and drugs and

● **FEARED** he had AIDS and persuaded doctors to test him.

Reggie received an underworld tip-off while behind bars that three former lovers were threatening to expose his gay lusts.

Terrified he would be branded a

EXCLUSIVE
By IAN EDMONDSON

"poof" like his gay twin Ronnie, he ordered two London hitmen to warn the would-be blackmailers they would be killed if they talked.

At Maidstone jail, Kent, he also gave me the letter, to be revealed before his death only if his ex-lovers spoke.

Reggie wrote: "The reason I am coming out into the open is because I have an intense dislike of blackmailers and all they stand for."

Truth

The letter also says: "'I prefer not to live a lie and I ask the reader to understand my predicament of having been in prison for 26 years with an all-male population.

"It is not sympathy I seek but that the public applaud me for telling the truth instead of giving me stick.

"My belief is that persons should be able to decide for themselves what they wish to do with their lives, be they heterosexual, gay or bisexual." The letter is signed: "God Bless, Reg Kray."

But the blackmailers never

blabbed. Reggie's henchmen visited one in Ranby prison, Notts, and warned him: "Speak and we'll f***ing shoot you in the face."

The young inmate, thought to have incriminating tapes and letters, signed a pledge of silence.

A former cell mate of Kray said: "Reggie was beside himself when he thought the truth could come out. It had been a well-guarded secret.

"He went to extraordinary lengths to keep his lovers happy. He bought them gold watches, bracelets, rings and carried on looking after them financially even when they were released from jail.

"Reggie always had a supply of booze and Ecstasy tablets which he shared with his lovers.

"The prison officers constantly told him about trying to chat up young inmates and he was even given a written warning.

"Other inmates treated Reggie's young men with respect because they were under his wing."

Empire

Reggie had already asked prison doctors for tests because his lovers might have given him AIDS. The tests were negative.

The jail source added: "It's very ironic. Reggie built his empire on terror and masculine power."

Reggie, whose funeral is on Wednesday, married Roberta Jones behind bars three years ago.

Roberta, 41, was with him when he died of cancer in a Norfolk hotel days after his release from prison on compassionate grounds.

Ronnie died five years ago. The twins were jailed for 30 years for murder in 1969.

Their downfall came after Ronnie shot dead George Cornell in the Blind Beggar pub. The small-time villain had called him a "fat poof."

● **People** HOTlinks

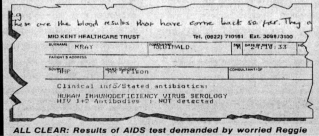

ALL CLEAR: Results of AIDS test demanded by worried Reggie | i.edmondson@people.co.uk

REG, RON, TEDDY AND FLOPSY THE BUNNY

ADVERTISER SPECIAL REPORT

BY PAUL MARINKO

Secret report says twins were Krayzy about furry toys

Ron Kray (left) and Reg (right) were said to be "friendly and pleasant" by a psychiatrist in Brixton Prison

THE Kray twins may have been known for their reign of terror in East End gangland but they were also good at making furry animals, a government report kept secret for 30 years has revealed.

They were also "friendly", "sociable" and "pleasant" according to a psychiatrist who examined them in Brixton Prison.

Denis Leigh was assessing their mental state in 1968-69 as they waited to be tried for their alleged involvement in the jailbreak and murder of Bow-born 'Mad Axeman' Frank Mitchell.

In the reports, released by the Home Office under the 30 years rule, the psychiatrist says of Reg: "Mentally he was alert, friendly, pleasant and indeed one might say charming.

"He was evacuated from London during the Second World War and he appears to have been a rather nervous boy who was a bedwetter till he was 10 years old who suffered from nightmares."

According to the papers Ron was good at making furry rabbits while Reggie preferred to turn his hand to furry bears, although both showed "extremely good workmanship".

Mr Leigh had to decide whether the East End crime duo were mentally fit for trial and concluded that they were.

Ron and his older brother Charlie were cleared of conspiring to secure Mitchell's escape and harbouring him, while Reggie was cleared of murder but sentenced to five years for conspiracy and nine months for harbouring.

But in a TV documentary on Monday former gangland hardman Freddie Foreman admitted murdering Mitchell on the orders of the twins.

Kray firm member Albert Donoghue admitted breaking Mitchell out of prison for the twins and said he was there when Foreman finished him off after pumping 12 bullets into him in the back of a van.

He said: "Foreman put the gun under his ear and that was it, pop."

Foreman said on the programme: "It was all over in seconds, done, finished."

The programme claimed the twins ordered the killing of Mitchell when he started getting restless and threatened to blow the whistle on the plot. Next Monday's programme tells what happened to Mitchell's body.

■ Former world heavyweight boxing champ Mike Tyson has told of how he got a letter of support from Reg Kray.

Boxing's bad boy made the revelation in an interview in which he described how much he loved Britain. He said he admired Reg because he had the respect of people in London.

Reg Kray preferred making furry bears while Ron had a liking for rabbits, says the prison report

---

KILLER

Part Two: In his own words, fro[m]

KRAYS WERE JUST A JOKE

THE Kray Twins, top criminals? Don't make me laugh.

In Liverpool there are several villains who are multi-millionaires. Men who have made a career out of crime but have never ever been nicked. I'm not saying it's something to be proud of, it's just a fact.

But Ronnie and Reggie Kray were a joke. They spent 30 years in jail for their stupidity and never did a bank robbery or any real lucrative villainy. All they ever did was terrorise people to extract a few quid.

If you did a bank job in their area in the Sixties they'd have come knocking on your door for a cut. They wouldn't have got a penny off me. They'd have had to kill me.

How could they have been clever? Ronnie Kray carried out a cold-blooded murder in front of witnesses.

They thought they were invincible and that no-one would ever dare grass on them. You can only keep people frightened for so long – they'll turn in the end.

The Kray funerals were a pantomime too. All those bouncers with sunglasses and shaved heads.

Crime never paid for the Krays – they were kings for a few years and clowns for three decades.

CLOWNS: Ron and Reggie Kray

BYE-BYE CHARLIE: Tony Lambrianou, Freddie Foreman, Joey Pyle, Wilf Pine, Roy Shaw and Johnny Nash at graveside   Picture: SIMEON FRANCIS

THE FINAL FAREWELL

Gangland veterans gather to pay last respects to Charlie

THE hair's turning grey and the eyesight is not what it used to be – but the bulging muscles under their expensive suits are still a real giveaway.

These are the ageing legends of London's East End gangland who gathered together for the last time at the family grave of the Kray Twins.

The six met a few days ago at a secret ceremony photographed exclusively by the Sunday People to pay their last respects to Kray brother Charlie.

The Underworld veterans viewed the newly-installed headstone which they had helped pay for and laid a wreath of lilies and carnations.

Then, hiding their massive fists in trouser pockets, they reflected on the dark past that had bonded them for nearly 40 years and brought them together for probably the very last time.

There was Tony Lambrianou, 58, and Freddie "The Enforcer" Foreman, 68, who were involved in Reggie Kray's notorious murder of Jack "The Hat" McVitie.

There was Roy "Pretty Boy" Shaw, in his early sixties, who killed a man in

**By Chief Reporter
ALEXANDER HITCHEN**

prison with his bare hands, shattered the jaw of the governor of Broadmoor and was once branded the most dangerous man in the British penal system.

There was gangland boss Joey Pyle, 64, who was cleared of murdering a night club boss after two trials.

There was Johnny Nash, 67, elder statesman of North London's Nash crime family and rival to the Kray Twins. And there was Wilf Pine, a close associate of all three Kray brothers.

Charlie, 72, died in Parkhurst prison last year after being convicted of plotting to smuggle £39 million of cocaine.

MOB: Reg (left) Charlie, Ron   One of the old villains at the graveside at Chingford Mount cemetery, Essex, who did not wish to be named, said: "Charlie was no angel, none of us are saints, but he was a loyal man and loyalty is a quality that seems to be disappearing rapidly."

The gang member added: "It is going to be the last time we will all be here together.

"My health is not too good and we seem to be going to more and more funerals for our friends these days."

KILLING SPREE: Kray twins Reggie (left) and Ronnie lusted for blood

KRAYS KILLED 30

THE Kray Twins killed over THIRTY people during their 13-year reign of terror, the News of the World can reveal today.

Sensational new evidence from close friend Colin Fry exposes an orgy of bloodletting that blows their 'hero gangster' image to smithereens.

Fry, a regular visitor to Ronnie in Broadmoor, also details grim ways Charlie Kray got rid of corpses.

Some were smuggled into funeral parlours, squeezed into coffins on top of the body already inside and then buried by unsuspecting families.

Others were jammed into oil drums and dropped into holes on a plot in Essex.

Fry said: "I've been told a garden centre on that site has difficulty planting deep-rooted trees."

Body

This week BBC1 broadcast a death-bed 'confession' from Reggie where he admitted to the killing of an unnamed victim besides gangster Jack 'The Hat' McVitie who he stabbed in October, 1967.

He was jailed for life in 1969. Ronnie got the same sentence for killing gangster George Cornell in the Blind Beggar pub in

DEAD: Isaacs

EXCLUSIVE

BY SARAH ARNOLD

Whitechapel, east London. But Fry said: "There were around 30 victims."

Among them were gangsters Jack Frost, 'Mad' Teddy Smith, Ernie 'Mr Fixit' Isaacs, Billy Stayton and Frank Mitchell.

There was also an anonymous rent boy killed by homosexual Ronnie.

"He was just a penniless lad from the streets," said 57-year-old Fry.

"Ron used him for his pleasure then shot him. Charlie disposed of the body." Fry added: "Someday the diggers will go in and corpses will pop up all over Essex."

DEAD: Mitchell

DEAD: McVitie

203

DID REG KILL MAD TEDDY?

■ Mad Teddy Smith was a psychopathic homosexual who had an affair with Ron Kray - but an argument with the twins led to his death

THE Advertiser can reveal the first picture of the man believed to be another of Reggie Kray's murder victims.

Limehouse-based Teddy Smith, who worked for the Kray Firm as a minder and debt collector, went missing in 1967 probably because he would not carry out a contract killing.

Ron Kray and Teddy, both psychopathic homosexuals, had been having an affair.

After a long weekend together an argument broke out followed by a fight. Smith went missing and was never seen again.

In an interview with the East End gangster to be shown on television tonight (Thursday) Reg admits killing another person besides Jack 'The

The first photo of Kray's last victim

SPECIAL REPORT BY PAUL MARINKO

Hat' McVitie, the man he was jailed for knifing to death in 1967.

During the interview Reggie was asked if he had killed anyone else besides McVitie.

He replied: "One, one."

He did not reveal the name of this second mystery victim although it is believed to be Mad Teddy.

Reggie died of bowel and bladder cancer last October just days after giving the interview in hospital.

Retired cop Leonard 'Nipper' Read, who gathered the evidence to convict the twins of murder in 1969, said that Reggie was probably talking about Smith.

Kray victim Lenny Hamilton said Reggie had killed Smith because he refused to kill his first wife Frances' brother Frankie Shea.

Frankie said the Krays asked plenty of people to kill him and Reggie only married his sister because he had spurned the gangster's homosexual advances.

But Smith refused to do the deed.

■ TURN TO PAGE 6

50 year secret of Krays and Princess Margaret

BY PAUL MARINKO

SECRET files thought to tell of how Princess Margaret visited a club owned by the Kray twins are being hidden from public gaze for 50 more years.

They could include the memoirs of Ronnie which he penned while serving life for the murder of George Cornell and are believed to tell of how he and twin Reggie, who ruled the East End underworld during the swinging decade, rubbed shoulders with royals and top politicians.

Long time friend to the twins, Les Martin, said: "Because Margaret stepped into the gambling joint it was a coup for them and it should be brought into the open.

"They (the twins) were over the moon."

Home Office minister Charles Clarke said eight police files on the late infamous pair would stay locked up for 50 more years and a further one would be kept secret for 30 more years.

The news came following a question from Labour MP Harry Cohen about the files.

He said: "These files should be made public.

"What secrets could Ronnie Kray have known to treat these files like Cabinet pa-

pers?"

A spokeswoman for the Public Record Office said files were kept locked away for a number of reasons, such as to avoid distress to victims of crime or protect police informants, but she could not confirm the reason in this instance. But she added that the decision to close the files was not reversible.

"The closure status of files can be reviewed on request to the department concerned. In this case that is the Metropolitan Police."

A spokeswoman for Princess Margaret said she did not know if the Queen's sister had visited the club because it was so long ago.

Kray widow's first visit to grave

TEARS FOR MY REG

By NEIL McLEOD

GANGLAND killer Reggie Kray's devoted widow Roberta tenderly lays flowers at his grave – her first visit to his final resting place.

Roberta, 41, had been too devastated to go to Reggie's grave since she wept for him at his funeral last October.

But she finally gathered up all her strength to pay her respects in an emotional visit.

Standing on the rain-soaked grass, she tearfully looked at the grave where Reggie is buried and lovingly placed her bouquet of flowers.

There is no mention of Reggie yet on the tombstone. Instead it reads: "Legend. Ronald Kray".

zSlaughters

But Reggie has been buried in the same plot at Chingford Mount Cemetery in East London as his brother Ronnie who died in jail six years ago.

In time the grave will be marked with a stone dedicated to the infamous twins who were jailed for life in 1969 for gangland killings.

Roberta leaned on her knee and carefully placed her wreath with a short message.

It said "Reg, You are always in my heart. All my love, Rob" – with three kisses. Her companion Wilf

EMOTIONAL: Roberta lays her flowers

TRIBUTE: Roberta's message at grave where Reg and Ron are buried

Pine, who walked her through the graveyard, also left a floral tribute to the Kray twins' elder brother Charlie who died last year in jail, convicted of drug smuggling.

One on-looker in the cemetery said yesterday: "Roberta held herself together extremely well – but it looked very tough for her.

"She paid her respects in a very dignified manner. The visit was very solemn and she looked deep in thought."

Loyal Roberta was by Reggie's side when he died of cancer at the age of 66 in the honeymoon suite of a Norwich hotel – having been freed on compassionate grounds

following a campaign backed by the Sunday People.

The university graduate had married Reggie in Maidstone Prison 1997. And she campaigned relentlessly for the ailing gangster to be released from the life-term handed to him for the murder of Jack "The Hat" McVitie.

Following her poignant visit to Reggie's graveside, Roberta was driven away in a blue car by a couple who had joined her in the cemetery.

One onlooker said: "Just at the end, the tears seemed to come – as if she could not hold back her feelings any longer."

205

I'M REGGIE KRAY'S SECRET DAUGHTER

Sandra tells of her mum's fling with gangster and a moving prison reunion

EXCLUSIVE
By MIKE HAMILTON

WHEN THE last of the notorious Kray brothers was laid to rest he took one final secret to the grave with him.

Among the thousands of mourners who gathered in London's East End to pay their last respects to Reggie Kray was the secret daughter he did not want to know.

Sandra Ireson, a 42-year-old mother and gran, was born after a brief romance between Reggie and cabaret dancer Greta Harper in 1958.

And she didn't discover who her real father was until 1995 following the death of Reggie's twin brother Ronnie.

For the next five years she tried to forge a relationship with Britain's best-known long-term prisoner.

But only once did she manage to meet Reggie, who was jailed for life in 1969 for stabbing small-time villain Jack "The Hat" McVitie.

Sandra, now 42, briefly hugged the ageing mobster after an hour-long chat inside Maidstone Prison two years before his death from bladder cancer, in October last year

But he later rejected his daughter's attempt to cement their relationship.

He had been devastated by the death of his elder brother Charlie in April last year and feared upsetting his young wife Roberta, 41.

But last night, speaking exclusively to the Sunday Mirror, Sandra said: "I am his daughter and I couldn't care less who knows.

"I don't feel any shame about who my real father is. It's time it was out in the open and the world knew the truth."

Sandra's existence was until now, a closely-guarded secret known only to her family and a handful of Kray's close associates.

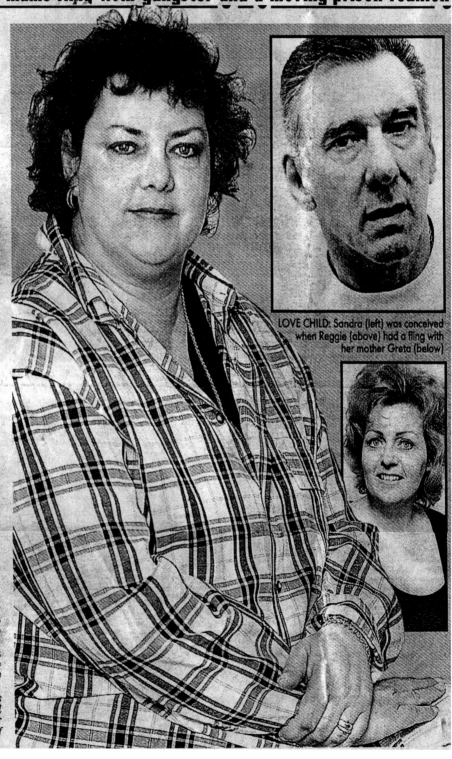

LOVE CHILD: Sandra (left) was conceived when Reggie (above) had a fling with her mother Greta (below)

Kray twin admitted gay killing – prison pal

A former prisoner claims Reggie Kray confessed to him that he killed a young homosexual. Peter Gillett says the confession was made in jail 16 years ago.

The claim was revealed in a Channel 5 documentary The Krays: Their Empire Behind Bars, last night and comes after the feared East End gangster made a deathbed admission that he committed an as yet unknown about murder.

Reggie died from cancer in October 2000 and his confession was revealed in a BBC documentary last March.

He refused to reveal the victim's identity but it was widely thought to have been Edward "Mad Teddy" Smith, missing since 1967.

Identity

Mr Gillett, who did time with the gangster at Parkhurst and Maidstone prisons, said: "Sixteen years ago Reg burdened me with the secret of this other murder he did.

"It was not a villain, not a policeman but a young boy, a young gay boy ... he was disgusted with himself for realising that he enjoyed that sort of thing, knowing he was gay or bisexual, and he shot the kid."

Reggie was released from prison in August 2000 after spending nearly 33 years behind bars for the murder of Jack "The Hat" McVitie.

AUTHOR Steve Wraith found organising guests for the launch of his book on the Kray Twins a bit like arranging the seat placings at the Middle East peace talks.

The bash for Wraith's The Krays: The Geordie Connection is to be held at an East End pub called the Blind Beggar, where Ronnie Kray murdered George Cornell – a heavy from a rival gang – allegedly for calling him "a big fat poof" in 1966.

"I decided against inviting Frankie Fraser on the sole basis that he'd just had a rumble with Freddie Foreman at a café in Maida Vale," Wraith tells me, "and while it might have made a nice splash

RUMBLE: Frank

in the newspapers – two gangsters having a fight at the launch of a book – I decided against it. I will send Frank a copy of the book, but I didn't think it would be too good an idea to invite him."

After all that, however, Foreman won't be at the Thursday night launch either. He and another Kray henchman, Tony Lambrianou, have turned down their invitations "out of respect for Cornell's widow". Thankfully for Wraith, hardmen Ray Shaw, Eric Mason, and Joe Pyle will be there.

KRAY'S GAY NOTE SALE

By NICK ALLEN

GANGSTER Reggie Kray denied being gay in unpublished letters about to be auctioned and even suggested getting engaged so the story could be sold to newspapers.

On his own headed notepaper Reggie, jailed with twin Ronnie in 1969, wrote to a journalist: "I'm not gay. My heart does not beat faster when I see a male – does yours?"

He asked if newspapers would pay a lot for the engagement story, saying he wanted "big money".

Reggie asked who the lucky girl should be and suggested a model he claimed had an affair with a marquis, a page three girl and a soap actress.

LETTERS: Ron & Reg

He said: "Tell me by return of post who is better. I can get a young model if necessary."

In one letter he said: "Let's do the engagement in style and go for top money."

The 80 letters from both twins were written in childlike, barely legible scrawl to Robin McGibbon, who got to know them after ghost-ing their brother Charlie's autobiography.

One of Ronnie's letters denounces a "diabolical" book by his wife Kate, saying if she does not stop publication he will divorce her.

And 28 letters written in 1993 chart his mental breakdown.

Also in the sale are letters Charlie wrote from Belmarsh jail during his drugs trial.

With other memorabilia they could fetch £10,000 next week.

RON 'KILLED REG'S WIFE'

GANGSTER Ronnie Kray murdered his twin brother Reggie's first wife, it was sensationally claimed last night.

An inquest at the time concluded bride Frances had committed suicide. But Bradley Allardyce, Reggie's gay lover in prison, says Ronnie **FORCED** her to take the pills that killed her.

Allardyce was released from prison three years ago after serving nine years for armed robbery.

He spent three of those years in Maidstone prison, four cells along the landing from Reggie Kray.

Kray, who died in 2000, was serving life for the murder of Jack "the Hat" McVitie.

But Allardyce told BBC Radio 4's Today programme that one night

BY **STEPHEN RAWLINS**

Reggie revealed the crime that haunted him the most – the apparent suicide of his first wife.

He added: "He put his head on my shoulder and told me Ron killed Frances. He told Reg what he had done two days after."

Although both Krays are dead, Scotland Yard have told the BBC they will investigate.

KISS OF DEATH: Reg, (left)Frances and Ron

'I spurned gay Reg Kray - so he wed my sister in revenge'

EXCLUSIVE INTERVIEW BY PAUL MARINKO

A toast on the wedding day - Frances and Reggie

REGGIE Kray's former brother-in-law has revealed the East End gangster married his sister because he spurned his gay advances.

In the same week that a former prison friend of the infamous gangland boss revealed a mystery murder victim was one of Reggie's gay lovers Frankie Shea told the Advertiser the mobster's marriage to his sister Frances was a sham just to get back at him.

Former thief Frankie - who used to work as a driver for Reggie and his twin Ronnie before they were caged for murder - said: "That geezer married my sister because he was in love with me.

"I was one of those baby-faced kids I suppose.

"He did the worst thing any man could ever do to get his revenge at not being able to get hold of me and that's what it's all about."

Marrying Frances was sham - geezer was in love with me, claims brother Frankie

Frankie, who was brought up with his sister in Ormsby Street, Bethnal Green, said he had to run away to escape the clutches of the Krays.

He said Reggie got Frances hooked on drugs so she was dependent on him and she eventually killed herself at the third attempt.

Dismissing claims by Reggie's former gay lover in prison, Bradley Allardyce, that Ronnie had murdered Frances by forcing pills down her throat, Frankie said: "We know she committed suicide but Reggie was the instigator of it all as far as I'm con-

cerned."

He claimed Frances was so desperate to get away from Reggie that in 1967 she even changed her name back to Shea by deed poll, adding: "That's how much she wanted to be away from that a***hole.

"She married him to keep the peace because he threatened to kill me and my father."

Frankie said his 85-year-old mum was still living with the memory of what happened to her daughter.

The revelation came as a Channel 5 programme revealed last night (Wed

16/01) that a murder Reggie admitted to days before he died two years ago was that of a young gay man killed before the gangster was jailed for life for murdering Jack 'The Hat' McVitie in 1969.

Peter Gillett met Reggie in prison and said the twin admitted he shot the man just after he had performed an intimate sex act on the gangster in the Kray home at Vallance Road, Bethnal Green.

"I think it was his disgust in himself that he enjoyed that sort of thing showing he was gay or bisexual and he shot the kid."

Keeping the legend of the Krays alive

MANY FANS: The Krays

HOBNOBBING with gangsters is not the kind of after-school activity most parents would like to see their child partake in. But a schoolboy obsession with the Krays meant that was exactly how Steve Wraith spent his evenings.

Steve said: "My first recollection of Ronnie and Reggie Kray was as a 10-year-old child as my mam and dad watched the news intently.

"Two middle aged men dressed in black were emerging from the back of green prison vans to attend their mothers' funeral in Essex.

"That news report and my parents interest had left its mark on my imagination."

Steve started writing to the twins and to his surprise he received a number of letters back. It wasn't long before Steve was welcomed into their protected circle of friends. Now aged 30, the Gateshead lad has taken his schoolboy obsession one stage further and has written a book about his experiences.

The Krays – The Geordie Connection

(www.thegeordieconnection.com) is a website dedicated to publicising his forthcoming work.

Steve said: "The idea was to produce a site that would help promote the book. We didn't expect the kind of feedback that we have received from Kray fans all over the world."

The site is divided into a number of sections and includes some real hidden gems for die-hard fans. There are loads of exclusive photographs, audio and video clips and a host of little-known facts. It is an alternative look at the lives of Britain's most notorious criminals.

RACHEL GRECIAN

THE NEW KRAYS

Cleared Damilola boys rule estate by fear, says top copper

By TOM WORDEN and IAN HEPBURN

THE teenage brothers cleared of murdering Damilola Taylor are violent thugs known to police as the "new Krays," it was revealed last night.

The two 16-year-olds lead a gang who rule South London estates through fear, intimidation, robbery and protection rackets. And the cop who led the Damilola probe, Det Supt

Continued on Page Four

Thugs in the clear . . . the brothers from hell, whose identity is protected by law

KRAYS MADE £10M FROM INSIDE JAIL

- **They ordered 30 murders from their cells**
- **They duped star Shane in charity con**
- **They paid for blinding the Ripper**

KILLERS:
Reg, left,
and Ronnie

EXCLUSIVE
**By LUCY PANTON
Crime Reporter**

GANGLAND killers Reggie and Ronnie Kray made £10 million while BEHIND bars, the Sunday People can reveal.

The notorious twins scammed more money on the inside than they ever did before they were jailed.

A startling new TV investigation into Ron and Reg has revealed that while they were serving life sentences for murder they...

- ●CONNED top entertainers such as Shane Richie and Steve McFadden into helping charity frauds.
- ●ORDERED up to 30 murders of rival criminals.
- ●PAID for Yorkshire Ripper Peter Sutcliffe to be blinded.

And according to new evidence, before they were jailed in 1969 they...

- ●BLACKMAILED Beatles manager Brian Epstein and tried
- ●GRABBING a share of the fledgling group for the Mafia.

The TV investigation reveals one of their most lucrative scams

DUPED: Star Shane Richie

was the phoney charity ball. Guests would pay £30 each to mix with stars like presenter Shane Richie, EastEnders' Steve McFadden and Leslie Grantham and The Bill's Billy Murray.

But instead of going to charity the proceeds of up to £3,000 a night went straight into the Krays' pockets to pay for their illicit booze and drugs in jail.

Menaces

Dumbfounded Richie says now: "I was never aware that the money was siphoned off and went directly to Reg."

The Krays continued to open clubs, pubs, betting offices, record shops and snooker halls from behind bars. They had 15 trusted lieutenants on the outside

STABBED: Ripper Sutcliffe

whose tasks included collecting debts with menaces.

Although Reg was convicted only of killing petty crook Jack "The Hat" McVitie and Ron of gangster George Cornell, it is now believed Reg murdered at least three more and Ronnie six.

And they ordered dozens more killings carried out by henchmen.

Business associate Colin Fry says: "They got rid of 30 all in all." The bodies were either dumped at sea or cremated in an aluminium smelter.

Reg also put out a murder contract on Yorkshire Ripper Peter Sutcliffe. He took revenge after the mass murderer attacked Ronnie in Broadmoor top-security hospital.

Ronnie had wanted to forget

it. But Reg got Ian Kay, already serving life for killing a Woolworth store manager, to strike. Kay rammed a pen into Sutcliffe's left eye but only succeeded in blinding him.

One of the Krays' scams BEFORE they went to jail involved Beatles manager Brian Epstein, according to the Channel 5 series starting tomorrow.

The Mafia's British representatives told the twins they wanted a share in the group's growing success.

Terrified

The Krays and business associate Sydney Vaughan, who knew Epstein had a weakness for drink and drugs, began to put pressure on him.

Epstein, terrified and out of his depth, started to pay the Krays cash to keep them sweet.

Vaughan, now 58, says: "We were bullies and he was very vulnerable. He must have given us a few thousand pounds but it never got us anywhere.

"In reality he wasn't in a position to give us a piece of the Beatles and our plan failed."

●The Krays: Their Empire Behind Bars, 10.50pm tomorrow and 11pm Tuesday and Wednesday, C5.

REGGIE'S KEEP-FIT VID FOR WRINKLIES

ONE of Reggie Kray's most bizarre schemes for making money behind bars was a fitness video for the over-60s.

The grey-haired gangster, then pushing 60 himself, arranged to be filmed training in the prison gym.

Reg was the brains behind the twins' money-spinning deals in prison. Although they once ruled London's East End they had been more efficient at violence than making big profits.

But their Old Bailey trial brought them nationwide notoriety and Reg was determined to cash in. He began commissioning mugs, tea-towels, pictures and T-shirts bearing the Kray name to sell on the outside. Reg pulled strings to get exclusive use of the prison phone and made up to 50 calls a day running the business empire.

Ronnie died in 1995 and Reg died 16 months ago aged 66 from cancer. He left the merchandising rights to his widow Roberta, 43.

GANGSTERS are gathering tonight to celebrate what would have been the Kray twins' 70th birthdays. However, Mad Frankie Fraser and his pliers have been blacklisted because he keeps "upsetting" the other hardnuts.

Steve Wraith – who handled the Krays' business affairs while they were banged up – tells me: "I invited Dave Courtney and Freddie Foreman and it's best not to have them in the same room as Frankie, so I didn't invite him.

"Frankie wrote on his website that Dave was a grass, which wasn't true. And Frankie said something nasty about Freddie... I can't remember what.

"Then Freddie saw Frankie in a café in Maida Vale and started dragging him out by his shoes. It was like a scene out of Goodfellas."

The party takes place at the Blind Beggar – the East End pub where Ronnie Kray murdered George Cornell in 1966 – and funds will be raised for the Bubble Foundation, which helps ill babies.

Pubs 'to pay for extra policemen'

BY DAVID HARDING

PUBS and restaurants will have to pay for extra policing to tackle late-night drunkenness under proposals by David Blunkett.

The Home Secretary, under growing pressure from Downing Street to tackle yob culture, is considering the levy in town and city centres.

The West End of London alone attracts 300,000 drinkers on a typical Saturday night.

At present, police can charge clubs and music venues for cover only for one-off events such as festivals.

The new levy, which would also apply to fast-food outlets, could be included in a White Paper on anti-social behaviour to be published later this month.

The plan was inspired by a pilot scheme operating in Peter Street, Manchester. The road is patrolled by two extra constables – one paid for

'The Krays thought of that years ago.'

by the police authority and the other funded voluntarily by clubs and bars.

But the proposed compulsory levy has provoked anger in the food and drink industry, which already gener-

ates £12billion from tax on alcohol sales each year.

Landlord Jason French, of the Akenside Traders pub in Newcastle, described it as 'another scam for the Government, another stealth tax'.

Mark Hastings, of the British Beer and Pub Association, which represents brewers and pub owners, said: 'Perhaps the Home Office should direct the police to arrest and prosecute thugs, rather than picking the pockets of publicans.'

Ministers also fear the Government may appear to be sending mixed messages amid moves to extend drinking hours.

The new licensing Bill about to enter its report stage in the House of Lords will introduce more flexible opening hours, which could pave the way for 24-hour drinking.

Last week, Mr Blunkett announced plans to force heavy drinkers into detox under a new mental health Bill.

WILL KRAYS BE CLEARED OF MURDER?

KRAY twins Ronnie and Reggie, the East End's most notorious gangsters, could be posthumously cleared of murder.

Two lawyers are disputing the twins' convictions in 1969 for the killings of Jack 'The Hat' McVitie and George Cornell.

The barristers, acting for Ronnie's widow Kate, say new evidence could mean the convictions were unsafe.

The evidence centres around documents released from the Old Bailey's archives, relating to the original trial.

According to a Sunday newspaper report, Kate Kray's lawyers have uncovered a 30-page memo written by prosecutor Sir John Leonard.

Written on the night before the trial began, the document reveals how Leonard altered statements from key prosecution witnesses.

In it, details are given of how he ordered pages of signed testimony

Legal probe may be held into twins' trial

by senior detectives to be removed, according to the Sunday Times.

He also edited the text of testimonies, removed and inserted passages, and changed names, according to the paper.

Reviewing the memo, Kate Kray's lawyers said that interfering in any way with witness statements was a clear breach of the law.

As a result, they concluded that the ■ CONTINUED P2

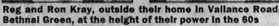

Reg and Ron Kray, outside their home in Vallance Road, Bethnal Green, at the height of their power in the 60s

Exhibition on the lives of notorious East End gangsters

ROUGH JUSTICE: Jannette Galtry, marketing manager of the Galleries of Justice, tries out Reggie Kray's bed from Nottingham Prison in 1991 and (above) a painting of the Kray twins on show   POSTPHOTO C161097TB4-1

Kray twins in spotlight

By JAMES KAY

THE Krays are the subject of an exhibition at the Galleries of Justice.

The Firm: The Media and the Myth of the Krays previews tonight with a visit from one of their closest acquaintances.

Laurie O'Leary was a long-standing friend and confidante of East End hoodlums Ronnie and Reggie Kray.

The twins, along with their brother Charlie, were the most powerful men in the criminal underworld of 1960s London.

Their campaign of protection rackets, beatings and extortion came to an end in 1969 when the pair were sentenced to 30 years for murdering two gangland rivals.

A long incarceration led to a campaign for their release in the 1990s.

But Ronnie died behind bars aged 61 in Broadmoor Prison in 1995, and Reggie died five years later aged 65 at a hotel in Norwich after a long battle with cancer.

Mr O'Leary, who ran nightclubs for the Krays and visited them countless times during their imprisonment, said: "The Krays were the last of that type of gangster, in an era before drugs. I saw the fear factor they created, but I never felt threatened myself, partly because I never got involved in their criminal activities.

"As young men, they were extremely courteous, had respect for their elders — like the rest of their generation. Ron was a shy man who became frustrated by his own lack of education, and that frustration tipped over into violence because of his schizophrenia. Reggie was always the controlling influence."

The exhibition includes dozens of letters written by Reggie Kray to Barbara Hall in Carlton.

Mrs Hall, 45, became fascinated by the twins when Reggie moved to Nottingham Prison for a year in 1990. After watching the biopic of their lives and reading their autobiography — *Our Story* — Mrs Hall wrote to Reggie, beginning a long friendship.

At its height, the pair used to talk on the phone twice a day, with Reggie sending her more than 120 letters and others items, such as clothing, signed posters and books.

Mrs Hall said: "He was an ordinary person — polite, a

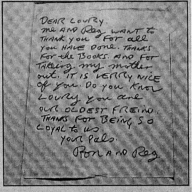

KIND WORDS: A letter from the Krays to Laurie O'Leary and (inset below) Barbara Hall

gentleman. He was an old school sort of person, really; he hated people swearing when there was a lady present. Unfortunately, the newspapers kept the myth of him being an evil man very much alive."

Mrs Hall sold the letters — plus eight scrapbooks of original newspaper cuttings — last year to the Galleries of Justice in Nottingham for £4,500.

The exhibition also features shocking photographs of their known victims — 'scenes of crime' material donated by Scotland Yard.

Curator Louise Connell said: "I want this exhibition to demonstrate how prison life affected the twins but also to show how crime may seem glamorous, but the consequences of a criminal lifestyle are extremely harsh.

"It is also interesting to see how popular mythology has made these men into cult figures and so representative of the gangster chic of the era."

Visitors will also be able to see two new linked exhibitions: *Inside Outside*, a community-based media display and visual dialogue between people in a Young Offenders' Institute and children at risk of getting involved in crime, and *Gun Crime*, which features firearms handed in to Notts during the gun amnesty earlier this year.

● *The Firm: The Media and the Myth of the Krays* opens to the public on Saturday.

THREAT: Ronnie and Kate

Kray death contract on wife Kate

GANGSTER Ronnie Kray tried to have his wife Kate killed — because she was seeing another man.

Kray, who died in 1995, put out the contract while serving a life sentence for murder.

The plot is revealed by author Steve Wraith in a new book about Ronnie and twin brother Reggie called The Krays: The Geordie Connection.

Wraith said: "Kate had just written a book but Ronnie wasn't pleased.

"She'd said she was having a relationship despite an agreement that they would lead a celibate life."

Ronnie issued the death threat when Wraith saw him in Broadmoor in 1993.

He said: "He put his hand on the table and said, 'I want you to take care of Kate'. I took it to mean he wanted me to arrange for her death."

Former kissogram girl Kate wed Kray in Broadmoor in 1989 even though he was gay.

213

STAR TO PLAY THE TWINS – AT THE DOUBLE

BY ROB MACKINLAY

EAST END urban myths are set for a serious smacking in a new film about the Krays.

The film plans to bury the 'St Krays' image fostered in the earlier movie which starred the Kemp brothers and will look at Ronnie Krays disturbed mental state.

East End–born Ray Winstone, star of Sexy Beast and Scum, who used to box at Repton Boys Club, is set to play both of the notorious brothers.

Ray Burdis, the writer and director for the movie - set to start filming in January - said he wanted to dispel folklore legend that the East End was safer when they were about, adding: "that's a load of old cobblers."

He said that Ronnie Kray was "unhinged" and that you only had to look at him the wrong way and he'd "rip your face off".

Pressure was put on Burdis in his role as writer and producer for the original Kemp brother's 1990 film, The Krays, because both Ronnie and Reggie were still alive.

Burdis was in direct communication with the brothers and it was they who pushed for the "St Krays" image that ended up putting the killers in a "goody-goody light."

The other myth set to take a hammering in the movie is the infamous 'wall of silence' that police still complain about.

According to Burdis, Det Supt Len 'Nipper' Read, smashed the wall in his plea to bring the Krays to book.

Bob Hoskins is set to play Nipper's role in a film that could finally shatter an enduring East End legend.

East End movie star Ray Winstone is all set to play the role of the Twins

REG, RON AND NOW IT'S RAY!

Claims rubbished

CLAIMS that former gangster Dave Courtney largely invented his criminal past have been rubbished by a Kray family friend.

In his book Wannabe In My Gang?, Bernard O'Mahoney labels Courtney a fantasist and police informant, who never killed anyone.

But Les Martin, an old friend of Charlie and the twins, said that Courtney had earned his reputation and had never talked to the police.

O'Mahoney's claims that Tony Lambrianou had never been on the Kray firm and later informed on them were also dismissed by Les.

He said that both Tony and his elder brother Chris had worked for the twins for at least six months and had been well respected.

The idea that Lambrianou talked to detectives about Reg killing of Jack 'the Hat' McVitie in 1967 was also ridiculous, said Les.

"Tony was on the Firm," he told the Advertiser this week. "He served 15 years for murder and he never once opened his mouth."

Les also pointed out that it was the media which built up the image of the Krays, following the funeral of their mother in 1982.

The murders which the twins were actually convicted for, of McVitie and George Cornell, were personal matters, he said.

McVitie had tried to con the twins in a deal, and Cornell was killed in revenge for the shooting of their friend Dickie Hart.

On the issue of Charlie Kray, Les stressed that the fight would continue to have him posthumously cleared of his conviction.

New book slams Kray gang fantasies

The Krays in their prime: Charlie (centre) is flanked by Reg (left) and Ron

'Fake villains seek glamour of the Firm' says Bernard

DAVE Courtney never murdered anybody and Tony Lambrianou was never on the Kray firm, according to a new book.

In fact, according to former Kray associate Bernard O'Mahoney, much of gangland folklore is pure fantasy and was never true.

The claims come in O'Mahoney's latest book Wannabe In My Gang?, a scathing account of his involvement in violent crime.

In it, he takes a swipe at all those who profited from the Kray name and the newspapers and reporters who glamourised them.

O'Mahoney tells how he first came to know Bethnal Green twins Ronnie and Reggie while trying to raise funds for crash victim James Fallon in 1989.

James, 10, had been the victim of a hit-and-run accident and after reading about it the press O'Mahoney says he wanted to help.

Reg Kray offered his services, and the event snowballed into a charity boxing

BY BARNY STOKES

match attended by London's underworld.

But O'Mahoney says the event was a shambles, full of "Kray clones" like Welsh twins Lindsay and Leighton Frayne.

Charlie Kray encounters former East End Page 3 girl Flanagan

He claims that many of the so-called gangsters, including Lambrianou, never even paid for their tickets for the event.

And he says the promoter the Krays put him in touch with walked off with the cash but Reg told him to keep quiet. **Lambrianou, who died in March, also comes in for criticism, as O'Mahoney claims that Ron Kray told him the henchman had never been on the firm.**

He prints the statement he claims Lambrianou gave to the police about the killing of Jack 'The Hat' McVitie at an East End flat in 1967.

In it, Lambrianou is quoted as saying he was never part of the twin's organisation and had never been asked to do anything for them.

O'Mahoney stresses Lambrianou went on to make money out of the Kray name and slams 'Dodgy' Dave Courtney as another fake.

He describes Courtney as a serial fantasist who got to know Reg by writing to him and then asking if he could visit him in prison.

Despite the hype, he says Courtney was in reality a petty criminal who milked his association with the Krays.

FOOLS

Ron Kray's funeral is described as a "macabre circus", attended by legions of fools, trying to promote themselves.

And O'Mahoney says he was sickened by the cheers for a "schizophrenic homosexual who had shot a man through the head."

The author is critical of the police sting operation that saw Charlie Kray jailed in 1997 for his part in a conspiracy to supply drugs.

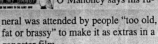

But only because Charlie was a sad and penniless man with no connections, and his funeral was also a media circus which he never wanted.

When Reg Kray died, O'Mahoney says his funeral was attended by people "too old, fat or brassy" to make it as extras in a gangster film.

CONCENTRATING

Finally, the media is slammed for giving publicity to the Krays and their hangers-on, and not concentrating on the victims of crime.

Krays blamed

SIXTIES gangsters the Krays have been blamed for the One-Armed Bandit killing.

Michael Luvaglio was convicted of shooting Angus Sibbett in County Durham in 1967 and, along with Dennis Stafford, was jailed for life.

But now Luvaglio, who has always maintained his innocence, has pointed the finger at the Kray twins.

Luvaglio is fighting for life after suffering a heart attack.

The 69-year-old has vowed to clear his name before his death and through his family said it was Ronnie and Reggie Kray who were responsible for the killing of Mr Sibbett.

From the Chelsea and Westminster Hospital in London, he said: "I do not want to die a murderer".

TO publicise his new autobiography, Jools Holland has been reminiscing in the Radio Times about a curious encounter with gangster Reggie Kray. "He wrote to me when I was doing The Tube on Channel 4 and complimented me on the suit I was wearing — so I wrote back and thanked him. Then he asked me to visit him in prison. I went with some trepidation but he was perfectly charming. He leant towards me at one point and said in a very serious voice, 'Do you need any help with anything?' I said, 'Well, I am trying to give up smoking.' He said, 'Well, that's easy. All you need to do is give me your word that you're going to stop.' I presume if I'd lit up in an East End pub, someone would have sidled up to me and said, 'Oi! We've heard you shouldn't be smoking, mate'."

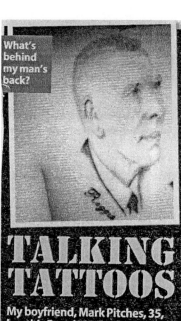

What's behind my man's back?

TALKING TATTOOS

My boyfriend, Mark Pitches, 35, has this Reggie Kray tattoo on his back. What does it mean?
Jo Davies, 38, Doncaster, South Yorkshire

DR ROSS GIVES HIS OPINION

Psychologist and tattoo reader, Dr Alistair Ross, says: 'The Krays represent brotherhood and security. Mark probably thinks blood's thicker than water. He's also likely to be territorial over what he sees as his own. Old-time gangsters also stand for control and authority. Perhaps Mark likes to get his way. He values respect both given and received. The villain's life can be a lonely one and he may value companionship above all else.'

Dignity's high hopes

THE company that buried the Kray brothers hopes to raise £150m in next month's share float. Dignity, the UK's biggest undertaker with 507 outlets, is expected to sell its shares at between 230p and 270p, valuing it at about £200m.
Dignity still handles big East End funerals like that of Tony Lambriano (pictured above) this week.

Krays' old pub is going gay

GAY weddings are to be held in the pub once used by gangsters Ronnie and Reggie Kray.

Ronnie shot dead gangland rival George Cornell in the Blind Beggar in Whitechapel, London, in 1966 after he was allegedly called "a big fat poof".

A barman said there were very few places in the East End offering gay weddings.

Kray's ghost is haunting hotel

GANGSTER Ronnie Kray's ghost is haunting the hotel where he died five years ago.

The spooky villain even spirits away other customers' booze and fags when they are not looking.

Josh Peak, manager of the Town House Hotel at Thorpe St Andrew, near Norwich, said: "It's very eerie and sends a shiver down the spine."

Farewell Lol

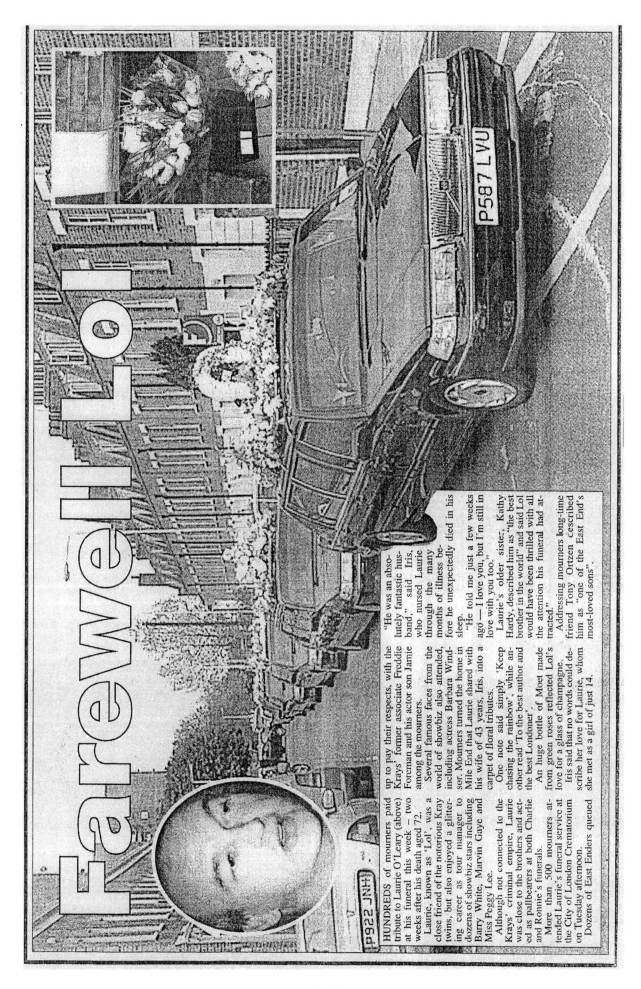

HUNDREDS of mourners paid tribute to Laurie O'Leary (above) at his funeral this week – two weeks after his death aged 72.

Laurie, known as 'Lol', was a close friend of the notorious Kray twins, but also enjoyed a glittering career as tour manager to dozens of showbiz stars including Barry White, Marvin Gaye and Miss Peggy Lee.

Although not connected to the Krays' criminal empire, Laurie was close to the brothers and acted as pallbearers at both Charlie and Ronnie's funerals.

More than 500 mourners attended Laurie's funeral service at the City of London Crematorium on Tuesday afternoon.

Dozens of East Enders queued up to pay their respects, with the Krays' former associate Freddie Foreman and his actor son Jamie among the mourners.

Several famous faces from the world of showbiz also attended, including actress Barbara Windsor. Mourners turned the home in Mile End that Laurie shared with his wife of 43 years, Iris, into a carpet of floral tributes.

One note said simply 'Keep chasing the rainbow', while another read 'To the best author and the best Londoner'

An huge bottle of Moet made from green roses reflected Lol's love for a glass of champagne.

Iris said that no words could describe her love for Laurie, whom she met as a girl of just 14.

"He was an absolutely fantastic husband," said Iris, who nursed Laurie through the many months of illness before he unexpectedly died in his sleep.

"He told me just a few weeks ago – I love you, but I'm still in love with you too,"

Laurie's older sister, Kathy Hardy, described him as "the best brother in the world" and said Lol would have been thrilled with all the attention his funeral had attracted."

Addressing mourners long-time friend Tony Ortzen cescribed him as "one of the East End's most-loved sons".

217

Day the gangsters buried the hatchet

HAD they met on the streets of London in their 1960s heyday, the result would undoubtedly have been violence at its most extreme.

But yesterday a small yet distinctive group of superannuated gangsters and their henchmen put bitter old rivalries behind them and came together to mark the passing of one of their own.

They were among more than 1,000 faces who attended the funeral beneath leaden skies of 69-year-old Joey Pyle, a man who uniquely ran with both the Krays and the Richardsons.

A one-time professional boxer and much in demand as hired muscle, Pyle had straddled both sides of the fence between two of Britain's most notorious and feared gangs. He had moved as easily in the Krays' East End fiefdom as he had in the Richardsons' ugly empire south of the Thames.

He was best man at Ronnie Kray's wedding but also a friend of rival South London mobster Charlie Richardson, and both families were present to pay their respects.

Richardson himself, balding and grey-bearded, mingled amongst the crowds of mourners as did Kate Kray, widow of Ronnie. Two of a sea of mourners who arrived at St Theresa's Church in Sutton, Surrey, for the funeral of a man who, against all odds, died of natural causes.

A fleet of 25 vehicles – plus a huge white Humvee stretch limo – ferried them to the church, where lines of hard-faced individuals maintained order.

One coach disgorged dozens of shaven-headed mourners and roads were jammed as Pyle's coffin, borne on a carriage drawn by black-plumed horses, made its way to the Catholic church watched by bemused passers-by. One lorry

'I know Ronnie and Reggie well'

trailed behind festooned in floral tributes.

Apart from the Kray and Richardson representatives, also present were Great Train Robber Bruce Reynolds, one-time gangland enforcer Freddie Foreman and hardman debt collector Dave Courtney.

Snooker star Jimmy White, former Coronation Street star Chris Quinten, boxer Gary Mason and actor Kenny Lynch also filed into the church.

To many of the survivors – and victims – of the sixties gang warfare, not to mention the police, the sight of so many one-time rivals on the same 'manor' will have caused a wry smile.

For 'Big' Joey Pyle was a canny criminal who for 30 years usually managed to stay one step ahead of the police while building an empire of protection, extortion and drugs across South London.

Shrewd and cautious, he normally gave his occupation as car dealer, street trader or simply businessman but in reality he was a professional criminal and drug dealer.

Born in the East End, he met the notorious Kray twins when they were all young boxers. 'I know Ronnie and Reggie well, but that doesn't make me a criminal,' he said in one rare interview.

When Pyle was 19, the courts won a rare conviction against him when he was jailed for three months for stealing cars.

Five years later he faced the Old Bailey charged with the murder of nightclub owner Selwyn Cooney and, if convicted, could have faced the death penalty.

The first trial was abandoned after jurors were 'approached' and Pyle was acquitted of murder during a second trial but jailed for 18 months after being convicted of assaulting Cooney moments before he was shot.

In the years that followed Pyle was repeatedly arrested – and repeatedly escaped prosecution.

Detectives suspected he was a key figure in organising the escape from prison of Frank Mitchell, the Mad Axeman of Broadmoor, and Jack 'The Hat' McVitie.

Both men were later murdered by, or on the orders of, the Krays.

Pyle's business methods of the 1960s and 1970s centred on gambling, extortion and protection rackets. Violent fights would break out in pubs and Pyle would step in and offer 'protection'. Publicans brave enough to refuse were made to regret their resistance. In some cases Pyle forced them to sell to him at knockdown prices.

By the 1980s police, frustrated at their inability to convict Pyle, resorted to objecting to his liquor licences but still he survived. Senior detectives turned up at one licensing application to magistrates and said he was a major international criminal with Mafia links – but admitted they didn't have evidence to charge him.

In 1987 a joint police-customs swoop arrested him after a £5million cannabis-smuggling plan was uncovered. The case collapsed when a key witness, a German ship captain, declined to give evidence.

Pyle's criminal reach stretched way beyond Britain and the FBI claimed it had evidence linking him to members of the Genovese and Gambino families.

Justice finally caught up with him in 1992 when he was jailed for 14 years after being convicted of masterminding a multi-million-pound drugs ring.

The first Old Bailey trial had been dramatically halted when three jurors claimed they had been threatened with death unless they returned not guilty verdicts.

For the second trial, costing taxpayers another £1million, the new jury were given a 24-hour police guard.

Pyle – whose sentence was later reduced to nine years – was the top man in an operation to supply heroin, opium and morphine sulphate in Britain but was trapped by a police informer who introduced the gangster to a 'buyer' for the drugs – an undercover policeman.

He was freed in 1997 and insisted he had 'gone clean' working with his son Joe Jr behind the scenes in the music industry.

Only days before his death Pyle was due to be questioned – as a witness – by police investigating a South London murder.

He promoted an unlicensed boxing event at Caesar's nightclub in Streatham last December, after which one of those attending, Sean Jenkins, was shot five times at a party.

218

BRUCE REYNOLDS, now 71, masterminded the Great Train Robbery in 1963 in which a gang escaped with a then record £2.4million.

A career criminal who enjoyed the high life and drove an Aston Martin, he was a well-known jewel thief and house-breaker who formed the robbery gang.

Using a series of aliases, Reynolds went on the run in South America before return-ing to Britain and being jailed for ten years.

He subsequently wrote a successful book on the robbery and featured in a film about it.

NOW 72 and decep-tively avuncular, Char-lie Richardson was the most feared villain in London. He developed an empire in the 1950s and 1960s which embraced fraud, gam-bling, protection rack-ets – and generated terror through torture. He was arrested on the day England won the World Cup in 1966.

At his trial he was alleged to have used iron bars, pliers and electrodes on anyone who crossed him. He was jailed for 25 years. Three years ago his life story was told in a film starring former pop star Luke Goss.

KATE KRAY is said to have had a contract put out on her life by her late husband Ronnie because he believed she was seeing another man.

The couple had wed in 1989 while Ronnie, who was gay, was in Broadmoor. They stayed married for six years but divorced three months before he died of a heart attack in 1995.

Despite the contract, there was no 'hit' against his ex-wife and the three-times-married crime author and journalist has a string of suc-cessful books behind her, including Diamond Geezers and Hard Bastards.

The 49-year-old, a former kissogram girl, is now mar-ried to Leo 'The Razor' O'Reilly, a publican.

FREDDIE FOREMAN was a key associate of the Kray twins. The 74-year-old was linked to two of the most infamous killings of the 1960s – the deaths of 'Mad Axeman' Frank Mitchell and Tommy 'Ginger' Marks.

Foreman has admitted he was asked by the Krays to get rid of Mitchell, a one time Kray ally, and shot him in the back of a van, arranging for his body to be dumped at sea. It was the same fate suffered by Marks, killed for arranging the shooting of Foreman's brother George.

Foreman was jailed for ten years as an accessory to McVi-tie's killing in 1975 and served six years from 1989 for his role in the 1983 £7million Security Express robbery.

CYCLOPATHS

Kray twins loved bicycling in country and buying antiques

Gang bosses ... Ronnie and Reggie

Fancy stopping for a cuppa and a McVitie?

Crime bling ... Ron ring

Kray sale you can't refuse ...

JEWELLERY, sunglasses and photos belonging to notorious murderers the Kray twins will be auctioned this month.

The collection, being sold by a family friend of the late East London gangsters, includes unpublished pictures from Reggie's 1965 wedding, silver-plated tankards, cufflinks, suits and Ronnie's trademark Ray-Bans.

There is also a letter from artist Francis Bacon thanking Ronnie for sending him some of his landscape paintings.

The items, going under the hammer at Chiswick Auctions, West London, on January 26, came from Broadmoor and Parkhurst Prison, Isle of Wight.

Gangsters ... Reggie, Ronnie

PSYCHO gangsters the Kray twins secretly enjoyed cycling in the country and browsing around antique shops, it was revealed yesterday.

Notorious hardmen Ronnie and Reggie — jailed for life in 1969 for murder — would get out of London's East End as often as they could.

The twins told of their country pursuits during interviews taped in 1989 which have never been heard before.

Ronnie said: "We were always going to the country. We used to go every weekend and cycle along country lanes, and go to antique shops and buy antiques. We bought clocks and ornaments — lots of different things."

Ronnie insisted they left their violent lives behind while touring Kent, Suffolk and Hertfordshire on their bikes.

He said: "There were no crimes. We got on with the locals very well. We used to go to inns.

"I had gin and tonics and brown ale and Reggie had gin and tonics and light ale.

"We found it very peaceful. The locals were very nice people — very genuine. We were not looking for any trouble.

"We loved the nice scenery and the quiet. We used to go for long walks along country lanes — it was smashing."

The twins even bought a country mansion just before they were caged for killing Jack "The Hat" McVitie and George Cornell.

Ronnie said they paid £11,000 for it, but later sold the home for £14,000 to pay debts and help out

By TOM WELLS

their mum Violet. He said: "It's worth a million now. We were inside — there was no point in keeping it."

The killers' love of the countryside began when Violet took them to Hertfordshire to escape the Blitz in World War Two.

Ronnie said: "We'd go sledging in the winter time and used to go scrumping for apples during the war."

The gangster also revealed they squandered their cash on booze, cars, jewellery and gifts for pals.

He said: "We got £1,000 each a week, but we've got no money stashed away. We spent it all."

Author Robin McGibbon interviewed Ronnie, Reggie and older brother Charlie for The Kray Tapes, released on CD next month.

Ronnie died of a heart attack in 1995 aged 61, and Reggie was killed by bladder cancer five years later. Charlie died the same year aged 73. t.wells@the-sun.co.uk

1GM 1GM

Cleaning up after the KRAYS

'Reggie Kray was my father'

By STAFF REPORTER

newsdesk@heraldexpress.co.uk

A NEWTON Abbot mum involved in a £1million fraud case has claimed she is the daughter of East End gangster Reggie Kray.

Linda Finnimore (pictured above), of Courtenay Road, was being sued by bare-knuckle fighter Roy Shaw who said she had deceived him out of a vast chunk of his fortune.

Yesterday in the High Court she was ordered to pay back almost £900,000, plus interest, including £643,000 for the disputed property transaction. She has already returned £50,000 to Mr Shaw. Her legal costs are expected to run to £700,000.

After the hearing, Ms Finnimore, a 43-year-old mother of three, said she only found out the notorious villain was her dad when he tracked her down in 1993.

Speaking to the Herald Express said: "I didn't know I was Reggie Kray's daughter until he tracked me down in 1993. I was seriously shocked when I found out.

"After I found out, I used to visit him in prison every day and I also organised his funeral.

"I've lived in this kind of world all my life, so it wasn't a big deal

Laundryman finds riches in Costa Rica after Aldgate

AN EAST END laundry business which began in Aldgate more than 40 years ago is alive and cleaning in a tropical paradise on the other side of the world.

What started out as Caroline's Dry Cleaners at 57-60 Aldgate High Street in 1967 is now Dry Cleaning International in a plush suburb of San Jose, the capital of Costa Rica.

While in the 1960s, owner Brian Kerr braved cleaning the clothes of the Kray twins, these days he serves the Costa Rican ruling class, with the likes of the country's foreign minister among his clients.

Caroline's was a fixture on the high street until 1971, before Brian got the opportunity to start a new venture in Canada.

That voyage across the Atlantic was the start of the globetrotting businessman, but it was in Aldgate he cut his teeth. And Brian recalled that his first forage into business after being de-mobbed was a gritty experience.

His business premises in Aldgate managed to attract an uncanny affinity with crime.

"We were in a building called Rennie House and beside us was an alleyway where it was purported that the last of Jack the Ripper's victims was found!" explained the 71-year-old.

"In the centre of this alleyway is a pub called 'The Still and Star' and from time to time the Kray twins

and their minders would drop in for a meeting and a drink because it was out of site of the main Aldgate High Street.

"They were actually good customers of the store and we always found them to be very polite in their requests."

One incident from the period – involving an apparent attempt on the twins' lives – occupies a particularly prominent spot in Brian's memory.

"One lunch time we heard a loud bang and thought our boiler had blown a gasket and ran to the back of the plant... it was the Krays' Jaguar which someone had placed a small explosive beneath and detonated.

"Apparently it was some sort of warning from the Richardson gang who were vying for their territory at the time. Anyway the Krays just opened the door of the Still and Star and shrugged and went back in to finish their drinks."

His days in Aldgate were marked by a number of colourful characters, he added.

"We also used to open on Sundays to serve the people who worked in Petticoat Lane. They were regular clients especially men like 'Tosher the Tie King' and the people who ran the china auctions.

"Also being so close to the Tower of London we used to get a lot of Beefeater uniforms in for dry cleaning – one would make up a full load for the machine."

■ **From Page 1**

to be related to the Krays."

Ms Finnimore told the Herald Express she will appeal the judgement.

Lawyers for 72-year-old Mr Shaw — who boxed under the nickname 'Pretty Boy' after serving time for armed robbery — said Ms Finnimore transferred £643,000 to her bank account in October 2007 after Mr Shaw sold a £2million property.

She claimed it was her fee for helping organise the sale.

It was Ms Finnimore's case that, when Mr Shaw sold land and property belonging to him, he gave her the £643,000 after promising she could have a 50

per cent share of any sale price over £1million.

But the Judge, Sir John Lindsay, said there was never such an agreement.

He also found Ms Finnimore had 'unduly influenced, deceived and misrepresented' Mr Shaw.

Although Ms Finnimore has not faced any criminal proceedings in relation to the case, Mr Shaw's lawyers said they would be passing the case to the Crown Prosecution Service.

Sir John described Ms Finnimore as 'clever and quick witted' and said the term 'feisty' could have 'been minted' for her.

Mr Shaw and Ms Finnimore became close after meeting in a

bar in Spain in 2006 and she moved in with him.

Sir John said their relationship was mainly platonic, although there was occasionally a sexual element to it.

The court heard Mr Shaw had spent 18 years in prison for criminal violence and dishonesty, and on his release he became a champion bare knuckle boxer.

Sir John said: "Mr Shaw was a well known figure in the criminal milieu which grew around the Kray brothers.

Funeral

"He was a pall-bearer at the funeral of one of them."

He added Ms Finnimore was also 'part of and familiar' with

the East End criminal scene, and at times called herself Linda Kray.

Between October 2003 and September 2005, she acquired 13 criminal convictions for, among other things, fraud, theft and drugs.

Outside court, Mr Shaw's lawyer Stephen Watmore said: "He had placed his trust in her as a friend to look after his interests and to give him advice and guidance in his business affairs.

"It has now been demonstrated in court Ms Finnimore fundamentally abused that trust."

THE KRAY TWINS' BLING & DIE SALE

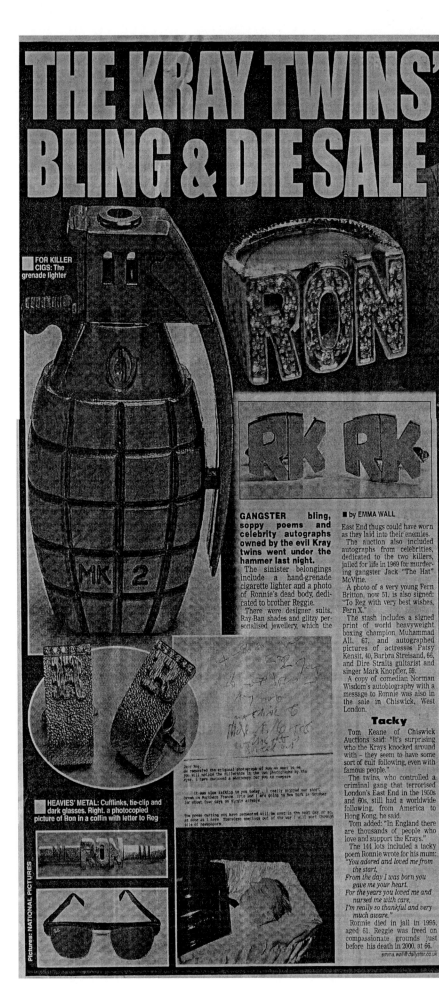

FOR KILLER CIGS: The grenade lighter

HEAVIES' METAL: Cufflinks, tie-clip and dark glasses. Right. a photocopied picture of Ron in a coffin with letter to Reg

Pictures: NATIONAL PICTURES

GANGSTER bling, soppy poems and celebrity autographs owned by the evil Kray twins went under the hammer last night.

The sinister belongings include a hand-grenade cigarette lighter and a photo of Ronnie's dead body, dedicated to brother Reggie.

There were designer suits, Ray-Ban shades and glitzy personalised jewellery, which

■ by EMMA WALL

East End thugs could have worn as they laid into their enemies.

The auction also included autographs from celebrities, dedicated to the two killers, jailed for life in 1969 for murdering gangster Jack "The Hat" McVitie.

A photo of a very young Fern Britton, now 51, is also signed: "To Reg with very best wishes, Fern X."

The stash includes a signed print of world heavyweight boxing champion Muhammad Ali, 67, and autographed pictures of actresses Patsy Kensit, 40, Barbra Streisand, 66, and Dire Straits guitarist and singer Mark Knopfler, 59.

A copy of comedian Norman Wisdom's autobiography with a message to Ronnie was also in the sale in Chiswick, West London.

Tacky

Tom Keane of Chiswick Auctions said: "It's surprising who the Krays knocked around with - they seem to have some sort of cult following, even with famous people."

The twins, who controlled a criminal gang that terrorised London's East End in the 1950s and 60s, still had a worldwide following, from America to Hong Kong, he said.

Tom added: "In England there are thousands of people who love and support the Krays."

The 144 lots included a tacky poem Ronnie wrote for his mum:
"You adored and loved me from the start,
From the day I was born you gave me your heart.
For the years you loved me and nursed me with care,
I'm really so thankful and very much aware."

Ronnie died in jail in 1995, aged 61. Reggie was freed on compassionate grounds just before his death in 2000, at 66.

emma.wall@dailystar.co.uk

PARTY: Charlie & Sam

Ronnie & Kray bro pal

THIS shows where Samantha Janus found her inspiration for tough EastEnders character Ronnie Mitchell —as she parties with Charlie Kray.

She posed with Ronnie and Reggie's brother at his birthday bash in a London pub in the '90s. The snap is among Kray memorabilia set to be auctioned.

Years later Samantha, 36, landed a part on the BBC soap—and likened her and screen sis Roxy (Rita Simmons) to the twins.

She said: "They are very Kray like. There's no coincidence that they are called Ronnie and Roxy.

"They are very chilling and very dark."

The picture was found in memorabilia belonging to one of Charlie's pals which is due to go under the hammer at Ludlow Racecourse in Shropshire next month.

Charlie died in 2000, aged 73, after being taken to hospital from Parkhurst prison on the Isle of Wight where he was serving a 12 year sentence for his part in a drugs plot.

KRAY ART CELLS

TWO child-like pictures Ronnie and Reggie Kray did while in prison are expected to sell for £3,000.

Auctioneer James Mander, of Clare, Suffolk, said of the watercolour and crayon pictures: "They look as if they took a few minutes. I'd describe them as 'naive'."

Krays' art sale is on

Seven paintings created by the Kray twins during prison art classes are expected to sell for thousands when they come up at auction today.

The works of notorious gangsters Reggie and Ronnie were painted in the 1970s when they were serving life sentences in Parkhurst Prison on the Isle Of Wight.

They are due to go under the hammer at Hampshire Auctions in Andover. Also up for sale is a portrait of the twins, done in Parkhurst and signed by G Young – believed to be poisoner Graham Young who murdered his stepmother and two work colleagues. The three landscapes by Ronnie all feature a small white cottage in rural scenes.

Ronnie Kray died in 1995 at the age of 61. Reggie died five years later.

Kray-zy clothes

GANGSTER Ronnie Kray's tailor has been signed up as Marks & Spencer's new clothes designer.

Mark Powell, 46 — who dressed East End villain Ronnie in jail — will create a 1960s-inspired line for M&S.

A store spokeswoman said: "We picked him because he has a certain style."

THE KRAY TEENS

First mugshots of villains at age 19

By ANDREW PARKER

THESE are the first ever police mugshots of the notorious Kray twins — taken as they were locked up in the Tower of London at the age of 19.

The black and white photos show Reggie and Ronnie glowering menacingly after being arrested for desertion during their national service in 1952.

They are set to fetch hundreds of pounds at auction next week after being put up for sale by an ex-Scotland Yard cop.

Auctioneers Mullocks, of Ludlow, Shrops, said: "There is a burgeoning interest in the history of crime, especially surrounding the Krays."

The twins – some of the last prisoners ever locked up in the Tower – were held there because that is where their Army regiment was based. They were sent to military prison for a month, then dishonourably discharged after repeatedly attacking guards and escaping.

It was their first taste of life behind bars, and marked the start of their reign of terror over London's East End. The twins went on to spend years behind bars for gangland murders and other crimes. Ronnie died in jail aged 61 in 1995, while Reggie was freed on compassionate grounds before his death five years later. a.parker@the-sun.co.uk

Caught . . Reggie, left, & Ronnie before crime empire

Feared . . the twins in 1966

Gangland shots, blood and missing body baffle police

January 10, 1965: Cal McCrystal reports as a 'respectable' man vanishes and his family is put under guard

THOMAS "Ginger" Marks, the 37-year-old small-time haulage operator who disappeared in Bethnal Green, east London, a week ago, was shot dead, according to persistent underworld stories.

It was about 30 minutes after midnight last Saturday when Marks, a smartly dressed man with red hair, freckles and horn-rimmed glasses, was walking past the Carpenters Arms pub in Cheshire Street. He stopped on hearing his name called from the darkness of an alleyway and turned to face a group of men.

Seconds later, there was a series of shots. One bullet hit Marks in the stomach. Before he fell to the pavement, other shots followed, one ricocheting off a 5ft wall behind him, and another entering his head at close range.

What happened then is anybody's guess. When police investigated reports of gunfire Marks had disappeared. They found blood, horn-rimmed spectacles, a 0.22 calibre cartridge case, a bullet mark on the wall and an apparently insoluble mystery on their hands.

Police have puzzled over the cartridge almost as much as Marks's disappearance (they see no reason his attackers should not have left him where he fell). The cartridge was of a type used in an outmoded gun, once popular for shooting rabbits. It was an unlikely weapon to use to kill a man.

Marks was born into a fighting family in June 1928. His father was a tough professional welterweight in the 1920s and his uncle Joe was a successful lightweight boxer.

Ginger did not carry on the tradition. He made up for his lack of aggression by dressing well, driving flashy American cars and giving lavish parties in his flat above a shoe warehouse in Redman's Road, two miles from where he was shot.

From the day he married Ann Sullivan, a local girl, she had accompanied him almost everywhere, except on business. Every Friday night and Saturday night, they went to the Blind Beggar, a pub in Mile End Road owned by one of Marks's closest friends, Patrick "Patsy" Quill.

For once Ann Marks was not with her husband last Saturday night. Just what Marks was doing in Cheshire Street is something of a puzzle. He did not frequent any of the pubs there, nor did any of his known associates.

Marks's friends are reluctant to believe that he is dead. Patsy Quill said: "He'll probably turn up like a bad penny. I can't see him being murdered. He had no enemies."

Marks was still in his twenties when he started up in business selling second-hand cars. He seemed to do quite well. Then, on an impulse, he left with his family for Canada. In 1959 he returned to London, took over the present flat at a rent of £4 a week and went into business again.

This time business did not come easily and Marks had a period of difficulty. He and seven other men were accused in 1961 of conspiracy to defraud finance companies of £44,000. All were acquitted.

Marks decided to concentrate on the haulage business. He bought a lorry and operated from Spitalfields market. He appeared to be doing well again. He was never known to be short of money. His flat is comfortably furnished, with a large, eye-catching cocktail cabinet.

Neighbours consider the Marks family respectable. His wife and children, Barbara, 16, and Michael, 14, attend mass every Sunday.

Ann Marks, said by neighbours to be suffering from extreme shock, is now guarded night and day by two detectives. Policemen escort Michael to school and Barbara to her office. Marks's friends who have visited the family since the shooting have been questioned before being allowed to enter the flat.

Not one person has come forward to say he saw the shooting. One man who lives within a few steps of the alley told me: "I must have been sleeping soundly. I heard nothing, but then we are used to cars backfiring."

Police have taken statements from all of Marks's known friends and associates. They are checking all rumours and local theories. But they are unable to confirm that Marks is dead and where he has gone.

After a tip-off, The Sunday Times hired three frogmen to search the Thames at Chertsey. Marks's body was never found. Freddie Foreman, 77, a gangster who worked for Ronnie and Reggie Kray, was acquitted of the murder in 1975. In an interview in 2000 he confessed to the killing and claimed the body was dumped at sea.

■ WHITECHAPEL, the drama featuring copycat killings by the Kray twins, has a lot going for it.
Best of all, however, was a reminder of just how vicious these gangsters were.
I say "best of all" because there's a tendency to glorify the Krays as Cockney wide boys. The passage of time has dimmed our perception of just how evil they were. Anything that helps to paint them in their true colours can only be applauded.

CORPSE IN GARDEN OF KRAY PAL

Arrest over patio grave

By MIKE SULLIVAN, Crime Editor

A BODY wrapped in carpet was found yesterday under a garden patio belonging to a dying pal of gangland boss Reggie Kray.

The rear garden of cancer-stricken Roy Heath was **DUG UP** after police were tipped off that a body was there.

A team of forensic cops led by an archaeologist uncovered the remains inside a rolled up piece of **UNDERLAY** at Heath's home in Fulham, West London.

Former underworld heavy Heath, 52, was arrested on suspicion of murder at the hospice in Lambeth, South London.

He was questioned there under caution in the presence of the solicitor. Heath — who has just weeks to live — was given bail until later this month.

But one source said: "There will never be enough time to charge and try him, and what's the point? He's already got a death sentence."

Friends said Heath met Reggie Kray, who ruled London's gangland in the 1960s with twin brother Ronnie, in prison and carried out work for the pair.

Cops were last night trying to identify the skeleton, which is thought to be male.

Det Insp Tim Dobson appealed for anyone who may have information to come forward. He said: "It is believed that the body

Search . . . forensic team at house

may have been at the scene between 15 and 20 years."

Police were told in 1997 that Heath had murdered a business rival, but nothing could be proved.

The new probe came after cops were tipped off about a remark Heath is said to have made in the past.

Police will be at the terraced property for at least week to see if **MORE** bodies could be there.

● **FOLLOWING** the discovery of the remains two men, aged 52 and 47, were arrested last night and were being questioned at a Central London police station. *m.sullivan@the-sun.co.uk*

Reggie . . . 60s gangland boss

THE KRAY TWIN TOURS

See the sites where Reggie killed Jack 'The Hat' McVitie and his brother Ronnie shot George Cornell (Bethnal Green, Whitechapel and Stoke Newington). Dr Jack was acquainted with the Krays in 1967 (13-14 years old), he was friends with the late Niki Faroue (Ronnies boyfriend, born May 29th 1952). It was at his birthday party (October 1967) that Jack 'The Hat' McVitie was murdered and Dr Jack was there. Learn more about the Kray twins with Dr Jack only at £9.50.

225

OH BROTHER . . . Kevin (front) and Vinny Mitchell as Ron and Reggie Kray (inset) *Picture: RICHARD PELHAM*

WE WERE 2 TEARAWAYS

Mitchells' Kray upbringing

KEVIN MITCHELL reckons he and brother Vinny had an upbringing every bit as tough as that of East End gangsters Ronnie and Reggie Kray.

But the Mitchells have steered clear of a life of crime thanks to boxing and now Kevin is on the brink of a world-title fight.

Unbeaten Kev, 25, takes on Ignacio Mendoza at Wembley Arena tonight in a lightweight contest that promoter Frank Warren has promised is a stepping

---

Q I HAVE a letter and a Christmas card from Reggie Kray which were sent to me in 1990 when he was in prison.

Are they worth anything? – Colin Monnaf, Kings Heath, Birmingham

A THERE is a market for Kray Twins memorabilia, as there is for other crime relics, such as items related to the £2.6million Great Train Robbery in 1963.

An autograph by the late gang member Buster Edwards, played by Phil Collins in a movie about his life, is quite desirable. Letters from the Krays, especially if they reveal personal thoughts about life in prison or other matters, might well fetch £150 or more.

Kray twins' secret files

By TOM MULLEN

tom.mullen@ncjmedia.co.uk

SECRET police files on the notorious Krays twins have been opened to help produce a documentary about the gangsters' rumoured links to the North East.

The film aims to explore whispers the feared brothers visited Newcastle with the aim of expanding their crime empire in the 1960s.

Almost every big city in England has some kind of shadowy link to Ronnie and Reggie Kray, but The Day The Krays Came to Town draws on the most authoritative sources yet.

For part of the film, Durham Constabulary gave the producers access to a file on the brothers which has remained unseen by the public for 40 years.

The documentary also draws on interviews from notorious crime figures including West End gangster

HARDMEN: Reggie, right, and Ronnie Kray at Reggie's wedding to Francis Shea

Paddy Conroy, London hardman Dave Courtney and the self-styled Geordie godfather Mario Cunningham – the brains behind a string of post office and bank raids and one of the only people ever to have escaped from Durham Prison.

The Chronicle's local historian Ray Marshall is also involved in the project, but the show's key producer is Steve Wraith, a former Newcastle doorman whose connection with the Krays began at the age of 17.

Steve became fascinated with the brothers' notorious past in London's East End and he regularly visited them in prison where they were serving life for the murder of Jack

'The Hat' McVitie in 1969.

In 1995 Steve was a security guard at Ronnie's London funeral and two years later was a character witness for Charlie at his Old Bailey trail when he was convicted of masterminding a £39m drugs ring. He remained in touch with Charlie and Reggie until they died.

He said: "Recording this documentary, I have now met a lot of these characters. I wish I could go back in time and ask Ron And Reg about their visits here. We are looking to put the record straight once and for all."

Anyone with any information, stories should visit www.kraysintown.com

Labourer, dog breeder, billiard hall keeper, wardrobe dealer, soldier..and murdering mobster

By ROBIN PERRIE

THE police record of infamous gangster Ronnie Kray has been found — listing a bizarre range of "occupations".

In this previously unseen prison mugshot unearthed with it, Ronnie stares menacingly straight at the camera.

The six-page record details his rise from teenage tearaway to the vicious crime king who ruled London's East End with twin brother Reggie in the 1960s.

It describes the convicted double murderer as the boss of a "ruthless and terrible gang" and an "extremely violent criminal who will not hesitate to kill".

Yet it also lists a strange variety of jobs as "club owner, labourer, dog breeder, billiard hall keeper, wardrobe dealer, soldier".

In a section giving his physical description, he is "5ft 7.5ins tall with a fresh complexion, brown eyes and dark brown hair".

Under "Peculiarities" it adds: "Eyebrows meet over nose".

The record — which also says Ronnie terrified even his own thugs — was found gathering dust in a box during an office clearout.

It had been consigned to the North Eastern Criminal Record Office after Ronnie was sent to high-security Durham Prison following his conviction in 1969 — and then forgotten about.

Revolver

The record begins in 1950, when he was 17, and says he was given one day's police detention for trying to take a car without consent.

The offences soon grow in severity, with two assaults on police for which he was given probation, and then his first jail in 1953.

It details a brief spell of National Service, during which he deserted and was such a troublemaker the Army kicked him out.

By 1956 he had moved up to wounding with intent and possessing a loaded revolver, for which he was sentenced to three years.

During the 1960s, as he and Reggie muscled in on organised crime, his charges included trying to bribe police, driving offences and breaking gambling laws. He was fined, banned from the road and put under good behaviour orders.

Then his record ends abruptly in 1969 with the stark entry: "5/3/69 — Murder. Life."

The record was found by Durham Police press officer Charlie Westberg during a sort-out of old cupboards and filing cabinets.

Charlie said: "I recognised Ronnie Kray straight away. We have no idea who put it in there."

Krays author Steve Wraith said: "It's an amazing document. The mention of his eyebrows joining is interesting because his aunt once said it meant he would hang."

Ronnie and Reggie were both jailed for life over the murders of George Cornell and Jack "The Hat" McVitie.

Ronnie was eventually sent to Broadmoor and died in 1995 at 61. Reggie served 31 years before being freed with inoperable cancer. He died in 2000 aged 66.

r.perrie@the-sun.co.uk

Tea for two . . . Reggie and Ronnie have cuppas, 1966

Menacing . . . Ronnie stares out from his prison mugshot, top, kept at record office

227

As ex-gang boss Eddie Richardson hires himself out as a raconteur, he sings like a canary to JANE FRYER

The Krays? They were both gay – and both brainless!

Gangland memories: The Kray twins with Reggie's bride, Frances. Inset: Eddie Richardson

---

CRIME FLICK HOPE ON MISSING HOOD

Kray twins and mystery of the Scots henchman

Crony . . . Barrie with Reggie Kray

By KENNY ANGOVE and
ROBERT McAULAY

A GRITTY gangster movie exposing the sadistic Kray twins could help solve the mystery of their missing Scots henchman.

Hardman John 'Ian' Barrie suddenly vanished in the 1980s when he was freed from jail after serving time for murder.

No one has since found a trace of the Glaswegian, who was caged in 1969 with Ronnie Kray over the shooting of villain George Cornell.

But experts believe big budget movie Legend – featuring Hollywood star Tom Hardy as both Ronnie and Reggie Kray – could finally unlock some clues.

Steve Wraith, who's written a book about the twins, said: "Ian was their right-hand man, he's a real man of mystery.

"He went into hiding after jail and disappeared off the face of the earth."

Steve, right, added: "It's a million dollar question – whether Ian is still alive. With the film coming out it would be incredible if he could be tracked down.

"I'd love to go and see him and ask him about his time with the Krays.

"It would be a crying shame if he was to vanish from this world without speaking about his time with the twins."

Barrie – played by actor Mel Raido, 36 – was a key member of the Krays' firm in London's East End in the 50s and 60s. Ronnie used him for back-up when he blasted Cornell in the head at the Blind Beggar pub.

Drinkers dived for cover as Barrie fired shots into the ceiling.

The film – out next year – also features fellow Scots accomplice Big Pat Connolly, the Kray's bodyguard.
kenny.angove@the-
sun.co.uk

Murder . . . Blind Beggar pub

Ray's Kray encounter

FILM hardman Ray Winstone has revealed he wet himself when he was introduced to gangster Ronnie Kray - although he was only six months old at the time.

The Sexy Beast star told Desert Island Discs host Kirsty Young he was a baby when Kray visited his dad in their East End home.

He said: "By all accounts he came round to see my dad and there was a few people there and he picked me up and I weed all over his raincoat, he had a brand new raincoat, and everyone kinda went quiet then Ronnie laughed and everyone laughed and I guess he went off then to have his raincoat cleaned."

Winstone said he spoke to Kray, who was jailed in 1969 for his part in the murder of two underworld rivals, about the incident years later when he visited him in Broadmoor high-security hospital.

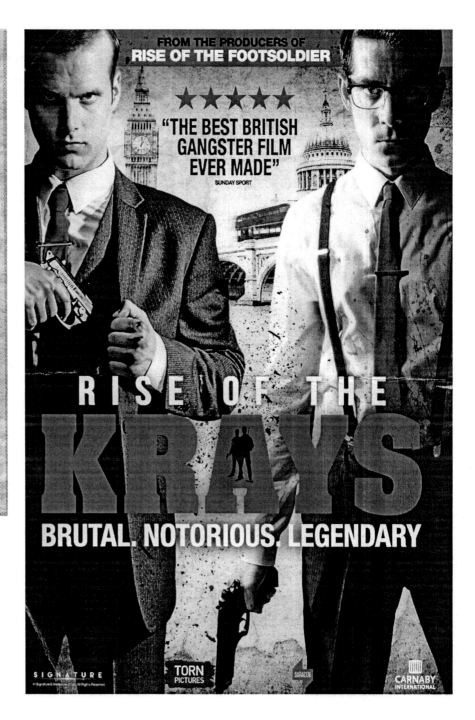

FROM THE PRODUCERS OF
RISE OF THE FOOTSOLDIER

★★★★★

"THE BEST BRITISH GANGSTER FILM EVER MADE"
SUNDAY SPORT

RISE OF THE
KRAYS

BRUTAL. NOTORIOUS. LEGENDARY

SIGNATURE   TORN PICTURES   SARACEN   CARNABY INTERNATIONAL

The right to tie the knot like Reggie Kray

PRISONERS have had the right to wed in jail since the Marriages Act in 1983.

They are also backed by EU human rights law. Marriage is considered a basic human right, alongside access to education, health care and freedom of religion.

Since the law changed, some notorious prisoners have tied the knot with brides from outside while doing time.

Gangster Reggie Kray, pictured left, wed English graduate Roberta Jones, then 38, in Maidstone jail, Kent in 1997. The Kray

Twin was serving a life sentence for the murder of Jack "The Hat" McVitie.

And Mickey McAvoy, leader of the gang which carried out the £26million gold bullion robbery at the Brink's-Mat warehouse, married his second wife Kathy in the gym of Leicester prison in 1986.

He was serving a 25-year sentence for masterminding the raid three years earlier.

Since gay marriage became legal in March last year, the authorities cannot deny gay prisoners the right to wed in jail.

BRIDE Roberta leaves jail after Kray wedding

LEGEND OF THE EAST END

Iconic Exhibition Brings Kray Legend to Life in the Heart of the East End

What defines the East End's unique character and spirit, and why have its streets and residents long captured the public imagination? With the East End now a place where creativity, commerce and enterprise mix as the wealth of the city spreads eastwards, *LEGEND OF THE EAST END* offers a snapshot of a bygone era and invites everyone to explore the East End old and new.

Legends? No, just a pair of fame-hungry psychopaths

As yet another film lionises the Krays, the sickening thing is it gives these sadists the very celebrity status they craved

HAVING broken into the house he'd targeted, the burglar wasn't content with mere theft. Grabbing hold of the owner's dog, he held it down on a hot cooker hob until its body was horribly burned.

When he was caught and hauled before a court, the magistrate demanded to know why he had committed this crime of 'incomprehensible cruelty'. Because, the crook explained — as if it was some sort of reasonable excuse — he wanted to be like those fabled torturers, the Kray twins.

They, the magistrate said with massive understatement as he sent him to jail, 'are not something very impressive to aspire to'.

Quite so. This tale of senseless sadism dates from 2003, by which time both Ronnie and Reggie were dead after decades behind bars for violent crimes. But their example — if that is what you can call it — lived on as an awful inspiration for those as mad and evil as they were.

For a pair of nasty low-life hoodlums, the Krays continue to hold a bizarre fascination, as potent today, it seems, as when celebrity photographer David Bailey immortalised them in the Sixties in their Savile Row suits, narrow ties and slicked-down hair. They stared menacingly into his camera at a time when, as Ronnie put it, 'me and my brother ruled London. We were f***ing untouchable'. It seems that half a century later they still — sadly — have the drawing power of stars.

Legend, a new film about them, had its premiere this week, to rave reviews for actor Tom Hardy who plays both twins. It follows in the footsteps of a 1990 film with Spandau Ballet's pop star brothers Gary and Martin Kemp as Ronnie and Reggie and award-winning actress Billie Whitelaw as their domineering mother, Vi.

Over the years there have been enough memoirs, books and newspaper articles about the Kray twins to fill an entire criminology section, and the new film has prompted more.

Veteran BBC broadcaster Tom Mangold told readers of The Times how, as a young journalist, he introduced himself into the Krays' orbit — but ended up taking an assignment in war-torn Vietnam rather than risk their wrath in London when they feared he might cooperate with the police against them.

He wrote: 'I've got be honest, there were nights with the twins and "The Firm" [their gang] that were just outstanding.'

Anyone with the smallest connection has a story to tell — even their mum's hairdresser, who happily chatted to The Guardian this week about how Vi Kray, sitting under the dryer, would be pestered by people wanting her sons to 'have a word' with someone on their behalf.

On the small screen, several more documentaries about them are in the pipeline. The Krays: The Prison Years will appear soon on the Discovery Channel, while The Krays: Kill Order, is released on DVD next week.

Yet another film, The Rise Of The Krays — whose executive producer is the pornographer and joint chairman of West Ham David Sullivan — came out last month and will be followed by a sequel later this year.

So it seems the macabre fascination is as great as ever. Yet, just like those who crossed their path in the East End all those years ago, we dabble in the lives of the Krays at our peril.

The danger is that the violence becomes sanitised and the hard lessons we should learn from their criminal ways are lost — as they were on that thug who felt empowered by their example to cook a dog alive.

KRAY? MY ARTS!
Forger's fortune flogging fake twins' paintings

A CONMAN raked in a fortune by selling art and letters he falsely claimed were the work of the Kray twins.

A painting purportedly

EXCLUSIVE by MIKE SULLIVAN

done by Reggie, who died in 2000, was still wet when the swindler tried to sell it earlier this year.

The hoaxer claims the gangster gave him the letters, trinkets and paintings when they became pals in the 1990s.

They included correspondence between Reggie and notorious prisoner Charles Bronson.

A Derbyshire couple spent £10,000 on items and took them to the Crime Through Time Museum in Cinderford, Gloucs.

Curator Andy Jones said: "The lot was fake. I know of three people who paid this swindler £10,000. Bronson knows and he's not a happy bunny. He never met Reg."

A 55-year-old man has been arrested and bailed on suspicion of fraud. *mike.sullivan@the-sun.co.uk*

LEGEND
OF THE
EAST END

FROM CRIME SCENES TO CAFÉS

A guide to
THE WORLD OF THE KRAY TWINS

REGGIE KRAY INSIDE

- We would drink with the IRA terrorists singing rebel songs
- Reg sent one cheeky youngster flying with a sweet left hook
- The Who's Roger Daltrey flew in on a helicopter to visit him

Double take: Tom Hardy as both Ronnie (in glasses) and Reggie (smoking) in their mother's kitchen, in a scene inspired by a photo of them taking tea, below

Tea but no sympathy: Krays on film and camera

Robert Dex
Arts Correspondent

PREVIOUSLY unseen photographs of the Kray twins are being shown in a new exhibition that organisers say goes beyond the clichéd image of the Sixties gangsters who ruled the East End.

The show, Legend Of The East End, opens tomorrow in Bethnal Green and features pictures from the twins' heyday, as well as photographs from Reggie Kray's funeral in 2000.

Also included are pictures by renowned photographer Brian Duffy, a contemporary of David Bailey. One shot from 1964, right, shows Reggie sparring with his grandfather Jimmy "Cannonball" Lee, who introduced the twins to boxing when they were children.

Duffy's son Chris, who helped organise the show, said many of his father's

PHOTO DUFFY ©DUFFY ARCHIVE

HULTON ARCHIVE/GETTY IMAGES

pictures of the twins were lost when he destroyed much of his archive. He said: "Duffy had a well-documented moment of madness and burned stacks of

negatives. Fortunately he was stopped by complaints from the neighbours and the council came round before he destroyed them all. I know him and

Bailey went for dinner with [the Krays] the night before they went to prison and I'm pretty sure he would have taken more photos but people didn't

realise how important it was. When he took photos it was just disposable, it was just a job."

The Krays were convicted of murder in 1969. Ronnie died in Broadmoor in 1995 while Reggie was released weeks before his death from cancer.

The show coincides with the release of Legend, starring Tom Hardy as b brothers. The family's Bethnal Gr home was recreated for the film an exhibition features the front roo

Curator Zelda Cheatle said: "W was conscious to do was not the cli thing to glamorise violence or make out the East End to be a terrible place full of violence. What I really hope is some of the joy and desire for life in the streets comes through."

■ *The Legend Of The East End runs Aug 28 to Sept 11 at 133-5 Bethnal Green Road. Legend is in cinemas on Sept 9.*

> Christopher Eccleston, who has criticised the lack of opportunities for poorer children trying to break into the acting industry today

Soon to be seen in Legend, a biopic about the Krays starring Tom Hardy as both twins, Eccleston has the pivotal role of Detective Chief Inspector Leonard 'Nipper' Read – the man who arrested the gangland brothers.

Talking about his part, he slammed the glamorisation of 1960s criminal gangsters Ronnie and Reggie Kray.

"They were vile criminals," Eccleston told Readers Digest.

"I'm dismayed at the way they're romanticised by some.

"I mean, it's all just nonsense."

Even as he condemns the sentimentalisation of the infamous hoodlums, he understands it.

"On a psychological level, the Krays were interesting," he said.

"I myself have identical twin brothers, eight years older than me, so I know how extraordinary that relationship can be."

As played by Eccleston, 'Nipper' Read is a man totally unsuited to the Swinging Sixties.

He said: "This is someone formed in the 1930s and 1940s in working class Nottingham, and wants things to remain that way."

Even as he condemns the sentimentalisation of the infamous hoodlums, he understands it.

"On a psychological level, the Krays were interesting," he said.

"I myself have identical twin brothers, eight years older than me, so I know how extraordinary that relationship can be."

As played by Eccleston, 'Nipper' Read is a man totally unsuited to the Swinging Sixties.

He said: "This is someone formed in the 1930s and 1940s in working class Nottingham, and wants things to remain that way."

"Benedict Cumberbatch, say, is never going to look like Ron Kray," says the director. "I had seen Tom in the film Warrior, which had a Reggie Kray quality"

METHOD IN THE MADNESS Tom Hardy takes on the role of the twin killers in the film Legend

233

FIRST KRAY FILM REVIEW...BY THEIR OLD PAL

NEXT week sees the release of Legend, the screen story of East End gangsters Ronnie and Reggie Kray.

The infamous twins and their gang, the Firm, terrorised the capital in the Sixties.

We took former Kray hitman Freddie Foreman, now 83, to see the film, starring Tom Hardy in both lead roles.

Here is his verdict.

TERROR... the Krays in 1965

ACTION... Freddie meets Tom

Legend's got it wrong...Ronnie and Reggie were BOTH gay

By FREDDIE FOREMAN, twins' enforcer

TOM HARDY plays both Ronnie and Reggie in the film — and watching him in action on screen was like seeing the twins reincarnated.

His physical likeness to both is uncanny. It was like watching their ghosts looming from 50 years ago.

But one thing the film gets totally wrong is the relationship between Reggie and his wife, Frances Shea.

It portrays him to be a Romeo who charms all the birds off the trees, and that could not be more wrong. He was gay, just like Ronnie.

The film gives the impression that Frances killed herself because she couldn't cope with Reggie being a gangster or being drawn into violence by his brother, and all that cobblers.

The truth is that their marriage was never properly consummated and she referred to him as "bacon bonce", which is Cockney rhyming slang for nonce. The film also gives the impression that Reggie was a fun-loving, cheeky chap who fancied himself as a businessman but got dragged down by his nutty brother.

It wasn't like that at all. Reg shot and stabbed people for next to nothing.

He took liberties. Once he went to the home of one guy on the Firm at 7.30am and shot him in front of his wife and kids. That was just for taking Ronnie's side in an argument. And the film makes Ronnie out to be a psychopathic lunatic, but actually he was a very warm person and capable of great kindness. He also had a very good sense of humour.

Yes, he did walk into the Blind Beggar pub and shoot George Cornell dead. But in the earlier days, Ron was still not as bad as the film makes out.

There was an aura of fear about both twins and the film gets that across well. If they were around, everybody was on their best behaviour.

But they were also polite and never swore in front of women or raised their voices in public. I'm not sure the film gets that across.

But the best thing about Legend is Tom Hardy and the special effects — they are brilliant. The story is not exactly how I remember it in true life and some parts are over the top — but that's cinema for you.

● Legend (18) opens on Sept 9.

'Kray dog' puts frighteners on a pigeon

By Eleanore Robinson

ACTOR Tom Hardy's dog Woody failed to stick to the script last night at the UK premiere of his new film Legend.

The 37-year-old British star brought his hound along to the Odeon in Leicester Square, London, to see him play both of the notorious Kray twins.

But the pet, ignoring the starry atmosphere, became distracted by a pigeon – which he proceeded to chase across the blue carpet.

Hardy, who plays both Ronnie and Reggie Kray, looked dapper in a three-piece navy suit as he posed with co-star Emily Browning, 26, in a floor-length orange dress.

The actor was accompanied by his pregnant wife Charlotte Riley, 33.

Co-star Christopher Eccleston, 51, who plays Det Supt Leonard "Nipper" Read, was also present. Earlier, he said he felt "jealous" of Hardy's dual role.

Hardy's pet Woody is distracted by a pigeon at the premiere

I MUTT BE IN THIS PIC!

Tom Hardy was supposed to be the star attraction at last night's world premiere of his film Legend... but he was upstaged by his own dog, Woody.

After posing with Hardy and his pregnant wife, Charlotte Riley, 33, the labrador-cross butted in when the actor tried to take a selfie with fans outside the Odeon in London's Leicester Square.

Hardy, 37, who plays both Ronnie and Reggie Kray in Legend, had no qualms about glamorising the gangsters. 'I just come to do a job. My job is to observe and reflect and anything that gets in the way of that has to go,' he told Metro. 'I'm a face-puller as opposed to a message bringer.'

Taking a bow-wow: Woody trying to get in on Tom's selfie last night

I dumped a body for the Krays but murder isn't glamorous and they were not legends

Legend stars Tom Hardy and Emily Browning last night. Inset: Real Kray twins Reg and Ron

They sipped champagne with celebrities such as Judy Garland and Barbara Windsor – but the Kray twins also ruled the East End with an iron fist, leaving a trail of blood and broken bones in their wake.

And gangster Chris Lambrianou was the man forced to clean up that mess. It was a dark and dangerous job.

Lambrianou came close to shooting two police officers to escape after he and his brother Tony were forced by the Krays to dump the body of hitman Jack "the Hat" McVitie in 1967.

The murder forms the chilling climax of the much anticipated new film about the twins, which stars Tom Hardy as both Ronnie and Reggie Kray, and opens in cinemas tomorrow.

The movie is called Legend, but despite the brothers living like stars, Lambrianou says they were far from that.

"The Krays have passed into folklore now," he says. "They are an industry and everyone wants a piece of it.

"But the Krays weren't glamorous or legends. There is nothing legendary about murdering a man in front of 16 people.

"A legend is somebody who does the right things, somebody you can really look up to. The Krays could have been legends, they could have made a difference. But they chose a different path.

"They destroyed so many families. And they really disappointed me." Speaking in depth about that night for the first time, Lambrianou reveals how he cleaned up the flat in Evering Road, Stoke Newington,

North London, after Reggie stabbed McVitie in the middle of a party.

Lambrianou mopped up McVitie's blood and poured it down the toilet.

But when he went into the bedroom to fetch a blanket to wrap the body, he found two young children asleep and realised the Krays had been babysitting for a friend when McVitie was murdered.

Lambrianou says: "What the Krays did was utter madness – murdering a man in front of 16 witnesses AND with two children asleep upstairs. I couldn't believe even the Krays would do something like that."

The Krays had lured McVitie to Evering Road to confront him about a hit he had failed to carry out.

Lambrianou saw Reggie pull a gun on McVitie to frighten him. And Lambrianou decided to leave before things got worse.

When he returned several hours later looking for Tony, he found what looked like a scene from a horror film.

Someone had handed Reggie a knife. High on drink and drugs and egged on by Ronnie, he leapt at McVitie and stabbed him repeatedly in the face and chest. The Krays then fled.

Lambrianou says: "I went downstairs and saw Jack the Hat lying there. There was blood everywhere.

"I went into the kitchen and got some socks from the wicker basket to wear as gloves, so there were no fingerprints. I went upstairs to get a blanket and found two small children sleeping in the bedroom. They couldn't have been more than five and seven years old.

"It was obvious that Tom wanted to play Ron — he kind of said, 'If you let me play Ron, I'll give you Reg'"

235

Left to right: Steve Wraith, Wayne Lear, Neil Jackson and Freddie Foreman
London, May 2015.